LYRIC AND LABOUR

IN THE ROMANTIC TRADITION

Lyric and Labour in the Romantic Tradition examines the legacy of romantic poetics in the poetry produced in political movements during the nineteenth century. It argues that a communitarian tradition of poetry extending from the 1790s to the 1890s learned from and incorporated elements of romantic lyricism, and produced an ongoing and self-conscious tradition of radical poetics. Showing how romantic lyricism arose as an engagement between the forces of reason and custom, Anne Janowitz examines the ways in which this romantic dialectic inflected the writings of political poets from Thomas Spence to William Morris. The book includes new readings of familiar romantic poets including Wordsworth and Shelley, and investigates the range of poetic genres in the 1790s. In the case studies which follow, it examines relatively unknown Chartist and republican poets such as Ernest Jones and W. J. Linton, showing their affiliation to the romantic tradition, and making the case for the persistence of romantic problematics in radical political culture.

Anne Janowitz is Reader in Romanticism in the Department of English and Comparative Literary Studies at the University of Warwick. She is the author of *England's Ruins: Poetic Purpose and the National Landscape* (1990).

CAMBRIDGE STUDIES IN ROMANTICISM

General editors

Professor Marilyn Butler *University of Oxford*
Professor James Chandler *University of Chicago*

Editorial board
John Barrell, *University of York*
Paul Hamilton, *University of London*
Mary Jacobus, *Cornell University*
Kenneth Johnston, *Indiana University*
Alan Liu, *University of California, Santa Barbara*
Jerome McGann, *University of Virginia*
David Simpson, *University of California, Davis*

This series aims to foster the best new work in one of the most challenging fields within English literary studies. From the early 1780s to the early 1830s a formidable array of talented men and women took to literary composition, not just in poetry, which some of them famously transformed, but in many modes of writing. The expansion of publishing created new opportunities for writers, and the political stakes of what they wrote were raised again by what Wordsworth called those 'great national events' that were 'almost daily taking place': the French Revolution, the Napoleonic and American wars, urbanization, industrialization, religious revival, an expanded empire abroad and the reform movement at home. This was an enormous ambition, even when it pretended otherwise. The relations between science, philosophy, religion and literature were reworked in texts such as *Frankenstein* and *Biographia Literaria*; gender relations in *A Vindication of the Rights of Woman* and *Don Juan*; journalism by Cobbett and Hazlitt; poetic form, content and style by the Lake School and the Cockney School. Outside Shakespeare studies, probably no body of writing has produced such a wealth of response or done so much to shape the responses of modern criticism. This indeed is the period that saw the emergence of those notions of 'literature' and of literary history, especially national literary history, on which modern scholarship in English has been founded.

The categories produced by Romanticism have also been challenged by recent historicist arguments. The task of the series is to engage both with a challenging corpus of Romantic writings and with the changing field of criticism they have helped to shape. As with other literary series published by Cambridge, this one will represent the work of both younger and more established scholars, on either side of the Atlantic and elsewhere.

For a complete list of titles published see end of book

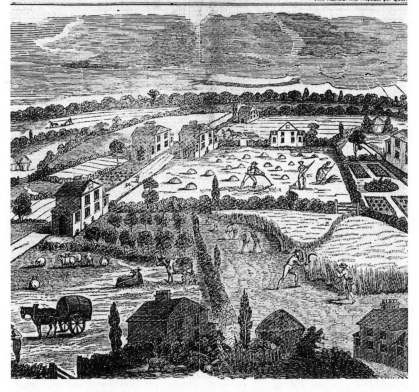

The Northern Star,

AND NATIONAL TRADES' JOURNAL.

NO. 458. LONDON, SATURDAY, AUGUST 22, 1846. PRICE FIVEPENCE or Five Shillings and Sixpence per Quart

Front page, *Northern Star*, 22 August 1846.

LYRIC AND LABOUR
IN THE ROMANTIC TRADITION

ANNE JANOWITZ

 CAMBRIDGE
UNIVERSITY PRESS

PUBLISHED BY THE PRESS SYNDICATE OF THE UNIVERSITY OF CAMBRIDGE
The Pitt Building, Trumpington Street, Cambridge CB2 1RP, United Kingdom

CAMBRIDGE UNIVERSITY PRESS
The Edinburgh Building, Cambridge CB2 2RU, United Kingdom
40 West 20th Street, New York, NY 10011–4211, USA
10 Stamford Road, Oakleigh, Melbourne 3166, Australia

First published 1998

Printed in the United Kingdom at the University Press, Cambridge

Typeset in Baskerville 11/12½ pt [CP]

A catalogue record for this book is available from the British Library

Library of Congress cataloguing in publication data

Janowitz, Anne F.
Lyric and labour in the romantic tradition/Anne Janowitz.
p.   cm. – (Cambridge studies in Romanticism)
ISBN 0 521 57259 2 (hardback)
1. English poetry – 19th century – History and criticism.
2. Politics and literature – Great Britain – History – 19th century.
3. Literature and society – Great Britain – History – 19th century.
4. Political poetry, English – History and criticism.   5. Social
problems in literature.   6. Labor movement in literature.
7. Romanticism – Great Britain.   8. Radicalism in literature.
9. Chartism in literature.   I. Title.   II. Series.
PR585. H5J36   1998
821′.809358–dc21   97–40831 CIP

ISBN 0 521 57259 2 hardback

for
Patrick
and
Alice and Ellen

Contents

Illustrations

Acknowledgements

Thanks to the Series Editors, Marilyn Butler and James Chandler, for encouraging my work in this study, and to Isobel Armstrong and William Keach who each read this manuscript at an earlier stage – both generous and enthusiastic readers. Mary Campbell, James Epstein, Kevin Gilmartin, Cora Kaplan, Michael McKeon, Jeremy Treglown, and David Worrall also read chapters and offered good advice.

Many thanks to Josie Dixon of Cambridge University Press. She is a brilliant and kind romanticist and editor, and I have valued her advice and encouragement. Thanks to Hilary Stock and to the staff at Cambridge University Press who made the final stages of production easy and pleasant.

My dear friend and colleague Michael T. Gilmore read the manuscript from start to finish. His work on early American poetry provided the starting point for this study. I have greatly benefited from his advice and help over many years.

I was privileged to present portions of this material as papers and lectures at Brandeis University, Rutgers University, the Center for Literary and Cultural Studies of Harvard University, the Universities of Zurich, Southampton, East London, Keele, Oxford, and my new home institution, The University of Warwick. I hope I have made good use of the comments offered on those occasions.

I would like to thank the following friends and colleagues for information, advice, and good cheer: Derek Attridge, Bridget Bennett, Marilyn Butler, Mary Campbell, Ed Cohen, Shirley Dent, Daria Donnelly, Maud Ellmann, James Epstein, Sandy Flitterman-Lewis, Neil Fraistat, Paul Hamilton, Henry Janowitz, Cora Kaplan, William Keach, Marianne DeKoven, Catherine LaFarge, Peter Mack, Emma Mason, Michael McKeon, Pamela

Mosher, Barry Qualls, Stephen Roberts, Nicholas Roe, Barbara Rosenbaum, Michael Scrivener, Pam Singer, Helen Taylor, Dorothy Thompson, Adeline Tintner, Jeremy Treglown, Deborah Valenze, Dror Wahrman, Carolyn Williams, Tom Winnifrith, Sue Wiseman, and David Worrall. Ulli Freer and others on the staff at the British Library, Bloomsbury Reading Rooms, made my work much easier. Thanks to John Hopson, British Library Archivist, for information on W. J. Linton's relation with the British Museum. I am very grateful to Barbara Rosenbaum for her conversation and her eye for detail.

I began work on this project while I held a National Endowment for the Humanities Fellowship in 1991–1992.

The article upon which parts of Chapter 3 are based was published in *At the Limits of Romanticism*, edited by Mary A. Favret and Nicola J. Watson (Bloomington: Indiana University Press, 1994); the article upon which parts of Chapter 5 are based was published in *The Politics of the Picturesque*, edited by Steven Copley and Peter Garside (Cambridge University Press, 1994).

This study is dedicated to Patrick Sikorski, and to my friends in the USA, Ellen Fitzpatrick and Alice Kelikian.

Introduction
Romantic studies as a unified field

Can we extricate ourselves enough from romantic presuppositions to produce a history of romanticism? This question has elicited equally impassioned replies from both literary theorists and literary historians. From those who write in the tradition of deconstructive theory, the answer is almost, but no: modernity is the utterance of romanticism, and romanticism as the literary anti-genre of 'becoming' draws everything into its individuating current.[1] From those who write in the tradition of literary history as science and morality, the Althusserian Marxism which was foundational for theories of the 'romantic ideology', the reply is yes: we must intellectually and ethically grasp our distance from romanticism in order to analyse it, and not be subject to its unrelenting myth of transcendence.[2]

This study focuses on the lyric in order to put the case for a dialectical history of romanticism which can make sense, within a unified field theory, of some of the countercurrents and antithetical movements in contemporary scholarly and critical academic work. And the purpose of hypothesising such a unified field theory is to reiterate and insist upon the power of romantic lyric discourse, not as an ideology of seamlessness, but as a matrix within which a debate about past and present was invented and persists. Romanticism is the poetic discourse that both names itself as totally different from what has come before – a revolution in poetics, politics, philosophy – and relies for its fabric on what has come before – enlightenment, accounts of primitivism, ancient models of democracy.[3] It is the rhetoric of an unrelieved tension between what came before and what will come after.

In our own period, and felt more acutely as the categories of post-modernism disrupt earlier models of thinking, romanticists are constantly working with and against the fact that the term 'romanticism' is used as both a period description and as a bundle of aesthetic characteristics. This is a point that Jacques Barzun made in 1944, and it remains true today.[4]

That is, we are always having to negotiate the problems caused by either the limits imposed by thinking periodically (1789,1798 or thereabouts to 1824,1832 or thereabouts) or those imposed by thinking generically (romanticism as a set of formal, aesthetic or thematic categories). Yet in the period from the 1960s through the 1980s, the exertion of pressure against these limits resulted in some very impressive work in the field, which led in turn to new areas of intellectual investigation, though now they threaten to disperse romantic studies altogether.

So, the interest in and exploration of the *persistence* of romanticism has shaped work as different as Frank Kermode's important work on the romantic image, Harold Bloom's theory of the tenacity of romanticism through the twentieth century, and more recently, Philippe Lacoue-Labarthe and Jean-Luc Nancy's characterisation of romanticism as the literary anti-genre of modernity. And their formulation can stand as a kind of redaction of the debates and history of deconstruction, itself a critical precipitation of romanticism.[5]

Equally, literary critics and historians remaining within the period limits of the field have forced major re-assessments of what we *can* mean by the romantic period in the study of British romanticism. These critics argue that the primacy of a slightly shifting but fairly solid and certainly very male set of poets – Blake, Wordsworth, Coleridge, Shelley, Keats – has been built upon a very wide set of exclusions, and upon a fairly narrow set of generic resemblances. The romantic period may not have been so romantic after all, goes one version of this investigation, which now exhibits a newly recovered, and wider-ranging set of texts, and retrieves a set of debates and concerns formerly unnoticed or marginalised. Marilyn Butler and Stuart Curran have redescribed the discursive and generic worlds of romanticism; and in a move towards greater coverage inaugurated by Roger Lonsdale's *New Oxford Book of Eighteenth Century Poetry*, we can now use and teach from Duncan Wu's very diverse anthology of *Romantic Poetry and Prose*, Jerome McGann's *New Oxford Book of Romantic Period Verse*, Jennifer Breen's *Women Romantic Poets*, Andrew Ashfield's *Women Poets of the Romantic Period*, and Isobel Armstrong, Joseph Bristow and Cath Sharrock's *Nineteenth Century Women Poets*.[6]

This revivified interest in the period has resulted from the combined influence of the 1960s and 1970s social history project (much of which was formulated through the work of E. P. and Dorothy Thompson), the power of feminist scholarship on both sides of the Atlantic, and both structuralism and post-structuralism in their less arcane, more historicised versions.

It was amongst feminist critics of the romantic lyric that the first substantial critique of the romantic canon was undertaken, and they made a case for how the male romantics had produced a poetic predicated on the silencing of women's voices. Through the work of critics beginning with Margaret Homans, we now cannot help but see the violence done to the possibility of the female imagination in such representations as Leila's sunken body in *The Giaour*, or Dorothy's rôle as mausoleum at the end of 'Tintern Abbey', or the reduction of Christabel's speaking voice to a brute hiss.[7] Another group of literary historians, including Donna Landry, Jennifer Breen, and Stuart Curran, has meanwhile been recovering the words of neglected women poets in the period, and the interchange between the two groups has resulted both in new anthologies, and in a new sense of the complexity of the romantic moment.[8] Feminist criticism has also altered the shape of romantic studies by foregrounding and taking into a new account literary texts until now marginal within romantic studies; most strikingly, by attending to novels of the revolutionary period, but also by introducing other kinds of texts as phenomena worthy of cultural study, including letters, pamphlets, and prophetic writings.[9] Perhaps most remarkably, these labours have decentred one of the chief figures of romanticism: the male solitary poet wandering the countryside is now crowded by an urban social network of readers and writers, often and significantly, women readers and writers. Jerome McGann's striking study of *The Poetics of Sensibility* has pursued and reintegrated the aesthetics of women's poetry into a larger view of the romantic poetic: the self-consciousness of romantic idealism throws into relief, as its precursor, an irrecoverable wholeness of bodily affect, derived from the poetic of sensibility.[10]

A corollary movement within romantic studies has been the dialectic between ideology theory derived from Althusserian Marxism and advanced in romantic studies through the work of Jerome McGann and Marjorie Levinson, and the more agency-orientated theory of cultural materialism, as theorised particularly by Raymond Williams in *Marxism and Literature*, which itself responded to Terry Eagleton's mid-1970s Althusserian formulations. For many scholars, a return to a Williams who had himself travelled far since the days of *Culture and Society*, has offered a way out of the radical scepticism which awaits the post-Althusserian.[11]

More recently, blending the insights and methods of cultural materialism and social history, a new group of literary historians of romanticism has developed what we might think of as an E. P. Thompson-derived theme of *plebeian* studies within romanticism. This work has brought to light texts of numerous urban radical popular writers and enthusiasts, and has created a much more complex sense of the cultural geography within which romanticism resided. With different emphases, critics and historians such as Malcolm Chase, James Epstein, Kevin Gilmartin, Iain McCalman, Jon Mee, David Worrall, and Thompson himself, have made the point that in the rich urban culture of London in the late eighteenth and early nineteenth centuries a remarkable encounter between past and present was played out in the rhetorics of custom and reason.[12] Enlightenment rationality did not only confront the *ancien régime* of ideas in a polemic against habits, customs, and precedent – it was also changed by it. A simple contrast between the world view of Burke and that of Paine is insufficient to a moment whose contradictions and complications make binaries appear even more reductionist than they would in less turbulent times. So the argument against custom that fuels Shelley's *Queen Mab* operates at one level of intellectual discourse, while what Thompson analyses as the recalcitrance of the inhabitants of customary culture in the face of the rationality of waged labour issues in a volatile counter-cultural language defending custom. And this contesting rhetoric impinges upon and marks the poetic of even those poets writing from and to the advocates of an age of reason.

The dissolution of boundaries between country and city, past and present, traditional society and the unmoored individual was an explosive and short-lived cultural phenomenon, which brought artisans into contact with middle-class scholars, saloop sellers with intellectuals, rationalist revolutionaries with utopian collectivists, ballad singers with ballad collectors. Chase, Mee, and McCalman have all mapped in a clear and geographical way the coming together of religious enthusiasm and millenarianism with Deistic rationality, the imaginary countryside with the limits of urban life, and the memory of mutuality with a compulsion towards self-actualisation. In the encounter, polite literature brushed against plebeian songs and doggerel, and romantic period poetry and poetics record the engagement of registers. In this context, Blake has been described as the exemplary 'bricoleur', constructing a momentary linkage between old and new epistemes.[13] And there is no doubt that in Blake's depiction of the very formation of identity we experience the difficulty and pain of this patchwork. The hideous declension into the limited body that Urizen undergoes in the *Book of Urizen* may stand as an emblem for us of the imaginary self in 1794 – torn from the fabric of customary culture and powerfully raging into individuality. As Urizen's utopian mirror image, Blake creates the Giant Man Albion, a self beyond selfhood, built out of the variety of possible persons and embodying the desire to be

differentiated without being individuated. We can also, as McCalman
has argued, hear the jostling demands of custom and the possibilities of
reason in the texts of Thomas Spence, radical rationalist and agrarian
communitarian. In fact, as literary and cultural historians have begun to
survey the range of voices whose conversations and harangues join and
contest the mandates of customary and enlightenment culture, the shape
of romanticism begins to look more and more like the literary form of a
double tension or engagement. Romantic lyricism not only serves as the
threshold of past and future, custom and democracy, Burke and Paine, but
it also prompts the meeting of the utopian possibilities secreted in the
customary language of the past (the 'futurity' seeded in the claim of an
embedded community) and the limits imposed by an ineluctable alienation offered by the individualist language of the future (the personal
isolation of democratic voluntarism).

My aim in this study is to notice once again what is so powerful about
romanticism, and why we cannot stop using the term, even when dispers-
ing its characteristics. My sense is that the modelling of poetic identity has
been under-explored by the cultural and intellectual historians named
above, but that it was shaped through and in concert with many of the
oppositions they investigate. What we call romantic poetics was one of
the important resources of and matrices within which the encounters of
customary and rationalist philosophical, economic, and political rhetorics
took place. Romantic period lyric forms explored identity as, on the one
hand, determined by external norms and values derived from the past,
ranging from the frightening tyranny of tradition to the wonderful
enchantment of the landscape; and on the other hand, as the source of a
newly theorised voluntaristic individual. The meeting of plebeian and
polite poetics opened an area for a conversation, a debate, a conflict, and
an interpenetration so powerful as to have residual influences well into our
own time. It is a tribute to that power that the question continues to arise as
to whether we are still too romantic to speak about romanticism. But it is
certain as well that the shape of this conflict has substantially shifted since
the early nineteenth century. For one legacy of romanticism, diffused into
the sentimentalism of the mid-nineteenth century, can be heard in the discourses of racism and domestic ideology; and a late twentieth-century
legacy of the romantic Promethean self has been the abstraction of self
from a social dialectic into the anomic self-regard that now characterises
the regime of 'virtual' identity.

The argument of this study, which addresses the question of romanticism
by asserting the centrality of the place and meanings of communitarianism

and individualism to romantic lyric poetry, is an attempt to engage with both contentions about the persistence in romantic problematics over time and the more clamorous debates about canonical inclusion and exclusion, about élite and popular rhetorical worlds. Drawing upon the adjacent discourses of social history and moral philosophy, in method, the intent of the argument is to make a literary bridge between social historians' analyses of the transition in the late eighteenth and early nineteenth centuries from customary culture into that of free wage labour, and those critical analyses made by moral philosophers such as Alasdair MacIntyre and Charles Taylor of the emergence of liberal subjectivity out of communitarian moral teleologies in roughly the same period.

Theorised and analytically developed in the work of E. P. Thompson and his colleagues, the social historian's investigation of eighteenth-century customary culture opens up a reclaimed sense of the purposiveness and generous mutuality of common practical knowledge, as against the alienation of the success of abstract 'free wage labour'.[14] These studies, including Thompson's *Customs in Common*, Janet Neeson's *Commoners*, Peter Linebaugh's *The London Hanged*, and Deborah Valenze's *The First Industrial Woman* exhibit a companionable discipline to the critique of liberalism advanced by a philosopher such as MacIntyre, who shares their interest in the ethical dimension of customary practices, as well as a critical interest in the paradoxical implications of the triumphant voice of enlightenment liberalism.[15] The analysis in social history and historical anthropology, then, of the shift from what Thompson defined as the practices and rituals of the 'moral economy' to capitalist wage relations can be understood, in the language of political and moral philosophy, as analogous to that shift from communitarian to individualist formations of personal identity, from moral value being located in external goods to its being located in inwardness. The senses of loss that MacIntyre and Taylor explore (MacIntyre rather more pessimistically than Taylor), are echoed in Neeson's study of rural enclosure in England, as she demonstrates the losses of tradition, habits, and sense of order within customary culture.[16] The 'common culture' shared by English peasants before their forced entry into a rural proletariat 'supported customary behaviour, joint agricultural practice, mutual aid, and on occasion, a sense of political solidarity'.[17]

But my aim is not simply to turn the claims of communitarianism and individualism around and assert a history of decline rather than an enlightenment; rather, my purpose is to trace out moments in an on-going interchange between the two formations, which is particularly acute in romantic lyric poetry. My attention will be on those moments where the communitarian lyric tips the scales of the dialectic and takes the form, for self-identified social and cultural groups, of 'some negative and critical power over against the larger and more diffuse demographies in which the group's current oppression is practised', as Frederick Jameson argues (about the utopian impulse in general).[18] These moments articulate together a tradition through the nineteenth century in which the relationship between communitarian and liberal versions of identity creates a lyric identity which is differentiated without being fully individuated, and in which residual communitarianism is inflected by the voluntarism of liberal subjectivity.

Nor is my aim to assert that the complete 'invention' of the modern subject takes place in the romantic period. Literary and cultural historians can and do claim this for every period, which poses the problem as if identity were a precipitate of the world, rather than an agent in making it. The dialectic of subjectivity within historical process demands that we recognise that the problem of the emergence of the subject is always on-going, though it takes diverse forms. The alienated reflexive individual has been a speaker in lyric poetry since antiquity, but the centralising of the lyric within the hierarchy of genres in the late eighteenth and early nineteenth centuries secures the claim for its particular efficacy in the romantic period. The embedded lyric speaker who knows the narrative of the world around him or herself has a complex relationship with the unencumbered lyric speaker who must know everything from within, and finds within everything there is to know. This is the terrain of self-possession, and much of the self-conscious history of radical working-class poetry in the nineteenth century is an attempt to repossess identity by making claims for lyric poetry as a possibility for collective, embedded experience. It is the nineteenth-century version of a dialectic within English poetry of a fundamentally oral stress (four-beat) metre and the syllable-stress (five-beat) metre of artifice, that is, print culture: the contest between the poetics of court and country, the possessors and the dispossessed.[19]

So the literary analytical bridge between the social historian's and the moral philosopher's versions of this period is built from the stuff of lyric poetry. That is, my argument focuses on the valences of the lyric, understood not as a secure poetic infrastructure for a transcendent self of lyric solitude – i.e., the version of lyric codified by John Stuart Mill in 1833 as 'feeling confessing itself to itself, in moments of solitude', and recently reiterated by Harold Bloom as 'the sovereignty of the solitary soul . . . the deep self, our ultimate inwardness' – but rather as a theatre of engagement for competing and alternate versions of personal, political, and cultural identity.[20] While Mill and Bloom may *describe* (and indeed help to create) lyric hegemony from the 1840s until its modernist and post-modernist dispersion, they do so by ignoring those versions of lyric and lyric voices upon whose ruin the *a priori*, autonomous and abstract speaker of the lyric of the aesthetic ideology is perched, just as wage labour was built upon the ruins of custom, and the paradoxical modern 'self' – compounded of disengagement and radical subjectivity – was built upon those of external moral narratives.[21]

Nonetheless, the social and aesthetic endowment of the romantic lyric is great, and it is the matrix out of which was born not only the high romantic argument but also a competing alternative version of selfhood. This is a lyricism of sociality, of transpersonality rather than transcendence, of achieved connections, and one which, embodying in poetic structure the argument between individualism and communitarianism, is both a literary and cultural site for the self-development and imagined instantiation of selves. So the study aims to understand the position of a communitarian lyric in the tradition of romanticism, and foregrounds those texts which themselves assert the lyric as a site for insisting upon the connections amongst persons above the assertion of the inwardness of a single subject.

But the intent of this study is also to move back towards a unified field theory of romanticism, to show the exchange between polite and plebeian forms. The recent models of inclusion and exclusion have served a purpose in pressing literary historians to locate and discover the varieties of literary culture in the period of romanticism. This study is meant to help provide an explanatory framework within which to situate the plurality of romantic 'exclusions' which are now being given their place.[22] Without such a comprehensive framework, study of the disparate materials of the period fragments into a set of competing and mutually incomprehensible 'free markets' of romanticism. If we suspend the inclusion/exclusion model, we can see more clearly both the self-divisions and the entwined elements in the literary culture of the late eighteenth and early nineteenth centuries, and thereby recover the tradition of what both Shelley and William Morris called 'hope', the dialectic of romanticism in its most liberating form.

PART I

A dialectic of romanticism

CHAPTER ONE

The communitarian lyric in the dialectic of romanticism

There is a peculiar discrepancy within the image of the British romantic poet. Figuring the poet as both an isolated consciousness, and as a socially orientated poetic radical, literary historians and critics ameliorate this constitutional doubleness by narrating it as a life history, in which the youthful radical turns into either an apostate or a 'Jacobin-in-recoil', who cultivates the garden of his interiority, or, more briefly, dies before that can happen.[1] But in the fabric of their lives and poems, the antithetical mix of self and solidarity has been as integral as it has been consecutive. Think of the example of Wordsworth, who tells the story of how, on his way to school, he had to grasp at the trunk of a tree in order to remind himself that there was indeed a world to encounter beyond the boundary of his already powerful, creative, and unencumbered self: 'I communed with all that I saw as something not apart from, but inherent in, my own immaterial nature.'[2] Coexisting with this radical solitude is Wordsworth the democrat, aiming in his poetical 'experiment', *Lyrical Ballads*, to speak out of and into a community forged through sympathetic links across the borders of status and wealth, and drawing on the counter-hegemonic metres of oral tradition. Or, turn to the second-generation romantic poet, Percy Shelley, in whose complex poetic identity we find the radical solipsist who shapes the beloved as the epipsychidion, or 'soul out of my soul', occupying the same poetic skin as the communitarian who exhorts the labouring poor of England to 'rise like lions after slumber' in a collective effort of rebellion.

I begin by repeating this cliché of the romantic poetic because my main subject matter here is the communitarian lyric voice in both the structural and historical modalities of romantic poetry, and it seems worth beginning with a reminder of the familiar fiction of the romantic lyric speaker as the extension of the poet's self in order to open a space for other versions of romantic identity. For the central argument that I will advance begins by folding the isolated romantic self back into its originary matrix, and showing how the dialectic of romanticism in its formation, and in its life through the nineteenth century, is linked to individualism and communitarianism as integrally related – neither fully opposed nor chronologically successive – models.

If the terms of the dialectic feel old, they are: the argument between the self and the community has been a shaping rhetoric of the past two centuries at least, and at moments of political and cultural crisis, the opposition of individual and collective is invoked as a habitual binary. Though our contemporary public debate takes place somewhat removed from the world of poetic form and meaning, the provenance of its terms are historically congruent with and culturally interdependent on the rise of the lyric modality we associate with romantic poetry. Though apparent in poetry since its origin, the singular lyrical voice came, in the romantic period, to be both centralised in the hierarchy of poetic genres, and taken as the voice of the political subject, the citizen, and hence, the human. At the end of the twentieth century, the assumptions and underpinnings of the universalising power of the liberal self have become the subject of post-romantic investigation. The liberal self and the lyric self were twin births from and accompanying voices to the revolutionary idea of a democratic voice in the age of revolution. But out of this same matrix arose as well the notion of a collectivised popular sovereignty, which drew upon customary culture and its popular poetic forms, which were then marked and modified by the languages of interiority. What we often encounter rhetorically as a stark opposition between individual and community is a flattening out of the historical dynamic whose attenuation has issued in our stale contemporary formulations. For when we return to the period when the romantic self was produced in lyric poetry, we find that the categories of self and community differentiate and depend upon each other, and out of their dialectic is woven the stuff with which succeeding generations will fashion what look to us like mutually exclusive claims of self and community. Linked to this distinction is that between oral and print culture: where we also find that the idea of print culture as supervening upon oral culture proposes a chronological succession belied by the on-going interaction between the two modes of poem-making. At the micro-level of poetic form, an assertion of the force of four-beat stress metre against the five-beat stress-syllabic metres of print culture encodes arguments about social and personal functions articulated at the macro-level of poetic thematics. In the romantic period, the exchange between oral and print cultures is energetic: on the one hand, democratising print-culture poetry, and on the other, reanimating the resources of oral poetic culture.

The history of liberalism and the history of romanticism are tied together through the voice of lyric individualism, and deployed through the poetic mechanisms of print culture. At the same time, however, the success of individualism has meant the shadowing of communitarian solidarity, and the triumph of lyric individualism has meant the sidelining of the communitarian tradition in romantic lyricism, and the relative neglect of the tradition of communitarian lyricism in nineteenth-century poetry, except insofar as it offers a minor strain against the major currents of romantic lyricism.

The proposition, then, at the centre of this study is that in analysing British poetry of the late eighteenth and early nineteenth centuries, the literary term 'romantic' ought to be used to describe neither (1) a set of literary functions nor (2) a set of ideological mystifications.[3] As readers of this study will know, the paradigmatic debate over romantic functions took place in discussions by Arthur J. Lovejoy and René Wellek about the reducibility or irreducibility of romantic structures and preoccupations such as imagination, nature, myth, and symbol; while the analysis of ideological mystification is the legacy of a psychoanalytically inflected Marxism, and in romantic studies is associated with the 1980s work of Jerome McGann and Marjorie Levinson.[4] The function debate, however, leaves us with an extremely restricted set of texts which can be considered under the rubric of romantic, and the trajectory of the ideology critique has been towards the dispersal of the category altogether, with, I believe, an accompanying impoverishment of literary resources.

Rather, we should consider romanticism to be the literary form of a struggle taking place on many levels of society between the claims of *individualism* and the claims of *communitarianism*; that is, those claims that respond to identity as an always already existing voluntaristic self, and those that figure identity as emerging from a fabric of social narratives, with their attendant goals and expectations. For a central conflict within British society as a whole, beginning in the mid-eighteenth century, reaching its height between 1790 and 1848, and persisting in various forms (as romanticism has persisted in various forms) well into the twentieth century has been the debate between voluntaristic individualism and embedded communitarianism as grounding social theories of the constitution of personal and political identity. In this sense, then, romanticism is the vehicle of one of the central contradictions of modern identity, whose implicit logic is given its late and explicit articulation by the communist-romantic, W. H. Auden, as our coexistent, contradictory desire for both 'universal love', and 'to be loved alone'.[5]

In making the case for this proposition, my work here undertakes a sequence of interrelated explorations: first, enlarging on themes outlined in the introduction, I briefly outline what I am calling here the dialectic of romanticism; after which I recuperate and trace out the occulted communitarian tradition emergent from within that dialectic. That is, the communitarian lyric in the tradition of romanticism recapitulates and repeats, in various forms, the foundational romantic engagement between communitarian and individualist versions of identity – subjectivity understood via a community and via a self. This communitarian lyric also enacts the problems of poetic vocation, interpreted through the exchange between oral and print cultures, and the entry of plebeian labourer poets into the terrain of polite and then 'literary' culture. The communitarian lyric in the tradition of romanticism also produces versions of public knowledge, distributed through a shifting set of rhetorics, including those of custom and reason, and self and sociality.

What follows is an historical account of poems and theories of poetry in the light of these issues. Chapter 2 begins by examining Wordsworth's theory and practice in *Lyrical Ballads,* and then traces the theorisation of the individualist lyric that gave the dominant contour to the romantic tradition, focusing on how John Stuart Mill forged a version of the lyric based on a very partial understanding of Wordsworth's poetics, and contrasting this with George Dyer's theory of the lyric. Turning then to the communitarian lyric itself, Chapter 3 looks at radical poetry in the romantic period. I then offer a series of case studies in Chapters 4 through 6, examining the elaborate relationship amongst the poetic projects of three significant Chartist poets: Allen Davenport, Thomas Cooper, and Ernest Jones. The study concludes with a discussion of the dynamic of republicanism and socialism in poems by W. J. Linton and William Morris, evincing a late nineteenth-century moment of this dialectic.

This sequence is both powered by and argues with E. P. Thompson's long-lasting project of analysing the relationship between romanticism and socialism, and I offer a riposte to his view, set out in both *The Making of the English Working Class* and *William Morris: Romantic to Revolutionary,* of romanticism and radicalism as following parallel but tragically unconnected paths.[6] At the end of *The Making of the English Working Class,* Thompson argues that Blake is the singular example of a poet who threaded together the discourses of artisan radicalism and romanticism: 'After William Blake, no mind was at home in both cultures, nor had the genius to interpret the two traditions to each other.'[7] The argument of this study revises Thompson's characterisation: though no minds were entirely at home in the two traditions, in fact there was an on-going and mutually constitutive practice which helped to shape both romanticism and plebeian radicalism, and whose exchanges were critical to both poetic and political history. By demonstrating this dialectic, a literary space is opened for the socialist poems of Blake's late nineteenth-century counterpart, William Morris. Thompson could not allow that space to exist, because his restrictive model of romantic growth and decay led him to argue that Morris's socialist poetry was a species of poetically belated and inferior romanticism.[8] Part of my purpose is to put in place a lyric provenance for Morris's utopian expectation in the 1880s that 'a reform in art which is founded on individualism must perish with the individuals who have set it going'.[9]

The premise upon which the following discussion is based is the phenomenal one experienced by anyone teaching romantic poetry – namely that even within the canon, poetic intention is deeply divided. This self-division is disclosed in the ways in which romantic poetry offers at times a poetic of transcendence, lyric solitude, and private meditation – what we have come to call the ideology of aesthetic autonomy; while at other times, romantic texts polemically call for a kind of poetical activism closely linked to social life, for as Blake contends, 'Poetry fetter'd fetters the human race'.[10] To pose this proposition more dynamically, romanticism follows a double-trajectory. Rather than observing developmental and organic rules of growth and decay (as in Thompson's long view of romanticism through the nineteenth century) or those of earthboundedness superseded by aesthetic transcendence (Harold Bloom's vision of the Apollonian supersession of the Promethean mode in his psycho-poetical analysis of romantic poetry), in fact romanticism proposes radically distinct paths at the same historical moments.[11]

It is true that 'Tintern Abbey' breathes fairly freely in the countryside, providing an aesthetic location within which to cultivate an individual private poetic of transcendence. But what we have, even if tacitly, agreed to call romantic poems also present a poetic of engagement and transpersonal voicing, as in the *Lyrical Ballads* when they engage with and respond to the rhetoric of custom, or in a poem such as Blake's stanzas 'The Fields from Islington to Marybone' from *Jerusalem*, which offer a version of a speaker originating in collective desire and seeking to intervene in the world as a collective agency, 'Mutual shall build Jerusalem, / Both heart in heart & hand in hand'.[12] These poems are grounded in, though traduced by, the tradition of oral cultural forms: the congregational lyricism of ballads and hymns are reinvented as print culture artifacts, replete with the ornament and artifice which distinguishes the high culture lyric presentation. Similarly, when we take Shelley's 'The Mask of Anarchy' as he asked us to, as his attempt to intercede in political affairs, with songs 'wholly political & destined to awaken and direct the imagination of the reformers', we enter into a poetic that belongs to an interventionist, communitarian strain, whose direct inheritors were the Chartist poets and poetic theorists of the 1830s and 1840s, and later William Morris, and later still, the poets of Anglo-Communism.[13]

In 'The Mask of Anarchy' (a poem which, against the backdrop of high romantic subjective lyricism, has been considered as a Shelleyan anomaly, even though it is in the form of a popular song, the central lyric form until the triumph of the individualist lyric) the 'selves' of political upheaval are generated from and come to know themselves through their collective experience of oppression. That is, they are what some of our contemporary critics of liberalism would call communitarian selves, persons whose identities are made through a set of traditions, goals, and social meanings. In the individualist mode within romantic poetry, by contrast, most often the self is pre-given and extremely vulnerable; the possibility of development, though inherent in each self, is understood in Wordsworth's poetry after 'Salisbury Plain' to be, as he remarks in *The Prelude*, 'in most abated and suppressed' by society.[14]

In other words, romantic poetry models experience in two distinct forms, the extremes of which I am calling the individualist and the communitarian. At one end are situated those lyrics whose voice is singular, most often masculine, and voluntaristic; at the other end are those which produce a lyric 'we'. But between these extremes, much romantic poetry engages with and ambiguates the two positions. For the Wordsworth of the aesthetic ideology is also the poet of the explicitly political, as in his poems on 'Liberty and Independence', though the very clarity of distinct poetic intention here exemplifies the growing separation of the two realms, evident as well in his own taxonomy of poetic forms. And the overtly aesthetic lyricism of Shelley's 'Ode to the West Wind', proving by its *terza rima* rhyme scheme its indebtedness to the foundations of print culture, works with the voices of transpersonality, in which other forces animate the poet's 'dead thoughts', and the wind's 'mighty harmonies' momentarily inhabit the speaking 'I', itself dispersed like 'withered leaves'.[15]

At the same time, the figure of the poet that Wordsworth constructed in *Lyrical Ballads* as a mediator between a language of the commoner and that of high culture, served as an important model and source of tension to plebeian and radical poets desiring to make poetry that would serve the collectivity but also fulfil their personal poetic vocations. Theirs was an ambition to prove the central rôle played by lyric in the on-going history of labour, redeeming the human effort in both industrial and poetic process.

Our ability to elicit critically this double intention within romantic poetry has been hampered deeply by the outcome of the contest in the larger regions of intellectual and political life. Because individualism won the larger debate, it has shaped the history of literary criticism, which for the most part either approvingly reads the romantic period backwards as the poetic which marks the separating out of poetry and politics, or disapprovingly exposes a mystifying 'romantic ideology'. As a result, the presiding spirit of the age has been Wordsworth rather than Burns; the characteristic form has been taken to be the blank verse paragraph rather than the choric song or the ballad; and the stance of identity taken to be solitude rather than that of solidarity in which, Burns sings, 'Like brethren in a common cause, / We'd on each other smile'.[16] Recently there has been a recovery of oral poetics in our cultural milieu. The four-beat and double four-beat line emerges in poetry slams, rap poetics, and all versions of poetic culture which aim to return poetic activity to a public activity. In a sense a recovery of this material from the romantic tradition helps to clarify the sources and resources of a post-print cultural tradition.

Though the intuition upon which the discussion builds comes from experience in the classroom, in recent work on the critique of liberalism there is intellectual warrant for making the argument. For if Mill reified the individualist facet of romantic lyricism in 1833, contemporary moral philosophers have provided the analytical apparatus for resituating it as part of a dialectic. In *Sources of the Self*, Charles Taylor describes the way in which the modern self develops as a contradictory version of an objectified 'punctual' self, which is, at the same time, increasingly reliant on categories of 'inwardness' for criteria of truth and value. Taylor writes of this punctual self: 'this ungrounded "extra-worldly" status of the objectifying subject accentuates the existing motivation to describe it as a self ... The punctual agents seem to be nothing else but a "self", an "I".'[17] It is in the triumph of individualism that the lyric is not only centralised as the genre of value in poetry, but that the lyric 'I', the universalised lyric subject, comes into prominence as a personal abstraction which every and any reader is to occupy while in the act of reading the poem. Making an argument against what he calls 'emotivism', Alasdair MacIntyre outlines a prolonged crisis from the middle of the eighteenth until the middle of the nineteenth century, in the break-up of moral presuppositions. He argues that this loss was not, however, conceived by moral philosophers as loss, but rather as a 'self-congratulatory gain' through the emergence of a freed, but as we have increasingly discovered, impoverished individualism, the one we still live with. Though MacIntyre is discussing the history of moral philosophy and not literary texts, his claim resonates with the complexity of poetic purpose within romanticism.[18]

It is helpful to recapitulate the story of the nineteenth-century lyric 'I'. For, enmeshed as it is in those moments when liberalism, as Anthony Arblaster argues, moved from being a dream into a 'dominant, dynamic political force', though before it had given rise to a named party, individualist romanticism provided a poetic of the unencumbered self, nourishing liberalism's valuation of the individual as separate, autonomous in will and reason, and crucially, *private*.[19] Liberalism's own contradiction is its presentation of a democratic sense of the individual, theorising society as an aggregate of autonomous selves, but suggesting at the same time that an élite layer of selves must rise to the surface to direct the mass. This self is, like Wordsworth's poet, a 'representative . . . man speaking to men', but somewhat more politically than poetically astute. Romanticism in this sense depends upon liberalism, which sanctions and, importantly, *protects* the inner space of subjectivity.

One of the most powerful images of this unencumbered self is the solitary reader and writer; the self who is constituted as a mental space of voluntary choices inhabiting the realm of poetic artifice, neither embodied nor localised, though capable of surveying and understanding a locality. The speaker in 'Tintern Abbey' recalls an embodied earlier self, who 'bounded o'er the mountains like a roe', but his present state is one which draws, by memory, that past into a place of consciousness in which the body is 'laid asleep'. What we have learned through the analysis of the romantic ideology has been that to produce such a vision, enormous amounts of data must be excluded from the scene.[20] But even having learned those things, we still find ourselves as readers identified with the lyric 'I' in a disembodied space of abstract consciousness. No matter how much one knows about the particularity of Wordsworth's situation and locale in the poem, the 'I' continually exerts its force as an abstraction or model of consciousness above its presence as any set of particulars. Wordsworth is always speaking from the place of the human abstract, and that is why, just as the site of 'Tintern Abbey' can never be fully historically recovered, so the shock of Dorothy's appearance at the end of the poem can never be fully assimilated into an interpretation of the text. Because the presence of another self in the landscape is both necessary to Wordsworth's poetic argument, and always seen from the outside, it is seen precisely *as* an embodiment, and shocking to the systematic abstraction of the speaking 'I'. Yet the simultaneous presence of both of these forms – the abstract consciousness of the speaker and the physical nearness of Dorothy – diagram a project that Wordsworth is absorbed in; namely, how to outline the self and situate it as representative of all 'men speaking to men'.

It is here, in this image of William finally speaking to Dorothy, but assuming that she had been overhearing him all along, that the space is created within which John Stuart Mill will construct his theory of lyric poetry. His theory renders explicit the links between the making of liberalism and that of the making of poetry, though both the intellectual and the lyric practice had already been established for some decades. What has been a dilemma between consciousness and sociality for Wordsworth is resolved, in Mill's theory, as the social setting is benignly severed from poetic intentions: 'the peculiarity of poetry appears to us to be in the poet's utter unconsciousness of a listener'. In Mill's theory, poetry, instead of serving a social function, is now the index of inwardness, of what he calls 'the delineation of the deeper and more secret workings of human emotion'.[21]

It is a commonplace of post-modern thought that the 'self' is not born but is constructed, and that the bourgeois self has a will to power, and a will to universalisation that has only recently been philosophically defeated, and not yet politically defeated. The democratic nineteenth-century citizen subject is enabled by the content and structure of romantic lyric poetry, and underpins such formulations as Harold Bloom's that poetry loses all subject matter but that of subjectivity itself with the work of Wordsworth.[22] That is why 'Tintern Abbey' appears as both the limit case for individualist romanticism and as its universal case as well. For that reason, it is often the site of contention, whether from a feminist argument about Dorothy's rôle, or a New Historicist one about the social realities erased from the frame of the poem, or a canonical one about what texts are left out in order to keep 'Tintern Abbey' in.

Of course, the solitary self in the landscape is not a romantic invention; it is the particular form that the pastoral retreat takes in a period when the political and the poetical are differentiating themselves within the lyric mode. If the 'I' of 'Tintern Abbey' appears characteristic of romantic lyricism, its attribute may inhere in its filling with the theme of interiority (to the point of excluding everything else), the place where, previously in pastoral, the political might exhibit itself. Michael McKeon has recently described the trajectory of English poetry of retreat into the early eighteenth century as a path in which 'writers consolidated the idea of pastoral retreat as an active agency, not the passive "privation" of merely private existence (for example the fortuitous absence of urban corruption) but the negative liberty of a chosen solitude.'[23] The 'liberty of solitude' may have been formed much earlier than 'Tintern Abbey', but Wordsworth's self in the romantic landscape offers a perfected version of the impulse. And as in pastoral preoccupation with what has been left behind, so Wordsworth's 'I' cannot elude the 'still sad music of humanity' that echoes in him as he surveys his 'pastoral scene'. That 'music' is transmuted from the articulate voices of urban radicalism into something more sonorous and less referential, and Wordsworth signals here what will be the growing distance between his poetry of nature and that of politics. For the intermingling of the voices of self and society, which characterises Wordsworth's *Lyrical Ballads*, comes undone and Wordsworth's poems of 'Liberty and Independence' reflect this alteration, in what Alan Liu describes as Wordsworth's 'flight from narrative'.[24]

Study of the range and the internal dialectic of romantic lyric subjectivity has been somewhat sidelined, both by the continuation of an insistent universalising notion of poet and reader (which now occupies Bloom in his new Canon formation), and more complexly, by the binary opposition between the canonical and the marginal. These two opposite tendencies are, moreover, mutually determining. For Bloom, the accession of the lyric self is shadowed, but not defeated by the dangerous spectre of solipsism. For M. H. Abrams, whose narrative of romanticism follows the shape of Christian conversion experiences, the happy fall of defeated revolutionary expectations is the ground upon which the transcendent spiral of romantic redemption is built.[25] There is hardly a place for either the residual voice of a community or the emergent voice of a collectivity in these prescriptive versions of a lyric self who, no matter how buffeted about, remains consistently committed to the defining view of the unencumbered self.

Yet the breadth of selves that we encounter in romantic lyric poetry ranges from deepest solipsism to an embracing collective social identity. Blake, for example, presents a version of identity which consistently deplores the liberal reduction. This is manifested prominently in the prophetic books: the difficulty as well as the utopian promise of Blake's resurrected Giant Man Albion inheres in his variousness. The reader's task is to imagine a 'one' who is also an infinitely differentiating and contracting set of variables:

> & every Word & Every Character
> Was Human according to the Expansion or Contraction, the
> Translucence or

> Opakeness of Nervous fibres. Such was the variation of Time
>   && Space
> Which vary according as Organs of Perception vary; & they
>   walked
> To & fro in Eternity as One Man, reflecting each in each &
>   clearly seen
> And seeing, according to fitness & order.[26]

This vision informs the stanzaic lyrics throughout Blake's œuvre, and his 'Mental Traveller' not only goes through the revolutions of identity formation, but is implicated in all other identities in the poem as well. In quite the other way, the perplexity and dystopic peril experienced by Coleridge's floundering identity in 'Dejection: An Ode', turns on such a severe sense of separation of personhood from conjugal sociality, such an ambivalent shaping of individual autonomy, that the 'I' becomes hermaphroditic, sending forth 'A sweet and potent voice, of its own birth', and claiming for itself not a materiality, but a 'fair luminous cloud', which we nevertheless know from the rest of the poem is more often the bearer of dark storminess.[27]

Less frustrating, and certainly less autonomous than either Coleridge's 'I' is the social selfhood of 'a little cottage girl' who, refusing to be instructed by the admonishing adult, 'would have her will, / And said "Nay, we are seven"' in defiance of the speaker's rationalist arguments. The interlocutor in Wordsworth's ballad 'We Are Seven' shows us how hard it can be for one 'I' to imagine another Self; but the theory in the 'Preface' to *Lyrical Ballads* does argue for such a connection, and for recognition of the ballad – derived from and addressed to customary culture – as central to that task. If we read Wordsworth's 'Preface' with attention to the ways in which it braids together the claims for a voluntaristic self (for example, when Wordsworth argues for the priority of feelings to incident) and claims of an embedded one (the poet who binds humanity together in song), we see how its power derives from being poised between two conceptions of creativity: one which grounds the work of the poet in a habit and soil; the other which describes the formation of modern inwardness, in which an autonomous self locates value within his or her own consciousness. The poems in *Lyrical Ballads* also work through competing versions of identity formation. In 'We Are Seven', the soil affords a tradition of humanity from which the voluntaristic 'I' is painfully excluded, though the poet distances himself from his narrator, positing and then learning from his naïve subjects.[28]

While the speaker in 'Tintern Abbey' abstracts himself from locale as

he intuits his connection to that 'motion and spirit that rolls through all
things', the landscape he uses as a *point d'appui* for meditation is construed
elsewhere in a more domestic and convivial manner. A 'sensible' mutuality
of domesticity produces a differentiated, but not individualised identity in
women's poetry of the period. Joanna Baillie inserts her speaker into the
sociality of rural life understood as a set of common and interlocking
activities, grounded in georgic conventions of traditional society: a
communitarian positioning of identity in relation to narratives of local
labour:

> Work proceeds,
> Pots smoke, pails rattle, and the warm confusion
> Still more confused becomes, till in the mould
> With heavy hands the well-squeezed curd is placed.

In Anna Barbauld's 1797 poem, 'Washing Day', the importance of sociality
and active mutuality turns the unencumbered and, as well, uninvited
visitor on washing day into an unwelcome distraction to those who do
work, and presses as a source of personal alienation upon the visitor: 'the
unlucky guest' who 'early slinks away'.[29] The benignity of domesticity
offered by Barbauld and Baillie coexists in lyric production with that
satiric martial mutuality in which personal identity is liberated through
social change: 'The burden of my song is a wondrous *transformation* . . . Lo!
a *Swinish Multitude* were chang'd to *men* and heroes.'[30] The lyric speaking
self can imagine itself entirely self-creating and self-delighting, or as part
of some larger social unity. Keats's voice in his sonnet 'On First Looking
into Chapman's Homer' balances the claims of a self whose autonomy is
assured by engagement with the world of poetry, and that of a self who is
in fact forged through the layering of selves whose collective poetic is
brought into the present in Keats's own sonnet.

   In these examples, I have been juxtaposing a range of possible positions
for the lyric self, for the initial movement of my argument is that what we
think of first as romantic lyric poetry, and secondly as romantic period
verse, and finally as the persistence of romanticism as a lyric modality *is*
the very contestation of communitarian and individualist identities,
alongside the mutual inflections of oral and print cultures, within the
shaping of both the aesthetic ideology and the interventionist poetics of
radicalism. The second movement of the argument is to claim that as we
articulate the links between romanticism and individualism, we see more
clearly the complicity between, on the one hand, that individualist aspect
of romanticism and *liberalism* as it developed in the nineteenty century, and
on the other, between the collective aspect of romanticism and *socialism* as

it developed out of an encounter between residual plebeian communitarianism and emergent democratic liberalism.

For though the romantic lyric subject is also the liberal subject, the two
arising together and in aid of each other, there is also a movement of lyricism in this period which models another version of subjectivity. This path
is one through which the subject of customary culture – a pre-capitalist,
communitarian, plebeian subjectivity – is dialectically engaged with the
emerging voluntaristic or unencumbered self. This takes place in lyric
experiments, such as lyrical ballads, in 'we' voices within lyric poetry, and
in lyrics which attempt to intervene in and not simply represent human
life. For as much as a particularly autonomous version of the self was made
in the period of the revolution, it came up against and interacted with earlier
and productively residual meanings of personhood and identity. Romantic
lyricism thus incarnates a turning point in the valuation of the self in its relation to a larger context and much of its power derives from its instability in
this regard, its perfection highlighting its vulnerability as well. It is the
central task of this study to elaborate the practices of that version of identity
which presents itself as conscious of social origins and aims, an embedded
identity committed to fulfilling itself in function of social responsibilities.

It is by way of the collective presentation of labour that this customary
self engages most fully with that of the solitary self. Labourer and poet
alike are charged with the task of making the world and finding themselves
in the worlds they have made. The image of the romantic poet stresses the
self making itself through its lyric capacity; and this serves as a redemptive
mirror to the alienation of self that is experienced in industrial labour. So
it is that images of non-alienated labour are presented as pre-industrial
agricultural labour, the customary self working the next ground over from
the solitary poet who locates identity in the isolation of self in the natural
landscape. Conversely, the poet as single self requires the model of labour
to justify the apparently idle activities of walking and contemplating. The
democratic poet is not represented as a figure of fashion or wealth, but is
engaged in that mental fight which shapes the liberal consciousness.

As an economic, social, and political ideology, liberalism linked enlightenment rationalism to capitalism as the most congenial soil in which to
develop the growth of liberty as non-interference. On the other hand,
what came to be called socialism, and was dispersed across many sects and
factions, and politically split into the reformist strategy of Labourism and
the anti-reformist revolutionary tradition, was, from its origins, bifurcated
by contradictory sources and goals, one in the direction of republicanism,
the other deeply anti-political, at times millenarian in its goals.[31] This

anti-political strain is the link to traditional, customary practice, and to a communitarian impulse which can be read through early nineteenth-century romanticism and followed to the end of the century.

If we look at the double intention within romanticism as a literary-historical trajectory, we can see that the engagement between liberalism (based on the rationalism of natural rights) and communitarianism (often grounded in community-derived notions of the customary rights of the labouring poor) yields, in the course of the nineteenth century, to both the triumph and the crisis of liberal individualism, and the consequent re-emergence of communitarianism in a socialist rather than either a Burkean or plebeian sense. As Terry Eagleton notes, socialism borrows from communitarianism its sense of the 'collective determination of meanings and values', but adds to it the political desire to contribute 'more rather than less plurality . . . [into] the sort of heterogeneous social order [that] the liberal most admires', for 'if everyone is able to participate fully in the moulding of that culture . . . the upshot is likely to be a culture far more heterogeneous than one bound together by a shared "world view"'.[32] The late nineteenth-century permutation of communitarianism *as* social-ism takes place, however, in the context of an historical reconfiguration after the defeat of Chartism between 1848 and the 1880s, and it arises again in the voices of the socialist movement at the end of the century.

The history of the communitarian lyric within the romantic tradition moves from the 1790s through the 1890s as a dialectic in which a deepening interior voice of the individual subject comes to reinhabit the external structure of ballads and customary popular poetics, transforming, for example, the external anecdotal lyric of the agrarian poet-radical Thomas Spence, into a revised and three-dimensional version of the identity of the 'we' in the Chartist poetry of the 1840s and 1850s. So it is that two poetic lines are both joined and differentiated. One is the canon instituted in the last quarter of the nineteenth century, reinforced today in the Western Culture debate and volumes like Bloom's *Western Canon*. The other is an alternative 'people's' poetic tradition which was built over the nineteenth century.

If the modern critique of liberalism offers tools for understanding the instantiation of the individualist lyric, it is from the work of social historians that we can see how the communitarian moment within romanticism is historically linked to the various and overlapping cultures of plebeian democracy, customary culture, radical enthusiasm, and agrarianism. In this language, the context for the lyric contest is the engagement between customary culture and the individualist culture of nineteenth-century waged labour. As I suggested in the Introduction, the work of E. P. Thompson and others has brought to light and given a historical shape to a set of practices which can roughly be called 'customary': including the tacit knowledge of plebeian culture, the practical uses of the common law, and the expectations of subsistence in a not fully-waged market economy, all adding up to what Thompson calls 'a whole vocabulary of discourse, of legitimation and of expectation'.[33] The study of the tacit knowledge embedded in customary culture and the conflicts between the economic regimes of custom and market, highlights custom's residual importance for oppositional culture in nineteenth-century class society. The analysis in social history and historical anthropology of the shift from what Thompson defined as the practices and rituals of the 'moral economy' to capitalist wage relations can be understood, in the language of political and moral philosophy, as analogous to that shift from communitarian to individualist formations of personal identity. Against this similarity of interest, however, runs the focus, in Thompson's work, on how customary culture in the transition to market culture exhibits an unruliness which adumbrates rebellious culture in the nineteenth century, while a philosopher such as MacIntyre aims to re-institute the conservatism of traditional society.[34]

In *The London Hanged*, a study of the criminalisation of customary practices across a wide range of trades in the eighteenth century, Peter Linebaugh makes explicit the interweaving of social, economic, and rhetorical forces. Linebaugh narrates the material losses entailed in the specific history of the suppression of 'non-monetary appropriation' in the everyday lives of the urban labouring poor: tailors, sailors, servants, etc.[35] And Linebaugh reminds us that the concepts of 'wages' and 'rights of man' were fundamentally linked among the English Jacobins. As a result of his analysis, we are left with a compromised version of the radical rationalists. The complexity of the period is such that what looks like the freeing of subjugated labour into free wage-labour can be understood as well as the breakdown of relations of mutuality and common interest. It is important, therefore, to generate more distinctions than only that between a Burkean reactionary sense of custom and tradition and a forward-looking Painite rationality. For though the rationalisation of both agricultural and urban production offered an entry into wage-labour for one sector of the labouring poor, it was at the expense of other sectors, whose members became, thereby, outlaws.

It is by way of these themes that I am situating the communitarian lyric as a romantic persistence in the nineteenth-century life of lyric forms. This lyric lineage formulated a version of poetic autonomy by drawing on a tradition of English popular sovereignty manifested in oral narratives and myths of origin, conveyed through metres associated with traditional culture. It insisted upon the importance of narrative elements within lyric form. The importance of the tenacity of oral poetic structures from within customary culture is apparent in the practices of romantic period ballads as both aesthetic and as interventionist lyrical objects. If the quintessential individualist lyric features an unmoored 'I' speaking from an atemporal 'spot of time', the communitarian lyric voice is anchored in labouring practices, narratives, and traditions, while proposing a future at which it is aimed for its realisation as an identity. In other words, the communitarian lyric is teleological in a way that the individualist lyric is not. In *Sources of the Self*, Charles Taylor discusses the way in which our sense of moral provenance has shifted over time from external to internal sources of the 'good'. In the same manner in which the constitutive goods which underlie liberal life reside in the depths of personal inwardness and find their significant poetic form in the meditative personal lyric, so do those external constitutive goods which shaped the world of customary culture reside with rhetorical ease in lyrics of temporality, solidarity, and futurity.[36]

Though this tradition, named during the Chartist period as the tradition of the 'people's poetry', would focus on the figure of Shelley, Thomas Spence was one of its first literary activists. Through his poems, songs, and the extracts collected and arranged in his 1790s journal and document for plebeian self-education, *One Pennyworth of Pig's Meat*, which served as a riposte to Burke's depiction of the crowd as a 'swinish multitude', Spence founded a line of poetic activism which made a claim for a semi-autonomous cultural tradition, and for the importance of poetry to political life, integrated into the Spencean Land Plan for the redistribution of wealth. After 1795, once the period of deep repression had set in, Spenceans increasingly turned to the interventionist possibility of poetry and song: 'Sing and meet and meet and sing, and your Chains will drop off like burnt thread.'[37]

Thomas Spence forged links between enlightenment rationalism and the customary heritage, and he acted as a lightning rod for the counter-improvement communitarian rhetoric of agrarianism. Although he denounced religion as a delusion, like Blake he drew heavily upon biblical rhetoric and contemporary millenarianism. Spence was born into the artisanal community in Newcastle, was involved in a political campaign against the loss of common grounds, and became a committed rationalist.[38] Once in London in the stormy 1790s, Spence found himself not only further radicalised, but drawn back to visions of social change which drew as much upon plebeian myths of community as on Painite ideas of Natural Rights.

Outflanking Paine to the left in his call for the rights of women and infants as well as men, Spence's Land Plan advocated the community distribution of all wealth derived from agriculture. The theory of 'Spensonianism' travelled back and forth from city to country via the extensive family and community links amongst agricultural and urban workers, endowing a legacy for the Chartist Land Plan and the socialist revival at the end of the nineteenth century. The theory of the 'people's farm' drew on a tradition of the 'freeborn Englishman', the 'Norman Yoke', and a sense of custom which differs markedly from the conservative Burkean version, and which advocates the community recovery of agricultural stolen property. The Spencean 'people's farm' lyric idealisation of the land differed from that proposed by the aesthetic ideology's poets of solitude and retreat, presenting in place of a landscape most noteworthy for its coalescence with pure consciousness, a landscape meant to feed the body. While Wordsworth's guardian Nature nourishes him 'by beauty and by fear', Nature bequeaths to the agricultural worker an 'entail' of abundance:

> When Nature her pure artless reign began,
> She gave in entail all her stores to man;
> The earth, the waters, eke the air and light,
> And mines and springs, men held in equal right.[39]

This is an important strain within popular ballads as well: 'In olden times the poor could on the common turn a cow / The commons are all taken in, the rich have claimed them now.'[40] The sublime landscape of individualist romantic lyricism presents an absolute distance between personal identity and nature; the communitarian strain demonstrates the inextricability of the human and the natural terrain.

It is in the ambience of Spencean communitarian lyrics that we can find a place for Shelley's 'The Mask of Anarchy', which, I will argue, displays a Shelley who, in this instance, fits less of a Godwinian and more of a plebeian model. The collective subject Shelley invokes in his poem on the Peterloo Massacre derives from customary myths about communal property which were rekindled amongst the second-generation Spenceans. The importance of the communitarian tradition to feminism is hinted at when we notice how, in this poem, Shelley refigures the romantic figure of the silent woman by invoking a voluble female Earth, the inside out of the female counterpart Shelley calls upon in his poems of solipsistic individualism, such as 'Alastor' and 'Epipsychidion'.

But, as Allen Grossman has argued, the paradox at the heart of liberal lyric culture is that the freedom of the lyric 'I' constantly threatens to become that of the 'we'. Those who possess the freedom of interiority fearfully anticipate its democratisation as unintelligibility and the unmooring of tradition.[41] Charles Kingsley's mid-century remarks about the effect of Shelley's poetry upon Chartist poets reflects this apprehension. He blames Shelley as one who had done Chartist poets 'most harm in teaching the evil trick of cursing and swearing ... and one can imagine how seducing such a model must be, to men struggling to utter their own complaints'.[42] On the other hand, in the maintenance of the isolation of the 'I', the singularity of self threatens to become isolated and autistic, wherefore comes in the end, as Wordsworth reminds us, 'despondency and madness'.

In the 1830s and 1840s, the Chartist movement displays the complex inheritance of the double-voice of romanticism. Activist Chartist poets and poetical theorists were particularly interested in, even preoccupied with, their inheritance from romantic poetry. Historians of the movement have on the whole neglected the force of poetry within the political project, and literary historians have only recently begun to track and taxonomise the varieties of working-class poetry.[43] It is clear, however, that Chartism fully engaged itself in the interventionist aspect of romantic poetics, and so provides a literary link between the communitarian strain evinced in the decades of romantic lyricism, and the socialist poetics of the end of the century. The Chartist poetic was indebted to Robert Owen and the Owenite interest in Shelley's poetic intentions, which Owen read as an early version of his own communitarian model of identity and sociality. Chartist poetry was not merely a reflex of the movement, however, for Chartists' desires to create a self-sufficient intellectual world urged them to formulate a poetic that would in turn fuel the political movement itself. The central Chartist goal of enabling full civic subjectivity through the objective demand for the franchise, was formulated, at least in part, through the shaping of a Chartist poetic.

Recapitulating the division between the individual and the communitarian within its own trajectory, Chartist poetry begins as a collective voice, and then throws forward a new version of the subjective lyric, and a group of 'labour laureates'. Early Chartist poetry is often anonymous and grounded in the norms of oral culture. Poetic texts which appeared in the main Chartist newspaper, Feargus O'Connor's *Northern Star*, range from lyrics based on popular ballad measure ('The Slave's Address to British Females', 'The Factory Girl's Last Hour') to great stretches of dramatic iambic pentameter ('Prologue to a New Drama, Spoken by a Druid, on John Frost and the Insurrection at Newport'), as well as poems which belong to a more meditative mode ('A Fragment for the Labourer', 'Sonnets Devoted to Chartism', and many others).

Importantly, however, Chartist poets did not only invoke the overt political poetry of romantic poets, but also drew on the meditative mode. Thomas Cooper and others may have relied heavily on models deriving from romantic poets interpreted as champions of the oppressed, but W. J. Linton borrows the lyric sweep of the 'Ode to the West Wind' and the sublimity of *Prometheus Unbound* to produce the metaphorical language of a communitarian movement. In *Prometheus Unbound*, Shelley's Asia invokes the power of Earth by analogy with that of the minds of humans:

> Hark! the rushing snow!
> The sun-awakened avalanche! whose mass,
> Thrice sifted by the storm, had gathered there
> Flake after flake, in heaven-defying minds
> As thought by thought is piled, till some great truth
> Is loosened, and the nations echo round,
> Shaken to their roots, as do the mountains now.[44]

Linton materialises this impulse: not thoughts, but masses of bodies build to the avalanche:

> Roll, roll, world-whelmingly! . . .
> Melt us away!
> Gather ye silently!
> Even as the snow
> Buildeth the avalanche
> Gather ye, Now.[45]

The late Chartist poet Ernest Jones draws on both external and subjective lyric forms, and opens up a liberated space of subjectivity within the realm of the exploited, emphasising the collective subjectivity of the operatives at their toil:

> 'Tis not to dig the grave,
> Where the dying miner delves;
> Tis not to toil for others
> But to labour for *yourselves*.[46]

For Jones, and other practitioners of Chartist lyricism, the legacy of plebeian communitarianism has been intertwined with the hegemony of lyric solitude: the song bears the mark of the inward subject. The communitarian lyric itself shifts and alters in the course of the century, under the influence of the principal generic centralisation of the solitary lyric speaker.

So it was that the power of the romantic lyric for Chartist poets drew on the figure of the poet as well as on the contents of poems. Imagined versions of Shelley and Wordsworth and Byron were crucial to the Chartists, for example, not because Chartists were dupes of some hegemonic poetic institution, and therefore too emulative of putative 'middle-class' poetic norms, but because in the romantic poetic were to be found elements of both traditional culture, with its sense of the centrality of a common voice, along with the developmental, self-authorising, autonomous subject of liberalism. The image of Byron as a romantic hero fighting for a democratic good was one such robust image, but the figure of the solitary contemplative worked as well, offering an ambiguous model of a self released from alienated labour, but perhaps then alienated from the collective struggle as well. Many Chartist poets uncomfortably wove together personal poetic vocation with collective political aspiration. And for Ernest Jones, as for many of the Chartist 48ers, the aim of solidarity was as social as it was political, the fight for the supplementary, as they called it, 'the Charter and something more'.

William Morris occupies a late and significant moment in the itinerary I have described here, when an explicit discourse of socialism is, in the 1880s and 1890s, jammed as a wedge into an emergency within the now dominant discourse of liberalism. The socialist revival offers a communitarian vision which, though carrying traces of the plebeian custom of the late eighteenth century, has mutated into something quite distinct through its encounter with and pressure on that aspect of enlightenment liberalism which had moved in an increasingly popularly democratic direction. For by the 1880s, Liberalism itself had become frightened of its theorisation of democracy.[47]

Morris's own movement from Gladstone's Liberalism to Marxist socialism offered to him, from within the dialectic of romanticism, an alternative set of poetic resources from which to draw. In the 1880s, when the old Chartists rallied round the new socialist movement, Morris found open to him that strand within romanticism which foregrounded the interventionist, rather than the meditative turn within lyricism. Morris's *Chants for Socialists* have much in common with Chartist songs and their endowment from romanticism.[48] In his biography of Morris, E. P. Thompson writes a narrative of romanticism in which he attributes to it a progressive anti-capitalist function which then atrophies and becomes nostalgic; and so Thompson is unable to find aesthetic or moral value in these *Songs*. I argue that in fact they present themselves not as a weak complaint against industrialism or a nostalgia for the past, but as part of a strategy for a future. And it is Morris's deployment of the communitarian aspect of the romantic tradition that provides the grounding for his extremely powerful and not frequently enough taught poetic sequence, *The Pilgrims of Hope*, a discussion of which completes this study. Thompson argues that in returning to Shelley's 'Ode to the West Wind' in 'The Message of the March Wind', the opening poem of *The Pilgrims of Hope*, Morris was trying to recover an outmoded poetic no longer adequate to the tasks required of it. Thompson is more or less forced to make this argument since he is himself committed to an organic birth, maturity, death model of romanticism, in which its high point is to be found in the rationalist republicanism of Byron and Shelley, who were themselves rekindling the values of the radical Wordsworth and Coleridge. This version of romanticism, Thompson argues, suffered aestheticisation and decline by the time Morris was writing. But if we think of romanticism not on this model but as the on-going theatre of contest between communitarianism and individualism, we see something different going on in Morris's poems. Morris's debt to Shelley is not antiquarian, but recuperative and revitalising; and it demonstrates the continuity of a communitarian, romantic poetic, which in the hands of the late nineteenth-century socialist movement, brings a poetic of lyric solidarity to bear upon the complex punctual and inward self of the liberal hegemony. Furthermore, the rurality which Morris evokes belongs less to what Thompson sniffs at as an 'idealized pastoral scene', than to the vernacular agrarian, the tradition of popular agrarianism, linked to urban radicalism, which produced the 'land' as a signifier of urban discontent.[49]

Communitarianism in the atmosphere of socialism in the 1880s represented an important advance upon the plebeian communitarianism which of course had also fueled the ideology of the radical Tories and the conservative Burkeans. The difference between these versions is the historical dialectic whereby plebeian communitarianism itself was transmuted into a socialist view of the *community* as the *collective*: a formation which depended on choice as much as birth. Voluntaristic identity offered the means for choosing positions of solidarity, which might take the form of socialism or the 'Red Republicanism' exemplified in the work of W. J. Linton. This movement pushed liberalism to accommodate aspects of a community vision of society, and put pressure on it to make sense of the developing self-consciousness of the 'new unionism' and working-class self-organisation in the 1880s and 1890s.

Though it is evident that it was individualism which won the larger debate, the communitarian poetic has continued to have its life in 'unofficial' culture, which has been and continues to act as its lyric repository. The poetic resources of what is often thought of as opposition or marginal cultural movements are steeped in a communal voice. The poetry of Anglo-Communism, the women's movement, and the poetry that appeared in the 1984–85 Miners' Strike all draw from the communitarian moment within romantic lyricism. As the contemporary meanings of individualism appear inadequate to our present political and social dilemmas, the urgency of communitarian values has re-emerged into calls for new manifestations of community. But it has been primarily versions of community in the lineage of Burke which are currently being seized upon as an antidote to the chaos of late capitalist individualism.[50] That is, the conservative communities of family and church are posed as antidotes to the loss of constitutive goods in the late twentieth century. The very recent appropriation of the term 'communitarian' by 'family value' ideologues, against the welfare state, threatens to overwhelm the important value of the communitarian criticism of liberal individualism as a conduit to thinking collectively and socially. For there is another genealogy of the communitarian tradition, whose history needs to be not only reiterated but seen as a present resource. As Alasdair MacIntyre points out (perhaps against his own conservatism): 'It is worth remembering that from the early 1840s onwards the recently coined adjectives "communitarian", "communitive" and "communist" were all used in much the same way.'[51] This other communal version has also had a rich life in the persistence of romanticism in poetry.

CHAPTER TWO

Ballad, lyrical ballad, lyric
Wordsworth, Dyer, and Mill

Both as a poetic practice, and as an object of study, the ballad was crucial to the founding of romantic lyricism: simultaneously dated and fashionable, oral and written, choric and monologic, the ballad expressed the pan-cultural possibility of a democratic poetry. Popular and ubiquitous, the ballad was the structure most obviously linked to an account of culture which relied on narrative coherence and the passing on of tradition, while being, at the same time, liable to the special claims made by Wordsworth for the 'lyrical ballad' as a poetic form suited to a project of cultural reformation. The ballad, like the broadside, had been a central form in eighteenth-century plebeian culture. It was the vehicle for political statement, poetic expression, and group identity.[1] By the very end of the eighteenth century, the popular tradition of ballads had met up with élite literary culture's fairly new interest in native balladry and song, while also being intercepted by and modified through the growth of congregational singing within dissenting and Methodist practices.[2]

While élite literary culture participated in acts of national identity formation through the recovery of documents of the past, poets from plebeian backgrounds who were themselves aspiring to enter print culture, described their initiations into the world of poetry through ballad and song, and as an aspect of the narrative of their personal identity formation. Allen Davenport, a significant communitarian poet linking Spencean to Chartist movements, and John Clare, who was notably, albeit briefly, integrated into London poetic culture of the 1820s through the *London Magazine*, were just two amongst many who attributed their social and cultural mobility to the impact of ballads. In his autobiography, Davenport recounts how he first encountered poetry by listening to his mother sing ballads; and Clare writes that his first attempts at poetry '[took the form of] imitations of my fathers Songs for he knew and sung a good many', which Clare then 'blushed' to write down 'but as my feelings grew into song I felt a desire to preserve some'.[3] Clare's anecdote presents an often-repeated memory of a sense of shame accompanying the plebeian poet's journey from oral into print culture, which forms part of the poet's narrative of vocational individuation. Clare's personal history is an index of how the contestation between communitarian and individualist norms of poetic identity produced astonishing poems which sear together the claims of self and of sociality, but also inflicted terrible hardship on personal identity.

Wordsworth's *Lyrical Ballads*, both the poems and the 'Preface', are generated from and riven by this engagement between plebeian and polite, customary and liberal, literary cultures. In the history of Wordsworth criticism, there has been much discussion of the meaning of the term 'lyrical ballad' as well as of the putative 'experiment' that Wordsworth carried out in the volume.[4] Twentieth-century critics have attended to the phrase 'lyrical ballad' as if it were an undecidable generic tag, and Stephen Parrish speaks for others when he remarks: 'No one knows precisely what a "lyrical ballad" was supposed to be.'[5] So it is worth reiterating the point made by a reviewer of the volume in the *British Critic* in 1801: 'The title of the Poems is, in some degree, objectionable; for what Ballads are not *lyrical?*' To the reviewer the lyric meant most obviously that form of poetry accompanied by music, ballads being an unproblematic example of such a form.[6]

But though this generic fact was obvious to the reviewer, it does not appear to be so to us, for the musicality of the lyric has, in the course of the nineteenth and twentieth centuries, mutated into a metaphoric cue for reading, rather than for reciting or singing. And this has taken place in the context of the lyric being directed into the centre of the generic repertoire of poetry.[7] It now often serves as a redundant term for poetry itself, used variously to denote a genre, a set of sub-genres, and, more diffusely, the poetic modality of *subjectivity in solitude*.[8] What we now miss in the peculiarity of the term 'lyrical ballad' is the extent to which it sews together the popular and demotic activity of the ballad with a classical heritage: the voices and choral collectivity of Greek tragedy.[9] By specifying the lyricality of his ballads, Wordsworth articulates a distinction between lyric and ballad in the same phrase that joins them to a classical tradition and history antedating the difference between oral and print poetic modes. This oscillatory title, which emphasises the closeness and the ineradicable distance between élite and popular, traditional and voluntaristic, embedded and unencumbered selves, is foundational for romanticism's work. Between *Lyrical Ballads* of 1798 and of 1800, Wordsworth draws out the implication of the separation of the lyrical from the balladic. In the 1798 'Advertisement', Wordsworth offers the notion that a lyrical ballad is a counter-intuitive or 'experimental' category, and by so doing, helps to mark out and introduce a distinction between what is properly lyrical and what is a ballad. He then goes on to reflect at length on his material in the 'Preface' to the 1800 edition; and the poems added to that edition, including, amongst others, the 'Lucy' poems, further extend the range of lyrical ballads, for they are poems which clearly belong to a print-culture definition of lyric, spoken in the lyric voice of subjectivity and individuality, but here contextualised by the lyrical ballad and the possibility of song. Incidentally, Wordsworth's displacement of Coleridge's poems from the volume also suggests a revision of the claim for impersonal collective authorship of ballads.

In élite literary culture, it was not until the mid-eighteenth century that theoretical links were forged to yoke the ballad to a classical inheritance of lyricism, when the great collections of Percy, Smith, and others not only made the poetic structure of the ballad fully visible to polite culture, but also formulated the represented figure of the bard, the ballad singer, as a mythic token of national identity.[10] The process of appropriating the ballad structure from within lived plebeian customary culture for the purposes of a campaign going on within élite culture – namely the campaign for the democratisation of art, of which Wordsworth and others were significant members – is the matrix within which the pseudo-enigma of the 'lyrical ballad' appears in romantic discourse. And while Wordsworth's 'Preface' organised the meta-discussion of the lyrical ballad, the difficulty of synthesising the now semi-autonomous realm of the lyrical with that of narrative is evinced as well in Mary Robinson's 1800 volume, *Lyrical Tales*, and in George Dyer's discussion of the term 'lyrical ballad' in his 'Essay on Lyric Poetry'.[11]

In investigating Wordsworth's presentation of the 'lyrical ballad' as an experimental form, Marilyn Butler has called attention to the ways in which Wordsworth's purposes serve enlightenment intentions. In her reading, it is Wordsworth's engagement with an aesthetic of simplicity, linked to an increasingly literate potential readership, that places Wordsworth's undertaking recognisably within enlightenment concerns. She shows that he was, in fact, somewhat behind in presenting his case, for the winds had swung away from those democratic arguments which, under the ideological pressures of the war, were increasingly identified as excrescences from France.[12]

Addressing the question of the 'lyrical ballad' in a more structural and less historical manner, both Tilottama Rajan and Don Bialostosky argue that Wordsworth's novelty is that he introduces elements of dialogue into the hitherto purity of the singular lyric speaker. Rajan maintains that the breaking of lyric solitude is a structure which, exhibited in a large number of romantic texts, may in fact be a hallmark of romantic lyricism.[13] Although these discussions make affective sense when critics are discussing the structure of dialogue in Wordsworth's poems as individual texts, it actually reverses the order of historical occurrence to argue that this represents a new phenomenon in lyric. It is more accurate to say Wordsworth had a larger hand in shaping lyric solitude than in breaking it, for ballads as lyrical forms have traditionally incorporated multiple voices.[14]

On the other hand, the elevation of the customary cultural form of the ballad into the range of generic visibility for polite literary culture found a particularly appreciative audience amongst the reforming and republican poets of the 1790s, in conjunction with the emergence of an interest in and appreciation of Burns's songs, and buttressed by congregationalist and Methodist hymnody.[15] While Wordsworth's yoking of the customary and the voluntaristic poetic self in *Lyrical Ballads* served as the matrix from which both the communitarian and the individualist lyric of the nineteenth century would emerge, Burns was by turns being claimed by a progressive, 'people's' poetic tradition and by a conservative one.[16] So, the process of reclaiming a ballad tradition both comes to its completion and undergoes a transformation in Wordsworth's attention to the lyricality of the ballad. In making explicit and then reflecting upon the tacit connections amongst oral culture, music, and choric voicing, Wordsworth's ventriloquising of customary culture authorises the theorisation of the 'lyrical ballad', at the very moment at which it is being superseded by the demands of individualism, print culture, and the modelling of an internal lyric voice whose constitutive goods are to be located, finally, within the self. Wordsworth's lyrical ballads are an elegy to what they signify.

When Robert Mayo first reinserted *Lyrical Ballads* within the literary fashions of their moment, he argued that there is a peculiar quality to Wordsworth's poems which renders them superior to the general run of ballads: a 'clarity, freshness, and depth'. Other critics, under the press of the individualist lyric, have also made a point of highlighting the individuality and subjectivity of Wordsworth's lyric speakers. In the subsequent trajectory of Wordsworth's poetic and its reception, critics often stress the manner in which the ballad side of the formulation more or less drops out, and an interest in the lyrical, as in the *subjective* side of it, rises into prominence, Charles Ryskamp's being a most distinguished example of this line of argument.[17] Both contemporary and later critics have found the 'Lines Composed a Few Miles above Tintern Abbey' to be the most successful and compelling of the 'other' poems in *Lyrical Ballads with a Few Other Poems* (1798); it is often cited as the example which reveals the coming into maturity of Wordsworth's poetic. The subsequent editions of the volume further modify its generic intentions: *Lyrical Ballads with Other Poems* (1800), and *Lyrical Ballads with Pastoral and Other Poems* (1805).

It is not, however, until John Stuart Mill's essays on poetry in the early 1830s that the apotheosis of the Wordsworthian lyrical subjectivity takes place; in 'What Is Poetry?' (1833) an article written for W. J. Fox's liberal *Monthly Repository*, Mill specifies what had been tacit in Wordsworth's own composition, articulating the link between the liberal subject and Wordsworth's lyrical œuvre.[18] Through Mill's presentation, the individualist side of Wordsworth's romantic lyricism was positioned as formative of poetic continuity in the period between 1800 and the 1840s, and that aspect of Wordsworth's poetic became the foundation for the 'distinctive character' of lyric poems in the nineteenth century that Palgrave would group together under the rubric of 'The Book of Wordsworth'.[19] Mill codifies a process which is undertaken in Wordsworth's poetry, but he significantly deprives Wordsworth's argument of its communitarian facet. Wordsworth's foregrounding of the lyricality of the ballad disengages the function of lyric from that of ballad, letting the possible meanings of lyricality float free; Mill's attention to the solitude of the lyric voice disencumbers Wordsworth's poetic of its own claim to the social, transpersonal voices of the ballad. Wordsworth himself, of course, participated in this reduction of his poetic towards the individualist mode: we might think of the 'spot of time' as Wordsworth's displacement of the ballad's embedded narrative of customary culture by the inward poetic moment of lyric time.

Over the past fifteen years, critical discussion of Wordsworth has been dominated by debate about his political commitments and their impact on his poetry and poetics.[20] One way to exemplify the debate is to juxtapose the positions taken on the one hand by James Chandler and on the other by E. P. Thompson. In this critical encounter, which recapitulates a larger division in the field of romantic studies, the question asked is whether Wordsworth's late 1790s poetry was that of 'Jacobinism-in-recoil', as Thompson argues, or rather, as Chandler claims in his very influential book, *Wordsworth's Second Nature*, the early appearance of the conservatism of Edmund Burke which then suffuses the whole of Wordsworth's œuvre.[21] Thompson defends Wordsworth's move as one from ideology, 'abstract political right', to 'something more local, but more humanely engaged'.[22] Chandler makes the case that, after a brief flirtation with Rousseau, from very early on Wordsworth was deeply influenced by Burke's categories of 'habit, custom, and tradition'.[23] Chandler makes a compelling presentation of these categories in Wordsworth's poetry, but since his study was published in 1984, intellectual and cultural historians have shown that in the 1790s, the notion of 'custom', like many other categories, was under great stress. Just as Burke wrestled the term 'patriot' to the ground, after which it signified an upholder of the crown after centuries of having meant precisely the opposite, so did he participate in the work on the term 'custom', and make it politically accountable, by way of his polemic against Richard Price, to an ideal of authoritarian traditionalism. In this way Burke formulated for the 1790s the strain of conservatism in Hume, whose use of the category of custom as the shaper of the order of experience, 'the great guide of human life', underpins the blossoming of Burke's conservative custom as a resource against cultural and political change.[24] Hume's own turn to arguments of behaviour and observation to make sense of human morality positions him as a preparatory figure to the focus on 'ordinary life' that Charles Taylor sees as central to the romantic view of identity.[25]

Chandler does not consider *Lyrical Ballads* as a volume in his otherwise exhaustive reading of Wordsworth's poetry, yet in those poems and the 1800 'Preface' the category of custom is presented in all its contemporary political volatility. The plebeian politics of custom, with its own logic and rationality comes up against and clashes with the logic and rationality of the economic shift which strangled the régime of common right: 'its loss played a large part in turning the last of the English peasantry into a rural working class'.[26] Often in Wordsworth's ballads the consciousness of the poet or narrator, formed in and through the culture of individualism – autonomous, self-exploring, and finding the good in personal choice – comes up against and must make sense of other identities formed in the culture of customary society: socially embedded, making meaning through narrative, and finding moral value in a set of external goods.[27] Wordsworth's stance in relation to these selves varies throughout the volume. In 'Simon Lee', the poet responds with a combination of despair and indignation to the degraded sense of self produced within the huntsman because of his displacement from his feudal and unreflective connection with the master of Ivor Hall. Simon Lee lives within and thinks through the relations of external customary culture; but the reader of the poem, Wordsworth suggests in the 'Preface', is meant to break through those mental habits: 'in the way of receiving from ordinary moral sensations another and more salutary impression than we are accustomed to receive from them'.[28]

'The Idiot Boy', which Wordsworth describes in the 1800 'Preface' as making plain the subjectivity of the self, the passage of 'the maternal passion through many of its more subtle windings' (241), shows just as clearly a straightforward sense of community responsibility amongst rural cottagers: interior and external constitutive goods are shown to occupy the same poetic space. That is, Wordsworth plays with customary and individualist modes of being and knowing, drawing on the languages of interiority as well as those of superstition and canniness, the most customary forms of knowledge. 'Goody Blake and Harry Gill' is a ballad which enacts most concretely the conflict between customary rights and the legislation that followed on from enclosure. Goody Blake, a poor cottager who lives by spinning, gathers fuel from Harry Gill's hedge, but what had been a custom is now judged to be a theft, and Harry Gill regards her practice as a criminal act. In revenge Goody calls upon the magical powers of the plebeian enchanted earth, and Harry Gill is henceforth afflicted by a palsy. In the 1798 'Advertisement', Wordsworth asserts the logic of customary culture when he writes that this poem 'is founded on a well-authenticated fact' (8); in the 1800 'Preface', however, he writes from a rather different epistemological position, first noting how 'rude' the metre of the poem is, and then offering an explanation from rational psychology: 'I wished to draw attention to the truth that the power of the human imagination is sufficient to produce such changes even in our physical nature as might almost appear miraculous' (261). Here Wordsworth modifies the customary voice from within a logic of scientific psychology. The voices of custom that Wordsworth draws on carry the weight of plebeian rhetoric, and as well, the residual power of 'customary culture' quite unlike its shape in Burkean conservatism. This strand within the romantic lyric tradition incorporates not only the forms of ballad and the shapes of collective identity, but also the customary themes of magic and canniness, which continue to inform romantic lyrics well into the mid-nineteenth century.

But in the prefatory remarks to 'Goody Blake' and 'Simon Lee', Wordsworth opens a breach between the customary consciousness within the poem and the individualist voice of the poet. What these examples suggest is that the legacy of Wordsworth's 'Preface' – its hardy perennial place as the originary text of a theory and practice of lyric dependent upon affect before event, interiority before experience, thinking and

feeling before narrating – depends upon a partial and retrospective interpretation, a reading whose values were instantiated in and co-ordinate
with the liberal poetic theory of John Stuart Mill in the 1830s. Read however in the context of its own genealogy, however, Wordsworth's argument
in his 'Preface' shows itself to be compounded of the paradoxical materials
of 1790s ideology. For the argument of the 1800 'Preface' is poised between
two conceptions of creativity: one which grounds the work of the poet in
a habit and soil; the other which describes the formation of modern
interiority, in which an autonomous self locates value within his or her
own consciousness. One side of the picture Wordsworth presents is the
poet whom Mill will regard as the voice of modernity, inward and
autonomous. But Wordsworth also argues that the resources of such a
position are found in the language and very geography of customary
culture, articulated by an habituated self who belongs to a set of habits, a
tradition, and is a character in a narrative of human practice.[29] So
although Wordsworth does call upon the tradition, habit, and custom of
the ballad form, he does so in an ideational and geographical space where
the term 'custom' had more caustic deployment, and was as indicative of
plebeian rebelliousness as of Burkean containment.

   E. P. Thompson's later work on customary culture offers a good point of
departure for questioning his earlier interpretation of romantic politico-
poetics. Thompson began by defending Wordsworth's poetry of
'Jacobinism-in-recoil' in order to save Wordsworth and Coleridge for a
particular version of a republican-internationalist tradition within
romanticism. But this commitment to the Painite line, tied to an
apparently inevitable sequencing of theoretical organicism, turns the rest
of nineteenth-century romanticism into a long movement of decline. Yet
Thompson's work in *Customs in Common* now allows us to see more clearly
how Wordsworth's politico-poetical journey exhibits and enacts the
conflicts and competing voices of nativist custom and internationalist
rationalism which name and shape a dialectic within romanticism. In fact,
the communitarian lyric in this tradition owes much to Wordsworth's
yoking of internal and external goods in *Lyrical Ballads*.

   In *Wordsworth's Historical Imagination*, David Simpson, writing in the
tradition of the work of Z. S. Fink, argues that Wordsworth's poetic was
underpinned by 'agrarian idealism', a theory of agrarian civic virtue
derived from the older models of native republicanism of Harrington and
others.[30] Returning to the question of Wordsworth's idea of the rural
polity in *Romanticism, Nationalism and the Revolt against Theory*, Simpson
argues that in the 'Preface' to *Lyrical Ballads*, Wordsworth attempts a

'synthesis of the otherwise antagonistic principles of Burke and Paine'.[31] In presenting the case for the complexity of Wordsworth's politics against what Simpson finds to be a lack of nuance in Althusserian-inflected New Historicist readings of Wordsworth's poetic history, Simpson argues that in poetics, Wordsworth was a Painite, while in politics, he was an 'idiosyncratically formulated ruralist'.[32] Simpson's argument brings us a step closer to the structure of feeling within which Wordsworth was living. Another way to specify this tension between the nostalgic and the progressive in Wordsworth's poetic is to place it within the larger cultural experience of the encounter bétween customary and individualist models of personal and social identity. We can see the power of the rôle Wordsworth assigns to the poet as a kind of articulate boundary between the cultures of custom and of reason, speaking on behalf of but not from the customary culture; and criticising, but engaged in, the enlightenment one. Drawing upon the common associations and functions of the ballad as a customary form, Wordsworth yokes the rationality of his poetic practice to the culture of plebeian rurality.

To encounter even more fully the structure of feeling within which *Lyrical Ballads* was written, it is worth thinking about Wordsworth's place in the urban public space just prior to his 1797 walks in the Valley of the Stones with Coleridge, during which he was planning the *Lyrical Ballads* volume. This is a thought made possible by Kenneth Johnston's work on Wordsworth's conjectured association with the journal *The Philanthropist*.[33] The account Wordsworth gives in *The Prelude* of his moral crisis and his return from abstract reason to a domestic language of the heart, now written by him in the light of Burke, may have been prepared for in the 1790s by way of the complicated claims for customary culture in a radical plebeian mode which was loose in the public spaces of London. In this milieu, which drew together radical artisans, rationalist intellectuals, and agrarian communists, Wordsworth's version of tradition may more easily be understood to include elements of the complex inheritance from the plebeian customary culture being fought over and articulated in both country and city during the revolutionary years, as well as the pure distillation of Burke's account of custom which Wordsworth did later come to adopt wholeheartedly. That is, Wordsworth's progress towards Burke may have involved a slippage from the more radical possibilities of custom as plebeian claims to identity, in addition to his repudiation of absolute Godwinism.

The meeting point of the epistemology of customary and voluntaristic régimes is apparent from the start in the 'Preface' to *Lyrical Ballads*, where

Wordsworth argues that a set of customary conditions organises the project of the volume, including (1) a 'soil' in which 'essential passions' can grow (239) ; (2) the repetitions of rural life, which, organically linked to the language used to describe it, stabilise that language; (3) the integration of human activity and the natural world. The poet, by his self-consciousness, mediates the presentness of rural experience, and the figure of the poet becomes an emblem of the link between consciousness and rurality: in making poetry, the man of 'organic sensibility' (240) must yoke his spontaneity to the process of thinking 'long and deeply' (240).

Wordsworth argues against 'habits of association' (237) in the opening of the 'Preface', but only those habits that belong to a deracinated urban literary culture which a return to rural custom is meant to moderate. The language of 'common life' (238) arises from 'repeated experience and regular feelings' (239), and this is a virtue because it situates speakers in a network of human associations, unlike poets who 'separate themselves from the sympathies of men, and indulge in arbitrary and capricious habits of expression' (239–240). In this strand of his argument, then, the poet is to be an exemplar of communitarian rootedness, who establishes links amongst persons through his lyrical work, as he articulates the 'strength of fraternal, or to speak more philosophically, of moral attachment' (242). The localism of association which is the attribute of the rural commons provides a ground for the narrative ballads in the collection, in which stories of selves are shown to emerge from their situation in space and their integral connection to the production of their livelihood. In 'We Are Seven', this association extends the claims of locale beyond life into death, as the child in the poem offers a narrative of inclusion which stands as an admonition to the analytically dissecting logic of the poem's speaker. The rational narrator of 'We Are Seven' is inanely unable to comprehend the cottage child's assertion that there are no geographical boundaries amongst her two dead siblings, the two who have gone 'to sea' (67), and the two who dwell at Conway, all of whom have been physically removed by illness, lack of work, and the power of the press gang or bounty.[34] Her family has submitted to the perils of the new socio-economic world, but they remain socially and narratively linked to the community of their cottage family, through the inclusive and trans-individual consciousness of the little girl. 'We Are Seven' details the meanings of the losses entailed in the shift into the régime of nationalist war, industrialisation of productive work, and changing rural demography. The poet scorns the narrator for his inability to break out of the logic of rationalism. It is interesting, then, that in the 1800 'Preface', which secures the 1798 poems to a reflective poetic intervention, Wordsworth describes this through a psychology which repudiates this poem's crash of customary and individualist mentalities: the child and the speaker now reside in the same logic, and the poem shows 'the perplexity and obscurity which in childhood attend our notion of death, or rather our utter inability to admit that notion' (241–2).

As many critics have noted, 'The Female Vagrant', 'The Old Cumberland Beggar', and others of the poems of human suffering in *Lyrical Ballads* dramatise the conditions of displacement of rural commoners and their communities.[35] But his use of this material is not merely conservative nostalgia, for Wordsworth's presentation of the 'common' was read in both reactionary and revolutionary periods as authorising a vision of the 'people' which, linked to later transformations in economy and identity, became a wellspring from which communitarian lyricality would draw. An article in the *Chartist Circular* in 1839 quotes Channing to confirm Wordsworth's place in democratic poetry, his 'prerogative, to discern and reveal the ordinary walks of life, in the common human heart'.[36]

The force of a poem such as 'The Female Vagrant' is that it underlines the ambiguous trade-off between custom and voluntarism: the Female Vagrant loses her place in the community, but she gains a three-dimensional subjective voice. 'The Female Vagrant' is written in Spenser's literary metre, exchanging what might be thought of as an atemporal ballad measure for an archaic one, and alerting the reader to the poet's place in high culture and in an English poetic tradition. But the poem takes the form of a soliloquy spoken by the Vagrant, offering her a place in this world as well. In an earlier version of the poem, 'A Night on Salisbury Plain', the Vagrant speaks directly to a traveller; in its form in *Lyrical Ballads*, the speaker – never named, and so representative – is situated in the disembodied, non-representational space of lyric consciousness.

She was born into the life of a rural cottager, and her family's troubles begin when an engrossing landlord claims their cottage. Her father is victimised when he refuses the landlord's offer of a cash settlement. The family's misery is compounded by the crash of the weaving trade, and they find themselves displaced from their rôles as traditional cottager labourers in the 'old hereditary nook' (line 44) and forced into the 'free' waged labour of the provincial town and then to America, where they suffer enormous deprivation and death. The Vagrant is picked up by a British ship, and though she is now travelling back to her place of origin, she is an alienated self, dreaming of herself as utterly landless, 'roaming the illimitable waters round' (line 175).[37] Returning to find that England is now a world which refuses to recognise or shelter her, the Female Vagrant manages her fate by recognising herself in the rôle of domestic alien, first as Gypsy and then as Jew, for the native cottager has truly become estranged through economic displacement. She travels first with a group of 'rude earth's tenants' (line 218). Amongst these Gypsies, the Female Vagrant is invited to become one of what appears to be a traditional and horizontal community where 'all belonged to all, and each was chief' (line 221). But though they are all vagrants together, she experiences a fundamental incompatibility with the group, for these are gypsy-outlaws, and she still maintains the values of the native customary community, 'brought up on nothing ill' (line 242), even though her community has been reduced to a population of one, and the authority for those values removed from the external world to her own subjectivity. So it is that (recognisable within the popular depiction of the period and echoing her vision of endless wandering on the ocean) she takes on the penitent figure of the Wandering Jew, because she has, she says, 'my inner self abused' (line 259). The Vagrant 'unaided and unblessed' (line 244) travels 'three years a wanderer' (line 262). When revising the texts for the 1802 edition, Wordsworth reinforced the connotations of the interiority of the Wandering Jew by altering the 1800 lines, 'I lived upon the mercy of the field, / And oft of cruelty the sky accused' (lines 253–4) to 'I led a wandering life among the fields, / Contentedly, yet sometimes self-accused' (lines 253–254, 1802). When the Female Vagrant opts for the identity she can *choose*, she moves out of the customary world and into the world of voluntarism and individual sufferings. Even though the Gypsy crew welcomes the Female Vagrant, she is marked by her separateness from them, because her identity has been forged out of her personal struggle of alienation from the cottager life. As a solitary, however, and like the many Wandering Jews who figure in romantic period poetry, she becomes a candidate for romantic transcendence. She exhibits that sense of autonomy, the need for self-exploration, and the goal of personal commitment which characterises individualist culture. The agony of the Female Vagrant suggests that at issue in the shift from customary to voluntaristic culture is not only the absolute good of forging a transcendent self, as in the voice of the speaker in 'Tintern Abbey', but the practical possibility of forging a self at all.[38]

'Custom', 'commons', and the story-telling function of ballads are all linked in one movement within both the theory and the practice of *Lyrical Ballads*. Communitarian identity is built upon a shared sense of history, conveyed in narratives which give direction to persons in social experience. Yet the poetics of the 'Preface' also articulate the unencumbered individual of romantic solitude, and presage the Wordsworth who will be praised for his invention of 'the poetry of the growing inner self'.[39] The yoking together of these two intentions of identity can be marked in places in the 'Preface' where Wordsworth converts the embedded narrative of social community into the transcendent lyric of a universal subject. In his presentation of the poet and his poetry as belonging to a world of subjective aesthetic liberty, Wordsworth makes the strong assertion that it is in the *priority of feeling over action* that the singularity of his poetic inheres: 'the feeling therein developed gives importance to the action and situation and not the action and situation to the feeling' (242). The purpose to trace and follow through 'the fluxes and refluxes' (241) of consciousness also suggests the priority of self over setting. That is, Wordsworth ascribes an autonomy of affect to his lyric creatures, disengaging them from the common culture to which they must nonetheless remain linked for his narrative lyrical balladic purpose. This is what we have seen in the voice of the Female Vagrant. One of the recognisably 'romantic' presentations of the duality is an abundance of madness in ballad characters, since that autonomy is unprepared for, as Wordsworth argues in the case of the Sea Captain in 'The Thorn' or the 'Mad Mother'. But what to the unencumbered self is the spectre of madness may be to customary consciousness the magic of the community, and the plebeian knowledge of the rurality, as in the case of 'Goody Blake and Harry Gill'. The power and the paradox of Wordsworth's assertions in the 'Preface' – that is, its romanticism – reside in his coupling together the links to custom and the break into free subjectivity. What functions within customary discourse as knowledge becomes superstition within individualist culture, and Wordsworth's mad people oscillate between the two poles of meaning. What becomes clear, however, is that insofar as free subjectivity *can* be conveyed without eccentricity – that is, as representative – it must be done through the presentation of a solitary 'I'. Through this 'I' the 'spontaneous [i.e. unencumbered] overflow of powerful feelings' (240) is given lyric shape. The lyric speaker can be representative insofar as any reader can occupy the space of its subjectivity, but to imagine the lyric 'I' as having an embodied identity will make that identification increasingly difficult, as in the troubling physical interruption of Wordsworth's meditation when he turns to Dorothy in the last movement of 'Tintern Abbey'. This increased need to theorise a represented, individualist 'I' to compensate for the disintegrating identity of the customary speakers of *Lyrical Ballads* may account for Wordsworth's addition in the 1802 'Preface' of a passage on the identity of the poet.

What makes Wordsworth's theorised poet so impressively the absolute of the romantic poet is that he is simultaneously the carrier of a customary tradition of the common life, the narrator of a tradition, as well as the model of the unencumbered individual. In the 1802 additions, the poet's powers as a voluntaristic individual are in evidence insofar as he can stir up in his consciousness feelings 'which are indeed far from being the same as those produced by real events' (250), though stronger and in some sense more real than those which people normally experience. So, the poet 'has acquired a greater readiness and power in expressing what he thinks and feels, and especially those thoughts and feelings which, *by his own choice, or from the structure of his own mind,* arise in him without immediate external excitement' (my emphasis) (250). This poet is disengaged as well from the weight of a poetic tradition whose élite dynastic encumbrances threaten to trap him, either by rendering his work indistinguishable from others', or equally vexing, rendering it unintelligible as poetry. For example, Wordsworth almost boasts that staying away from the falsity of personification 'has necessarily cut me off from a large portion of phrases and figures of speech which from father to son have long been regarded as the common inheritance of Poets' (245). In his presentation of the poet as a representative 'man speaking to men' (249), who has the talent for 'conjuring up passions', the figure of the lyric poet is shown to be not one amongst many versions of the abstract subject, but its very exemplar and highest version, as well as, paradoxically, the exemplar and highest version of the poet as socialised subject. What Wordsworth uses from customary culture is modified by his access to self-exploration, which launches him into the sense of autonomy which in turn generates an argument about the representational function of the poet who is more attuned to the nuances of experience, 'with a great promptness to think and feel without external excitement' (255). The communitarian worker poets that this study explores in its later chapters, take on and embody this ambiguous version of the poet and the lyric speaker that Wordsworth formulates in his 'lyrical ballads' and in his 'Preface': aiming to be a voice of the people, and also increasingly aware of and responsive to the claims of their own vocation and the individuated inwardness that indexes poetic vocation in romanticism.

Therefore, it should be noted that Wordsworth's liminal sense of this lyric subjectivity – disengaged yet engaged, autonomous yet common – is held up as a model to the readers of these poems. He requests of his reader that 'in judging these Poems he would decide by his own feelings genuinely, and not by reflection upon what will probably be the judgment of others' (270). But he also argues that such judgements should be brought within the purview of the larger community, 'for an *accurate* taste in Poetry and in all the other arts, as Sir Joshua Reynolds has observed, is an *acquired* talent, which can only be produced by thought and a long continued intercourse with the best models of composition' (271). In this statement Wordsworth appeals to a class of *readers* as opposed to those plebeian *listeners* he had referred to when describing the reception of 'Goody Blake and Harry Gill', writing that he had had 'the satisfaction of knowing it has been communicated to many hundreds of people who would never have heard of it, had it not been narrated as a Ballad' (267). Wordsworth produces the particular eccentricity of romanticism here, claiming a democratised readership through drawing on the ballad form (267), with its assumptions of the oral culture, while speaking as well to the literary élite of print culture.

These differential values of individuality and customary community regulate each other in Wordsworth's theory, and they also lead in different directions. Democratic radicalism in its individualist form bifurcates the poetic project: leading Wordsworth towards a wider audience, but also exacerbating the gap between the poet and those he represents, and hence more fully developing the solitary figure of the poet, whose being *as* poet grows closer to a 'self as mind', in Charles Rzpeka's phrase.[40] Alan Liu argues that Wordsworth's poetry after 1796 'produces by inversion a private lyric of presence: imagination . . . where collective loss can be reimagined as individual gain'. Liu feels that this lyric mode 'was not so much any particular kind of lyric as an *émigré* flight from narrative.'[41] But the values of customary culture as they operate as conductors of narrative were also agents of contradiction, implicating Wordsworth in the communal forms of plebeian life, and as well towards that Burkean paternalistic conservatism which he would later embrace fully.

It is poignant to check the meaning of common right within a very different Wordsworthian perspective. In an 1800 poem, 'Point Rash Judgement', Wordsworth begins by refining agricultural labour to a pleasant background hum, against which the interiority of the poet's Fancy develops. But the placidity of the poem is interrupted by the appearance of an emaciated peasant exercising his customary fishing right. From within the 'privacy' of a narrow ridge where Wordsworth and his friends saunter, they hear the productive labour of agricultural workers, whose crop 'feeds' the idlers' 'fancy'. The ramblers are comfortable in the social gap between their wandering and the labourers' work, and are then distressed to find their private space already inhabited by a 'peasant' significantly distinct from a 'labourer'. They first assimilate the fisher to the régime of capitalist agriculture, calling him 'improvident and reckless . . . when the labourer's hire / Is ample'. But once they see him face to face they are chastised by his poverty and his obvious redundancy in the brutal relations of contemporary agricultural production. Though Wordsworth does not invoke the loss of the 'pescatory' right, the poem performs the bifurcation of moral and capitalist economies. But the best response that the speaker of the poem can manage is, as in other of his post-1797 poems, one that devolves upon the cultivation of 'My single self'.[42]

The period during which the ballad was of interest to the literary élite was brief, and was prior to the discursive fashioning of an autonomous 'people's' literary tradition articulated with class struggle rhetoric, characteristic of the post-1832 period. As Albert Friedman asserts of the late eighteenth-century ballad fashion, 'in its latest development the ballad of simplicity became one of the principal means through which the sentimental humanitarianism of the period expressed itself'.[43] The passing of the ballad style was neither the simple end of an arbitrary fashion, nor evidence of the super-saturation of a form, but an example of a generic exclusion after the convention had played its part in the reformation of polite poetics, and was tied to changes in polite politics in the declension of reform into anxiety in the 1790s. Of course, the ballad does not entirely drop out of élite cultural life; poems continue to be written in ballad form, but for the most part it runs to ground as a significant instantiation of the lyric, though balladic elements continue to be incorporated into print-culture art poetics.[44] Wordsworth continued to pay homage to the impact of Percy's collection: 'I do not think there is an able writer in verse of the present day who would not be proud to acknowledge his obligation to the *Reliques*.'[45] But with its roots in customary plebeian culture, the work of the ballad shifts in the course of the century, re-emerging along with other lyric structures such as the hymn to benefit the print-culture poetics of the working-class movement of the later 1830s.

The lyrical ballad, then, serves as an icon of romanticism and its constitution as the engagement between communitarian and individualist models of poetic making: subjectivity displayed concurrently in time (narrative) and out of time (lyric). While the transit from ballad to lyrical ballad to lyric was one path through which the individualist liberal lyric came to control the central trajectory of romanticism, other ideas of lyricism were simultaneously being tested which also theorised a democratisation of poetry. Counterpoised to Wordsworth's account of the poetic self who stands in for and represents other selves, is a notion of poetic identity as a space within which other identities can proliferate.

For in the period prior to the 1832 Reform Bill, when the categories of 'democracy' and 'liberalism' *appeared* to be congruent, they were, in fact, moving on distinct trajectories, evidence of instability at the centre of the liberal project; namely, the desire both to protect the hierarchy of private property and to extend political equality. Anthony Arblaster argues that this shaped the two themes which were to be 'dominant in nineteenth-century liberalism: a concern to structure the political system in such a way as to protect property, and an abiding fear and anxiety about democracy'.[46] Arblaster finds that the power of American and French revolutionary ideas 'which assured the future of liberalism, also inspired a range of political developments and movements situated outside and beyond liberalism, all of which were to grow up to challenge liberalism's brief hegemony'.[47] The project within poetry to name a value for subjectivity which would coalesce with a new political citizenry fuels the discourse on democratic poetics.

The régime of liberalism was in formation long before its political party was seated in Parliament. In *Keywords*, Raymond Williams follows the course of the meaning of the term 'liberal', bifurcated from the mid-seventeenth century on the one hand as 'generous', on the other as 'unrestrained': so 'open-minded' can be read as 'unorthodox' by Tories, and as the potential guarantor of freedom by Whigs.[48]

It was from within a deep sense of the 'liberality' of lyric poetry in the 1790s, its openness and lack of uniformity, that the lyric mode was understood to be crucial to the democratising stance of republican and reform poets. For alongside the freedoms of privacy and of voluntarism came an untrammelling of generic definition as well: the notion that each person is their own yardstick is mirrored in the notion that each genre accomplishes its own organic form. And it was precisely such implications of liberality which became troubling later in the century as working-class poetry develops as an autonomous vein within literary culture. As Brian Maidment points out, throughout the nineteenth century there was an extended discussion in the periodical press over the values and drawbacks of working-class poetry, 'expressing widespread anxieties and ambiguities felt by the middle classes at the appearance of voices from the industrial working labouring classes'.[49] As noted earlier, Charles Kingsley feared that Shelley's influence would be a source of agitation and unrest in working-class poetry; F. W. Robertson, on the other hand, advocated working people's poetry as a means of deflecting political agitation, arguing that: 'It is a mistake to think that Poetry is only good to nurse feeling ... It is the safety-valve to the heart.'[50] The poetic activists of the Chartist and Socialist movements gathered their strength from economic and ideological crises between the 1830s and the 1890s, for the liberalism around them was unable to meet the demand for complete democratisation, and the residual elements of the communitarian lyric of customary culture offered a poetic site for recovering the poetics of democratisation.

Given the indicative value of the lyric, then, it is of some interest to turn to two 1802 essays by the London radical republican, George Dyer. These essays, probably influenced by Wordsworth's 'Preface' to *Lyrical Ballads*, address issues of generic formulation, balladry, and the rôle of poetry in a liberal reform movement. In discussions by Wordsworth and Dyer, the analysis of lyric functions sits comfortably with notions of liberality that partake of both aesthetics and politics, and their essays situate the lyric flexibly between the privatising of the aesthetic ideology, and the democratising spirit of a common culture.

In the essays on 'Lyric Poetry' and 'Representative Poetry', Dyer theorises the lyric with the intention of showing the liberality of lyric forms within established literary culture, with an emphasis on the ballad, and he also aims to focus on the range of voices available to lyric structures. Dyer is eager to argue from the freedom of the lyric as a generic form to the freedom of people generally. And he supports a rendering of subjectivity in which the poetic voice is not an assertive 'I', but available to other voices, a kind of poetic 'representation' in which the poet of the best lyric poetry 'resigns his individuality'.[51] Dyer produces a theory of the lyric subject as differentiated but not individuated.

Dyer was an accomplished political pamphleteer as well as a theorist of poetry. His work in the 1790s appeared in a range of radical periodicals, including the *Monthly Magazine* and Thomas Spence's *Pig's Meat*. As was the case for many other radicals and republicans, Dyer's reputation in the nineteenth century was subdued into that of an eccentric and ineffectual intellectual, and he has been remembered principally as the foolish, kind, and unhygienic friend of Charles Lamb. Thomas Noon Talfourd, in his *Final Memorials of Lamb*, describes Dyer's life as 'an Academic Pastoral', his personality blessed by a 'bland unconsciousness of evil'.[52] But Dyer probably knew rather more about the world than many of his friends and companions. He came from an artisan family in Wapping, where his father worked as a watchmaker. He went to Christ's Hospital and then to Cambridge, where he was drawn into the circle of radical dissenters at Jesus College, and in the close connections between radical dissent and political activism, when he arrived in London in 1792, Dyer dived immediately into the reform movement.[53]

So Dyer was fundamentally an urban radical, coming from the London artisan milieu and, after Cambridge, living permanently in London.[54] In politics, Dyer drew from and contributed to both the artisan and the middle-class intellectual milieux. And he knitted together rationalist internationalism and nativist structures of thinking and feeling, linking the historicist mythology of English liberty and the rationalist logic of Painite republicanism. For example, Dyer's conception of natural rights does not exclusively belong to enlightenment categories, nor to the rhetoric of either Paine or Rousseau; rather, rights for Dyer arise from their being embedded in the domestic soil. Natural rights are 'claims arising out of our present situation, our mutual relation, and our common equality. Whoever attempts to violate them encroaches on the common privileges, and supports the cause of tyranny'.[55] One can hear in Dyer's claim that natural rights derive from 'the soil where you received your origin', the traditional narrative and ideology of the 'Freeborn Englishman', whose ancient constitution had been broken by William the Conqueror.[56] Writing on the English Constitution, Dyer indulges in the historicist idea of ancient rights undone through the Norman Yoke: 'The restoration of long-lost rights . . . is now imperiously demanded by the times.'[57] As James Epstein has shown, the linking of historicist to rationalist arguments did not feel contradictory to those making the arguments, rather they seemed to reinforce one another:

Plebeian democrats might have revered the memory of Tom Paine, but as often as not they ignored his strictures against invoking the legitimating force of the past. They turned more often to a radicalised British constitutionalism than to the language of the French revolution in order to draw legitimacy for their own democratic claims and actions and to censure the claims and actions of their social betters.[58]

Dyer wrote a series of political tracts, beginning with one in favour of the repeal of the Corporation and Test Acts, his 1789 *An Inquiry into the Nature of Subscription to the Thirty-Nine Articles*. Acutely aware of the contemporary problem of the engrossment of wastes, in his 1793 *Complaints of the Poor People of England*, Dyer offers a description of the state of the labouring classes and practical plans for the reclaiming of waste lands for common use. His discussion of the 'GREAT DISPROPORTION between crimes and punishments', with its attention to the incommensurate values of property and life, articulates the causal links which led from the engrossment of land and the cessation of customary right to the legislating of customary into criminal acts.[59] Dyer was, nonetheless, a committed republican, and he mixed with the radical intelligentsia around Godwin,

was published by Johnson, and supported Mary Wollstonecraft's positions
in her *Vindication of the Rights of Woman.*[60] Dyer was active in the Society for
Constitutional Information, but was attracted as well to the more radical
and artisan London Corresponding Society.[61] Some of Dyer's positions
derived from Paine, but like many radicals in the period, and in particular
those living in London, the rhetorics of radicalism that Dyer drew upon
were culled from many traditions, and had an active, *ad hoc* quality about
them.[62] His political interests were not sectarian, and he was a supporter of
the United Irishmen. While his language and sense of right were based in
the organicist and historicist version of the past, what he calls 'the good old
tree of English liberty', Dyer's was a Painite vision of an improved society,
in which the main fault of the English Constitution, that it is 'defective
in political liberty', might be remedied through reform and increased
representation.[63]

It is worth rehearsing Dyer's radical credentials and the seriousness of
his political purposes in the face of the myth of the man as silly, weak, and
intellectually marginal.[64] For in the context of Dyer's work as a radical
republican, we can make significant sense of his interest in the lyric as a literary form of cultural liberation. Dyer's theory of lyric is interesting in
part because in it an implicit conversation takes place with Wordsworth
about the value of poetry in social life. And Dyer's own poems take on added
interest in the light of his theory of lyric poetry, which is linked closely to
the politics of reform and the idea of liberality.[65] Some of Dyer's poems,
such as his song 'While venal bards attempt to sound', are song lyrics, drawing on constitutional historicism, and invoking the image of the freedom-
loving bard of Justice; while his more explicitly elegiac poems such as
the 'Ode to Major Cartwright' and 'Gilbert Wakefield' belong to the
traditions of public lyricism and articulate the language of republicanism.

A telling example of how Dyer's democratic theory of poetry was mis-
interpreted as a simpleton's benevolence can be found in Charles Lamb's
good-naturedly denigrating remark that according to Dyer, 'All Poems are
good Poems ... All men are fine Geniuses.'[66] Dyer's commitment to and
interest in processes of democratisation suggest, however, that this notion
of poetic competence was the unfolding of a political position about
democratic capability, rather than simply being the result of lack of
aesthetic discernment. While Wordsworth's poet was a man speaking to
men, to Dyer all men might be poetic speakers.

Dyer published a volume of poems with Joseph Johnson in 1792, and his
satiric assessment of the place of poets in public life, *The Poet's Fate*, in
1797.[67] He also included a series of critical essays, including one on 'Lyric

Poetry', and one on 'Representative Poetry' with his two-volume *Poems* (1802).[68] The essay on lyric poetry begins by stressing how the lyric has moved into the central position amongst the genres in his literary milieu:

Critics, and no bad ones, have pronounced lyric poetry to be more elegant in its structure, more lofty in its spirit, more difficult in its contrivance, than any other species; and poets unite with critics in ascribing to it excellencies of the highest character. (I, viii)

Dyer goes on to catalogue the variety of lyric forms, and then makes a case for the importance of those lyrics which come from the aesthetic of simplicity, the enlightenment strain of humanitarian sentimentality. These poems are an important addition to those from the classical literary tradition:

There is a species of lyric poetry that may be thought somewhat different from these already mentioned, and to have obtained but little sanction from such as we consider the models of this sort of composition, the Greek and Roman poets: I mean that, which studiously searches for subjects in what are deemed the most ordinary concerns of life, and where the language is characterized by greatest simplicity. We have of late years had many attempts of this kind, and some have been made with success. (I, xxxix)

Dyer acknowledges the fashions around him, and given that he knew Wordsworth, and says that he has rewritten his essay in the light of new thoughts about lyric, it is probable that he is here referring to *Lyrical Ballads*. In his political reading of the lyric, Dyer follows on from and understands the fashion for simplicity, and he links it to the kinds of genres associated with plebeian cultural forms. Dyer argues that

The tender balad, the sprightly song, and even the humorous tale, possess the character of lyric poetry, no less than compositions of higher pretension, as to subject, and of more magnificent appearance, as to structure. (I, xxxii)

Dyer's insight into the importance of the ordinary to lyricism signals both his acuity about the culture of democratisation and the impact, within a radical democratic politics, of the norms of oral culture upon print culture. But Dyer takes the enlightenment focus on simplicity and ties it even more securely to republican politics. His argument states first that lyric poetry is the most 'liberal' poetic form, and then that the current state of poetry is diagnostic of the state of freedom in a society. He argues that the political sentiments of his poetry are of a piece with the purposes of lyric in the life of a polity:

An apology for such pieces as savour of enthusiasm for liberty, would come with an ill grace from me ... The principles of freedom are too sacred to be surrendered for trifles; too noble to be exchanged for song. Good policy is founded in justice, and ratified by experience. It is, as it were, the fostering nurse of great and good men. It inspires a dignified magnanimity; it teaches the sublimest sentiments: it awakens the most generous passions: it gives splendour and brilliancy to language. (I, liv)

Just as freedom is directly linked to brilliant language, so a decline in poetry can be indexed to a decline in liberty: 'To the loss of freedom, therefore, Longinus justly attributed the decay of genius, and the departure of all that is great and sublime in writing, from the Grecians' (I, lvii–viii). Good poetry is lyrical poetry, lyrical poetry is liberal, and liberal poetry can only thrive in a free and liberal society, notwithstanding the difficulty of crafting it: 'Nay, that ease, freedom and unrestrainedness, which characterizes lyric poetry, is not among the smallest of its difficulties' (I, xii). In Dyer's construction of a poetic tradition, it is political principle which carries the burden: 'Under the influence of good political principle, Milton, Marvel, Akenside, Gray, and Mason, raised their most rapturous notes, and produced their most finished compositions' (I, lvi). Dyer's reading of poetic tradition articulates a public version of liberalism, and brings that eighteenth-century public idea into a productive counterpoint to the internalisation associated with Wordsworthian 'Jacobinism-in-recoil'.

In his 'Essay on Representative Poetry', Dyer argues for the variety of subject positions that a poetic speaker can occupy, again emphasising differentiation rather than individuation, focusing on what he calls the 'representative' poem. Here, Dyer appears to be responding to the narrowing of the lyric category into that of solitude and individuation, and Dyer makes as his central claim the necessity for the representative poet to *disarm* himself of his individuality:

For though poetry, by its very nature, is a species of creation, and possesses in itself a degree of magic, giving the writer new eyes, new ears, new feelings, and lifting him above his ordinary material self; yet after all, if the poet is but speaking his own person, he is confined by his own individuality: his own system of sensations and passions, his own assemblage of associations, sentiments, and manners, mark out his proper boundaries. (II, 4–5)

This passage suggests a possible source for Keats's remarks about the 'poetical character': '(that sort distinguished from the Wordsworthian or egotistical sublime; which is a thing *per se* and stands alone) it is not itself – it has no self ... A poet is the most unpoetical of any thing in existence, because he has no identity'.[69] It is likely that Keats encountered Dyer's works at the Enfield Academy where he studied as a boy, for Dyer was part of the dissenting circle associated with the school.[70] In identifying himself with the liberalism of the Dyer version of representative poetry, and specifying this as that which is *not* Wordsworthianism, Keats participates in a different rendering of the privacy of the lyric 'I', similar to that formulated in the sonnet 'On First Looking into Chapman's Homer'. This is an argument about the lyric speaker as a singular abstraction or as a multiple particular. Dyer argues that in representative poetry, 'the poet . . . of necessity resigns his own individuality . . . He ceases to be himself' (II, 6). This poetic intention does not substitute the self for the world, but opens up the self to the world. Dyer makes a crucial distinction between the poet who imitates reality, and one who represents it:

The mere imitator, being confined by his own individuality, moves, as it were, within a given circle; whereas, the REPRESENTATIVE poet is bound by no circumference, except the characters, which he borrows, for the time. (II, 25)

Dyer's poet represents by opening up space to other consciousness, and he emphasises the value of this by distinguishing between the work of imitative and representative poetry:

Those poems, in which the speaker wears a fictitious character, differ from such, as are merely imitative, on this ground: the latter still reserve the personality of the author; whereas the former go out of the poet himself, and come forward as representative of another. (II, 26)

And for Dyer, '*representation* is the only true measure of political liberty'.[71] In his scheme, the representative poet offers the poetic stage to other voices; in Wordsworth the poet, as representative, speaks on behalf of others whose 'first poetic spirit' has been 'in most abated and suppressed' by society.[72]

I have been arguing here that Wordsworth's theory of lyric straddles the claims of individualist and customary culture: the 'Preface' to *Lyrical Ballads* owes much of its power to the way it balances the claims of custom and voluntarism, a poise which cannot ultimately be sustained. In the fluidity of the rhetorics of the 1790s, poetic theory, no less than political theory, juxtaposed aspects of the ideologies of the moral economy and of the new world order of liberal individualism, creating the space within which a great flowering of poetry took place. As Stuart Curran has pointed out, 'the most eccentric feature of [the] entire culture [was] that it was simply mad for poetry'.[73]

Dyer's theory of representative poetry articulates the lyric within a republican framework, holding on to eighteenth-century norms of public poetry, and retaining a space for a social lyric speaker, but unmoored from the confinements of the specificity of traditional culture. This foregrounds the second point I am arguing here: that the 1790s matrix from within which liberal individualism grew was also that from within which a democratic as opposed to a customary communitarianism grew. The place for the social lyric speaker is variously opened and modified in the work of later poets, both those associated with canonical romanticism, namely Keats, Shelley, and perhaps less securely, John Clare, and those associated with marginal oppositional poetic rhetorics, namely Chartists and Socialists. Nevertheless, while Dyer and Wordsworth shared certain values and began with similar premises about the social efficacy of poetry, it was the asocial, unencumbered individualist side of Wordsworth which was consolidated and enlarged within his work as a lyric poet, and which was upheld in the hegemony of print-culture individualist lyricism in the nineteenth century.

The third part of the argument of this chapter looks to the shaping of the poetic voice into the nineteenth century. My claim here is that in his 1829 debate with John Arthur Roebuck on the values of poetry, and in two 1833 essays for the *Monthly Repository*, John Stuart Mill codified the individualist view of the lyric, reducing dramatically its range, and claiming its functions exclusively for liberal identity.[74] This is a textual locus where liberalism and the romantic poetic of individualism are used explicitly in each other's support, by way of the Wordsworthian poetic.[75] The first of the two essays, 'What Is Poetry?' (1833), has become famous for Mill's analysis of the difference between eloquence and poetry as being that between being 'heard', and 'overheard' (71); it offers a structure of lyricism shorn of either social intention or musical accompaniment. Though Mill presents his critical statement as if in a direct line from Wordsworth's theory of the lyric, he is most unlike the Wordsworth of *Lyrical Ballads* in articulating a version of poetry as essentially without audience. If the individualist lyric speaker is always an *a priori* speaker, never named but always given, so the lyric listener now disappears into an abstract eavesdropper, for 'all poetry is of the nature of soliloquy' (71). Instead of serving a social function, poetry is now the index of inwardness, 'the delineation of the deeper and more secret workings of human emotion' (67). Mill argues that poetry is the diagnostic tool for discovering subjectivity. So, its rôle is an instance of asocial individualism purveyed as an aesthetic desideratum.

But beyond offering lyric *structure* as the proof of liberal subjectivity, Mill argues that the unencumbered self of the lyric provides the only true *subject matter* of poetry as well: 'The poetry of a poet is Feeling itself, employing Thought only as the medium of its expression' (83). The poetic self is asocial and voluntaristic; the narrative one is socially embedded: 'The truth of poetry is to paint the human soul truly; the truth of fiction is to give a true picture of life' (67). He then goes on to secure this link between the self and poetry at the expense of a social context by dispensing with the audience function: 'Eloquence supposes an audience; the peculiarity of poetry appears to us to be in the poet's utter unconsciousness of a listener' (71). Alone, speaking before entry into a social world, and having for an audience only his own mind, the poet of Mill's essay is the perfect embodiment of the voluntaristic self, generating a personal language of inwardness:

Poetry is feeling confessing itself to itself, in moments of solitude, and embodying itself in symbols which are the nearest possible representations of the feeling in the exact shape in which it exists in the poet's mind. (71)

Mill's retrospect in his *Autobiography* of how reading Wordsworth helped him through his moral crisis is fundamental to the association of romantic poetics with the shaping of individualist lyric culture in the mid-nineteenth century. Reading Wordsworth helps Mill because Wordsworth locates goods in the self, indeed he presents as a highest good what Mill calls 'the very culture of feelings'.[76] Raymond Williams has argued that what appears to be a separation between the claims of utilitarian rationalism and subjective feeling in Mill are really two sides of the same dilemma.[77] It is not the case that Mill refuses the category of the social, but rather, that he reads the social as the aggregation of voluntarily associated individuals. Looking back to the early 1830s, Mill argues that this resource of feeling in Wordsworth is accomplished 'not only without turning away from, but with a greatly increased interest in the common feelings and common destiny of human beings'.[78] Yet this is a different sort of common feeling from that which issues from the language of the commons itself in the 'Preface' to *Lyrical Ballads*. Mill's formulation returns us as well to Charles Taylor's exploration of the twinned trajectories of inwardness and empiricism as constitutive of modern selfhood:

[Rationalism] joins a lively sense of our powers of disengaged reason to an instrumental reading of nature; [romanticism] focuses on our powers of creative imagination and links these to a sense of nature as an inner moral source. These forms stand as rival, and the tension between them is one of the dominant features of modern culture.[79]

It is important, however, to distinguish between the account of Wordsworth that Mill shapes and the more complex and contestatory argument of the 'Preface' to *Lyrical Ballads*. For Mill has unhooked from

Wordsworth's theory the poet's insistence upon intimate links with the larger population of which he is to be representative and to which he wishes to speak. So, when Mill recapitulates Wordsworth in the formulation 'What *is* poetry, but the thoughts and words in which emotion spontaneously embodies life' (79), he stresses that aspect of Wordsworth's theory which prioritises the self over its social rootedness, but neglects the part of the argument which sees the rhetoric and meanings of poetry as best being drawn from the rural customary life. And when articulating a representative theory of the poet, Mill exacerbates the singularity of the poetic self, reversing Wordsworth's view of the poet as presenting a more intense version of everyone's experience. Instead, Mill isolates the poet from a social environment: 'Great poets are proverbially ignorant of life. What they know has come by observation of themselves' (67).

But Mill skilfully draws on Wordsworth's own contradictory presentation of the speaking self. Defining the difference between a poem and a novel, Mill writes: 'In one, the source of the emotion excited is the exhibition of a state or states of human sensibility; in the other, of a series of states of mere outward circumstances' (65). Wordsworth's use of the resources of narrative to make lyric sense, through the tradition of the pathways of common life, is here stripped away, leaving only the subjective atemporal space of consciousness. As Mill peels away Wordsworth's narrative from his lyric, he also narrows the range of what might be considered to be lyric. Significantly, he considers ballads to be of all poetry 'the lowest and most elementary kind' (66). At the same time, Mill participates in the centralising of the lyric within the hierarchy of poetic genres: 'Lyric poetry, as it was the earliest kind, is also, if the view we are now taking be correct, more eminently and peculiarly poetry than any other' (85).

Mill's radical reduction of all poetry to that of the autistic lyric is a distorted mirror of Wordsworth's taxonomy of his own poems in the volumes of 1815, the volumes which had succoured Mill in 1828 during his breakdown.[80] In that catalogue, Wordsworth organises his poems by way of the operations of the mind: 'Poems founded on the Affections', 'Poems of the Fancy', 'Poems of the Imagination'. And the one category which locates a 'kind' in relation to the landscape, 'Poems on the Naming of Places', nonetheless suggests the philosophical priority of *naming* to *placing*. Though Wordsworth acknowledges poetic generic distinctions in the 'Preface to 1815', he replaces them with those which proceed from the *a priori* creating mind of the poet. This substitution of subjective criteria for generic ones presents the lyric as a cultural counterpoint to the social production of the private self.

In 1829, the year following his Wordsworth therapy, Mill presented his newly developed 'theory of poetry' in a debate with Roebuck, wielding Wordsworth's poetry against Byron's, and the poetry of interiority against that of 'action and struggle'.[81] In that debate Mill drew heavily upon Wordsworth's atemporal lyrics, citing 'The Highland Girl', 'The Solitary Reaper', and 'Tintern Abbey', and disparaging Byron as a 'story-teller'.[82]

Using the division between narrative and lyric poetry, between external and internal motives, as a wedge, Mill formalises the distinction between a communitarian and an individualist theory of poetic identity. In the absolute difference he maintains between persuasion and poetry, Mill sidelines the side of the liberal argument put forward by Dyer and, subsequently, Shelley, of poetry's importance to the working of 'a great change' in social and cultural life; rather, 'Poetry . . . is the natural fruit of solitude and meditation; eloquence of intercourse with the world' (72).

When we contextualise Mill's argument within the world of interventionist lyric poetry being written throughout the nineteenth century, his refusal of the lyric of intervention begins to look as much like a strategy against the force of that poetic as it is the restorative for his personal affliction. For the essay affirms the absolute of the unencumbered self and its nurturance in the 'culture of feeling', by associating feeling with intention:

that capacity of strong feeling, which is supposed necessarily to disturb the judgement, is also the material out of which all *motives* are made; the motives consequently, which lead human beings to the pursuit of truth. (92)

Mill needs the poetry of solitude to validate the politics of liberalism, but he must also refuse the poetry of solidarity in order to argue for sociality as the aggregation of individuals.

It is interesting, and ironic, then, that Mill praises Ebenezer Elliott,' the 'Corn Law Rhymer'. Perhaps this is a recuperative move, in which Elliott is meant to be understood in the light of the theory Mill has just elaborated, and is thereby deprived of the social aspect of his poetic force. Mill quotes Elliott as having written 'Poetry is impassioned truth' (70). But what Elliott had actually written was 'Poetry is impassioned truth; and why should we not utter it in the shape that touches our condition most closely – the political?'[83] Or it may be that Mill is carried forward by the power of his own argument into its own dialectical opposition. Perhaps in Mill's fulfilment of an aesthetic of lyric solitude a newly understood liberal sociality appears in this allusion to Elliott as the return of the repressed.

Mill performs something equally peculiar and interesting when he turns at the end of the essay's argument to take Wordsworth's notions and use them against Wordsworth's practice, elevating in its place the 'lyricism' of Shelley (83–94). Mill argues that Wordsworth's was a laboured and intellectual lyricism, while Shelley's was a pure lyricism, blessedly empty of ideational material! Wordsworth's genius, Mill writes, is 'essentially unlyrical' (85), the product of thought rather than feeling. The great lyric poet on the other hand, 'is a poet, not because he has ideas of any particular kind, but because the succession of his ideas is a subordinate to the course of his emotions' (90). And Mill argues that Shelley is the exemplar of this poetic type, refiguring the most explicitly radical and political of poets into an image of ineffectuality:

It is only when under the overruling influence of some one state of feeling, either actually experienced, or summoned up in the vividness of reality by a fervid imagination, that [Shelley]writes as a great poet; unity of feeling being to him the harmonizing principle which a central idea is to the minds of another class, and supplying the coherency and consistency which would else have been wanting. (86)

Mill recasts both Elliott and Shelley, then, in the image of the lyric poet he wishes to encourage, and dispossesses each of their claim to a robust social and political poetic intervention.

In 1859, Mill published *On Liberty*, the central text for liberalism as a philosophical and political explanation and programme for modernity.[84] Mill formally distinguishes individuality from society in this text, but he has a harder time separating individuals from their customs. He also fears that the dialectic of individual freedom is such that mediocrity will prevail unless some superior persons rise to the surface: 'the counterpoint and the corrective to that tendency would be the more and more pronounced individuality of those who stand on the higher eminence of thought' (63). The momentum of rationality will be towards mediocrity, and the superior individuals must arise in much the same way as Wordsworth's representative poet will arise. For Mill, only more individuality will redeem the drawbacks to individuality.

But having argued for the unencumbered self, Mill must make sense of the fabric of social existence through which people make their lives. He sees this as a kind of encrustation over that twinned faculty of rational thought and deep feeling. Custom is the name Mill gives to this encrustation, which for him has become a brake on progress rather than a rich soil out of which individuals can grow. That is, he defines society as a set of abstract rules about rights and non-interferences; while custom is the social stuff which continually hampers the free flow of individual genius and prosperity.

The despotism of custom is everywhere the standing hindrance to human achievement, being in unceasing antagonism to that disposition to aim at something better than customary, which is called, according to circumstances, the spirit of liberty, or that of progress or improvement. (66)

Because Mill cannot allow custom, subjectivity, and rationality to be all mutually shaping, he cannot get past the problems which community as custom will impose on individuality. Here a line of continuity from Wordsworth through Shelley to Mill is clear: they share this critique of custom. But Wordsworth, and as we shall see, Shelley, also adopt from their view of customary culture a critique of the isolations provided by individualism. What had been a productive engagement between custom and reason in 1790s politics and poetry has become an impasse for the liberal theorist of 1850.

At the same time, however, one aspect of customary culture increasingly interested Mill: while he had once been fiercely Benthamite, from the mid-1830s he took an interest in Owen's ideas of co-operation.[85] But if Mill came to regard himself as a social thinker sympathetic to some version of socialism, his public formulations about poetry in 1829 and 1833 remained central to what ensued in the formulation of theories of lyric. In the individualist lyric can be traced the figure of the liberal self retreating into 'a private world of individual self-cultivation and personal relationships'.[86] The long-term trajectory of this can be read in the 1861 *Golden Treasury*. Here Palgrave declares that the lyric poem is one which 'turns on some single thought, feeling, or situation', and that the anthology excludes 'narrative, descriptive, and didactic poems'. Reproducing in practice the theoretical claims of Mill's essay, Palgrave includes a preponderance of poems by Wordsworth and Shelley in the nineteenth-century portion of the volume, which he calls the 'Book of Wordsworth'. These poems are made to preside over lyric nationalism and imperialism, for Palgrave aims to make his a 'true national anthology', appreciated 'wherever the Poets of England are honoured, wherever the dominant language of the world is spoken'.[87]

CHAPTER THREE

The sun and the tree: lyrics of liberty

But the work of the lyric in the nineteenth century also followed another significant path. When we turn in space and time to the peopled streets of the city, and away from an imagined rural isolation and capacious interior space of the voice which inhabits the solitary lyric, we can follow a different trajectory within romantic poetics, as it conducts and influences the social and political work of Radical London. The British intellectual debate about the French Revolution, which for a short period knitted together various voices aiming for domestic revolution or reform, began with Richard Price's address to the Revolution Society at the (delayed) 100th anniversary celebration of the Glorious Revolution of 1688, and continues today in the unending hermeneutic of the meaning and implications of the theme of 'popular sovereignty'. This was a debate which formulated in the register of the objective self tensions discernible within the poetics of the subjective self. This political debate drafted the terms of other, later discussions about personal, social, and national identity.[1] Was political identity to be understood as a function of habit and custom or was it to be based on the abstractions of reason? Would 'the people' be a true universal, or the embodiment of patterns and narratives rooted in past practices? Was the Glorious Revolution itself the guarantor of monarchical continuity, or the 'forerunner in a glorious course' of principle over practice?[2] Distilled as the debate between Paine and Burke, this argument has been the touchstone for analysis of not only the meaning of the French Revolution to Britain, but also of the histories of British liberalism and conservatism through the twentieth century. In this analysis, Paine is the emblem of liberal reason, Burke of conservative custom; Paine's is the voice of principle, Burke's of practice. Recently, this sketch has been subject to revision, and both Burke and Paine reveal greater complexities than such a binary opposition would allow. Anthony Arblaster, for example, recalls us to an intrinsic ambiguity in Paine's stance, demonstrating how Paine's arguments give rise to the socialist as well as the liberal strain in

British politics, and suggesting that issues of responsibility and community were as much part of Paine's political theme as were those of individual freedom from habit and custom.[3] After exploring the complexity of Paine's political positions, Arblaster concludes, 'the boundary between bourgeois or liberal on the one hand, and radical or socialist on the other, however clear it may be in theory, is constantly being crossed and re-crossed by the revolutionaries and radicals of the 1790s'.[4] As for Burke, C. B. Macpherson has persuasively argued that Burke's was fundamentally a voice of bourgeois capitalism: Burke was an advocate of the waged relation between farmer and labourer, and against the plebeian demands of customary right, but he also believed that 'the laws of the market were divinely ordained', and he relied upon a version of custom deprived of any commoners' content, and useful mainly as a means of perpetuating notions of subordination.[5]

In the pristine chambers of intellectual history, the argument between Paine and Burke has been abstracted into the distinction between custom and reason, precedent and principle. But in the cultural experience of the period, these abstractions are harder to keep in place. J. M. Neeson calls attention to the fact that Price, the exemplar of middle-class dissenting radicalism, was deeply committed to maintenance of customary right: his defence of the commons, *Observations on Reversionary Payments*, went into six editions.[6] What had looked like clear lines of descent from Paine and Burke into liberalism and conservatism show themselves to be, rather, tissues of conflicting and overlapping intentions and rhetorics.[7]

When cultural historians restore these intellectual traditions to their places in the life experiences of those debating in the 1790s, they find that the opposition between historicist and rationalist logics was not secure on street level, where rationalists borrowed from and contributed to the languages of both custom and millenarianism, and, significantly, the meaning of custom itself was far more dialectical and internally various than the élite version purveyed by Burke. What we abstract as a conceptual public sphere has been analytically deepened and complicated by maps of a *counter* public sphere, occupying the same public geography, where, particularly in London, the development of opinion and idea was as much influenced by the accidents of which bookstalls stood near which taverns, as by the logic of political argument.[8]

As the exemplary figure of the cultural exchange between Paine's and Burke's formulations, Malcolm Chase and Iain McCalman have drawn the complex lineaments of the agrarian communitarian Thomas Spence, who espoused a blend of rationalism and millenarian enthusiasm, and who

fashioned an image of a bountiful landscape within the confines of the city.
Elsewhere, E. P. Thompson's reading of Blake's 'London' as the conjunction of Painite logic and an imaginative anti-systemic impulse is a brilliant
presentation of the same dialectic of rationalism and millenarianism, and
Jon Mee's analysis of Blake's place in his intellectual milieu shows the
astonishing range of interacting rhetorics in the radical culture of the
1790s.[9]

The complex relations between the rhetorics and models of identity
grounded in reason and custom do not structure only the languages of
those in the plebeian and artisan milieux. George Dyer's theories of
government, derived from both Norman Yoke radicalism and rationalist
natural right theory, were no less an engagement between autonomous
rationality and customary practice than was his anti-individualist theory
of poetry. In the discourse of rationalist feminism one can locate a similar
interchange between voluntarism and embeddedness, with women from
the Dissenting tradition, such as Anna Barbauld and Helen Maria Williams
casting the light of reason on some of the patterns and mutualities of
female lives in family and community, while an anti-republican poet such
as Anne Grant, in her 'Familiar Epistle to a Friend', brings together issues
of aesthetic ideology as practised by women and the lures of individualist
ratiocination and sensibility, which however must 'give place / To duties
domestic'.[10]

In the interventionist poetics of the 1790s, songs and lyrics which in
form and theme straddled oral and print cultures, and yoked together the
languages of reason and custom, were constitutive of that moment's structure of feeling. Radical and reform poetry from the 1790s through the
1820s, particularly as it gained access to the public geography dominated
by the juxtaposition of taverns, bookstalls, and lecture halls, was one of the
vehicles through which was carried out the transmission of communitarian and individualist values.[11] The claims, then, that I am making for
romantic lyricism as the medium of a contest between communitarian
and individualist structuring of identity can be folded back into more
general cultural and intellectual history. The intention of this chapter is
to understand the work of poet-radicals who worked with and gave
immediacy to the tradition of communitarian ballad and song, and who
proved to be a vehicle of continuity to Chartist and Socialist poetics. Later
in the nineteenth century the recovery of the communitarian impulse
from within Wordsworth's and other romantic poets' œuvre enabled the
formulation of a sense of tradition, which kept that communitarian poetic
in play as part of a 'people's' literary tradition. So the bifurcation into a

democratic, or 'people's' lyricism and a 'liberal individualist' one was never complete or unproblematic, which is why both canons claim their poets from the same pool.

While the central theme of this investigation is the way in which the occluded communitarian poetic was shaped in the nineteenth century, it is no less the case that the poetry of individualism was, at least for a time, fuelled and energised by the poetics of popular democracy. This powerful urge of democratic universalism was employed within narratives expressing the newly recognisable twin goals of objectivity and empathy, seen for instance in the sentimental humanitarian ballad that is ubiquitous in the radical and reform press.[12] We find the unencumbered self urged forward to find a new and distinct kind of narrative to make sense of both itself and the world it chooses. But for the unencumbered self to know itself in order to make meaning requires, in Mill's analysis, the making of a deep self, incubated in the stasis of 'lyric time', and exemplified in his story of his initial despair and subsequent recovery through a sympathetic reading of Wordsworth's poetry. The embedded self's place in narratives that move across time is superseded by a shift from narrative temporality into lyric spatiality, focusing on the growth of self, in which successive moments of self are plotted as a thickening of identity. The unencumbered self inhabits lyric time, and then constructs a narrative of immanent development in poetic shapes of intensification and deepening. The lyrical ballad, in which the requirements of intensification and movement over time are superimposed on the temporal succession of ballad time, is a significant transitional generic form in this poetic structuring, and the genre identified by M. H. Abrams as the 'greater Romantic lyric' incorporates and extends this strand from the lyrical ballad.[13] Wordsworth's psychologising of customary affect in *Lyrical Ballads* can be taken as a sign of the transition.

In the interventionist poetry of revolution and reform, the poetic of reason is often focused through a familiar enlightenment image of the sun, which evaporates the miasma of superstition: 'The sun arises, and his light / Dispels our gloom away', decreeing that 'the *magic spell* is *broke*'.[14] But crossing this image is a persistent trope of nativist antiquity, the continuation of popular sovereignty encapsulated in Southey's image of the 'Oak of our Fathers, that stood / In its beauty, the glory and pride of the wood', but which has now

> received its incurable wound,
> They have loosen'd the roots, though the heart may be sound;
> What the travellers at distance green-flourishing see,
> Are the leaves of the ivy that poison'd the tree.[15]

In the 1790s, the sun nurtures the tree, and aims to transform the oppression of the Adamic curse of precedent and the prohibition against knowledge of Eden's 'Tree of Mystery' into the true tree of knowledge, the 'Tree of Liberty'. The 'Tree of Liberty' reminds us how differently configured can be the notion of custom and rootedness. Thomas Paine published a song on the Liberty Tree Elm in 1775 in the *Pennsylvania Magazine*, and the image moved with him from America to France and then to England.[16] In the 1790s Burke's oak contends with Paine's elm. And as Jon Mee has pointed out, Blake's 'Tree of Mystery', which metamorphoses into Albion's Fatal Tree – Tyburn – is the negation of the Liberty Tree.[17] In the late 1840s, the Liberty Tree will still have enough salience to be invoked by the Chartist poet Ernest Jones as an emblem for the Charter: 'Liberty is a tree of long growth in England. It was planted at Runnymede . . . and now it is beginning to bloom beneath the fostering of the Charter.'[18]

While the advance of reason in its utilitarian and expressivist forms – the peculiar mix of disengagement and interiorisation that names the individual of modernity – soon hegemonises identity formation, the régime of custom continues to build its own double life. This takes place within the hegemony as the abstraction of precedent in conservatism, and within oppositional radicalism, first as plebeian recalcitrance and rudimentary self-organisation, and later as socialist self-organisation. Arblaster makes this point: 'There is a significant continuity between the pre-capitalist notion of a moral economy and later socialist ideas of economic equality and a planned or controlled economy.'[19] In *Customs in Common*, E. P. Thompson argues that the process of capitalisation throughout the eighteenth century loosened the ties of customary practice from those of tradition, freeing the subjects of paternalistic, patrician culture from their economic bonds, while maintaining some of the ideology of the 'moral economy'.[20] In other words, a large body of persons was acting as a proletariat, though experiencing their conditions in the terms of community and custom derived from rural life. The meaning of custom to them, then, was distinct from that excoriated by Shelley in *Queen Mab* as custom's 'heart-withering . . . cold control'. The residual life of custom as opposition, in the atmosphere of an urban domestic reform movement and the French Revolution, had a significant impact on radical cultural practice. The dangerous mix of a language of custom with a logic of radicalism provided activist cultural theorists such as Thomas Spence with the assets to formulate a logic of custom understood *as* reason. Thompson argues:

when the ideological break with paternalism came, in the 1790s, it came in the first place less from plebeian culture than from the intellectual culture of the dissenting middle-class, and from thence was carried to the urban artisans. But Painite ideas, carried through by such artisans to an ever wider plebeian culture, instantly struck root there.[21]

Thompson concludes his discussion by drawing on the power of lyric, using Burns's long-lived lyric: in the 1790s, 'it suddenly appeared that the world was not, after all, bounded at every point by their [landed gentry and aristocracy] rule and overwatched by their power. A man was a man, "for a' that"'.[22]

Burns, the ploughboy-poet, would serve through the following century as a powerful emblem of the congregating force of song, derived from the embedded identity of commoners. While Wordsworth's mix of communitarian and individualist elements was interpretively skewed in liberal poetics towards lyric time and depth aestheticism, Burns, more clearly defined as the plebeian poet, became the name to characterise the voice of lyric as song. But neither Burns nor Wordsworth served to define only one tradition. Mill extracted from Wordsworth his voluntarist individualism, and left the rest aside; working-class poetics recovered the balladic side of Wordsworth later in the century. At the outset of his posthumous reputation, Burns was given a genealogy as a marginalised poet. Liberal poetic culture fitted him into the model of the isolate. Unsurprisingly, the crystallising location for this was in Wordsworth's 1802 'Resolution and Independence', which yoked Burns and Chatterton to the downward personal spiral of 'despondency and madness'. This version of Burns describes his experience as a tragic intersection of unencumbered and embedded identities. In the 1790s middle-class Dissenting reform periodical, the *Monthly Magazine*, an elegy to Burns inhabits his own lyric stanza in order to inscribe the dead poet as both the herald of the common man and as a singular voice. Burns is cast in the image of the bard, the lost voice of public poetry, reanimated after death as the 'sweetest minstrel, nature's child.' Though the poem asserts that Burns's genius will be recognised, it also offers a reproach. Whereas the glory of the poet is meant to be the glory of the nation, in Burns's case, the poet who builds a 'deathless name' is both 'Thy Country's glory and her shame!'[23] Burns's reputation in polite literary circles in the late 1790s was built on his native genius, which erased his connections to historical thinking: Coleridge named him 'Nature's own beloved bard'.[24] Scott and Jeffrey were eager to distance themselves politically from Burns, and so focused on his dissoluteness. In a note written in 1842, Wordsworth wrote that the 'immorality' of Burns's poems was 'the ebullition of natural

temperament'.[25] In the individualist lyric tradition, Burns occupied the
rôle of the author of what Hazlitt called 'pathetic and serious love-songs
... in the manner of the old ballads'; Carlyle described him as author of
an œuvre 'beautiful and sad at once unfinished and a ruin'. But later in the
nineteenth century, when the claims of a self-identified working class had
been separated out from the more manifold 'reform' movement, the discourse of Chartist poetics would name Burns as a figure to be admired far
more than pitied. Built from the local practice of celebrating the birth of
Burns on 25 January and singing his political songs, Burns became known
as a people's poet.[26] In that context, Burns was invoked as a revolutionary,
and his songs sung as toasts during political dinners.[27] A mid-century Tory
version of Burns linked him to the later Wordsworth, Southey, Moore,
Scott, and Rogers, all poets providing what Isobel Armstrong calls
'unmediated access to self-evident moral truths' of nationalism, chivalry,
and Christianity.[28] But what was narrated as personal tragedy in the growing nineteenth-century sentimental appropriation of Burns was to be
interpreted as strength by those creating a poetic counter-tradition. This is
the Burns who rails against the oppressions enforced by Church and State:

> Liberty's a glorious feast
> Courts for cowards were erected,
> Churches built to please the Priest.[29]

Taking up the image of the 'Liberty Tree' which carries 'buds and blossoms'
of freedom, Burns writes a democratic song which works up the tropes of
both nativism and enlightenment, blasting against 'Superstition' and calling
for 'equal rights and equal laws' which can flourish beneath the Liberty
Tree. 'Wi' plenty o' sic trees, I trow, / The warld would live in peace, man':

> Like brethren in a common cause,
>   We'd on each other smile, man;
> And equal rights and equal laws
>   Wad gladden every isle, man.

But the poem discloses its customary as well as its rationalist roots, for
this is a tree which has the magical powers of traditional medicine: unlike
the biblical tree which grants the knowledge of good and evil, Burns's
Liberty Tree is a sentient being, and offers the judgement of the forest:

> It clears the een, it cheers the heart,
>   Maks high and low gude friends, man;
> And he wha acts the traitor's part
>   It to perdition sends, man.[30]

Burns served as an on-going figure in the formulation of communitarian poetry. For example, the refrain of an 1840 Chartist Land Plan song joins together the heritage of plebeian song, agrarian rationalism, and mid-nineteenth-century poetic inwardness by repeating Burns's earlier refrain, 'For "a' that and a' that"', by way of an earlier radical agrarian Spencean song, 'The Spencean Plan for a' that'. This song was written by Thomas Evans, who had appropriated the lines by Burns:

> The rights of man then's in the soil,
> An equal share and a' that,
> For landlords no one ought to toil –
> 'Tis impositions and a' that,
> Yes a' that and a' that,
> Their title-deeds and a' that,
> How'er they got them, matters not,
> The land is ours for a' that.[31]

But what appeared to Chartist poets as a tractable tradition, open to appropriation as part of a class struggle, was far more inchoate and volatile in the 1790s. Before the 1832 Reform Bill split off from within the movement those with property from those without, radical poetic culture was as complex and multiform as the ideologies of rural and urban radicalism that it worked up. From the 1780s through the 1820s, the poetry of liberty included those poets most obviously linked to the middle-class reform movement, such as John Thelwall and William Wordsworth, as well as those exponents of plebeian radicalism, such as Thomas Spence, E. J. Blandford, and R. C. Fair, and those like George Dyer and Percy Bysshe Shelley, who moved between and made links amongst various elements in what Mark Philp calls the 'fragmented ideology of reform'.

We can juxtapose Thomas Spence and George Dyer as dialecticians of the sun (image of enlightenment rationality) and the tree (image of nativist liberty). Both men were active on the delegate committees of the London Corresponding Society, that mixing together of artisan and middle-class, deistic and millenarian supporters of the French Revolution. Unlike many of their contemporaries, neither Spence nor Dyer took cover from the reaction in the later part of the 1790s. As a result, both have had to bear the weight of being considered 'eccentrics' by liberal intellectuals and politicians, a familiar way of diminishing the opposition by caricature. As noted in the last chapter, Dyer was made fun of by Lamb and others, while Francis Place characterised Spence as 'extremely simple minded and unbelievably impractical'.[32] But Dyer was an important pamphleteer and held a secure place in the middle-class London milieu, and while

Spence's earlier foray into the polite world of letters in Newcastle ended in uproar, by the time he got to London Spence was wary of the middle-class allure.

It is instructive as well to place Dyer in relation to John Thelwall. Thelwall, who has recently been recovered as both a political theorist and poet, was a central figure in the Treason Trials of 1794: he was found 'not guilty' along with Thomas Hardy and Horne Tooke. But that event appears to have effectively marked the beginning of the end of middle-class radical commitment to the reform agitation. The son of a silk-mercer, Thelwall moved through various jobs but from an early age was seriously committed to a poetic vocation.[33] Gregory Claeys notes that Thelwall became progressively more interested in political questions and it seems probable that his steeping in the humanitarian poetics of sensibility was instrumental in his politicisation.[34] The humanitarian expression within poetry was a vehicle of personal politicisation for many persons, and it continued through the nineteenth century. Ernest Jones, for example, found his way into the political movement through his poetic vocation. Thelwall entered the same reformist milieu that Dyer had joined, and boldly first threw his lot in with the plebeian and volatile London Corresponding Society rather than with the more sedate and cautious Society of the Friends of the People and the Society for Constitutional Information.[35] Thelwall and Dyer were equally wedded to Painite ideals, but Thelwall's poetry turns in a far more uniformly meditative mode after the Treason Trials, when he abandons any interventionist poetic, enacting the increasingly split notion of the claims of poetry and of politics. Though Thelwall remained involved in political life, lecturing in the Beaumont Buildings to a more middle-class audience than he had addressed in the London Corresponding Society, his poetry had shifted away from interventionism earlier than his 1797–98 exile from public life.[36] Thelwall's verse exemplifies 'Jacobinism-in-recoil', moving towards the poetic lyricism of individualism, and adopting the resolutely print-culture form of the five-beat blank verse paragraph: 'Ah! 'twould be sweet, beneath the neighb'ring thatch / In philosophic amity to dwell, / Inditing moral verse or tale or theme', he breathes to Coleridge in 1797, three years after his release from prison.[37] Thelwall's *Poems Chiefly Written in Retirement* reiterate the themes of elegy and meditation, and his 'Effusions' echo Coleridge: 'Well, thou art gone – gone to the City's throng . . . '[38] When he tried to recover his radical constituency in 1818 and 1819, Thelwall was reviled by the new radicals as a deserter.[39] For his part, Dyer's poetry does not so much fall into a 'before and after' as it splits into the discernible clusters of nativist and internationalist republican lyrics, each with its own set of formulae and images, the nativism evident in imagery that summons up a democratic past of Alfredian Anglo-Saxon 'equal laws', and the internationalism apparent in Dyer's language of rational right. In the second wave of early nineteenth-century radicalism, which recovered and re-animated many of the rhetorical forms and images of the 1790s, Shelley, amongst others, was for a time drawn to these dated poetic conventions of reason and custom, and to the communitarian poetic of intervention, evident in the agrarian poetics of the 'Mask of Anarchy'. At the same time, Shelley's poetry of intellectual scepticism was also fuelled by ultra-radical rationalist contemporaries such as the poet-shoemaker, R. C. Fair, a fellow contributor to George Cannon's free-thinking journal, *The Theological Inquirer.*

If the radical and reform poetic formulated in the urban centre leads out into the countryside in the landscape poetic of Thelwall and Wordsworth in the later 1790s, it receives materials from the countryside as well. Our understanding of the romantic theme of nature is interestingly complicated by comparing the value of 'nature' in the poetry that links the Spenceans to the Chartists as against the versions of nature proposed by the refugees from the city chaos. Poets such as Allen Davenport and E. J. Blandford, closely associated with the Spencean Philanthropists, invented a landscape poetic which aimed to feed the body rather than the mind. In their work, we can follow the claims of a communitarianism grounded in the language of the landscape, and in contest with the power of the individualist assertion constitutive of the aesthetic ideology.[40] For the tradition of customary practice is most closely associated with the rights and customs of the commons, and the period we have come to designate as 'romantic' coincides exactly with the years of the greatest number of Parliamentary enclosure acts, in particular the enclosure of wastes and commons.[41] What is best in what we call nature poetry often lies on the borders of, or acts out, the contest of communitarian and individualist construals of nature. And this most often takes place in the context of a poignant awareness that the custom of the commons is at its moment of dispersal.

As cultural and literary historians have begun to define the romantic period by reference to plebeian as well as literary culture, the importance of Thomas Spence has been increasingly recognised. Spence is now understood to be seminal for the articulation of a lengthy tradition of agrarian radicalism, which began as a response to both industrialisation and the erosion of customary rights in the late eighteenth century, and which has been reanimated recently in road protests.[42] Standing at the juncture of city and country, urban and rural radicalism, Spence's 1790s intervention in London politics gathered into a movement which influenced later generations of communitarians. Immediately after his death in 1814, a group of Spenceans led by Thomas Evans set up a Spencean Philanthropic Society, and various Spenceans were implicated in a series of ultra-radical events, including the Cato Street Uprising.[43] In the history of the origins of British socialism, Spence figures as an important link between different constituencies in the 1790s reform movement: we know, for example, that he worked with Thelwall in the London Corresponding Society in 1793.[44] Spence is also a link between an attenuating plebeian culture and the Chartist communitarianism of the 1830s and 1840s, conveyed through the recovery of his songs and arguments, and carried out in the work of the political activist and poet, Allen Davenport. Spence's works were reprinted in the *Northern Star* during the Chartist agitation, and were a significant influence on Feargus O'Connor's Land Plan. In the 1880s, the Marxist Socialist leader H. M. Hyndman wrote a centenary tribute to Spence and his ideas.[45]

Spence's poetic intervention also offers an entry into the dialectic of romanticism in the nineteenth century, for though the poetic communitarian tradition would come to toast Burns as its patron saint and martyr, Spence was amongst its first self-conscious literary activists. Through his poems, songs, and his anthology-periodical, *One Pennyworth of Pig's Meat; or Lessons for the Swinish Multitude*, Spence articulated a poetic activism which valued a collective voice, made a claim for a cultural tradition, and directed poetry into the centre of political life.[46] As a polemicist, Spence designed a democratic plan for the repossession and redistribution of the wealth of the land, in which collective good was understood to pre-exist and form the needs of the individuals within the collectivity. As a poet activist, Spence designed an interventionist programme for lyric poetry, and always alert to the politics of language while employed in the work of both economic and educational reform, Spence marshalled the resources of the lyric to make literary culture, and thereby political culture, accessible to those persons hitherto excluded from the literate order.[47]

Spence achieved notoriety in London radical circles in the 1790s as part of the pamphlet war. As the editor, writer, and compiler of extracts for *Pig's Meat*, he gave polemical and satirical shape to the anti-Burkean rhetoric associated primarily with Paine, a rhetoric infused with the metaphors of enlightenment republicanism:

> No more the grinding hand of Power,
> The op'ning bud of Reason blights;
> On eagle's wings fair Truth shall tower,
> For *Man begins to know his Rights*.[48]

But Spence was only able to produce his compelling republican tone by being steeped as well in a communitarian politics which he had experienced in an early engagement in Newcastle over the privileges of custom. Spence had first entered radical politics in the mid-1770s in a nativist mode, well before the debate about the French Revolution had begun the process of introducing its internationalist theme. Spence's major contribution to political thought was his Land Plan, premised in the tradition that the commons are the space that belongs to the commoner. He then articulates the logic that all land is by natural right common land, therefore all land belongs to the commoners. The massive resurgence of parliamentary bills of enclosure in the very late eighteenth century, and in particular that part of common land – the wastes – which had traditionally been the site for customary rights of gathering and fishing, provided the soil within which Spence's theory took root.[49] But Spence did not wholly rely on the narrative of the commons to justify his proposals. He simultaneously invoked popular enlightenment ideas derived from Harrington and Locke to offer the rational logic for what amounts to a communal version (at least in terms of circulation and distribution of agricultural surplus) of social and economic life.[50] Though in places Spence relies on the narrative of the Norman Yoke, with its shadowy and magical ideal of an original Anglo-Saxon constitution, he reasons together issues of natural right and custom.[51] The 'agrarian fellowship' is a 'natural inheritance', and the claim for the natural right of ownership of the 'common farm of the people' is rooted in the by now very precarious customs of the commons. Spence's follower, Allen Davenport, will argue: 'So long as the common field remained in the possession of the people, the principle of the people's right in the soil was recognised, and the natural rights of man, though in a slight degree, remained in existence'.[52] For Spence, identity itself emerges from the explosive contact between the traditional narrative of labour on the land, derived as much from biblical as from historical sources, and the new focus on the unencumbered person, born from the double framing of the self as inward and punctual. In the following passages, one can hear the rhetorical force of this juxtaposing of the rhetoric of biblical prophecy with that of enlightenment:

O, you bloody landed interest! you band of robbers! ... soon shall those auda-
cious emblems of rapine cease to offend the eyes of an enlightened people, and
no more make an odious distinction between the spoilers and the spoiled. But,
ladies and gentlemen, is it necessary, in order that we eat bread and mutton, that
the rents be received by you? Might not the farmers as well pay their rents to us,
who are the natural and rightful proprietors? If, for the sake of cultivation, we are
content to give up to the farmers our wild fruits, our hunting grounds, our fish
and game; our coal-mines and our forests, is it not equitable that we should have
the rents in lieu thereof?

   Hear me! ye oppressors! ye who live sumptuously every day! ye, for whom the
sun seems to shine, and the seasons change, ye for whom alone all human and
brute creatures toil, sighing, but in vain, for the crumbs which fall from your
overturned tables ... The groans of the prisons, and the groans of the camp, and
the groans of the cottage, excited by your infernal policy, are at an end! And
behold the whole earth breaks forth into singing at the new creation, at the breaking of the iron rod of aristocratic sway, and at the rising of the everlasting sun of
righteousness.[53]

What Spence had constructed was a rights theory with a customary
valence.

   In Spence's personal history the clash of custom and reason was incar-
nated, for the impetus for his move to London around 1788 was his having
been expelled from the Newcastle Philosophical Society for publishing his
levelling Land Plan lecture. Spence had been brought up in the artisan
world, his father being a net-maker in the sailing trade.[54] Under the
influence of the Scottish Presbyterian James Murray, Spence moved from
artisan practice into schoolteaching, and, in his *Grand Repository of the
English Language*, he invented a reformation of English to make reading
easier for the uneducated.[55] Central to Spence's life project were his
interest in and concern for the intellectual experience of the poor – forging
them into an entity through literacy and through the fashioning of a
cultural tradition, using what he called 'the Progress of Reason aided by
the Art of Printing'.[56] Spence stands on the cusp of oral and print culture,
and the orthographic innovations of the *Grand Repository* are guided by
norms of pronunciation, designed 'especially for those who are but
indifferent Readers from not having been taught to pronounce properly'.[57]
It was through his connection with Murray that Spence came to join the
Newcastle Philosophical Society, the centre of enlightenment thought in
the city.[58] It was through the same source of Scottish Presbyterianism that
Spence's brother Jeremiah joined the radical Christian communist sect of
John Glas, who was a proponent of congregational singing, which
becomes an important strand in the Spencean poetic intervention.[59]

Spence's transit across intellectual and social boundaries provides a provincial microcosm of the productive pathways between social and cultural groupings in radical urban culture in the last years of the eighteenth century.

In the early 1770s, a polarising political event in Newcastle had been a suit prosecuted by the Newcastle freemen against the Corporation of the town over the distribution of revenues gained from renting a section of the Town Moor.[60] Allen Davenport writes that Spence later said that the Town Moor suit was the source of his arguments for the redistribution of wealth from the land.[61] The tension between custom and reason detonated in Spence's naïve assumption that his indignation over the destruction of customary rights would be endorsed by the property-owning members of the Philosophical Society. In his Land Plan lecture, Spence argued that privately owned land should be returned to the parish as whole and all the wealth earned be distributed according to need. Later versions of the Plan, written in London and engaging with Paine's work, in particular his *Agrarian Justice*, would propose even greater democratisation, distributive decisions to be based on a franchise given not only to men, but to women and children as well.[62] Not surprisingly, the enlightened interests of the Philosophical Society were more concerned with the capitalisation and improvement of agriculture than a popular redistribution of surplus, and Spence was forthwith expelled from the Society, though not before he had published and distributed his lecture on the streets of Newcastle, both as a reading text and in a ballad version sung to the tune of 'Chevy Chace'.[63]

This ballad, which may be Spence's most compelling song, describes the way the landlord claims the things of the commons as his own: the speaker lists animals and fruits that can no longer be hunted or gathered:

> To fish then you will them allow;
> The river's not my Lord's.
> Do not mistake, *the water's his,*
> And all that it affords.

Against the cruelty and unnaturalness of the landlords, Spence elaborates the notion of an Edenic communality on earth, produced in the strains of congregational hymnody:

> O! There is a land, as I hear say,
> Where landlords none there be!
> O! Heavens! might I that happy land
> Before I die but see.[64]

His double-pronged assault, through the anaphoric style of biblical prose and the oral culture of ballad, would structure Spence's cultural work for the next twenty years.

Spence arrived in London sometime between 1788 and 1792.[65] Here his idiosyncratic plebeian brand of Newcastle enlightenment thought, mixed with his own family traditions derived from Scottish Independent worship, came into contact with the more various and, in places, more unreasonable claims of millenarian radicals and enthusiasts.[66] From this point on, Spence's rhetoric is increasingly influenced by the voices of late eighteenth-century prophetic and apocalyptic writings, and the Land Plan gathers layers of Edenic metaphorisation.

The Spencean vision is a crazy quilt built from disparate references and associations, and the content of his pedagogical periodical, *Pig's Meat*, appears to be a trough into which are tossed all kinds of texts, without much thought as to their theoretical consistency. Yet *Pig's Meat* sets a precedent for organising and inventing a cultural tradition, laying claim to texts from the past, and juxtaposing them in such a way as to generate new meanings which fasten these texts to the social and political claims being made by the unenfranchised and the labouring poor. The title page of the second edition of *Pig's Meat* asserts that this compilation is intended to show 'the Labouring Part of Mankind' that they are the object of concern of 'the best and most enlightened of Men in all Ages'.[67] Spence brings together political extracts from Locke and Harrington to shape the political heritage, and poetical extracts from Milton and Goldsmith to establish a poetic lineage. In *Pig's Meat*, Spence advances a concept of tradition which, though not posed in the language of class, will define a 'people's' literary heritage, even while claiming figures from the hegemonic culture. Using the form of Knox's *Elegant Extracts*, in *Pig's Meat*, Spence pries loose Shakespeare and Goldsmith from one position in culture and shapes them into another, situated alongside more contemporary works, such as the first English translation of the *Marseillaise*. In 1839, W. J. Linton's monthly, *The National*, will create for the generation of Chartist activism a similar kind of educational compendium of passages.

In his study of satire between 1780 and 1829, Marcus Wood points out that Spence took full advantage of the technological possibilities of urban cultural life, making use of the many communicative vehicles available to him – printed prophecies, tokens, songs, poems, narratives, and prints.[68] In this period, Kathryn Sullivan has argued, 'in an emergently literate society like working-class England, reading [was] primarily an associative activity, and therein lay its danger'.[69] Wood notes that by juxtaposing Goldsmith to

Price, for example, Spence was inviting an associative politicisation of the poem.[70] Associative activity is as much about links between readers as well as writers, and Spence exploited both sides of this equation, writing songs and poems based on the oral ballad and printed broadside forms, aimed at involving the listener or participant singer in a sense of choric communality. Spence's ability to engage the possibilities of song and poem provided the culturally material basis for his work as a stallkeeper in Holborn, where he sold his own pamphlets and numerous other popular broadsides and ballads of London culture. There is some evidence that he worked for Charles Cooke, and distributed various numbers of Cooke's 46-volume *Pocket Edition of Select British Poets*, bridging the worlds of polite and plebeian poetic culture in a manner that will be fully articulated in the next generation by the poet Allen Davenport.[71]

The three volumes of *Pig's Meat* evince changes in the way in which Spence used the gathered poetic materials. In Volume I, Spence includes excerpts from Goldsmith and from Dodsley, along with what may or may not be his own songs, including 'The Year 93' and 'The Progress of Liberty'. These are impersonal satirical songs, with choral refrains.[72] There is a large gap in register between the extracts from polite poetic culture and the putative Spence songs. But in Volume II, which is notable for its more internationalist republican flavour, Spence includes quite a few poems written by contemporary urban radicals, such as the bookseller 'Citizen [Richard] Lee', and W. D. Grant, in which the radicalism of republican politics is matched by a closer attention to print-culture poetics. Lee's poetic voice is that of revolutionary millenarianism, calling on God to 'Tumble the *blood-built* thrones of *despots* down, / Let dust and darkness be the tyrants crown!'. In his 'Sonnet to Freedom', Lee speaks from within a renaissance generic convention, and in a more subjective and suppliant voice, 'Come then, dear FREEDOM, come, reside with me, / And I shall sing, tho' in a lowly cot.'[73] In this volume, Spence introduces some experimental poems, often unsigned, including a pastoral poem describing the amatory conventions of Chloe and Palemon, which is interrupted by the contemporary forces of empressement.[74] Spence appears to be expanding his idea of what poetry can accomplish to include the development of a print-culture poetry that can perform similar functions to those of song.

Volume III of *Pig's Meat* appeared after Spence's agitation activities in the London Corresponding Society led to his detention on 20 May 1794, during which time he was repeatedly questioned and only released from custody on 22 December 1794.[75] The poetry of this third volume has a retrospective cast to it, and for the first time, *Pig's Meat* carries humanitarian ballads on the lyrical ballad model, with their particularly elegiac tone. 'The Peasant's Lamentation on the Exportation of Corn' clearly belongs to the lyrical vein of the sentimental humanist ballad. This is an unsigned narrative ballad, in which an individual 'I' tells a tale of exile and separation from the soil which gave him his identity. Juxtaposed to the polemic of land reform which has been Spence's main lyric intervention, this poem is chosen and placed to demonstrate an internalised version of this social claim as an individual's story. However, the crisis of personal identity which the poem narrates is shown by the context of *Pig's Meat* to be resolvable only by social, and not individual means. The cottager has been turned off his land through the work of agricultural improvement, which has consolidated fields, raised the price of wheat, and driven the peasant into landlessness, while the crop is sold abroad. The peasant forfeits his identity by losing his place in the social narrative from which embedded selfhood is built.

In 'The Beggar's Petition', another lyrical ballad in Volume III of *Pig's Meat*, probably by the same author, the loss of customary rights similarly results in the disintegration of family identity:

> A little farm was my paternal lot,
> Then like the lark, I sprightly hail'd the morn;
> But ah! oppression forc'd me from my cot;
> My cattle seiz'd, as also was my corn.[76]

Here the 'I' recalls his past as a cottager: in the coherence of that life, his relation to labour had been immediate and tuneful, as he went forth to work singing like a lark. Now his lyric voice has been 'seiz'd' along with his corn and cattle. P. M. Ashraf attributes these poems to Spence, but it is more likely that Spence's keen sensitivity to the differential displays of poetic rhetoric and the audiences which they invite led him to choose rather than write this poem.[77] Both poems belong to the same thinking about the loss of custom that fills the voice of Wordsworth's 'Female Vagrant'. The bitter life of the deracinated urban poor made the memory of customary right a weapon in the fundamentally enlightenment-grounded theories promoting social change.[78] The joining up of narratives of custom and of newer claims for universal individuality find a particularly apposite shape in the lyrical ballad. The tension between a foundational self as embedded and one as *a priori* and free operates as a motor of lyric development in poems like 'The Beggar's Petition' and 'The Peasant's Lamentation', which call upon the customs and traditions of the past to make palpable the desires of a plebeian selfhood speaking for itself.

Social historians often turn to the poetry of John Clare to find a lyric voice speaking out against the erosion of customary right and enclosure, and this chapter will conclude with some consideration of Clare's indignant articulation of how 'Inclosure came and trampled on the grave / Of labours rights and left the poor a slave.'[79] But Clare inhabits an already constructed lyric position of a fully formed private self encountering its singular identity in the context of some larger sociality, and he feels himself to be a direct legatee of Wordsworth's formulation of that identity. The lyrical ballads in *Pig's Meat* encapsulate that voice as it is beginning to emerge from, on the one side, the generality of both an abstract 'peasant' and, on the other, from the non-personalised protest songs and poems of the tavern and broadside. The first was an imaginary version of a peasant spoken by a sympathetic print-culture poet; the second an impersonal and non-differentiated presentation of political claims and utopian desires.

For the greater part of the lyrics in this milieu are impersonal in a manner that is characteristic of the conventions of oral poetics. In his political interventions, Spence was able to bridge the gap between the worlds of rationalism and plebeian culture by way of his poetical interventions, which conveyed enlightenment concepts through customary lyric forms. The songs which fill *Pig's Meat*, such as 'The Progress of Liberty' and 'Kings Are Great Blessings', may have been circulated through the various media of print culture, but their form belongs to oral modes: additive in structure, aggregative in theme, and as Walter J. Ong characterises oral events, 'redundant or copious' in lexical elements.[80] This is the common experience of group singing throughout history. As David Lindley argues, 'To a group of singing people the arrival of "the chorus" generates a sense of release into the known and shared, and symbolises community.'[81]

In all the works that Spence circulated in London, song lyric and poetry always play some rôle, either as a coda or a representational example, or as a performative exhortation. For example, in his pamphlet *The Rights of Infants*, a satirical critique of Paine, Spence interpolates a verse paragraph, which concludes with an exhortation to 'Mortals, join to hail great Nature's plan, / That fully gives to babes those Rights it gives to Man'.[82] The song concludes with a chorus, 'to the Tune of "Sally in our Alley"': 'Then let us all join heart in hand, / Through country, city, town; / Of every sex and every age ...' etc. In his utopian version of life within Spensonia, the ideal version of an England which had achieved his Plan, Spence again makes explicit the rights of women: 'The women, yes, and

Children too, / Alike share with the Men / For why? They of the Species
are, / And as such owned again.'[83]

And it was the power of the choric connection, whose roots may well
have been in Spence's memories of the collectivism of the Glasites, that
sustained him and his followers over the period of the post-1795 reaction
within the radical movement. For the Glasites were communist in their
practice, and they foregrounded the significance of singing as a pathway
to the new life: 'To prayer is annexed the ordnance of SINGING.'[84] In
Spence's formulation, the utopian end of his Plan would result in a society
without distinction; in the lyrical life of the new community, even the
aristocrats would be invited into the collective:

And when you shall hear of the blessed decree being passed by the people, that
the land is from that day forth parochial property, join chorus with your glad
fellow creatures and joyfully partake in the universal happiness.[85]

Although he established his distinctive voice amongst the mix of artisans
and intellectuals who made up the London Corresponding Society, when
the aftermath of the Treason Trials resulted in the more or less complete
abandonment of the London Corresponding Society by middle-class
radicals, Spence was fairly swiftly characterised as an eccentric excrescence
of the liberal reform movement. But Spence maintained his bitter commitment to change even while excoriating those 'people's friends' who
'Prudently give up reform'. In Volume III of *Pig's Meat*, juxtaposed to a
song by George Dyer which celebrates the positive outcome of the trials of
Hardy, Thelwall, and Tooke, Spence predicts the difficulties that the freed
men will face:

> But sighs now follow prison groans,
> And duns and landlords, in their turns,
> The place of gaolers stern supply,
> And crush the heart late doom'd to die.[86]

The title page of Spence's *The Meridian Sun of Liberty* reprints and revises a
'Song' first printed in *Pig's Meat* in 1793. The 1793 song had described
Burke as being blinded by the light of the French Revolution: 'Let Burke,
like a bat, from its splendour retire, / A splendour too strong for his eyes.'[87]
The 1796 *Meridian Sun of Liberty* now links Thelwall and Burke, 'Let
Thelwall and Burke from its splendour retire, / A splendour too strong for
their eyes.'[88] This is an unfair criticism of Thelwall, who later insisted that
though he had 'abjured all politics', he had never 'shifted sides, like a
common prize fighter'![89] But the poem indexes the fragmentation that
beset the movement.

When faced with the disintegration of the democratic movement under the force of state repression, resilient Spence accommodated his enlightenment project to plebeian oral communicative forms, which were deployed through the communities of tavern and bar, and through the political congregations of hymn and song, ballad and broadsheet. He remained unperplexed by the clash of modes or registers. Spence, Iain McCalman writes, 'was a man so personally ragged, socially unexclusive, ideologically revolutionary and culturally plebeian that he attracted the insecure and declining, the casualized, pauperized and criminalized'.[90] Within the domain of radical London, appeals to commoners' rights, even conveyed through agricultural rhetoric, were appeals which foregrounded the losses experienced on the way to free wage labour. The argument of the Land Plan required continued references to commoners' rights, for example, those of pescary and hunting: 'To fish or hunt we have no Right / Since we no land can claim'.[91]

Unlike the 'Jacobins-in-recoil', once the period of deep political repression had set in, Spence turned more fully to the interventionist possibilities of poetry and song, and to the cultural pathways to consciousness raising. In 1801, he began promoting evenings of song and discussion, meetings 'after a Free and Easy manner'.[92] Thomas Evans, who founded the Society of Spencean Philanthropists after Spence's death in 1814, had been the editor and compiler of a series of pamphlets of 'Spence's Songs', printed between 1807 and 1811. Evans contributed his own songs, and wrote some prophetic-poetical passages. *Spence's Songs* begins with an elegiac call to preserve the elements of the 'Mighty Struggle'. Evans takes over Spence's work of ordering a tradition out of the materials of the past, and fashions an order in which Spence's own materials are a critical part of that tradition:

Let us then gather up the Fragments that nothing may be lost, and let the Wellwishers of the Human Race, bind up such valuable Tracts as fall in their way, thereby giving them a Chance of Preservation to future Generations, who will doubtless profit by the more than we have done, and avoid our Mistakes.[93]

In 'Spence and the Barber', the political efficacy of singing is the topic of the song:

> When all feel alike in a cause,
> Small trouble's requir'd in teaching,
> A song that attracts their applause,
> Is better than speeches or preaching;
> Let's hear then no more of despair,

> But sing your dear rights to each other,
> 'Till all think alike every where,
> Even from one Land's end to the other.[94]

Evans had a musical ear and a gift for the prophetic: he writes here of the political valence of congregational song:

Even under the modern tyrannies of China, France, Turkey etc. what could hinder small companies from meeting, in a free and easy Manner, and singing their Rights and instructing each other in Songs? Can Tyrants hinder People from singing at their Work, or in their families? If not despair no longer but begin immediately, too much time has already been lost. Sing and meet and meet and sing, and your Chains will drop off like burnt Thread.[95]

The experience of defeat and the opening of a retrospective shapes the second wave of Spencean poetics. A space hollows out for a version of collectivity which is introspective while not being individualised. Evans's remarks show that the function of lyricism as a mode of intervention is now much more self-consciously understood and invoked.

For it is the case that the political lyricism of *Pig's Meat* operates at a high level of generality, working both as congregational exhortation and as satirical narrative, both of which preclude the particularity of inwardness, the voice of the romantic self. Part of the reason why it is hard to authenticate Spence's own lyrics is because they belong to a rhetoric shared by many. And the impersonal lyric, ubiquitous in the reform and radical periodical literature of the 1790s, is most often rhetorically deployed through the historical conventions of oppositional patriotism, the language of the Norman Yoke, interacting with enlightenment notions of reason. As Christopher Hill has argued, Norman Yoke ideology fed both revolutionary and Whig arguments that English Constitutional rights predated the Norman Conquest. Debate about royal prerogative versus parliamentary privilege spoken in the metaphor of the Norman Yoke remained part of English political rhetoric, even after its heyday in the period around the English Revolution. The debates about the Norman Yoke, like that explored by J. G. A. Pocock on the antiquity of the Constitution, were in intent originally movements within juridical and constitutional theory.[96] Recent work by James Epstein has made clearer how very long-lived that rhetoric was, and how complexly the debate resonated throughout the eighteenth century in more widely spread cultural terms.[97] In radical and reform poetry the communitarian aspirations voiced by the commoners metamorphosing from plebeian into proletarian circumstances often takes on this rhetoric. In these poems, the enlightenment sun nurtures and shines on the customary tree, the oak now figured as the Tree of Liberty.

In Spence's 'The Downfall of Feudal Tyranny', written 'When a Prisoner in Newgate, under a charge of High Treason, in the memorable Year 1794', the Norman Yoke is used to describe feudal oppression, after which 'reason's ray' shows man 'his dear rights once again':

> That conquering blade, who did us invade
> Ev'n William the Norman by name,
> Among his proud band he divided our land,
> Nought leaving but slav'ry and shame.[98]

The poem 'Alteration', which appeared in the journal in 1794, begins with an embrace of a typical enlightenment trope, and then immediately couples it to the historical, customary narrative of the suppression of the Anglo-Saxon freedoms:

> No longer lost in shades of night,
>   Where late in chains we lay!
> The sun arises, and his light
>   Dispels our gloom away.
>   . . .
> The pomp of Courts *no more* engage;
>   The *magic spell* is *broke*;
> We hail the bright reforming age!
>   And cast away the yoke![99]

In identifying oppositional patriotism with the productivity of the land, Spence opens up a pathway from urban poetics to a counter-picturesque poetic. National identity is located on the land described through the customary privileges of production on the land, rather than as an élite aesthetic garden. As we will see, however, the agrarian nature poems of the second-generation Spenceans, Allen Davenport and E. J. Blandford, are inflected by the rise of the meditative landscape poem a few decades later in the nineteenth century.

Spence, of course, was not alone in poetically working the rhetoric of the Norman Yoke and the rights of the freeborn Englishman. Within the radical and democratic poetry of the period, we find an ample amount of this language, often as part of the even more general presentation of the 'patriot' in war poetry. A set of transformations of the representation of the 'patriot' take place in this poetry which follows the shifting of lyric pre-occupations. While Chartist poetry of the 1830s weaves into one fabric the voices and visions of romantic subjectivity and a collective lyric voice, there is an appreciable contrast between that richly elaborated sense of identity and the more formulaic and externally narrated presentations of collective selfhood in the republican poetry of the 1790s.

In the earlier radical and reform poems, the image of the patriot is narrated as a figure of identity within an historical community saturated with popular power. This nativist poetic, entwined with the language of the oak and Anglo-Saxon freedom, persists through the nineteenth century, often in contrast with its maimed twin, the governmental patriot of Burke and the francophobes. But the republican patriot as an inhabited identity is drawn schematically and opaquely. So, for example, a poem such as 'Tribute to Liberty' by W. D. Grant, which appeared in the second volume of *Pig's Meat*, takes a popular tune and makes the general point:

> Generous PATRIOTS, nobly daring,
> *Regal ruffians* rage defy;
> Ev'ry toil and peril sharing,
> In pursuit of LIBERTY.[100]

An 'Ode on Liberty' which was read aloud on 14 July 1792 in the Mitre Tavern, Aldgate, to celebrate the anniversary of the French Revolution, is another example of a 'patriot' poem which calls on the narrative of popular power. In this case it is linked to the theme of poetic identity, calling upon the myth of an ancient political bard who will be able to speak the voice of liberty, and whose presence will confirm a restitution of a popular culture: 'Yet shall the times be found / When BRITAIN'S BARD shall wake no venal strain.'[101]

The imaged patriot emerges from the idealisation of the British Constitution, which it is the patriot's duty to defend, because it is the matrix from which he derives his identity. This sense of the constitution belongs to the customary historical idealisations which interact with and repel the rationalist idealisations of Paine. For example, Joseph Gerrald, in his tract *A Convention Is the Only Means of Saving Us from Ruin*, called for a convention as a form of revival of the Anglo-Saxon constitution of King Alfred, when the 'Mycelgemot, Folk-Mote, or Convention' had met annually on Salisbury Plain.[102] Here the image of Salisbury Plain is the site of custom and popular heritage, while in Blake's *Jerusalem* it is the point of origin for the druidical and juridical oppression of the many by the priest and the king. Though Wordsworth first writes about Salisbury Plain from a democratic perspective in 'A Night upon Salisbury Plain', he refashions the scene in Book XIII of *The Prelude*, turning it into the site of his poetic self-consciousness, and entry into his aesthetic commission, as he witnesses 'Our dim ancestral Past in vision clear'.[103] The Alfredian image follows its own path into the nineteenth century, and second-generation Spenceans even named one of their publications *The London Alfred*.[104]

The residual longevity of the Alfredian narrative brings us back to

George Dyer, and to his poems published in the democratic press. As noted earlier, Dyer belonged to the educated dissenting milieu, but he also drew as well on nativist rhetoric, and Spence excerpted and reprinted a section of Dyer's *Complaints of the Poor People of England*. Though he might be closer in politics and social life to John Thelwall, and to the London radical intelligentsia where he met, amongst others, fellow republicans and erstwhile pantisocrats Coleridge and Wordsworth, Dyer shared with Spence a link to the constitutionalist idiom of reform, as opposed to Thelwall's purer Painite views.[105] Thelwall argued that 'Establishments cannot decide upon First Principles; but First Principles must decide upon Establishments.'[106] Dyer's poetry, though not as interesting as his political and literary theory, mimics his double genealogy, by falling into two main sorts of poems: on the one hand, nativist lyrics which belong first to the language of oppositional patriotism, with all its antiquarian and customary resonance; and rationalist republicanism, marshalled in the rhetoric of sentimental humanitarianism, and hinting at the interior life, on the other. In an 'Ode', first published in 1799 and then reprinted in 1824, Dyer invokes the widespread 'death of the bard' theme as a counterpoint to the contemporary European ruins of war. He images a society in which a bard would again sing the narratives of a popular sovereignty, as in the Anglo-Saxon myth:

> See Britain rising from her seat,
> Proud of her rights, and equal laws,
> Ardent in freedom's sacred cause,
> Proclaims thee, Alfred, wise and good and great.
>
> . . .
>
> They ceas'd – and cease the lyric strain –
> For Alfred lives to bless no more:
> Though still, its day of splendour o'er
> Downward the sun sinks but to rise again.[107]

It is, of course, the sun of the enlightenment that will now rise and re-animate the temporality of the Alfredian narrative as the present of rationalist republicanism. In a 1796 'Song', Dyer joins together the themes of oppositional patriotism, the necessary poetic function of the bard, and the collective song of the democratic movement: the singular bard is challenged by a chorus of republicans.

> While venal bards attempt to sound,
> Through years remote the trump of fame,
> And call the wondering nations round,
> To learn some haughty conqueror's name,
> Justice demands a purer song,
> Let Freedom's sons the strain prolong.[108]

The poetry of oppositional patriotism often invokes the familial language of the 'Sons of Liberty', 'Sons of Britain', and 'Freedom's Sons', to express an only sporadically particularised collectivity. In the context of these examples, one gets a sharper sense of both the satiric and the straightforward use Blake makes of these idioms. For from these he will build not only his image of the collectivity in unity, the Giant Man Albion, but also the sons and daughters who populate *Visions of the Daughters of Albion*, *Vala*, and most complexly, *Jerusalem*, Blake's epic of oppositional patriotism, where Blake takes on the myth of Britain and critically differentiates it into a utopian myth of liberation.

The lyric poetry of nativist patriotism not only alludes narratively to the rôle of an oral poetic in the figure of the bard, it was itself extremely public and social, both in themes and in mode of reception. While some lyric forms – the ode, for example – were given a social resonance by virtue of being read aloud to a group in the tavern or at a meeting, in the tavern toasting song, the function of bard, audience, and singers are all fused: 'Then Britons join chorus, and nobly advance / The glass and the song, to the Genius of France'.[109]

While some of the lyric enactments of the 'patriot' derive from the pleasures of customary culture allied to companionable drinking and toasting, from the enlightenment, rationalist side of the equation we find a developing emphasis on the self, which invokes a different version of the 'patriot', who serves less as the emblem for a community than as a vehicle for creating and defining the identity of inwardness. The affective bridge between the two shapes is 'sympathy', which not only forges mental links from individual to individual, as it does in the greater romantic lyric such as Coleridge's 'This Lime-Tree Bower My Prison', which naturalises into the vernal the urban experience of Patriots incarcerated in Newgate, but equally forges social links of identification. 'We hear our brethren's dying cries, / We feel their pangs, – and sympathize.'[110] The self here extends and makes contact with other atomistic selves; this is quite a different construction from that of the collectivity of 'Sons' or 'Brethren' whose first attribute of relation is through embeddedness in family and nation, or more correctly, the family of nation. The collective poetic speaker sympathises with the imaged patriots, and makes a congruence of identity.

While in prison in 1794, Thelwall wrote a series of *Poems Written in Close Confinement in the Tower and Newgate*: excellent examples of the political poetry of sensibility, which articulate the bonds between an inward and an external set of constitutive goods. Imprisoned 'within the Dungeon's noxious gloom', 'The Patriot'

> unaw'd by guilty fears,
> (To Freedom and his country true)
> Who o'er a race of well-spent years
> Can cast the retrospective view,
> Looks inward to his heart, and sees
> The objects that must ever please.[111]

Prison poetry leaves a legacy to the mid-nineteenth century, as Thomas Cooper and Ernest Jones take up and extend the meditation of the political prisoner, whose retrospection binds him to the struggle going on outside the prison walls. In his introductory remarks to the volume, Thelwall describes this productive exchange between inward and external resources:

The Patriot, immured in the walls of a bastille, is called upon, by important duties, to repel every enervating sensation, and cultivate those habits of reflection only which may increase the energy of his mind, and enable him to render his sufferings ultimately beneficial to mankind.[112]

In this politico-poetical vehicle for exploring inwardness in relation to the group, the more social and generalised image of the patriot transmutes into the image of a subjective revolutionary. An increasingly 'lyrical' political subject is introduced into this poetic, with the result that the individuated meditative lyric becomes distinguished from a previously more impersonal genre of war and public poetry.

A set of poems from the respectable Dissenting reformist family of John Aiken and Lucy Aiken, brother and niece of Anna Barbauld, gives a more focused and personalised version of the political patriot, but even though the patriot is specified, as in these poems written to and about Gilbert Wakefield (a republican who was jailed during the sedition law period, and who died almost at once upon leaving prison), Wakefield's individuality is diffused through the more general category of 'Patriot'.[113] In Dyer's poem for Wakefield, we see the workings of the sentimental rationalist idiom, which gives a more convincing version of inwardness. 'Meditated in a Garden', this poem somewhat crudely reproduces tropes and themes of 'Lycidas', but it closes by focusing on a sympathetic identification between speaker and patriot:

> But, in the Summer of his life I knew him,
> And call'd him friend: for in our hearts did dwell
> Some kindred likings and some kindred scorns:
> The tyrant's state, the pontiff's pomp and pride,
> The hireling's meanness . . .
>   together we did hail

> The star of Freedom, rising on a world
> Of slavery-goaded men; we liv'd to see
> France rise to something of the new-born man,
> Snapping her fetters off, enlarg'd and free.[114]

Given that Dyer and Wordsworth knew one another, it is plausible that Wordsworth had this poem, or poems like it, in the back of his mind when in 1805 he wrote about his 1791 relationship with the French patriot, Michel Beaupuy. In that reminiscence, Wordsworth fashioned a central image of the moment of sympathetic identification. Bridging the national boundary between France and England, Wordsworth's access to Beaupuy's subjectivity is gained through their mutual understanding of the 'hunger-bitten Girl' walking before them: "Tis against *that* which we are fighting.'[115] An object in their vision, the child leading her heifer is all but inanimate in her 'heartless' mood, but she is the catalyst for a communication between the two men, in which the work of the patriot is understood as a condition of heartfelt democratic consciousness, transcending both national and martial claims. Wordsworth conveys an importantly internationalist claim for republicanism; but the incident also encapsulates the trajectory by which the withdrawal of consciousness from a collective lyricality (in which the poet speaks the patriotism of the group), helps to build the private lyrical voice which enacts its own consciousness on the ruins of the poor and the displaced, who are then constituted as the objects of representation. Wordsworth's purpose in 1805 is to show how his true, inward nature reasserts itself in the language of the heart by breaking through the abstractions of analytical reason, which had been the topic of discussion between himself and Beaupuy up until the moment when the girl moved into their view. In many of the lyrical ballads, as we have seen, Wordsworth braids the claims of reason and custom into forceful presentations of identity, in which custom resonates with popular belief and claimed popular rights, while reason offers conduits for subjectivity to be conveyed. But in his narrative retelling of his experience in France, Wordsworth takes up Burke's custom as a cudgel against the insistence of both popular claims and those of rationality.

In her discussion of British war poetry, Betty Bennett points out that the greater part of published poems in the period between 1793–1815 were about the war with France. Her point suggests a new context for thinking about the figures from everyday life in Wordsworth's poetry when she writes, 'Wordsworth and Coleridge, Shelley and Byron celebrated the individuality of the common man, but it was the popular war poetry that, for the first time in British literary history, put the common man centre-stage'.[116] Bennett also states that through the publication of so many war poems and songs, 'the simple stanza-plus-refrain form acquired a poetic respectability which it had not previously had'.[117] In the complexity of war, the plebeian ballad met up with the martial lyric song, and opened another crossway between élite and popular poetics. Bennett's remark also casts a different light upon the value and meaning of the blank verse intervention of Wordsworth and Coleridge at the end of the 1790s. The movement away from public forms of war poetry into meditative poetry, the shift within the social function of the lyric, and the advocacy of a private individual voice over the communal forms of ballad and broadsheet were all features of the reorganisation of genre in the romantic period. The alteration in the status of the chief public lyric, the ode, in the second half of the eighteenth century is another component in this movement. The declension of the ode from public to private issues follows the theorisation of lyric as the site of solitude rather than sociality.[118] In his *Poems Chiefly Written in Retirement*, John Thelwall chooses the meditative blank verse paragraph over both the odal organisation of earlier poems and the popular stanzas of his earlier radical lyrics, electing representational over interventionist poetics. Thelwall makes a poetico-political gesture when he set out for the landscaped elegies of his verse effusions, leaving behind his raucous bar song, 'News from Toulon; or, the Men of Gotham's Expedition. Sung at the Globe Tavern, at the General Meeting of the London Corresponding Society', in which he lambastes the reign of the '*crucifixes, relics, shrines, apostles, saint, and martyr*', which the revolutionaries now melt down to pay 'for beef and brandy'.[119] It may be that in this separating out of lyric functions in the context of war and republican poetry that we find another strand in the prehistory of the 'cockney rhyming' scandal of 1819. That is, the manner through which Wordsworth became associated with blank verse can be traced back to his prosodic choices in the late 1790s, and those choices were to reverberate when, as William Keach has argued, Hunt's and Keats's liberal political voices were derogatorily linked to liberality in poetic couplets.[120] In 1822, when Thelwall anthologised his essays and poems from *The Champion*, he included an essay on 'English Songs', in which he theorises the song as an apolitical genre:

The diction must be graceful, elegant and simple – equally remote from the turgid and the low; from the quaint and the familiar. It must not be colloquial: neither must it be pedantic or obscure, technical or abstruse.[121]

His view of songs as 'cabinet pictures for minute inspection; or gems

which require an equal polish at every angle', erases his own comic contributions to the vital life of tavern song and agitational singing of the
1790s:

> But these are petty sheerers all,
>   And fleece a little flock;
> Behold where *haughty ministers*
>   Fleece the whole nations stock:
> The while *pretended patriots*,
>   A still more venal race,
> With liberty and bawling cant,
>   Would fleece them of their place –
>   When a fleecing they will go, etc.[122]

If patriot poetry leads us, in the individualist mode, to the Beaupuy
episode of *The Prelude*, it also moves us towards 'Tintern Abbey'. The
meditative lyric voice of 'Tintern Abbey' in this context actuates the withdrawal from the scene of war, and the withdrawal from the lyric forms
associated with the public life of war. The love of one's country as a
political site is metamorphosed into the love of one's country as an
aesthetic experience. The stanzaic lyric is associated with the forms of war
poetry; the meditative verse paragraph with those of aesthetic retreat.
The society within which the lyric is capable of invoking sympathy is thus,
in this poetic, significantly reduced and reshaped from the solidarity of
those generalised patriotic brothers, whose family resemblance inheres in
their social constitution and the patriotic narrative within which they all
engage and from which they derive their identity. Rather, we find a lyrical
community of unencumbered friends who reach out, voluntarily, to make
contact aesthetically and transcendentally, meeting in the shared landscape of their minds, as in Coleridge's 'This Lime-Tree Bower My Prison'
(or, failing to do so, as in his foiled attempt to make a sympathetic connection with his wife in 'The Eolian Harp').

If we consider, in the light of this withdrawal, Wordsworth's revisions to
the meaning of 'Old Man Travelling' as it turns into 'Animal Tranquillity
and Decay', we can get a deeper sense of how a poem which had belonged
to the genre of anti-war poetry is transmuted into an aesthetic vehicle for
the solitary speaker. In the first version of the poem, Wordsworth had
shown an ancient, stooped man walking a great distance through the
countryside on his last visit to his sailor son, a casualty of war, 'Who from
a sea-fight had been brought to Falmouth, / And there was dying in a
hospital'.[123] The poem begins in a purely natural scene, where nature is
composed, if not kind, and the old man is ordered and 'led' by the native

environment, and it ends by revealing an ecology of nature and culture, father and son, locality and the larger world. But Wordsworth revised his poetic intention in this poem along with his political intention, omitting the final explanatory lines of the poem from all versions after 1805. The connections between the old man and the world are thus cut off, and he is reduced to a state of brute nature, becoming the occasion for the growth of a poet's mind. His placement in a narrative of history is transformed into an image out of time.

It would be wrong, however, to suggest that the communitarian impulse is entirely eclipsed in the landscape poetry of individualism. If the customary practice visible in *Lyrical Ballads* tends to dissolve into varieties of Wordsworth's own subjectivity, it remains true that he articulates his development in 'Tintern Abbey' as a dialectic in which the rural site feeds him when he is in the city, while what he has learned in society allows him to hear, when once again out in nature, 'the still sad music of humanity'. When we look, however, at the Spencean poetic and its inheritors, we find an unambiguously luxuriant growth of communitarian rural poetry, poised against the transcendence and disembodiment of individualist romanticism. For the centrality of the land to Spencean ideology gave rise to a current of landscape poems committed to collectivity, whose impact would be felt in Chartist poetics later in the century.

Another way to model this contrast is to describe the dialectic of romanticism as comprising two poles of attraction in the landscape: a pole of personal transcendence, figured in the landscapes and conversations of Wordsworth and Coleridge, and a pole of natural instantiation, in which the material riches of the earth provided a site for communitarian identities to flourish. This tradition can also be linked to the work of Blake. Though *Jerusalem*, his communitarian epic, is a deeply urban poèm, Blake threads through it images of nature as a productive, abundant resource. As a poet of London, and one with links to artisanal conceptions of human labour, Blake was able to pierce through the increasingly mystified version of nature, and poetically recover it, not as a vista to be surveyed, but as a dialectic between human labour and earth, in which a distinction between society and nature is meaningless: 'Where Man is Not, Nature is Barren.'[124] When Blake does represent nature, he always introduces the practice of labour: even when his poetic language is at its most mythic and apocalyptic, Blake renders persons working the land and cultivating the soil analogous to the labour of making the permanent products of art. Participating in a counter-discourse to the capitalist one of improvement, Blake satirically produces a counter-capitalist picturesque aesthetic: 'Improvement makes strait roads, but the crooked roads without improvement are roads of Genius.'[125]

Within Spence's agrarian poetic, the counter-voice to the isolated self in the landscape was offered through the image of the 'people's farm', a trope which reintegrated the landscape garden back into its agricultural surrounding. The result was a utopian georgic, which recovered the narrative of farm and commons from the atemporal myth of the landscape. In his 'History of Crusonia', Spence gives a lovely vignette of the landscape of abundance:

I can never enough admire the Beauty of the Country: it has more the Air of a Garden, or rather a Paradise, than a general Country scene; and indeed it is properly a Continuation of Gardens and Orchards. For besides the infinite Number of real Gardens, all the Fields, even for Meadow and Pasture, are strewed very thick with Fruit-Trees and appear like as many Orchards; and the Corn is cultivated in Rows and as carefully as Garden-herbs.[126]

So the language of the country interacts continually with the motives of the urban milieu. The radical poetry of the 1790s is most prominently activist and interventionist, and centrally urban in its construction. In the wave of radicalism associated with the period from 1815 to the mid-1820s, second-generation Spenceanism is claimed by a group of activist-poets who elaborate a neo-Spencean version of landscape poetry against the ruralism of meditative poetry. These poems present a version of the past that Chartist poets draw upon to fashion their history of a popular poetic tradition. The story of Allen Davenport, Spencean and Chartist, belongs more properly to the next chapter, but he and fellow Spencean poets such as E. J. Blandford not only provide transitions between generations of radicals, but also between generations of romantics. The poetic of agrarian abundance in Southey's *Wat Tyler* took on a vital after-life in pirated and reprinted editions, outside and within the Spencean culture. Though split off from the trajectory of the poet himself, Southey's claim, 'Abundant is the earth', was invoked as a poetico-political continuity between the two generations.[127] David Worrall's excellent discussion of 'Agrarians against the Picturesque' has made clear to us how boldly Southey's poem was appropriated during the Spa Field rising of 1816 to indicate both the theory of a landscape of abundance, and to mark out the entropic path of those Jacobins-in-recoil.[128]

The poems which appeared in the short-lived but vivid *Medusa*, an urban radical weekly which ran from 20 February 1819 to 7 January

1820, articulate the next moment in the making of the counter-tradition of interventionist poetry. As Worrall points out, the poems in *Medusa* offer a more 'sophisticated poetic discourse' than that elaborated in 'the clumsier efforts of earlier Spenceans'.[129] It may be that as the tacit rights of the commons are disrupted, and then recalled as explicit rights, a recollection that simultaneously signals their suppression, these customary claims become more easily rendered in poetic conventions that belong to the larger lyric heading of the elegiac. So, in a poem by a 'Spencean Philanthropist', 'The Wrongs of Man. Or, Things as They Are', the poet claims that the customary right 'To hunt or fish, or grow a plant' has been displaced from the Divine to the Landlord's authority:

> Nor may you trespass on his ground,
> To nothing you can name,
> *To kip, nor haw, nor nul, nor sloe*
> Have you a *legal* claim.[130]

The stanza calls attention to the now superseded language of custom: all these are names of common rights of the agricultural peasantry: sleeping on hills, picking wild plums, gathering from hedges. The poet here repeats part of Spence's earlier song, 'The Rights of Man', in which he describes the erosion of right: 'Nor hip, nor haw, nor nut, nor sloe, / Nor ought that you can name'.[131] The power of second-generation Spencean poetry derives from its elegiac strain, which opens a space for a more reflective personal voice to inhabit. So the transaction between the individualist landscape lyric of romanticism and the interventionist urban lyric of the Spenceans becomes interesting and complex in the years around 1818 and 1819. If it is the case that the romantic meditative lyric alters and highlights one area within the junction of external and internal constitutive goods, it is also the case that the power of the individualist lyric, with its elegiac strain, makes a mark upon the next wave of political protest lyricism.

E. J. Blandford, a second-generation Spencean, was a hairdresser, musician, and poet.[132] He drew upon the rural resource which, from the loco-descriptive poem through the moralising poem through the landscaped elegy, took its most recent shape as the romantic meditative lyric composed by the solitary self. But Blandford holds onto the claims of a communitarian ethos in order to cultivate the 'people's farm' in place of an unproductive ornamental nature. Malcolm Chase has investigated the provenance of the phrase, the 'people's farm', finding it first in some remarks by Thomas Evans, Spence's lieutenant and propagator of Spencean song, as well as in this 1816 broadside ballad:

> A Nation is the People's Farm,
> They build, they plant, 'tis their strong arm,
> That till the clod, defend their clan.[133]

David Worrall points to the trope's place in a poem written three years later, 'The Rights of Man, or Things as They Were Intended to Be by Divine Providence':

> Thus all the world BELONGS TO MAN,
> But NOT to kings and lords;
> A country's land's the people's farm,
> And all that it affords:
> For why? divide it how you will,
> 'Tis all the people's still;
> The people's country, parish, town;
> They build, defend, and till.[134]

The poem is notable as well for a rhetorical juxtaposition, which begins in the 1790s and continues through the nineteenth century, of nativist and internationalist claims for this common ownership. While the idea of the people's farm is born from nativist historicism, it opens up into a global view:

> Thou gav'st the *earth, one common farm*,
> For them to dress and till,
> To make *this* globe a *paradise*;
> Such was thy HOLY WILL:
> Thou gav'st them laws, and covenants,
> To regulate the whole,
> *One* great *republic* to create,
> 'From Indus to the pole'.

That is, just as rationalism and millenarianism cohabit in the rhetoric of the period, so do a national and international sense of brotherhood. This begins in the idea that the French Revolution is an international revolution, even as it marks out the moment when nationalism becomes fully functional; the rhetoric of the nativist historical claim for change is revitalised as a way of claiming domestic sources for radical demands. The theme continues through the century, weaving an uneven fabric of nationalist and internationalist versions of the people's identity.

Blandford takes up the trope, and works it as an oppositional force against the narrative of feudal tyranny and expropriation. Blandford's first poem to appear in *Medusa* was 'Nature's First, Last, and Only Will! Or, a Hint to Mr. Bull', a miniature epic of paradise lost. Nature's bounty is familial, and equally distributed:

> The earth, the waters, eke the air and light,
> And mines and springs, man held in equal right
> For ever . . .

But having given 'in entail all her stores to man', 'Despots' and 'priestmen' take over the land: 'barefac'd pillage grasp'd the common soil, / And only poverty rewarded toil'. The language of commonality supports the narrative of the poem: 'All in her abundance share the same . . . common cause [and] common soil', but Blandford makes it clear that the resolution to the crisis can only be made through an alliance between Reason and Nature. The strength of Nature's 'sacred will' undermined by 'barefac'd pillage', she is now framed as a passive female: 'Suffering Nature shed her useless tear.' But Female Justice, who 'is not dead', awakens Reason who then calls upon Nature to become combative.[135] This martial peasant female Nature is a typical feature of the Spencean poetic, and she also appears in Shelley's agrarian song, 'The Mask of Anarchy'. Spence's advocacy of the rights of women as well as those of men, which put him well to the left of Thomas Paine back in the 1790s, is itself grounded in the identity of customary culture. Deborah Valenze has shown how the modernisation of agriculture changed the value of women's labour and hence their place in the working culture: 'Changes in property ownership and land use made women's customary work in agriculture illegal if not impossible.'[136] The 1819 Blandford poem performs the bridging of the languages of custom and reason as Reason encourages Nature to arise into struggle.

In 'A Real Dream; or, Another Hint for Mr. Bull', Blandford draws on the conventions of the poetics of the solitary, offering a dream poem, which turns into a ventriloquising of the oppressed through his voice. The poem opens with an epigraph from Blandford's own work, establishing his poetic voice as one which might be linked to a tradition, evoking the transformative power of poetic language: 'The dumb shall speak; and speak with voice so loud, / That e'en the deaf shall hear and be advised.' The poem begins by describing a landscape of peaceful equality,

> Where all the equal gain of produce shar'd;
> Where old and young an equal balance held,
> And each with fruits an equal measure fill'd.[137]

Blandford then goes on to describe the reality of everyday life in the present, where 'The slavish multitude starve, and seem to fear, / Lest wolves and vultures, their complaints should hear.' He participates in and appropriates the power of interiority for a revised sense of collective identity: against those who 'war 'gainst useful labour's common right; – /

Rouse men, cried I, and for your freedom fight!' The authority of the
Dreamer in this poem is of a different species to that in the other songs of
impersonal republicanism which appeared in *Medusa* in 1819 and 1820.
This poet has learned from print-culture poetics how to shape his polemic
through a version of a self who stands both within and outside the milieu
to which he speaks. The poet becomes a leader in this poem, and there is a
transaction between the voice of the collective and its orchestration. But
the assertion of control over the movement of the mind is complex, for
the speaker, at the end of the poem, finds that what he had assumed
(and asserted) to be the work of Fancy within his own mind was in fact the
lightning rod for an external collective will, of which he is a recipient. Yet it
is the result of the outward press of his fancy into the milieu around him
that precipitates that collective volition. As his epigraph urges that 'the
potent magic of a dream' might rouse 'The dumb to speak', so the poem
ends as Fancy, startled by its own work, dislocates 'the cords of sleep' and
'I found 'twas real, – no mistake, / A REAL DREAM, – for I was
wide awake.' Michael Scrivener links this poem to Shelley's *Queen Mab*, but
it also seems to be a precursor to his 'The Mask of Anarchy' as the
exchange of singular and collective voice motivates the movement of the
poem.

In 'A Terrible Omen to Guilty Tyrants; or the Spirit of Liberty',
Blandford continues Spence's appropriation of literary heritage, by drawing on Shakespeare for the epigraph to his poem: 'When the blast of war
blows in our ears, / Let us be tigers in our fierce deportment!' The
inference is that Blandford's own self-referential epigraph places him in a
lineage from Shakespeare. This is a tactic that continues in a spirited
manner in the elaboration of a Chartist poetic, and is part of the polemic
which will tie together communitarian claims for the unity of class,
literary, and national identity under the banner of poetic tradition.

In 'A Terrible Omen', Blandford works from the traditional poetic topic
of inspiration, and the power of invocations, but he materialises the
abstract relation between power and voice, articulated for example in
Wordsworth's 'correspondent breeze', and in Coleridge's storm in
'Dejection':

> SPIRIT OF LIBERTY, now 'midst the throng,
> In awful grandeur dost thou move along;
> From east to west, from north to south, behold
> Thy power extended, moving uncontrol'd,
> Tremendous rolling through the swelling tide
>   . . .

Each British breast is warmed; and all unite
In manly movement to assert their right,
With brave, collective, and o'erwhelming might![138]

It is reasonable to conjecture that Shelley had these issues of *Medusa* sent to him in Italy, after which he wrote his 'Ode to the West Wind' and 'Ode to Liberty', for there is a fascinating and short-lived confluence of oral and print culture, communitarian and individualist poetics, in Shelley's 1819 poetry.

Poetry as a collective voice, poetry as issuing from a communitarian sense of identity, and poetry as a political intervention for a popular politics are all linked: this is the case for the Spenceans, with their call to 'Meet and Sing', and for Shelley, who found poetic resources *in* the communitarian tradition, which he later donated *to* it, as the post-1832 working-class radical movement returned to Shelley's lyrics, and made them a ubiquitous part of the Chartist poetic scene.[139] In twentieth-century critical discussions, Shelley's political poetics have most often been linked to the traditions of radical liberalism learnt from Godwin and Paine.[140] But 'The Mask of Anarchy' and Shelley's other 1819 lyrics draw upon an already established mythology and imagery of a communitarian traditionalism, one which cuts across the rationalist scepticism of much of Shelley's poetic epistemology. The joining together of a poetic and a political intervention, which Shelley calls for in his response to the Peterloo Massacre of 1819 carries the lyric forward in its communal version, and makes this poem as critical as Wordsworth's *Lyrical Ballads* for describing the foundational significance of customary and enlightenment rhetoric, communitarian and individualist identity, to the constitution of the romantic tradition. Shelley's poem sits within the milieu of the popular radical song in much the same manner that Wordsworth's *Lyrical Ballads* sat amidst late eighteenth-century sentimental humanitarian ballads. The radical revival of 1815–24 recovered the Spencean lyric and reinvigorated it, and Shelley's 'The Mask of Anarchy', as well as his 'Men of England' stanzas make their appeal within the conventions of the radical song. But though the power of the song was manifest in the radical revival, the 'lyrical ballad' had lost its valence, and this is highlighted by Shelley's unpublished attempt in that genre, his 'Ballad of the Starving Mother', which, with its appeal to the pathos of the impoverished mother and child, sounds very dated within the poetical geography of 1819. The atmosphere of crisis and political immediacy which permeates Shelley's 1819 popular songs and lyrics – 'England', 'A New National Anthem', 'Two Similes' – provides a

counter-spirit to the elegiac tone of his lyrical ballad. Shelley described his
1819 communitarian lyrics as belonging to 'the exoteric species' – i.e.,
addressed to the populace at large rather than to a set of initiates.[141] They
are certainly distinct from the forms and rhetoric of the wilful and creative
Self of his philosophical poems, but this does not make them marginal to
his œuvre, and it is instructive to read them as a second-generation working through of the issues of romantic lyricism, entailing the contest of
voluntaristic and embedded identities. We can see how Shelley learned
from the customary tradition of plebeian recalcitrance, and how this
inflects some of his larger concerns.

The argument of 'The Mask of Anarchy' is straightforward: a 'vast
assembly' (LXXIII) coming 'From the corners uttermost / Of the bounds of
English coast' (LXVII) can 'Rise like lions' (XCI) because they establish their
identity through their act of solidarity.[142] Identity is clearly indicated as a
plural and a social mode. The act of solidarity produces action dialectically out of passive resistance, as the mass demonstration will provoke the
State to intervene and propel the demonstrators towards a revolutionary
retort:

> And that slaughter to the nation
> Shall steam up like inspiration,
> Eloquent, oracular,
> A volcano heard afar. (LXXXIX)

The language of the poem will occupy and then transform oppression into
resistance, the words

> Like Oppression's thundered doom,
> Ringing through each heart and brain,
> Heard again – again – again. (XC)

'These words' (XC), moreover, do not belong to the represented 'I' of the
text, for his voice is that of a scribe; nor do they unambiguously belong to
the Earth, for they are so attributed through an act of similitude, 'As if her
heart had cried aloud'. The source of that language is unfamiliarly fluid
and social compared with the romantic individualist poetics of the self.

So, although it may at first appear odd for Shelley to commemorate an
event in an industrial city with a vision of an agrarian utopia, in fact, he
was writing right out of the mixture of visions that characterised the
plebeian radicalism of the beginning of the nineteenth century and
provided the lexicon of Spencean agrarianism. The image of 'a comely
table spread' (LIV) that Shelley produces within his imagined community
was part of the communitarian and Spencean vision of a good life for a

labouring class very newly arrived in the cities and slowly being turned into the industrial proletariat, and not simply the idealised feudal fantasy of a landed aristocrat expatriated to Italy and filled with *ressentiment* about new industrial and financial wealth.

All the poems which Shelley wrote in the months after learning the news of the massacre at St. Peter's Fields draw upon the language of urban radicalism and utilise the rhetoric of constitutionalism, Anglo-Saxon rights, customary right, and non-Godwinian rationalism. 'England', which Medwin later renamed 'Lines Written during the Castlereagh Administration' when printing the poem in 1832, in a stroke historicising its purchase on contemporary politics, calls upon the theme of the 'Sons of Albion', though deployed here within a metaphorisation of birth and abortion that is characteristically Shelleyan.[143] Shelley's communitarian lyrics sound uncannily Blakean, and we are reminded of Blake's 'rocky druid shore':

> Her sons are as stones in the way –
> They are masses of senseless clay –
> They are trodden, and move not away –
> The abortion with which she travaileth
> Is Liberty, smitten to death.[144]

The congruity between Blake and Shelley in these lyrics is a function of their use of urban ballad forms, the rhetoric of oppositional patriotism, and the poetic construction of embedded identities. In his 'Similes for Two Political Characters of 1819', Shelley conceives a contemporary version of that perversion of the English Oak and Liberty Tree which Blake had named the 'Tree of Mystery', and which in Shelley's verses is pictured as the perch for the 'empty ravens' who 'scent the noonday smoke / of fresh human carrion.' These are the bodies of the labouring poor, the 'Men of England' who

> With plough and spade, and hoe and loom,
> Trace your grave, and build your tomb,
> And weave your winding-sheet, till fair
> England be your sepulchre.[145]

These lyrics, and the 'New National Anthem', which proclaims 'Liberty' as England's 'murdered Queen' in the same rhythms and accents as those tavern songs and anthems which appropriated tunes and rewrote the words, sound very like those of the urban agrarians. And ever since Kenneth Neill Cameron's work in the 1950s, there has been a link made between Shelley and Spence's agrarianism, though to date no one has made an exhaustive study of mutual influences.[146] In his analysis of the vicissitudes of Spenceanism in London radical circles between the 1790s and 1820, Iain McCalman has not only demonstrated the links between Spence's agrarianism and Paine's rationalism, but also suggests that Shelley must have had some intellectual relationship with the Spenceans. And William St. Clair has narrated the encounters between Shelley and George Cannon, an important second-generation Spencean, who, as 'Erasmus Perkins', first published *Queen Mab* in his free-thinking periodical, the *Theological Inquirer*.[147]

It is interesting then to read Donald Reiman's forceful argument that Shelley was linked closely to what Reiman calls 'reactionary agrarianism'. Reiman looks at the ways in which Shelley's personal position within the English estate system made it impossible for him to break with the aristocracy, and argues that *this* accounts for the particularity of the radicalism of 'The Mask of Anarchy'. Reiman presses his point by out-lining the antagonism between Shelley's positions and those of the 'new' financial interests, whose wealth 'was newly created by the need to fund the national debt, the issuing of paper money and credit, and the expansion of governmental bureaucracy during the American and French Wars, 1775–1815'.[148] But in fact most of the targets in 'The Mask of Anarchy' (taxonomised by Reiman as: abolition of the slave trade and the Court of Chancery; criticism of the Church hierarchy, lawyers, the House of Lords, spies, agents provocateurs, the standing army, royal prerogatives, the Bank of England, the Tower of London, the unreformed Parliament, the practice of hiring workers at subsistence wages; and hatred of paper currency) are equally those that would have been shared by the radical agrarian movements that helped to secure for the industrial working class a sense of an inherited and shared tradition, and so buttressed the growth of working-class consciousness.[149] For example, Shelley's attitude towards paper money in 'The Mask of Anarchy' was shared by both the agricultural aristocracy and popular radicals. Thomas Evans argued that it was the parasitism of the privileged classes which led to the poor being mired in debt and financial bondage.[150] It is impossible to know exactly which papers and journals Shelley read in Italy after the Peterloo Massacre, but 'The Mask of Anarchy' might have been published immediately had he sent it to Thomas Davidson's *Medusa*, rather than sending it off to Leigh Hunt, who kept it unpublished until 1832. Kevin Gilmartin suggests that it may have been Shelley's own timidity that led him to send the poem to Hunt rather than to one of the more radical periodicals.[151] Many of the ephemeral radical periodicals published both satirical and passionate poems about Peterloo. *Medusa* printed 'An Address to "The Rabble"' that also invokes a collective and interventionist poetic voice against the massacre:

> Britons, now your voices join;
> Britons, with your souls combine,
> T' avenge the infernal deed.[152]

When Shelley writes 'The Mask of Anarchy' in the discourse of agrarian radicalism, he links himself to the plebeian political tradition that runs outside and athwart Godwinian rationalism. This enables him to redirect his sense of what it is that poems can do: namely, it allows him to shift from a representational to an interventionist project in the poem. An unpredicted aspect of Shelley's engagement with communitarianism in his poem is an encounter with women and with the problem of the representation of women that is markedly different from his address to this question in his poems of the voluntaristic self. It is quite stunning to find that the Shelley who is the author of an idealised self-projection of the female, linked to solipsistic individualism in 'Alastor', the essay 'On Love', and 'Epipsychidion', is, in 'The Mask of Anarchy' equally the author of a fierce and autonomous female interventionism. The communitarian poetics in 'The Mask of Anarchy' link Shelley to a feminism of a different character from that of Wollstonecraft's rationalism. As E. P. Thompson has pointed out, the Spenceans were not only the historical link between the revolutionaries of the 1790s and the radicals of 1818, but they were also the link on the question of women's oppression. Though the intellectual circle around Wollstonecraft, Godwin, and Blake had been interested in the cause of sexual liberation, Spence was one of the only English Jacobins to address explicitly women from the labouring classes.[153]

While the response to Peterloo in the ultra-radical journals was unambiguously revolutionary, middle-class outrage turned on the issue of the involvement of women. One response to the massacre of women and children was an indignant sense of an assault on innocents. A Cruikshank engraving, 'Massacre at St. Peter's or "Britons Strike Home"' depicts the slaughter of women and children by the Loyal Manchester Yeomanry, their banner reading 'Be Bloody, Bold, & Resolute' (*Macbeth* IV, i).[154] But this benevolent patriarchal response was matched amongst the pro-Government forces by an equally severe condemnation of the women themselves. The women reformers of Peterloo were labelled as prostitutes, and Dr. Stoddert, editor of the *New Times*, argued that legislation should be passed so that women might not attend popular meetings.[155] It makes

sense that the depictions of women in the press in the immediate aftermath of Peterloo (which Shelley read in the papers which reached him
in Italy) would have raised for him the question of how to link the philosophical rights of women to the actual interventions of women activists. In
a letter to Hunt on 3 November 1819, Shelley refers to the troop of 'master
manufacturers' who 'cut off women's breasts & dash the heads of infants
against stones'.[156]

The version of femininity implied in the separating out of women from
men in this rhetoric makes a particular kind of sense within the discourse
of individualist romanticism. Margaret Homans has theorised the fabri-
cation of the feminine in the nineteenth century as a discourse of, and an
anxiety about the *literal*. 'For the same reason that women are identified
with nature', she writes, 'women are also identified with the literal'. Literal
meaning, she goes on to argue, 'would hypothetically destroy any text it
actually entered by making superfluous those very figures'.[157] Within the
individualist poetry of aesthetic autonomy, this is a very grave problem
indeed, since the translation of the unrepresentable into the figural is a
major stimulation for poetic production itself. One might invoke this
insight as the source of the not surprisingly female 'Maid of Mount
Abora', in 'Kubla Khan', whose song (luckily for the poetic speaker) *cannot*
be recreated. If it could, it would thereby usurp the place of Coleridge's
own presumptive poem, which is forecast from within the text as the as yet
deferred product of the poem's invoked male manic poet. Feminist critics,
developing Homans's insight, have seen the literalising of the female at
work amongst all the canonical romantic poets: for example, in 'Tintern
Abbey', Wordsworth 'addresses Dorothy in the manner of an address to
nature, as if conflating her with nature'.[158] And Shelley is not usually
exempted from this discussion of the figure of the female: Meena
Alexander, in her survey of *Women in Romanticism*, sees Shelley as transforming women's otherness into a figment of his own imagination. The
feminine as a 'purest symbol is intoxicating, fiery and finally in Shelley's
vision a catalyst for the longed for self-combustion.'[159]

But when we foreground Shelley's interventionist poetic, a poetic fused
not to aesthetic autonomy, but to poetic and political collective agency, we
see how the usurpation of the figurative by the literal turns into an asset,
not a liability. This opens up a space for a construction of the feminine as
an articulation rather than a suppression. Imagine now the passionate
qualities of the manic poet of 'Kubla Khan' – he who stands inside the
holy circle and cannot be touched – merged with the singing Maid of
Mount Abora. Such a merged agent *would be* the 'maniac maid' of 'The

Mask of Anarchy', who can turn her body into the source of a spirit of active change, and invoke the voice of the earth itself. In such a way words *do* 'rise up like things', as they did in Coleridge's reverie before he sat down to write 'Kubla Khan'. Unlike the ill-matched relation between the Maid of Mount Abora and the manic poet within Coleridge's text, the 'maniac maid' in 'The Mask of Anarchy' is invoked in order to participate in social processes. Nor does Shelley appear anxious that the fulfilment of deferred desire (namely, human liberation) will lead him out of his poetic reverie and into the diminished literality of the world (the usual charge against romantic poets), for in this case he is attempting to legitimate the literal, which leads him easily to present this through the vehicle of the female.

To literalise figures, then, is a central intention of 'The Mask of Anarchy', and this rhetorical step bears a necessary relation to the occasion upon which the poem was written. For it is in the very nature of mass demonstrations that symbolic actions are transformed into literal, engaged ones. When a public demonstration (a mass of people symbolically representing, by their mass appearance on St. Peter's Fields, their demand for political representation) is intruded upon by external authority (the Loyal Manchester Yeomanry), it shifts from having a symbolic to having a literal and potentially insurrectionary meaning. John Berger argues,

Almost invariably, authority chooses to use force. The extent of its violence depends upon many factors, but scarcely ever upon the scale of the physical threat offered by the demonstrators. This threat is essentially symbolic. But by attacking the demonstration authority ensures that the symbolic event becomes an historical one.[160]

This is precisely the structure of the Peterloo massacre. A mass symbolic demonstration in support of political representation was literalised by the actions of the authorities, who swept into the crowd to 'Slash, and stab, and maim, and hew' (LXXXIV).

We are authorised to read the 'maniac maid' of 'The Mask of Anarchy' as a strong riposte to the various maids who people romantic lyric poems. Not only does she speak, but she also acts, reversing the relation between figural and literal in a manner which completes the linkage between the worlds of poetic and social intention. Her passivity, 'Expecting with a patient eye, / Murder, Fraud, and Anarchy' (XXV), is the ground upon which the symbolic life of demonstration, of the masque which inhabits the realms of the representational, is transformed into the world of action and combat.

And contrary to the contention that for the male romantic poet the literal is always an inferior mode to the figurative, this poem invokes the literal as its own triumphant conclusion, and is thereby able to re-symbolise the massacre as a potential insurrection. Significantly, when the maid is freed from her mania and 'walking with a quiet mien' (xxxii), a transpersonal, communitarian voice rises from the unspecified spot. Now figuration is reintroduced, but in such a way as to efface entirely the boundary between the representational and the literal: the transpersonal voice arises,

> As if their own indignant earth,
> Which gave the sons of England birth,
> Had felt their blood upon her brow . . .
> Had turned every drop of blood . . .
> To an accent unwithstood,
> As if her heart had cried aloud. (xxxv, xxxvi)

The power to speak here is directly linked to a gendered power: the widespread voice of the people is assimilated to the female voice.

What occurs on the level of a poetic configuring of the woman is operative as a function of the communitarian, embedded notion of identity grounding the poem's work. Shelley's 'indignant earth' in 'The Mask of Anarchy' is a voluble peasant, defending her children against the social injustice that is judged to be inextricable from the manage of the soil. In the customary economy, the practical work and place of women was integral to the on-going stability of material life. Shelley's 'earth' is a traditional wise woman. But she, like her 'sons', is ravaged by the displacements of agrarian capitalism.

Shelley's communitarian female is distinct from his solipsistic figuring of the female elsewhere. In like manner, one can cite instances in Wordsworth's *Lyrical Ballads* where his presentation of the women of customary culture, often used to embody the effects of agrarian displacement as madness and alienation, nonetheless attaches a kind of agency to those women quite unlike what occurs in his later poetry. In his post-*Lyrical Ballads* work, Wordsworth's Nature is a rather proper teacher, whose major charge is to spur on the individual to locate his autonomous yet integrated imagination, which will then lead to a love of humankind. Wordsworth's Nature, however, is peculiarly withdrawn from, though catalytic within, social human affairs, while the Earth of 'The Mask of Anarchy' knows that it is the process by which humans dominate nature that determines the quality of their lives. The very term 'Earth' has a material concretion to it, while 'Nature' suggests a conceptual matrix rather than matter.

Shelley's 'I', who gives voice to both 'maniac maid' and 'Earth' is himself a very different kind of 'I' from the individualist one of either his own 'Alastor' or his precursor's 'Tintern Abbey'. Alert to the issue of a traditional versus a voluntaristic identity, Shelley makes the point, right at the outset of 'The Mask of Anarchy' that inwardness is *not* the point of origin for his poem:

> As I lay asleep in Italy
> There came a voice from over the sea,
> And with great power it forth led me
> To walk in the visions of Poesy. (1)

The voice of the mass activity for political change is the source of poetical vision. The process Shelley outlines is dialectical: action gives rise to poetry, and the inspired poem will, in turn, give rise to action of a particular sort; namely, to the literalisation of its figures in mass passive resistance. The poem re-symbolises the event in order then to be drawn into a discursive intervention.

The meanings intended in this poem dovetail with issues of the aesthetic ideology, for if the poems written in the aftermath of Peterloo were meant to 'awaken & direct the imagination of reformers', they were also meant to subvert the function of a representational aesthetic of the figural, and to enter into the literalisation of figures in the minds of reformers. The links between poetry and action are explicit in this intention, an intention utterly different from the one that will be enshrined in the aesthetic ideology, which demands and depends upon the separation of the literal and the figural, the poetic and the political. It is no wonder, then, that in the poetics of the Chartist movement, Shelley is invoked as a forerunner in the 'people's' literary tradition, via both his rationalist republicanism and his visionary movement, but framed within the overarching centrality to Chartism of the communitarian politics of 'The Mask of Anarchy'. It is instructive to note the dates of first publication of Shelley's 1819 songs. 'The Mask of Anarchy', 'England', and 'Similes for 2 Political Characters' were all first published in 1832; in 1839, the 'Song to the Men of England', 'What Men Gain Fairly', and 'A New National Anthem'. When 'The Mask of Anarchy' and the 'Men of England' stanzas were reprinted in Chartist publications in the 1830s and 1840s, the popular lyric was returned, via romanticism, to Chartism. The inefficacious 'Ballad of the Starving Mother' was not reprinted until 1926.[161]

But it is no less true that Shelley's voice in the solitary mode helps to define the modern 'I' that both aims for and experiences its distance from life as a narrative. Shelley has a peculiar and not yet entirely specified relation to the second-generation Spencean political activist and poet, R. C. Fair.[162] Fair was a shoemaker-poet, and he had been around the London Corresponding Society, becoming a follower of Spence in 1814.[163] Michael Scrivener, who has recently been working on Fair, writes that Fair was schooled in 1790s radical literature, and was at Spence's funeral in 1814.[164] Fair wrote a commentary on *Queen Mab* when Cannon published it in the *Theological Inquirer*, and Iain McCalman comments rather too harshly that Fair not only praised the poem, but 'later imitated it at tedious length'.[165] In 1821 Fair was one of the group who pirated *Queen Mab*, and he considered himself to be the 'Editor' of the volume.[166] While McCalman's remarks focus on Fair as a shadow of Shelley, it seems just as likely that the young Shelley, as a reader of the periodical which had published his poem, would have been influenced by its chief poetical critic, Fair. It makes sense to conjecture that Fair's 'Ode to Religion' published in the *Theological Inquirer* in 1815 was a model for Shelley's 'Hymn to Intellectual Beauty', written in 1816. In that poem, Fair's speaker questions religion with a sceptical sense, defining its lure and its horror:

> What art thou, phantom of caprice,
>   Veil'd in the rolling clouds of Doubt,
> Now singing to the lute of Peace,
>   Now trumpeter to War's wild rout?[167]

While Fair's 'Ode' may owe something to *Queen Mab*'s depiction of oppression, its radical interrogation of religion's multiple presences lights upon that interrogative poetic strategy that shapes Shelley's 'Hymn', and emerges again in the questioning that closes 'Mont Blanc'. Shelley's poem moves beyond Fair's anti-clericalism, and creates an alternative universal source in 'intellectual beauty' itself, which is prior to religion, but subject to the same questions, '– why has man such a scope / For love and hate, despondency and hope?'[168]

Fair's next significant poetic text is the long poem, 'The Ruined City', which belongs to the genre of ruin poetry. It engages with the problem of the destruction wrought by contemporary war and, as well, with the famine resulting from agricultural ruin. There is a lot of ruin imagery in *Queen Mab*, but it seems that exchange, rather than influence, might be the appropriate term for thinking about Fair in relation to Shelley. In fact, 'The Ruined City' may be one source for Shelley's 1818 sonnet 'Ozymandias'. Oriental in its location, around Fair's ruined city, 'Far to the east the desert waste extends', like 'The lone and level sands' that 'stretch far away' in Shelley's poem. Fair's narrator comes upon a 'mouldering monument of death' and reads the epitaph:

> 'Here lies immortal.' – Who? No name appears;
> Lost in the gradual ravages of years;
> Placed to commemorate a hero's fame,
> This stone is powerless, even to keep his name.
> Perhaps some warrior; who, in valour's prime,
> Great only by the magnitude of crime;
> Blew glory's bubble through the trump of war,
> And spread the terror of his name afar.[169]

Fair's presentation of the conventional trope of the ruins of time differs from its antecedents in that the poet's radical position leads him to place the conqueror beneath contempt: 'A petty robber I would less detest.' Shelley's sonnet improves this to link the anti-authoritarian positions of the radical ruinist to the claims for the immortality of poetry associated with the sonnet form, making an ironic version of his reiterated claim that the power of poetry may be to trump tyranny. 'The Ruined City' is built around an isolated consciousness who wanders through the world, aiming to comprehend a global totality. Therefore, while it may be the case that in 1819 Shelley was influenced by a communitarian poetic when he experimented in the 'exoteric' and 'didactic' poetry that he was soon to abandon, it may also be true that the radical milieu offered to him resources for his internationalist poetry of 'beautiful idealisms' as well.[170]

If Shelley offers a strong limit case for the presence of the communitarian poetic within canonical romanticism, he also presents one of the strongest instances of voluntaristic personal identity. Wordsworth's poetic of the egotistical sublime is the 'I' of aesthetic transcendence; he is matched in the next generation by Shelley's fashioning of the isolated 'I' of philosophic transcendence. The figure of the Wandering Jew, who appears often in Shelley's poems, is a late-born and fiercely radical version of Wordsworth's Female Vagrant. The man who has been punished by the Christian God is a site of political and philosophical identification for Shelley, who transforms the legendary Jew who sinned against Christ into a victim of the *ancien régime*. In *Queen Mab*, Shelley's Ahasuerus breaks from God and is heroic in that absolute of self-making and self-identity – his is the purest form of voluntaristic selfhood:

> Thus have I stood – through a wild waste of years
> Struggling with whirlwinds of mad agony,
> Yet peaceful, and serene, and self-enshrined,

> Mocking my powerless tyrant's horrible curse
> With stubborn and unalterable will.[171]

Shelley's isolate here foregrounds the tenuous valence of voluntarism as well as its power. The difficulty of asserting identity in a cosmos where thought is dominant is spoken by another of Shelley's Wandering Jews:

> Thought
> Alone, and its quick elements, Will, Passion,
> Reason, Imagination, cannot die;
> They are, what that which they regard appears,
> The stuff whence mutability can weave
> All that it hath dominion o'er: worlds, worms,
> Empires, and superstitions. What has Thought
> To do with time, or place or circumstance?[172]

Amongst Wordsworth's customary creatures, the break out of embeddedness into a world of isolation is often accompanied by madness. Wordsworth seeks to cure that madness by recourse to a psychology grounded in voluntarism itself. Shelley's view is starker and less comforting, not as fitted to the confidence Wordsworth displays about the mind's ability to understand itself. When Shelley abandons the model of embedded culture, he aims to conquer the consequent model of inwardness and isolation by submitting it to an endlessly sceptical appraisal. The other side of Shelley's engagement with customary culture is his headlong attack on 'the icy chains of custom' as a mode of oppression.[173] It is 'Custom' which gives birth to the 'hydra brood' that wages war with 'Justice and truth', and against which is poised the potentiality of 'the lamp of hope', whose legacy is heard in Morris's *Pilgrims of Hope* at the end of the nineteenth century.[174]

By closing with a differential appreciation of Shelley and Wordsworth, this discussion shadows and varies the ending of Mill's 1833 essays on poetry. But though a comparison of Shelley and Wordsworth is ineluctable, it is not conclusive. The recurrent presence of madness as ancillary to the thrust into the modernity of the voluntaristic self, invites a brief consideration of the poetic of John Clare, whose work illustrates another moment in the vicissitudes of the romantic lyric. Clare is positioned at an interesting crossroads between, on the one hand, the kind of collective agrarian poetics articulated and developed in the work of Shelley's 'Mask' and poems by Allen Davenport (first a Spencean and then a Chartist advocate of land reform), and on the other hand, the transcendent lyricism of Wordsworth in his post-Jacobin period.

Wordsworth and Clare might be said to embody the oscillating impulses of romantic individualism and communitarianism. Wordsworth's lyrical ballads present and play with the form of the common measure, the ballad stanza, and he intends them to present content that delineates an emergent individual subjectivity. John Clare employs the voice of the solitary speaker, but he is always ill at ease in its rhetoric, and he uses it to define themes of land enclosure and community dispersal. So Clare comes to resemble Wordsworth's characters: obsessional, mad, lyrical. Wordsworth's commoners are mad because their versions of identity cannot be accounted for in the language and logic of psychological individualism. Clare, quite differently, uses the language of self-discovery and inwardness to plumb his place at the meeting point of plebeian and polite culture. That language spins into itself, and then out into a painful poetic of longing, issuing from the voice of deracination. Like Wordsworth, Clare articulates the tacit knowledge of customary society, but unlike Wordsworth, he is thrown out of balance by that explicitation, because it is the ground on which he has stood. In poems such as 'Helpstone', written well before his madness and confinement, Clare is poised on the edge of tacit and explicit knowledge. The poet speaker is both part of and separated from Helpstone, the traditional village, 'Unknown to grandeur & unknown to fame / No minstrel boasting to advance thy name'.[175] His elegiac call to an earlier native community, where the only bards were the birds, 'wood minstrels', is crossed by Clare's desire to fashion his own poetic place. In a competitive burst against other 'peasant poets', Clare declared, 'I fancied [Helpstone] my Master piece (it may be) but my hopes are vanished since I am told that Nat Bloomfield has far outdone me in a piece of a Similar subject.'[176]

Clare's poetry attacks the privatisation of the land in the name of a communitarian ideal of liberty, but it is also traversed by the individual claims of his poetic identity, which places him outside his subject matter. In 'The Mores', Clare describes a rurality of 'Unbounded freedom', where no 'fence of ownership crept in between / To hide the prospect of the following eye'. The link between aesthetic freedom and economic freedom is self-evident: 'Inclosure came & trampled on the grave / Of labours right & left the poor a slave.' Dividing and parcelling the land breaks the ecological continuity between animals and humans as well. The cows have their 'common right' as do humans. Agricultural rationalisation accomplishes the disenchantment of the customary world: 'Each little tyrant with his little sign / Shows where man claims earths glows no more divine.'[177] The traditional world which 'glows' and holds familiar knowledge is similar to that presented in Wordsworth's 'We Are Seven'. But Clare's own consciousness has been formed in the narratives of this world, and so he is far more vulnerable than either the insouciant speaker of Wordsworth's poem, who is the wry mirror of the poet himself, or the poem's confident child. Clare grapples with his dilemma of being a speaker both inside and outside the customary régime. In one instance, he assimilates Wordsworth to customary protocols in an autobiographical fragment:

I[n] my days some of the pieces of the modern poets have gaind this common popularity which must be distinguished [from] fame as it may only live for a season – Wordsworths beautiful simple ballad 'We are seven' I have seen hawkd about in penny ballads.[178]

Yet Clare is divided in his idea of poetic vocation, which straddles the dominions of oral and print culture. Clare's ambivalence about the status of the two arenas is marked in this passage:

the common people know the name of Chatterton as an unfortunate poet and the name of Shakespear as a great play writer but the ballad monger whose productions supplies hawkers with their ware are poets with them and they imagine one as great as the other so much for that envied eminence of common fame – on the other hand there is somthing in it to wish for because there are things as old as England that has out lived centurys of popularitys nay left half its historys in darkness and lives on as common on every memory as the seasons and as familiar to children even as the rain and spring flowers – I alude to the old superstitions fragments of l[e]gends and storys in ryhme that are said to be norman and saxon etc.[179]

After Clare's confinement, his poetry of rurality is transposed into a different elegiac tone: more formal and 'poetic', less particularised, summoning 'a land of endless joy / And everlasting bliss'; though in poems like 'The Bean Field', in which there is no represented 'I' at all, the particularity of imagined place is vivid, and the integration of natural and human values complete:

> The pea bloom glitters in the gems o'showers
> And sweet the fragrance which the union yields
> To battered footpaths crossing o'er the fields.[180]

In Clare's 'I am' poems ('I am – yet what I am, none cares or knows', and 'I feel I am; – I only know I am') the break of identity from rootedness is absolute.[181] The sonnet 'I am' imagines the freedom of a self who exists before place, the pure being of transcendent solitude:

> I was a being created in the race
> Of men disdaining bounds of place and time: –
> A spirit that could travel o'er the space
> Of earth and heaven, – like a thought sublime.

From this vantage, the earth, once enchanted, now is 'dull and void: / Earth's prison chilled my body with its dram of dullness'. The other poem, 'I AM', also begins from inside the bewilderment of absolute autonomy, where the 'I', neither recognised nor cared for, is 'the self-consumer of my woes', and without kin, 'Even the dearest, that I love the best / Are strange – nay stranger than the rest.' In these poems, Clare becomes the victim of his situation as an unencumbered self. In a doubling back of his alienation from customary culture, Clare now images a return to earthly solidity as a 'vain and soul debasing thrall', and its escape as a landscape of unearthly character, a 'scene, where man hath never trod'.

Clare's isolation speaks the plangent voice of the romantic self, but it also demonstrates how claiming the tacit world of custom may be reduced to a nostalgic reflex. In a letter written in 1832, Clare describes the gap between the poetic of the commoners' culture and that of print culture, and the breach it opens within his own identity. He is wrenched into the dizziness of the unencumbered self: he expresses astonishment that a reviewer should 'imagine I had read the old Poets & that others should imagine I had coined words which were as common around me as the grass under my feet – I shrank from myself with extacy & and have never been myself since'. In 1832, this gave him great joy: 'the pinnacle of my ambitions is attained – & I am so astonished that I can hardly believe I am myself', but he was soon propelled into a deep depression.[182] From the asylum he complains in 1848 that there 'all the peoples brains are turned in the wrong way', the coercion of inwardness doubles the walls of the asylum which 'is called the Bastile by some and not with[out] reasons'.[183]

Towards the very end of his life, Clare figured his confinement in the language of politics, fuelled by a desire for political freedom. Though most of Clare's letters and journals are empty of topical political discussion, and do not engage with political categories, a letter written some time between 1849 and 1850 employs the agitational rhetoric of the 1790s. The madhouse is:

the English Bastile a government Prison where harmless people are trapped & tortured till they die – English priestcraft & english bondage more severe than the slavery of Egypt & Africa ... not dareing to show love or remembrance for Home or home affections living in the world as a prison estranged from all his friends.[184]

In a powerful turn, Clare uses his anger to discover another possibility within individuality – though he has been torn from his embedded identity, and experiences his singularity as a mode of estrangement, he also hangs on to the Painite formulations of individuality, which sanctions another view of freedom:

Still Truth is the best companion for it levels all distinctions in pretensions . . . when done & said with them truth is truth & the rights of man – age of reason & common sense are sentences full of meaning.[185]

Clare's poetic vocation propelled him from the community of the commons to the isolation of the madhouse. His fellow plebeian poet, the subject of the following discussion, Allen Davenport, travelled to the social maelstrom of urban culture, where he defended his poetic calling by yoking his customary inheritance to a political intervention.

PART II

Interventionist poetics in the tradition of romanticism

CHAPTER FOUR

Allen Davenport on the threshold of Chartism

The example of Shelley, in both his democratic internationalist and his domestic communitarian voices, pervades the radical poetics of the 1820s and the Chartist poetry of the later 1830s and 1840s.[1] After the 1815 publication in the *Theological Inquirer* of sections of the poem, *Queen Mab* had been printed in pirated editions from 1821, and when 'The Mask of Anarchy' was published in 1832, coinciding with the passage of the Reform Bill, Shelley's poem was thought to speak directly to the argument that British labourers had been poorly done by the terms of the Bill, most importantly by the requirement of an annual value for borough households of £10: only one in five men in England would now possess the vote.[2] Shelley was first significantly heralded as a voice for contemporary communitarian politics in the periodical press of the Owenite Socialists. Commended as 'a great moral, political, and social Reformer', Shelley provides, via Owenism, an overarching figure of the link between high romanticism and Chartism.[3] And Owenism itself, as a communitarian millenarian movement, joins the millenialism of the 1790s to the 1830s and 1840s.

While Shelley travels the poetic high road, the poet Allen Davenport (1775–1846) offers a grounded, practical example of a poet who absorbed Shelley's model, as well as those of tavern singing, Methodist hymns, and eighteenth-century satirical verse. Davenport practised his commitment to the connections between poetic and political craft within the chief political and social movements of his time as they modulated from broadly plebeian into recognisably working-class formations: Spenceanism, Owenite Co-operation, and Chartism.[4] 'I see', he says in a poem written in 1846, the last year of his life, and marked by the weariness of a life spent in the Cause,

> or fancy that I see,
> Through the dark vista of futurity,
> A shadowy twilight of a brighter day –
> A day when every working man shall know,

Who is his truest friend and who his foe –
A day of union and of moral might –

. . .

A day when working men of every state,
Shall feel as brothers in their common fate.[5]

By considering examples of Davenport's œuvre from the earliest to the last, and in relation to his narrative of himself as a poet, we can observe not only some of the various and, in places, competing elements within the self-definition of the communitarian lyrical tradition, but also see how available to poetic purposes were the chief political issues of the period: land reform, political enfranchisement, 'communitive' desires, the rôle of England as tyrant and oppressor of Ireland, as well as the struggles for national self-determination in other countries such as Italy and Poland. Because Davenport wrote an autobiographical account of his experiences as radical-poet, we can get some measure of the importance to him of his poetic rôle. For in keeping with the Spencean admonition to 'Sing and Meet', the radical shoemaker Davenport affirmed the impact of poetry on forming political character. In the last year of his life, when he was aged seventy-one, Davenport eulogised his fellow Chartist poet, Thomas Cooper, asserting that Cooper's 'heavenly genius'

with a golden pen,
Came to write 'TRUTH' upon the hearts of men!
The world awoke – from its profound repose,
A shout was heard – a monument arose.[6]

Like Spence before him, Davenport aims to contribute to the naming of a self-consciously counter-hegemonic poetic tradition. But even as he augments and extends lyric range within the impersonality of the Spencean song, Davenport also evinces the influence of the subjective voice that we associate with the innovations of the romantics, allowing doubt and hesitation to form part of the interventionist lyric, and naming and carving out an inward space for both self, and in the democratic mode, the self of the commoner.

When Davenport wrote his 1845 autobiography, he posed the centrality of poetry to political intervention via a narrative of the importance of poetry to *his* particular literary development, and literature is used as the index of interiority. Yet Davenport's narrative goal is to make a match between his personal depth and the claims of his constituency, the class of unenfranchised labourers. Right from the opening of his *Life and Literary Pursuits*, Davenport exhibits this tension, as he writes of himself as both a commoner, producing a 'plain simple, an authentic tale', and as a unique kind of poet, who had to overcome 'almost impossibilities', 'without a literary friend to encourage or instruct' him. The man of the 'common fate', as he called it in 'The Poet's Hope', also asserts of himself, 'I stand alone.'[7] That is, Davenport works ambivalently within the lyric problematic of shaping a version of subjectivity that can model civic subjectivity for the Charter, and be responsive to the claims of interiority that such civic subjectivity will legitimate for a mass population.

The Life and Literary Pursuits of 1845 was not Davenport's first foray into biographical writing. Nine years earlier, in 1836, he had written *The Life, Writing, and Principles of Thomas Spence*, a pamphlet opening with an elegy to Spence which, as explained in the text's accompanying note, was 'recited at the last anniversary of Mr Spence's birth-day, held at the Navy Coffee-house, Catherine-street, Strand, 1819'.[8] Davenport's biography of Spence links Spence's political plan to the radical present. Spenceanism, inflected by the 'communitive' ideology of Owenism and the system of Co-operation, draws close, in Davenport's narrative, to the National Union of the Working Classes, a foundational organisation for Chartism in the 1830s. In fact, the publisher of the pamphlet, Richard Lee, was an active participant in the NUWC.[9] A commemorative dinner was held to honour Spence soon after this publication, and Malcolm Chase argues that this was the moment when older radicals, such as Francis Place, and those who would become the leading lights of the Chartist movement, such as George Julian Harney and Bronterre O'Brien, conceived their genealogy through a Spencean inheritance.[10] The biography of Spence specifies Davenport's rôle as a poetic conduit between movements. The prefatory elegy presents Spence's positions as if they were poetic analyses in which his understanding conforms to metrical rules: 'All nature's laws he freely, clearly, scann'd, / And found the *summum bonum* in the land!' Davenport uses the iambic pentameter, rhymed couplet rather than a song form, and so exemplifies both ties and separations between Davenport and Spence as poets.[11] Spence's songs remain within the conventions of satirical squibs and congregational singing, while Davenport enlists the heroic couplet of the eighteenth century to mark his place within print culture. Davenport's elegy articulates the central principles of Spence's Plan, and locates Spence as an element in a larger narrative of 'agrarian fellowship': Spence 'show'd that justice planted in the earth, / Gave man new rights and liberty new birth'.[12] But in addition to presenting Spence's ideas, Davenport as *poet* performs the task of elegiac writing, which is to secure his own place as successor to the elegiac subject. The poetic gesture suggests a political continuity as well. The elegy opens with the conventional denial of elegiac powers: 'how inadequate [the poet's] language flows / How poor the tribute that his zeal bestows', but makes the point that he is, as well, 'A kindred spirit!'[13] Davenport's assertion of kinship with him opens a channel between the two men as politico-poets, while it also raises the status of Spence's lyrics as being singular and inimitable. The strength of Davenport's assertion of his own subjectivity within the conventions of elegiac formal protestations, as he 'reveres' and feels 'inadequate' to those attributes he credits Spence with – 'genius, judgement, wit' – helps to shape a genealogy for a poetic tradition. In the *Life of Spence*, Davenport modulates from elegiac reminiscence into a prospect of transformation. He regrets that Spenceanism has been overshadowed by Owenism, but his own vision of a future commonality updates the earlier Spencean version of land reform, drawing on a more contemporary vocabulary of self and sociality, heavily indebted to Owen's formulations: 'Such a people would be so wedded to their country, that on such an occasion all *self* would be lost in the glorious blaze of *social* love.'[14] Davenport, in fact, insists on the continuity between Spenceans and Owenites: 'For, even admitting that Mr. Owen's plan is superior to the Spencean system, it must be acknowledged that the latter is the very foundation of the former.'[15] Yet as a public figure Owen, Davenport complains, is somewhat pallid beside Spence's fervour and commitment.[16] Davenport is closer to Spence, both in his personal history within the radical artisan community in London, and in enthusiasm: 'Nothing appears more easy to me, than the commencement of this new state of society.'[17]

Davenport delivers Spence, and is the conduit in Chartism as well for the Owenite interest in Shelley's poetics. In 1816, Hazlitt had remarked on the links between the spirit of Robert Owen's ideas and those of the 1790s: 'The same scheme, the same principles, the same philosophy of motives and actions ... were rife in the year 1793 ... got into the hearts of poets ... were published in ... plays, poems, songs, and romances ... and turned the heads of almost the whole kingdom.'[18] Importantly, Robert Owen's plan for a 'new moral world' based on the analysis that 'the character of every human being is formed for, and not by, the individual', opened the way for plebeian communitarianism to be re-understood in the contemporary world of industry through economic discussion and 'scientific' analyses.[19] Robert Owen had known Godwin and turned the individualism of radicalism towards a reconception of the collectivity: it was within Owen's Socialism that the terms 'communitive' and 'communitarian' were coined to describe the project.[20] This project was cultural as well as social, and in claiming Shelley as a socialist precursor, Owenism participated in that formulation of an 'alternative' poetic heritage that took on its largest shape within Chartism as a whole. In the 1850s, Owen, now in very old age, still asserted that identity 'does not form [itself]', and furthermore asserted that Shelley had appeared to him in a séance, eager to help usher in the new world.[21]

While Davenport's 1836 *Life of Spence* performed the cultural work of establishing connections between the poetics of Spenceanism and that of Chartism, its companion text, Davenport's own 1845 *Life and Literary Pursuits*, enacts the interchange between an ever more residual plebeian customary culture and the newer worlds of the individuated, punctual self. In his autobiography, Davenport describes how his passion for self-improvement was indistinguishable from his love of poetry, and in his narration he demonstrates the complex interweaving of the exigencies of both oral and print cultures.

While the outer boundaries of Davenport's poetic can be marked by these two narratives, the shape of his own poetic life falls into three periods: first, his vocational entry into Spencean politico-poetics, characterised by the urban poetics of ultra-radicalism; second, a period of retrospect in the 1820s, in which Davenport blends together philosophic materialism and landscape imagery; and third, a reinvigoration of his interventionist poetics in the 1840s, participant in the late Chartist poetics of solidarity, internationalism, and land reform.

Davenport was born in 1775 and raised in 'the small and obscure village of Ewen . . . about three miles from Cirencester'.[22] His family was entangled in the economic and cultural transition of customary life. Casualised agricultural wage labourers, depending on cottage industry (Davenport's mother was a spinner) and using the residues of custom to supplement 'free' proletarian wages, Davenport's parents deplored the hegemony of the spinning jenny: 'as [fast looms] advanced every vestige of that beneficial domestic manufacture which had been a little mine of wealth to the poor cottager, was for ever annihilated'.[23] Davenport himself had no schooling as a child, but early on he desired to 'acquire the art of reading and writing', and he drew upon his local culture of song to do so:

I learnt, as most children do, a number of songs by heart, and having acquired, as best I could, a knowledge of all the letters of the alphabet, I saved up all my halfpence and bought up all the printed songs that I could sing, and began with those that appeared the most easy, my new process of education. I proceeded to match all the words in my printed songs, with those I had previously stored in my mind, and by remembering the words thus learnt, by comparing notes, I knew them again whenever they met my eye.[24]

Davenport's 'eye became the pupil of the ear': thus he theorises the super-vention of print upon oral culture.[25] Davenport's poetic corpus will be marked throughout his career as working with both the rhythms he brings with him – oral four-stress metres of English song, ballad, and hymn – and the five-stress ones he learns from English print culture. Davenport's auto-didactical method of repetition soon gave rise to invention, and his 'next attempt was to *write* a song, for my constant reference to metrical com-position, had inspired me with something like the spirit of song, and created an impression in my mind that no change of situation, or fortune in after life could obliterate'.[26] Amongst the range of identities which Davenport has accumulated by 1845 – Spencean, Co-operator, Chartist, Radical Shoemaker – he asserts here that his identity as poet is founda-tional, forming the matrix through which he will make sense of all his experiences. Having written his first song, Davenport 'stuck it up against a well known tree that stood in the middle of the village, and in a day or two I had the supreme delight to hear it sung by many a lad and lass'.[27] Davenport arranges his song to be almost a part of the natural environ-ment: the tree is the location of the song, and it crosses the boundary between an enchanted and a demystified natural world. It feels like part of village customary practice, linked to superstition and song, but linked as well here to the ambitions of the young poet. About forty years later Davenport would commemorate and transform the incident in a poem in which an apprentice writes poetry directly on bark. But in the later text enchantment is displaced by urbanity: 'The silent tree proclaims the writer's name, / And as it grows bears up his *rising* fame.'[28]

While Spence was devising his songs and polemics in London in 1794, Davenport had been 'a patriot', and, wandering from transient job to job, was easily recruited as a soldier.[29] Nonetheless Davenport situates himself in a literary culture, and models himself on that plebeian 'nature's child', Robert Burns. As a soldier, Davenport is marched to Scotland, the 'land of *Burns*', where, in emulation of that poet, he falls in love: 'It was not a "*Highland Mary*", but it was a *Highland Jane*, fair as the lily, and sweet as the opening rose.'[30] While recounting these anecdotes of his youth, Davenport constantly has recourse to a language of the 'poetical': he describes the gap between his anticipations and reality as a fall from poetical dreams, while his experiences of landscape in Scotland are recounted in the language of the 'beautiful and the sublime'.[31] But across these elevated thoughts run some grimmer realities: given the vaccine against smallpox, Davenport 'suffered severely', going blind at one point, and at another, 'my flesh stuck to my clothes and came off by bits'.[32]

Nonetheless, Davenport arrives in London in 1804, armed with lyric self-confidence as well as the trade of a shoemaker.[33] In an Edgeware Road workshop, he and a fellow artisan subscribe to Cooke's edition of the *British Poets*, then publishing in numbers at six pence each. And here, as he is initiated into the world of urban print culture, Davenport experiences his first crisis of poetic vocation: 'These standard Poets' works, especially those of Pope, were complete dampers, and went very near to extinguish every spark of my poetic genius. I felt ashamed of my own, as I now thought, wretched doggerel.'[34]

In these opening pages of his autobiography, Davenport tells the story of his access to communitarian lyricism as a prelapsarian narrative. He suggests that he had been raised in an authentic and customary tradition of song and poetry, one in which he might participate without self-consciousness, in a world where trees and songs were part of one organic environment, and in which speech and writing were helpmeets and not competitors. But in his rehearsal of loss and gain, the same source that had given him the means to read and write, and which constituted his primary means of self-identity, now, once he is in London, propels him into a world in which he feels shame. In London, expelled from a poetic Eden, his poetry appears to him to be mongrel, dog-rhyming; while Pope's is human, elevated, self-aware.

As is frequently the case, however, this lurch from Innocence into Experience, from country to city, turns out to be a peculiarly happy fall. The man who delivers the installments of Cooke, one day in 1805 'brought also a book, which he said ought to be in the hands of every Englishman in the country.'[35] It was the *Spencean System*, that by turns rationalist, enthusiastical, and customary plan for reappropriating the fruits of the earth and returning them to those who labour. Such a book would, Davenport writes, 'make the world a paradise! I read the book and became an out and out Spencean'.[36] The delivery man, it appears, may have been Thomas Spence himself, who had been working as a numbers runner for Cooke for some time.[37] So, Spence and Davenport meet at the crossroads of poetry and politics, Spence using the *British Poets'* subscription list to recruit supporters to his political programme, and Davenport gaining access to politics through his poetical desire.

Malcolm Chase somewhat critically suggests that Davenport's aim in his 1845 autobiography to be understood as 'literary' is the source of the many elisions in his narrative (for example, Davenport's almost total suppression of reference to the Chartist movement). While it may indeed be true that the Davenport of 1845 was reticent about his political activities, it is wrong to analyse this in tandem with his literary ambitions as a bid for respectability, for Davenport here acknowledges being an active partisan in the establishment and growth of an independent literary tradition, carrying forward Spence's politico-poetic into the next generation of activists. The idea that poetic vocation merely emulates the literary élite rather than being part of an important discourse of self-actualisation within the radical movement underestimates both the practical and the utopian power of lyric intervention.

We can understand Davenport's moment of self-recognition and shame as an illustrative event in the confrontation of customary and enlightenment modes of identity and identity formation. Spence's pamphlet explains Davenport to himself, and offers him an identity which is no longer unselfconscious, but does not fix him in a position of inferiority or emulation to the hegemonic poetic tradition. Rather, it offers him a place in *another* tradition, one which organises poetry in relation to plebeian aspirations and in relation to political intervention.

For however coincidental the juxtaposition of Cooke and Spence might have been, as Davenport shapes his narrative he suggests that his access to Spenceanism also afforded him access to a revised poetic vocation. Davenport briskly moves on to narrate the continuation of his literary life, jumping from 1804 to 1814, as he finds outlets for making poetical interventions. He makes evident to his readers that he is analysing a class distinction and divergence within the cultural purposes of poetry. Spence's plebeian radicalism offered to Davenport a radical and democratised view of social life which then allowed him to recover his vocation and desire as a poet, but now understood as a politico-poetical vocation and desire. Writing in 1846, Davenport recalls that back in 1805, 'I told all the reformers that I met with, that no other form of reform [besides Spence's Plan] was worth fighting for, but they generally laughed at me, and called me a visionary.'[38] The terms of politics and poetics interpenetrate each other here. The central trope of individualist lyrical visionary poetics in mid-century liberal cultural life resonates with Davenport's claim of visionary politics, and Davenport wears the charge lightly, for it places him next to a poet like Shelley as well as Spence. By reorientating his poetic vocation in relation to his political one, Davenport is then able to reclaim some of the attributes of the poet of polite culture. And as Davenport tells his story, just as his political energy rose, so did, apparently, the quality of his poetic productions. 'During the perilous years of 1818 and 1819, I strained every nerve, and called every faculty into action, to inspire the people with the spirit of Reform; and to expose the deceit, the treachery, and the base doings of the higher powers.'[39] Here Davenport echoes, in a more democratic key, Shelley's remarks in his letter to Leigh Hunt that he wished to write a set of political songs 'destined to awaken & direct the imagination of the reformers.'[40]

Describing his poem, *The Kings; or, Legitimacy Unmask'd*, printed and published at his own expense in the year of Peterloo, 1819, Davenport writes:

being written in a bold and democratic style, it became a little popular among the radicals, some of whom got it by heart, and recited or rather acted it in small assemblies, and with some applause. The booksellers thought it too strong, and refused to sell it in their shops, and whenever it was exposed, it was suppressed by the new police.[41]

Where once he had captured songs into writing, now fellow radicals unmoor his poems from the printed page, and memorise and even embody and enact them in assemblies, circumventing the world of printed texts, and trumping it in the process. Spenceanism has given Davenport an entry into poetic vocation, and in so doing, has also reopened the space for customary oral tradition in the urban centre of pamphlets, bookstalls and broadsides. Davenport tells us that errors which riddled the original printing, 'errors in manuscript ... doubled by typographical errors and blunders', are transformed through the oral presentation of the text, redeemed in the culture of urban radicalism. *The Kings; or Legitimacy Unmask'd*, is in the form of a dialogue, as the history of monarchical tyranny is traced simultaneously on a global scale – from 'Mighty Nimrod down to the fourth George' – and on a national scale: 'From good old Alfred down to George's days'.[42] It is worth juxtaposing this public effort, which was got off by heart by radicals, to William Blake's *Jerusalem*, which has a similarly global and national communitarian epic intention, tracing the history of English tyranny and oppression, and which was being written during the same period as Davenport's more conventional satirical text. Blake draws upon the prophetic rhetoric of biblical anaphorism, while Davenport produces set after set of rhyming couplets, unalleviated by even the looser 'cockney rhymes' so annoying to the critics of Keats and Hunt. Yet Blake's poem, because it was so deeply immersed in the protocols of not only print culture, but the print culture of artistic reproduction, languished in its printing-house, while Davenport's easily became assimilable from memory. That is, Blake's model of prophetic anti-metre is fundamentally a visual representation of what a spoken metre would be. Blake represents voice, but doesn't produce it. While Davenport's couplets appear to derive from élite print culture, high

culture, they are, in fact, extremely easy to memorise. The impulse of
Jerusalem is mythic and sublime, that of *The Kings* is urbane and ironic.
Jerusalem ends where it began, in Albion's 'Ancient Druid Rocky Shore',
while *The Kings* establishes a republican internationalism which leads to
America. Blake's Jerusalem is the transformed body of Britain, in which
every individual and every organ of every individual is given space and
identity:

> And they walked
> To & fro in Eternity as One Man. Reflecting each in
>   each & clearly seen
> And seeing, according to fitness & order.[43]

Davenport's end employs a very different rhetoric:

> Her laws accord with nature's glorious plan,
> By which her sons enjoy their rights of man.
> There all unite in one great family,
> Resolving to be happy, and be free.[44]

We see in these instances how an image of a communal, millenarian voice
is modelled by Blake, but is actually without an aperture for communal
entry: prophets speak in rolling periods, but people cannot and do not
memorise these long lines, so prophecy stays tightly connected to the
original utterer/writer, even when meant to be an oracular vessel. (It
would not be until much later in the nineteenth century that Blake's
stanzas from *Milton*, set to music as 'Jerusalem', would become a hymn,
and then sung both in borstals and at trades union meetings!) Davenport,
drawing on a convention of the polite genres, opens it up from within to
become newly accessible to a willing public. Davenport's poetic career
performs the weaving together of his rural plebeian origins with the
rational democratic poetics of radical London.

  The Kings represents one central strand in Davenport's lyric output in his
poetically prolific years as a Spencean and urban radical between 1817 and
1822. In poems built out of units of four beats, such as 'The Topic', he
draws upon the increasingly clichéd accents of the campaign against Old
Corruption, imagining a reformed time 'when vile placemen shall cease',
lines that might have been written in 1780 as easily as in 1817. Like
Cobbett, and like the Shelley of 'The Mask of Anarchy', in 'The Topic',
Davenport deplores paper currency, 'the Pitt-coined paper on which we
have stranded'.[45] Davenport's own 1819 contribution to the Peterloo
poetic corpus was a song, 'Saint Ethelstone's Day', sung to the tune of
'Gee-up Dobbin', jokingly called 'the Prince's favourite'. Davenport's

poems in this vein belong to the robust strain of political stanzas and satirical choric songs of the vivid years of the 1790s.[46]

In the political downturn of the later 1820s, Davenport's poems also turn: in this second period, they bridge and explore, within the urban radical milieu, the rifts between the communitarian politics of Spence and the developing vision of Owenism on the one hand, and, on the other, the ultra-rationalism of the Painite Richard Carlile and his comrades, who formed themselves into a group called the Zetetics, from the Greek word, 'to seek'.[47]

Davenport's 1820s poetry is inflected by Shelley, underpinned by the political commitment and theory of Owenism, and built from the imagery of the gardens at Tollington Park, where Davenport lived as a building supervisor from 1822 to 1828, and from which environs he developed a Spencean-cum-ecological poetic.[48] The embodiment of the landscape through both a rhetoric of natural abundance, derived from a customary notion of production, and the materialist enlightenment version of interdependence, becomes the field on which the contests of romanticism are played out in his poems. Davenport's poetry here exhibits the strains experienced in his rôle of being both a voice of the populace and a singular self, and these tensions make these texts more complex than his earlier poems.

It is certain that Davenport would have known Shelley's work, either via Richard Carlile's *Republican* or through the publication and circulation of *Queen Mab*, which went through many pirated editions in the 1820s, in addition to those of Shelley's poems which appeared in Hunt's *Examiner*.[49] Though 'The Mask of Anarchy' was not published until 1832, it is reasonable to conjecture that it circulated in radical circles before its publication.[50]

In an 1823 'Sonnet', published in Carlile's *Republican*, Davenport borrows elements of Shelley's 1818 *Examiner* poem, 'Ozymandias', using a 'ghastly visage' and a 'grin' signalling 'dire command' to describe the creature 'Persecution', who, much like 'Murder', 'Fraud', and the other 'Destructions' who inhabit Shelley's 'The Mask of Anarchy', drives her car of destruction through the land, while

> in her front a thousand jailors dance
> With instruments of torture, whips, and chains,
> To dungeon all who dare to truth advance.[51]

'Words to the Wind' combines the interrogative mode of 'Mont Blanc' with the sense of power of Shelley's 'Ode to the West Wind': 'What power impels thee through thy dubious course, / And gives my nerveless wings almighty force?'[52] Davenport's poetry in the period leading up to his 1827 collection of poems, *The Muse's Wreath*, is noteworthy for the presence of a pervading Shelleyan tone, which Davenport never entirely loses; much later, in his 1846 poem of praise to Thomas Cooper, Davenport dreams of the Chartist poet also in Shelleyan tones, as the spirit of truth,

> Bursting into light,
> And chasing far away the shades of night;
> His glorious track became a milky-way,
> Which so extended into boundless day.[53]

'An Elegy on Mr. Shelley, Written Soon after His Death', and published in the atheist journal, the *Oracle of Reason* in 1843, incorporates Davenport into the lineage of poets which includes Shelley as well as Spence. Shelley, the poem tells us, 'conquered prejudice and broke her fetters', but did only half the job, as he 'Half reformed the dreaming world of letters'. The work left to do is an inheritance, to be taken up 'Through an eternal chain of future ages', implying that Davenport the elegist is the next link in that chain.[54]

This strong Shelleyan strain within Davenport's poetic in the 1820s is interlaced with his support of Owenite Co-operation, and his retreat from the centre of London to Tollington Park, in Hornsey. His poetry reveals a changing sensibility, in which the communitive desire begins to thread itself more clearly into his poetic, and he carried this into the 1830s and 1840s, when intervening as a Chartist. In 'Co-operation', in which Davenport uses Owenite ideas in addition to Spencean ones, we again hear a counterpart to Blake's communitarian vision of the Giant Man Albion, but in a more contemporary and explicitly political rhetoric of improvement and self-organisation:

> Give the great body politic a soul,
> Unite all parts, and make a glorious whole!
> And as your senses, limbs, and faculties,
> Your physical and mental energies,
> All act on the co-operative plan,
> To feed and clothe, and civilize the man,
> The glorious system of co-operation
> When put in practice by the population,
> Shall furnish every necessary good,
> Clothes for the back, and for the belly food.
> Thy children shall enjoy a happier lot,
> Nor shall their education be forgot;
> The arts of life shall rapidly improve,
> And *sordid* self be lost in social love.[55]

This outline of the organism of the social whole is prefaced by a personal lament, in which alienation of labour is the theme, and is presented in the voice of the alienated labourer, 'with feelings only to be tantalized', 'I live an exile in my native land.'[56] This self stands as a representative of a collective subjectivity, 'Nor I alone, for more than half mankind / the more they toil the more they are left behind.'[57] In this volume Davenport displays the tension between his own persona as a solitary, now rural poet, and as spokesperson for the labouring class.

Davenport's poems may well have influenced the Owenite press, for Owen's *New Moral World* (1834–45) abounded in articles which assert the importance of Shelley to a 'community' poetry, and numerous poems attesting to the values of the communitive life, including John Barmby's 'The Poesie of Community', and a gathering of *Social Hymns, for the Use of the Friends of the Rational System of Society*.[58]

In a brilliant sequence, Davenport's interest in enlightenment material-ism leads him to consider issues of interiority and identity. 'However matter changes all agree, / It loses nothing but identity', he argues in one poem, answering his query about humanity in another: 'On man no two philosophers agree, / So indefinite is humanity.'[59] This sense of self is not the voluntaristic identity of Mill's poem-maker; it derives from an atomic theory, which allows for a more fluid construction of identity. This also makes it possible for him to produce a theory of mutuality, in which subjectivity is redeployed as community. For '*sordid self*' to be lost in social love', it must first know itself as an identity, which is then liable to mutation: 'Examine human nature and you'll find / No friendship's to be found unmix'd with self.'[60] In 'The Irish Emigrant', Davenport investigates the subjectivity of the self who is alienated from his land as well as from his labour. Necessity compels the speaker to move: ''tis that that cuts my heart / Shakes every feeling – weakens every nerve.'[61]

Davenport's poetry in the mid-1820s is marked by its attention not only to subjectivity, but to the divided subjectivity of alienated labour. Davenport had worked in William Bainbridge's shoe workshop from 1810 until 1822, when Bainbridge brought him out to Tollington Park, near Finsbury, and Hornsey Wood, to caretake a building development of cot-tages for labourers commuting into London to work. Davenport found himself again at the crossroads of city and country.[62] Here was rurality becoming suburban capital investment. Neither agricultural labourer nor owner, Davenport is poised, though alienated himself, as a voice of inte-gration. He returns in the poems of these years to the rural concerns of his youth, framed always by his involvement in and proximity to London, which stimulates a materialist ecological poetry. 'Hornsey Wood' is not a very successful pastoral poem, but it harbours within its prim and quaint set of mythic anecdotes a surprising ecological power: the poet figure is stimulated by 'philosophic fire' in the Wood, and he:

> Views Nature's revolutionary state,
> Observes her decompose and re-create
> And sees . . .
>
> . . .
>
> That not a grain in nature's ample frame,
> For one short moment can remain the same!
>
> . . .
>
> And by a process, easily to scan
> That which was grass becomes a living man!
> Thus, matter works, and subjects to its powers,
> Men chang'd to grass, and women chang'd to flowers![63]

The materialism of rational thought, reinvigorated by the language of landscape, underlies the distinction of Davenport's poetry. This is an augmented recapitulation of the Spencean link between city and country. The urbanity of some of Davenport's poems is refabricated into a Spencean poetic *redux*, and the productivity of the land is insisted upon as part of the ecological materialisation of an *anima mundi*: 'Is not nature the common mother of all mankind? And is not the earth the common field on which she incessantly labours to produce plenty for all, even for the noxious reptile?'[64] Davenport writes in an article in the *Republican* in 1824 that:

the moment a mechanic lays down his tools, every prospect of gain is suspended; nothing supplies his absence, to facilitate the conclusion of what he had begun: while the man who possesses land, has only to put his grain into the ground and leave it to the creative hand of nature, - who will not fail, in due time, by a mysterious operation, to raise it up and multiply it by fifty or a hundred fold, with little or no assistance from the hand of the labourer.[65]

The deadness of mechanical labour is contrasted with the fecundity of agriculture. The natural abundance of the land is both magical and empirical at once. Davenport's desire to recover the commoners' land-scape marks him as one who stands between enchantment and interpreta-tion. In places, the result is a recapitulation of alienation itself. 'Rural Reflections' mimics the tone of Goldsmith's 'Deserted Village', with Davenport speaking from outside the experience of agrarian hardship in order to reflect upon it:

> How poorly do the owners of the soil
> Appreciate the hardships, cares, and toil,
> Of those whose task it is to till the ground.[66]

But in the ballad, 'The Cottage in Which I Was Born', Davenport produces the feeling of displacement from the inner experience of the cottager, which is then juxtaposed to the ideals of abundance which secure Davenport's Co-operative optimism: 'The earth shall yield a triplefold increase, / And want be banish'd from the human race.'[67]

In the only literary discussion of Davenport to date, David Worrall argues that 'to some extent, Davenport's eagerness to be fully incorporated into the growing myths of Romanticism in the mid-1820s shows how fully he had relinquished some of the earlier violence of his revolutionary views'.[68] Yet if we acknowledge the double life of romanticism, its individualist and its communitarian possibilities, Davenport's claim for the visionary capacity of poetic intervention is part of what allows him, in his interweaving of Owenite communitarianism and his Spencean agrarianism, and then in his Chartist poetic, to draw from the individualist vision of romanticism and then work it back into a social, collective vision of political change. In places Davenport is able to bring together the urban romanticism of Shelley's democratic charge for poetry with the visionary thematic of the romantic landscape, fashioning a communitarian version of landscape democracy, grounded in the premises of Spencean agrarianism. In 'London', Davenport provides a foil to his Spencean embrace of rurality, for here he articulates an anxiety about the urban expansion which will obliterate the productivity of the countryside:

> London, when will thy encroachments end?
> Must every valley rise, and mountain bend?
> Must fields and gardens yield on every side,
> And shall no boundaries restrain thy pride?[69]

But unlike the landscape in which Coleridge, Thelwall, and Wordsworth found freedom from the urban press of too many consciousnesses and bodies, in Davenport's poetic, rurality is not equated with solitude; rather, it is the site of transpersonal solidarity. Ten years later, in his *Life of Spence*, Davenport will argue that the domestic love which would grow up from an 'agrarian equality' would recover the sort of collective identity necessary to a democratic nation:

What energy, what courage, what determination, would not be found among a people who had the sense to possess themselves of their rights and liberties, by planting the standard of justice in the earth, and enjoying all the glorious benefits arising from an Agrarian equality![70]

Davenport as solitary poet draws upon Wordsworth's project of speaking across the registers of polite and plebeian culture, but his aim to make that singular voice serve the communitive political endeavour returns the meditative impulse to interventionist goals.

1832 leaves an indelible mark across the history of radicalism. The Reform Bill reorientated the middle-class radical movement from the issue of the ballot to that of the Corn Laws and the claim of free trade: from political to economic freedom.[71] The principle of exclusion of the £10 franchise meant that it was now possible from within and without to describe a working class as an identifiable cohort. This sense of isolation gave a massive impetus to an impulse of self-definition, to reinscribe as a language of solidarity what was objectively a political exclusion. Within the ensuing revival of popular radicalism in the course of the 1830s, Davenport became increasingly linked to those groups which coalesced into the Chartist movement. Chartism, which drew together disparate working-class sectors under the banner of universal manhood suffrage, began in the realm of political reform to recover the impetus which resulted in 1832, but took off into social, economic, and cultural directions which sustained a sense of working-class interests and identities through the 1840s. While Davenport joins Spenceanism to Chartism, he does not foreground, in either his autobiography or his poetry, the explicit six points of the Charter (annual Parliaments, abolition of the property qualification, secret ballot, payment of MPs, equal parliamentary districts, and universal [male] suffrage) as many other Chartists will. But he provides a foundation for a lyricism of collective solidarity, and offers an example of a poet who draws upon oral and print culture, customary and rationalist rhetoric, and identity concerns of communitarianism, newly attached to the preoccupations and rhetoric of alienated labour by way of Owenite socialism.

By the mid 1840s, now in his late sixties, Davenport was the old man of the popular movement, itself a fluid and reformulating set of groupings. Sonnets dedicated to him appeared in the *Northern Star*, with excerpts from his autobiography, as well as a tribute and obituary from the editors in the year of his death, 1846.[72] That same year, Davenport published a valedictory series of poems in the *Northern Star*, which, taken as a group, evince his poetic range.

'The Patriot' opens in the constitutionalist idiom of the earlier decades of the century, in which the oppositional patriot

> Stands foremost in the battle for Reform!
> And who, with principles of freedom rife,
> To free his country risks his life.[73]

He refers to both Irish and English patriots, Emmet and Paine, and also to the martyrs of the Chartist Newport Uprising of 1839 – all are linked in their patriotic desire to rid Britain of tyranny. 'The Patriot' speaks the language of the 1780s and 1790s. Davenport's poetic career may be said to conclude where it began, in the idiom and with the preoccupations of the Spencean programme. In 'The Land, the People's Farm', which may have been written in earlier versions, but was published in the *Northern Star* in June 1846, Davenport invokes the values of customary agricultural life. Here the claim of custom is powerfully transformed, and helps us to mark the distance from the 1790s to the 1840s. On the one hand, there is clear reference to those oppressive laws which deny customary practices to rural commoners, but the argument has been transmuted into one which now figures the communitarian inheritance of the 'people's farm' as deriving as much from Rousseau as from plebeian guerrilla tactics of resistance:

> The savage has his freehold home,
> And hunting park wherein to roam;
> No laws of 'trespass' there restrain,
> The child of nature scorns the chain.

This mid-century song also bears the mark of colonial expansion and the images and narratives now available to the communitarian imagination. In fact, many of Davenport's 1840s poems are resonant with the imperial projects of Britain, and are marked by the contradictions of a domestic subaltern poetically making sense of these projects in relation to the larger globe. Davenport again and again turns to an experience outside England to provide the model for community at home. This is both a response to and an accommodation of the pressure of English imperialism, in the context of working-class self-definition.

In 'The Poet's Hope', Davenport binds together the land reform poetic with that of national liberation, specifically that of Poland. The poem images two kinds of outsides to Britain, an untamed world of 'the savage who can dig and plant his field, / And reap the fruits that his own labours yield' and the possible world of Poland, when 'Poland shall again be free and plant her fields with trees of liberty.' In the progress of the poem, the natural environment turns from physical place to symbolic landscape, while the abstract savage is replaced by the immediacy of Polish 'brothers in their common fate' and this 'common fate' is predicted as the possible transformation of the 'common road' of England, from which the agricultural labourer, 'the poor white-skinned slave . . . nor dares to wander'. The ideas of 'The People's Farm' poem are embedded now in a more internationalist fabric, which furthers the notion of community, but begins to unmoor it from a domestic plebeian casing.[74]

For by 1846, issues of internationalism made it easier to take up the issue of Ireland, and in 'Ireland in Chains', Davenport yokes the tune of the *Marseillaise* to the contemporary issue of Ireland and the famine: 'Behold them struggling for existence.' Davenport urges 'Britons' to move beyond their definition as Englishmen, and to forge the political link between Irish liberation and the Charter: 'You who hold the People's Charter, / And who would seal it with your blood / . . . [Ireland] is your sister still.'[75]

In 'The Iron God', a poem rendering the sublimity of the printing press, Davenport demonstrates his sense of the critical rôle of a public culture for the making of a national political movement. A free press, he argues, is the 'great regenerator of mankind', to whom 'we owe the moral power of man'.[76] 'The Iron God' alongside 'The Land, the People's Farm' attests to the workings of both the plebeian and the rationalist in Davenport's poetic trajectory, the country and the city, the agricultural and the mechanical, the song of oral culture, and the heroic couplet of print culture.

CHAPTER FIVE

The forms of Chartist poetry and poetics: 1838–1846

Allen Davenport's narrative is the relatively happy one of a man whose political dreams and poetic output spanned the period from the 1790s through the self-organisation of the first nation-wide working-class movement for the voting franchise. The poems which appeared in the year of his death in 1846, and the eulogies to him as a lifelong poet-activist mark his rôle as a shaper of Owenite and Chartist poetry and poetics between 1839 and the mid-1840s. The narrative of Davenport's poetic and political vocation moves us towards a central moment in the dialectic of romanticism: when the interplay between individualist and communitarian poetics issued in the poetic exuberance of Chartist poetry.

The poetry of urban radicalism and Spenceanism was an outcrop from the centre ground of lyric poetry in the first decades of the nineteenth century. The flowering of Chartism as a political, social, and cultural move-ment organised and endowed a programme and rhetoric to disparate groupings and persons agitating for political and social reform throughout Britain. Here the legacy of romanticism worked in a particularly produc-tive manner, illuminating and extending the communitarian elements within the first and second generation of romantic poetics. Though he was one of only a few Spencean poets, Davenport was one of *many* Chartist poets, whose multiform poetic œuvre not only celebrated and enacted the encounter of self and solidarity, but formed a collective lyrical corpus, working in the modes of both song and poem.

The first significant period for Chartism was the last few years of the 1830s, when those who had gained nothing by the 1832 Reform Bill grouped and regrouped in various bodies, and then merged into the campaign for the six points of the Charter: annual Parliaments, abolition of the property qualification, secret ballot, payment of MPs, equal parlia-mentary districts, and universal (male) suffrage.[1] The 1832 settlement had left most people still without the voting franchise, and as middle-class reformers turned increasingly to issues around free trade, the service rendered to property owners by the mass support of the labouring constituency was now disregarded by the legislators and Reformers.[2] The Charter was presented as a petition three times to Parliament, and was refused each time: 1839, 1842, and 1848. 1838–48 were the main years of active Chartism, whose parameters are usefully defined by Dorothy Thompson as (1) a sense of class (2) a unifying leadership and (3) a national press.[3] The range of activities which took place under the banner of Chartism included gathering signatures for the petitions, raising funds, holding celebrations, lectures, and mass meetings, in addition to strikes and even insurrection, most notably in the defeated Newport Uprising in the autumn of 1839, in which South Wales Chartists marched on and attempted to seize Newport.[4] Internal debates and hostilities defined the movement as much as did its overarching coherence, and the political and social culture of Chartism has been the subject of much research and debate over the last sixty years.[5] For any individual associated with the movement, defining oneself as a Chartist might be more or less essential to their sense of identity, and of course, that meaning would also shift and change over time. So, a central cultural task of the leadership was to encourage a sense of common identity. But though Chartists might also at times name themselves as Free Traders, as Liberals, as Owenites, as Spenceans, one of the chief vehicles through which a Chartist version of a collective project and identity was forged was through the project of Chartist poetry. Romantic poetics, where inwardness was tested and forged, was an apt forum for fashioning Chartist identity, and for describing that subjectivity which demanded a civic entitlement. The formation of Chartism as a political movement drew on the languages not only of radical politics, but also those of print culture literature and cultural nationalism.[6] Compounded of artisans, radical reformers, displaced agrarian workers, and industrial workers, Chartism was the first movement in the name of the working class to render explicit and democratise the links between cultural and political efficacy.

Thompson writes that though many Chartists who later moved in other circles wrote retrospectives of their radical lives, 'for personal memories of the first years we have to rely mainly on fragments'.[7] While memoirs of the early years may be scarce, poems written by men and women identifying themselves as Chartists are abundant, and in them we can read the identity of the movement. There was a vast number of poems written and posted to the *Northern Star*, enough so that in 1839 and 1840 each week a page in the paper was devoted to literary, and in particular, poetic interventions. The editor William Hill wrote in the 'To Readers and Correspondents' column: 'The poets must excuse us ... We have received more Chartist election songs than we could read in an hour or sing in a week.'[8]

Turning from Davenport's individual experience, then, to the meanings of Chartist poetics generally, the discussion which follows outlines the contours of the shifting fortunes of Chartist poetry in the period of the mass movement, until the 'collapse of the mass platform', when Chartism fragmented into different constituencies, and a large sector was drawn into the liberal political and cultural project.[9] As the radicalism of the 1830s built up towards the Chartist organisation and then dispersed outwards again, it was accompanied by the growth and dispersal of a Chartist poetic. Throughout its history, however, from the anonymous ballads and songs of the first days of the agitation, through the prison poems of jailed Chartist leaders such as Thomas Cooper and Ernest Jones, the poetic not only displays the double movement of romanticism described earlier in this study, but also formulated itself as a literary tradition which might position itself against the individualist, and increasingly, self-consciously named 'liberal' poetry of the mid-nineteenth century. Poetry was both a flattering mirror to a movement-in-formation, offering conventions for group identity, and a social matrix within which people could discover themselves as belonging to an on-going set of traditions, goals, and expectations. The work of Chartist poetry was both to excavate and invent that sense of tradition.

In the period leading up to the first and second petitions and the actions and imprisonments of 1840 and 1842, Chartist poetry was chiefly engaged in trying to formulate an independent people's poetic. Many of the subscribers to the *Northern Star* were factory workers, and the mix of artisans and industrial proletarians ensured that many elements of the communitarian and customary traditions would underpin Chartist poetry in its earliest days, along with the new vocabulary and issues of industrial exploitation. The alienation of displacement from the land is matched by the subjective experience of alienation at the workplace. Chartist poetry in this period is abundantly collective, often anonymous, and draws on the oral tradition of hymns, airs, and broadsides, to be sung to familiar tunes: 'Chartists and Liberty', 'The State Pauper's Soliloquy', 'Nine Cheers for the Charter'.[10] As early as 6 January 1838, a poem appears, the first of a series of 'Working Men's Rhymes', to which is attached the instruction, 'To be Committed to Memory', an example of the exchange between oral and print modes.[11] Chartist poetry is also inflected by the theories elaborated by Robert Owen of a communitarian politics located within an industrial environment. But centrally Chartist poetics calls on the world of literary romanticism, in particular imitating and citing Shelley, and invoking the language and traditions of enlightenment rationalism. So Chartist poetry re-complicates the categories already concentrated within romanticism which were engaged in the radical poetics of the 1790s, and the not-quite binaries of individual/communitarian, print/oral, custom/ reason are redeployed through the poetic and political engagements of the 1830s and 1840s.

The crises which took Chartism into the arena of confrontation with the State in 1839, 1840, and 1842 were accompanied by changes within Chartist poetry. After the defeat of the Newport Uprising, meditative poems – poems of exile and loss – began to enter the press more frequently, augmented by a richer sense of lyrical possibility, learned through the romantic presentation of self. These were resistant strains of individualism, which nonetheless preserved collective values: individualism offered a view of subjectivity which endorsed and deepened the meaning of subjective identity, and built upon a notion of the dignity of the self which was a fundamental tenet of enlightenment thought. As Welsh Chartists were tried and then sent to penal servitude in Australia, a Chartist picturesque poetry developed, which learned from and altered the romantic landscape of solitude.

As the leadership worked to maintain a sense of national identity after 1842, the importance of the press took on even greater significance. Feargus O'Connor, the most influential and popular national leader of the Chartists, was the central force here, and with both the *Northern Star* and his Land Plan, O'Connor made it possible for Chartism to remain an organisational shape for the interventions of the unenfranchised.[12] The rôle of Chartist occasional poetry in this period is less militant and more analytical. In this period, the enthusiastic promoter of poetry, Thomas Cooper, puts together a *Shakespearean Chartist Hymn Book* which collects songs and ballads of the indigenous rank and file 'Chartist Poets'.[13] Davenport's rural poetry and the Land Plan poetry which reinforced O'Connor's scheme builds upon the elements of a Chartist picturesque from the Newport Uprising period. At the same time, the developing influence of a growing liberal politics invoked a desire to get 'democratic' middle-class poets involved. The movement then distils a series of writers, who become known to a larger public as the 'Chartist Poets', who write both agitational Chartist hymns and more 'respectable' but democratic verse. The image of a Chartist nationalist culture, a 'people's' poetic tradition, which was created in the earlier phase, is transmuted into the possibility of an internationalist poetic, elements of which lead into both socialism and liberalism as the century moves on. Here the work of Ernest Jones is of great interest. 1846 is a critical year in the history of Chartist poetry, as Davenport, Thomas Cooper, and Ernest Jones find their places in the hierarchy and myth building of the movement. A later section of this discussion will look at the juxtaposition of their poems in the pages of the *Northern Star* in 1846, in which Davenport's rôle is presented as a nostalgic exemplar of a heritage in the land, Cooper is heralded as 'Labour's Laureate', and Jones, outlaw from the gentry, formulates a Chartist poetic which makes critical the question of subjective identity.

Yet there has been until very recently scant literary or historical attention paid to Chartist poetic culture, though it is rich, various, and startling in its claims about cultural efficacy. Social historians of Chartism have tended to focus on other areas of experience and textuality, including political speeches and newspaper articles. The most important contribution to the collection and analysis of Chartist poetry was published in the Soviet Union in 1956 by Y. V. Kovalev, whose *Anthology of Chartist Literature* is the source of much of Peter Scheckner's recent *Anthology of Chartist Poetry*.[14] Kovalev wrote the first critical survey of Chartist poetry in his introduction to the anthology; but his commitment to showing that Chartist poetry adumbrated the theories and practice of socialist realism compromises his acuity when he discusses the relationship of Chartism to romanticism. Kovalev's social realist norms were only slightly modified by P. M. Ashraf in her prodigious 1978 work on English working-class literature, inflected by her steeping in New Critical terms to produce what she calls 'aesthetic realism'.[15] Martha Vicinus was truly pioneering amongst the new social historians of the 1970s in attending to working-class poetry, and her volume, *The Industrial Muse*, opened a site for studying these documents, which was not taken up until recently. Her best legatee has been Brian Maidment, whose annotated anthology, *The Poorhouse Fugitives*, surveys a range of working-class poetry in a way which places Chartism as one amongst many strands of artisan and autodidactic poetics.[16] The growth of cultural history in the 1980s has, however, opened up avenues for locating the importance of Chartist literary production. In her paradigm-breaking study of Victorian poetry, Isobel Armstrong is the first literary historian since the 1890s to think about Chartist poetry as a facet of poetic production in general in the period.[17] Social historians have tended to neglect Chartist poetry, perhaps because it appears to be too emulative of high cultural norms, and hence less authentic. I aim to elicit from Chartist poetic practice its value for social and cultural identity in the movement as a whole.[18] My claim is that Chartism as a social and political movement made itself culturally intelligible to its constituencies *through* its use of poetry.

By their neglect of Chartist poetics, social historians produce a distorted mirroring of the nineteenth century's ruling élite conception of Chartist literature (in the widest sense) as existing outside the boundaries of recognisable genres. For at the time there was quite a lot of discussion within literary circles which anxiously responded to Chartist cultural capability. Unlike the marginal status of the ultra-radicalism of the previous decades, Chartism's mass character made it the object of attention from the literary hegemony itself. Yet to read Carlyle, Mrs. Gaskell, or Disraeli, even in their more sympathetic displays, one would think that Chartists were unkempt ignorant animals, as in Carlyle's description of Chartists as 'wild inarticulate souls' whose voices are in 'inarticulate uproar'.[19] The persistent nineteenth-century literary depiction of Chartism as a movement of the sub-literate, almost sub-human is, however, a good index of the dialectic of anxiety provoked in the British middle class by this autonomous working-class movement. Writers like Carlyle, who knew more of the Chartist press than he revealed, intended to foster an image of Chartists as being without interiority, and so unfit to take up civic subjectivity. Poetry, the index of inwardness in liberal culture, would display the activists in too human a perspective.

This élite literary version of the intellectual life of Chartism as brutish is a particularly telling misrepresentation of the movement, since Chartism placed literature and literary practice near the heart of its political agenda. When we look at the actual literary artifacts produced within the Chartist movement, we are offered a glimpse into a culture which continually asserted the importance of literature, and poetry in particular, to political intervention and to the making of a collective identity based on the universalising of the working class. What had been inchoate in Spence is explicit in Chartism. And as Chartist poetry offers a cultural vehicle for self-identity, it helps establish working-class identity by drawing on traditions of English popular sovereignty and English poetics.

The poetry column in the *Northern Star* offers an immense array of poetic forms. Running from the late 1830s until 1850, the paper ran a weekly poetry column throughout its life. In 1839 the weekly circulation ran as high as 36,000 copies paid per week, and given an illiteracy rate of about one-third of the working class, the estimate is that each copy served between fifty and eighty readers/listeners in radical coffee houses, working-class taverns and reading rooms and working people's clubs.[20] Poetic texts range from lyrics based on nursery rhymes ('Little Jack Horner – New Reading'), acrostics, and ballads ('Flowers and Slaves'), to great stretches of dramatic iambic pentameter ('Prologue to a New Drama, Spoken by a Druid, on John Frost and the Insurrection at Newport'), as well as poems which belong to a more meditative mode ('Lines Written in Prison', and many others).[21] Throughout Britain, Chartist political leaders used poems as political interventions, not just to represent political situations. William Sankey, a spokesperson for Scottish operatives, built upon Shelley's 'Men of England' stanzas in a public address recorded in the *Northern Star*, revising them to make the lines even more topical. The integration of the poetic with the polemical was a regular feature of public Chartist meetings.

Critical to the political power of Chartism was its centralising social function, and one national use of Chartist poetry may be exemplified by a set of 'poetical enigmas' printed in the *Northern Star*, in which rank and file Chartists exchanged political riddles and replies. Henry Dunn from South Molton in Devon writes a riddle poem printed in the first week of May 1840.[22] On 13 July, the *Northern Star* printed a reply, written by a Chartist from Newcastle with the answer, 'Justice':

> Chartists, unite to haste the happy hour
> When Justice shall again resume her power
> Unite, unite in one vast patriot band
> To gain our Charter and to free our land.

The poem is here a vehicle for communicating and linking together Chartists from North and South. One correspondent sent in verses, 'Suggested on Reading' a poem from the previous issue.[23] Some poets even produced texts with collective authors, such as a 'Song for the People' by 'Two Ultra-Radical Ladies'.[24] The presentation of poetry as an intervention within a larger political dynamic is dramatised in an anonymous 1839 poem, 'Chester Gaol', written in response to the imprisonment of a group of Chartists accused of treason, which directs the reader to make practical use of the text:

> Whoe'er you be that find this scroll
> Let our desires prevail,
> And send it to the *Northern Star*,
> That our complaints may spread afar.[25]

The life of poetry in Chartist periodicals was not limited to the *Northern Star*. W. J. Linton's 1839 *National* aimed to produce a sense of a poetic tradition by culling bits of poetry from the past which bore on contemporary questions, and the Glasgow *Chartist Circular* ran a long series of articles on 'The Politics of Poets' throughout its life. Part of what is striking and exciting about Chartist culture is not simply the large number of poems printed in Chartist publications, but also the importance assigned to poetry as an instrument of social change. So, an 1839 article in the *Chartist Circular* warns:

Statesmen would do well to feel the throb thus swelling [from poetry] from the pent-up breast of society ... like the feather [poetry] tells which way the wind blows. It points the dial-hand of time with unerring certainty to a coming period, when a deep and sweeping change must take place in all our institutions.[26]

It was primarily through the *Northern Star*, however, that the culture of Chartism asserted itself as a national culture, and that the forum was opened out of which individual and achieved Chartist poets would emerge. It was itself a collaborative endeavour, dependent in all of its departments, for the reports of local activists. Reading through the weekly poetry page in the paper, one finds emerging from within the Chartist cultural milieu a few mature poetic voices from a wide field in the course of the history of the movement. Stephen Roberts, one of the few social historians to investigate Chartist poetry, has indexed the poets whose work appeared in the *Northern Star* between 1838 and 1842, and has found over seventy different hands, some local activists, such as George Binns, author of the 'Chartist's Mother's Song', as well as men who were extremely important in the political voice of the national movement: Julian Harney and Feargus O'Connor.[27] Some of these poets had only one poem appear; others, like William Hick, who was part of the *Northern Star* staff published many, and also published a free-standing volume, *Chartist Songs and Other Pieces*.[28] A few of the poets of the early years who did not become part of the pantheon of Chartist poets – Cooper, Jones, Linton – were nonetheless represented by more than ten poems each in the *Northern Star*. The earlier years kindled spontaneous and anonymous poems and songs, often derived from song forms, printed with accompanying airs, much in line with Spencean tradition, and also independently from the hymn tradition of Methodism. These texts, choric and oral in origin and intention, often coincide with critical reflections on the importance of Burns as a patron saint of collective poetry. For example, an article on Burns in the *Chartist Circular* states,

Burns was the friend of humanity, the brother of man, the scourge of the oppressor, the soother of the oppressed – a republican, a democrat; and in principle and practice, an honest Chartist ... Every Chartist mother should repeat his patriotic songs, and sing his melting songs to her children, in the winter evenings, by the cottage hearth. His writings should be familiar to every young Chartist, and constitute part of his juvenile education.[29]

In 1852 Charles Kingsley looked on the rôle of Burns in working-class culture with some trepidation. He noted that 'the field in which Burns' influence has been, as was to be expected, most important and most widely felt, is in the poems of working men'. He then goes on to note how unsettling this may be:

The critic, looking calmly on, may indeed question whether this new fashion of verse writing among working men has always been conducive to their own happiness.[30]

Part of what animates and drives Chartist poetry is its advance along two axes: that of ballad and song, and that of poetry shaped within the conventions of print-culture 'aesthetic' poetry. The range of Chartist lyrics which were meant to be sung to popular tunes, and which conform to song metres is vast and these lyrics linked the world of newspapers and periodicals to people's experience in oral traditions and plebeian activities, as in Davenport's description of his own entry into poetic vocation. But Chartist poetry also made claims for poetic importance within print culture, through the five-beat metre whose most noteworthy feature, Derek Attridge argues, is that it 'resists' the pull of four-beat poetics; that is, its difference signals that what it is, is *not* derived from the traditions of pre-print-culture measures.[31] Drawn from an enlarging and increasingly literate population, brought into being by, and also defined against, the ruling élite, Chartist poets inaugurated their public life through the work of a vivid array of activists, whose poetry was by turns lucid, sentimental, repetitive, unusual, moving, and boring.

One version of this engagement between oral and print cultures was the *Northern Star*'s quarterly 'Feast of the Poets', a page filled entirely with poems, as a holiday insert, translating into print the customary practices of group singing and poem recitation. So many poems were sent into the paper that Hill had to request, 'The poets must give us some respite', and asks 'fifty poets to wait their turn'.[32] Soon one finds the growth of a more self-conscious and meditative strain, associated with a small group of writers who increasingly define themselves *as poets* with an eye to a place in literary as well as political institutions.

This double claim of interventionist and aesthetic poetics echoes the conjunction of oral and print cultures worked upon Spence by Davenport. This bifurcation is a tendency which has become paradigmatic for the lyrical projects of later political and social movements. As Adam Cornford has argued, the spontaneous work of the opening cultural moves in a political advance becomes the source of a progressive demarcation of aesthetic standards and values, as well as of the emergence, within the movement's poetry, of 'ambivalence and ambiguity . . . formal experimentation and complex personal statement'.[33] Cornford is writing about post-World War II American social/cultural movements, such as Chicano poetry associated with the Farm Workers' Union, and the Black Arts movement of the 1960s, so he takes for granted the place of personal meditation in this second stage of political poetry. But it was in the formation of the Chartist poetics of the mid-nineteenth century that we can watch the instantiation of the deep self as a vehicle for public liberation, and as the cultural shape for that civic subjectivity that the Charter demanded. As a corollary to the emergence of a literary aesthetic within the movement, a differentiation takes place into more narrowly specified generic purposes, and the consequent distillation of poems and poets from the more polymorphous poetic activity.

The issue of romantic lyric influence urges itself forward as one explores Chartist poetic identity in relation to the plebeian communitarian poetics of the 1790s and to the socialist poetry of the end of the century. What is of interest to the literary historian attempting to trace the power of romantic lyricism, is that activist Chartist poets and poetical theorists were *particularly* interested in, even preoccupied with, their inheritance from romantic poetry. If we return to the resonance of the ideology of aesthetic autonomy which was crucial to the making of the liberal lyric, and to the separating out of the political from the poetical, then Chartist poetry begins by refusing such a separation and asserts itself as action, while explicitly claiming and analytically revealing an equally romantic inheritance. So, an anonymous poem tells us that 'The Voice of the People'

> [It] rushes still on, like the torrent's loud roar;
> And it bears on its surges the wrongs of the poor.
> Its shock, like the earthquake shall fill with dismay,
> The hearts of the tyrants and sweep them away.[34]

And a journal article makes this interpretative point:

The gentlemen critics complain that the union of poetry with politics is always hurtful to the politics, and fatal to the poetry. But these great connoisseurs must be wrong if Homer, Dante, Shakespeare, Milton, Cowper, and Burns were poets.[35]

In refusing the separation between the aesthetic and the political, however, Chartist poetry does not abandon the romantic poetry of meditation, even when it eschews the notion of a solitary consciousness. Chartist poetry offers a utopian counter-statement to the notion of lyric as the terrain of landscaped solitude and secular transcendence through the extension of the unencumbered self, and whose conventional representations are modelled on the romantic poets. The trajectory of Chartist poetry over time is towards distinction, condensation, and complexity. In the poems of Ernest Jones, the Chartist poetic draws upon the power of subjectivity and meditation to invigorate the voice of the collective:

> We bear the wrong in silence.
> We store it in our brain;
> They think us dull – they think us dead:
> But we shall rise again.
> ⁓ . . .
> We'll cease to weep by cherished graves,
> From lonely homes will flee.
> And still as rolls our million-march,
> Its watchword brave shall be.[36]

But the meaning of romanticism as an element within Chartist poetry is romanticism as the contest of individualist and communitarian poetics. This means that Chartist romanticism is made up of both emergent (individualist) and residual (plebeian communitarian) elements. And these residual cultural meanings derive from *before* the self-definition of the working class: Chartist visionary communitarianism, with its imagined community of working-class national identity, often drew upon anachronistic utopian models, those visions of community that had been central to radicalism in the seventeenth century and which persisted in circles of artisans. We hear this, of course, also in the peculiar lexicon of Blake's poetry. Chartism's own mix of artisans and industrial workers, who then engaged with textile outworkers and refugees from middle-class radicalism – all this was the uneven ground on which images of community were built which referred back to agrarian utopias (the Chartist land-scheme being one example) and forward to a revolutionary working-class movement. And a central aspect of this mix of these cultural materials was the familiar and romantic poetic elaboration of the landscape as the site of personal meditation, which became for Chartist poets the site of a potentially transformed collective identity.

The rhetorical scaffolding within which the Chartist poetic intervention was built was the notion of a repressed 'people's' national literary heritage, which Chartist poets and poetic theorists both excavated and invented. For Chartist poetry is centrally a contestation of the received shape of literary tradition, within the larger context of the class struggle over the questions, 'Whose nation? What people?' in which the issue of the nation was often congruent with, because figured as, the landscape. That class struggle over the proprietorship of the nation was clear to William Benbow, who first called for a general strike as soon as the betrayal of the 1832 Reform Bill had become apparent, and who speaks on behalf of the working class: the middle class and aristocracy are, he writes, 'the *jugglers* of society, the pick-*pockets* of society, the *plunderers*, the pitiless *Burkers*.' The working classes, on the other hand, 'do everything and enjoy nothing. The people are nothing for themselves and everything for the few. When they will fight for *themselves* then they will be the people'.[37] On the other hand, Henry Brougham, Whig Reformer and founder of the Society for the Diffusion of Useful Knowledge, is equally confident: 'By the people, I mean the middle-classes, the wealth and intelligence of the country, the glory of the British name.'[38] In other words the definition of the nation was up for grabs, just as the two classes making their competitive claims for universality were in the process of dynamically defining themselves, of dialectically discovering and developing their class identities.[39]

For in an important sense, in the late 1830s a confident bourgeois literary culture was only shaping itself and gathering strength as an aspect of what would become the liberal, political, and intellectual hegemony later in the century. Chartist poetry quite interestingly exhibits the strains of a struggle to define itself literarily in a context in which the working class was also just coming into being as a coherent force. Chartist poetry and literary culture took on the task of wresting away the middle class's own claim to universality by providing its own alternative, though equally purposive genealogy:

The voices of Burns, of Campbell, of Shelley, of Byron, and Elliott have echoed through the Universe, Liberty! and that cry has been continued, and will not cease to be heard till tyranny is no more.[40]

In what one might think of as a pyrrhic victory for the Chartist literary theorists, by 1842, the term 'the people' was primarily used by parliamentary politicians to describe the lower orders, devaluing its universality.[41] So it was the strength of hegemonic class discourse that circumscribed the meaning of 'the people' to the labouring classes, and a function of the weakness of working-class discourse that its claims for universality with that term were never instantiated.

Importantly, and here we hear the echoing of the plebeian communitarianism, the Chartist poetic notion of popular sovereignty aimed to define a nation; and the nation would be born not from pure Painite and rationalist first principles, but out of and in relation to an inherited tradition, a tradition linked to the land, a tradition named and diffused through first- and second-generation Spenceans, and finding form again in the Chartist Land Plan of the later 1840s. The nationalism of Chartism awkwardly but affectively intertwined the nationalism that we associate with the French revolutionary-democratic movement, and the earlier radical patriotism of community.[42] For within that earlier notion of the 'commons' is an idea of abundance which predates the aestheticisation of 'landscape' as handmaiden to nationalism. The abundant countryside asserts the vitality and mutuality of nature and humans across political boundaries; the picturesque landscape asserts an idealised stable yet ancestral homeland, offering objects of contemplation to the native eye. The claims of abundance form one strand in the foundation of the internationalism of Davenport's later poems, and for the openness of Chartist poetics in the later 1840s to the new poetics of internationalism. But in 1840 William Hick admonishes his fellow Chartists to think in national terms: 'Trust alone in *native* thought, / For deeds of honour yet to come.'[43] And this intertwining of older with contemporary ideas of the nation is itself linked both to the importance of the landscape as the site of community *and* to the jostling of human elements within Chartism itself: a movement made up of artisans, with their local traditions and customary practices, radical reformers, and new industrial workers, naming themselves as something new – the working class – but just as eager to give themselves an historical ground. So, Chartist poets and literary theorists tried to define working-class identity by yoking it to a national poetic tradition in which, they asserted, the history of the labouring poor had always been woven into poetic purpose. In aid of that intention, the *Chartist Circular* ran a year-long series of articles in 1839 on 'Politics of Poets'. This elevation of a 'people's' intellectual tradition against a vaguely formulated but deeply felt notion of a hegemonic or élite tradition is an inheritor of the *Pig's Meat* literary intervention:

When the people shall have their own authors and press, to do them justice, they will sweep away the corruptions of literature from the haunts of social life, and the proud motto of Knowledge and Equality shall wave triumphantly on the noble banner of Literary Reform.[44]

Poetry has a particular place in this realm of literature, because:

Poetry is a lever of commanding influence when it grasps the subject that interests, or the elements that move the popular will. It penetrates to every nerve and fibre of society, stirring into irresistibility its innermost current, and spiriting into life and activity the obscurest dweller of the valley.[45]

Of course as Chartist poetry claims a past as well as a future, it finds that past only partially, fitfully, and with a necessary reliance upon the texts and poets from the culture from which it was seeking to distinguish itself, insisting that Shakespeare, Milton, and Marvell were the ancestors of the contemporary Chartist poetic aesthetic. So, for example, the *Northern Star* ran a series in the spring of 1840 of what it called 'Chartism from Shakespeare', culling passages from the plays with which to exemplify Chartist principles and issues. One such column is titled 'Frost and Physical Force', referring to John Frost, the leader of the Newport Uprising of 1839, and to the debate within the Chartist movement on 'physical' versus 'moral' force. The title 'Frost and Physical Force' heads a set of quotations from *Henry the Fourth, Part ii*.[46] That the dramatic sequence which culminates in the presentation of Henry V as the embodiment of absolutist coherence should be appropriated by the working class to describe its own will to national power is a good measure of the contestability and inextricability of both national and poetic claims in the early nineteenth century. Elsewhere, a squib in the *Chartist Circular* asks 'Was not Shakespeare one of the enslaved and despised people, a poacher and a vagabond player?'[47] In the *Northern Star*'s obituary for Allen Davenport, the mixing together of poetics and politics into a people's inheritance is a powerful potion:

[Davenport's] name deserves to be gratefully and proudly remembered by the people, as the name of another of the great nobles of nature who, with Shakespeare and Burns, Paine and Spence, have sprung from the ranks of labour.[48]

The language of aesthetics here enacts a contest of class antagonism. Chartists and popular radicals were heavily engaged in rhetorical battles to appropriate the discourses of religion and of constitutionality; and they were also in one to take hold of the discourses of literature and tradition to make a plausible case for that civic subjectivity which might mirror the civic objectivity of the franchise.[49]

Kitson-Clark, defining the romantic element in the literature of 1830–50, asserted that what he called 'romantic nationalism' was irrelevant to Chartism; he was as wrong as Engels was when he asserted that 'all feelings of patriotism have been crushed in the heart of the worker'.[50] The internationalism Engels desired was in actuality to emerge from within Chartism's domestic nationalism, for the Britain to which the Chartist felt patriotic duty was less Peel's than Blake's sleeping Albion and Shelley's 'Own indignant Earth / Which gave the sons of England birth'. The importance of traditions of the past for the formation of progressive collective identity ought not to be underestimated. From the revolutionary agrarians of the nineteenth century through the Red/Green networks of today, these claims must be distinguished from a Burkean or pure Painite tradition, offering a notion of nationalism freighted with international fraternity:

> See the banner of freedom, now proudly unfurl'd –
> Hear the glad voice of liberty sound through the world;
> And it calls on the sons of oppression to rise;
> Hark! it reigns through the earth, and it enters the skies;
> And it bears on its mighty breath on high
> The resolve of a people to conquer or die!
> Then up! for behold, on the wings of the blast,
> The spirit of vengeance is hurrying fast;
> And the cloud that now darkens our once happy isle,
> Shall burst on the foes of the children of toil.[51]

Some of the radical power of the interventionist goal of Chartist poetry can be measured by comparison with the apolitical autodidactic poets, whose roots were in the labouring classes, but whose thematically more acceptable literary accomplishments gave them entry into the culture of higher social ranks. In the essay 'Our Uneducated Poets', written in 1831, before the upheavals occasioned by the Reform Bill, Robert Southey was able to theorise poetry as social control. Writing of the servant-poet John Jones, Southey remarks: 'this exercise of the mind [i.e., writing poetry], instead of rendering the individual discontented with his station, had conduced greatly to his happiness'.[52]

In a recent discussion of Southey's essay, Kurt Heinzelman argues that in figuring the autodidact, Southey produces an image of a prototype for the romantic solitary poet, 'free enfranchised and at large', symbolising 'at the social level his auto-genesis as an aesthetic producer'.[53] Taken in isolation within a purely literary history, this is a convincing argument. But Southey's 1831 intervention either bypasses or suppresses the lively interventionist tradition. While Heinzelman is right that Southey's essay is a critical foray into the important issue of to whom literary tradition belongs, he does not do credit to the self-authorising traditions around which run athwart the 'uneducated poets' theme.

For the figure of the poet as a specially marked person in the ranks of the Cause is evinced throughout the history of the movement, and indicates one of the paths through which the Chartist poetic modified the meanings of the poet as romantic solitary. The example of Chartist and communitarian radical Thomas Frost's *Recollections* of forty years of activity in politics illustrates the close intertwining of the principles of poetic and political continuity from the 1820s through the Chartist movement and into the late 1870s. Frost, like Davenport, writes about the links between ultra-radicalism and Chartism, describing a history of radical politics from the 1820 Cato Street conspiracy to blow up the Cabinet, into Owenism, through the 'Communist Propaganda' and then into Chartism, following the fortunes of what he calls, using the Owenite vocabulary, the 'communitive project'. In the course of his narrative Frost allies his political awakening to the persistent influence of Shelley and Coleridge on his mental and political formation. When Frost first hears Owen speak about the possibilities of Co-operation, Owen's words lead Frost back to reread Coleridge's 'Religious Musings': 'The scheme of the philosopher seemed to be the due response to the aspirations of the poet.'[54] But, 'It was not until after I had read the grand and wondrous poems of Shelley, two or three years later, that my mind became impressed with the connexion between the influence of circumstances in the formation of character and the new organization which Owen desired to give society.'[55] And later, when Frost is drawn to the Chartist agitation, he is primed for this by his Shelleyan formation: 'The poetry of Coleridge and Shelley was stirring within me, and making me "a Chartist, and something more", as the advanced reformers of that day were wont to describe themselves.'[56] Frost was an exponent of communitarian living and of that 'something more' (a slogan developed in 1850 by Chartists aiming to transform the demands of the Charter into social as well as political ones) that reached beyond the aspiration of the six points of the Charter: 'We were unwilling to waste our strength in agitating for any thing less than the reconstruction of the entire fabric of society.'[57] The romantic poet's model served for daily life as well as poetic insight: Shelley's vegetarianism becomes a provenance for the Concordists' menus of 'rice, sago, and raisin puddings, potatoes, carrots and turnips'.[58] While Shelley provided materials for the content of the communitive world, Byron was the model of fashion: many of the agitators Frost refers to are signalled by wearing their hair 'à la Byron'.[59]

What links the two histories of poetry and of politics in Frost's narrative is the appearance throughout of a poet-shoemaker, Jem Blackaby who, much like a folkloric trickster figure, serves as a periodic point of contact as Frost recounts the various groupings within the radical movement. The image of this poet-radical is a powerful figure in Frost's account, and Blackaby serves as a voice for the movement as a whole, and always in opposition to the élite; a very different position from the peasant-poet described and patronised by Southey.[60] Frost tells a story of Blackaby at an outdoor meeting debating from the crowd with Cobden, the Free Trader. Cobden cannot believe that the young poet is an organic intellectual, and harangues Blackaby from the platform, accusing him of being an outside agitator. But everyone in the meeting crowd knows Blackaby and his authenticity as local poet, and so Cobden's own credibility is compromised. In the 1840s, Frost helps Blackaby get published in *Reynold's Miscellany*. Blackaby punctuates the whole of Frost's life story; Frost meets him again after the Kennington Common demonstration of 1848 which marked the defeat of the 1848 Charter petition. In Frost's narrative, Blackaby's poetic life ends in failure:

Whether he continue to court the Muses, or had all the poetry crushed out of his nature by the severer labour rendered necessary by an inferior description of work, I know not. If he left any manuscripts they have probably been used to light fires, or are stowed away, dusty and cobwebby, in some obscure corner of the house in which he died.[61]

This is, of course, a romantic narrative, and Blackaby is presented as a neglected poet in a romantic mould, but Frost locates his poetic purpose in the sociality of popular politics and its social collectivity.

In the mid-century, Charles Kingsley, speaking as an ameliorative Christian Socialist, was quick to point to the social dangers of poetry. He admires Burns because he sees the Scots poet as one who has been defeated, but nobly, by his struggle to find a poetic voice: Burns's poems are 'hints of a great might-have-been'.[62] But that status transforms Burns's history into a 'sad story'. On the other hand, he blames Shelley and Ebenezer Elliott as poets who, unlike Burns, had engendered 'bitterness' in 'working poets'.[63] So the Chartist affiliation to romantic poets was as much a cultural assertion of entry into an arena from which they were meant to be excluded as it was a species of emulation. And Chartist poets did often cite as their closest forebears the previous generation's apparent martyrs to liberty, Shelley and Byron. It is certain that Chartist poets felt a complex sense of debt to Byron and Shelley, whom they continually quote and allude to in the pages of their periodicals.[64] As a radical aristocrat, whose effectively marginal class position made him liable to produce a critique of the politics and culture of the bourgeoisie, Byron's poetic prestige was as high as Shelley's within the movement, and his influence is felt chiefly in the satirical verse of the *Northern Star*. Byron the individual is presented as an icon of the conjuncture of national and poetic aspiration: 'The poet and the patriot met in Byron', one article declares, and another tells us that as he 'had mixed extensively among mankind' he was able to trace 'through its ramified complications the development of the democratic principle'.[65] In an 1846 poem in the *Northern Star*, 'Byron Defended', the poet W. L. Warren thanks another poet who has earlier defended Byron in the paper, and places Byron in a religio-political context whose rhetoric is reminiscent of Shelleyan polemic:

> The well-paid priests for sordid gain
> Would fain have crush'd him with their thunder;
> . . .
> When will this world have done with cant
> And humbug priests call 'true religion'
> Never, while they are paid to rant,
> And mystify our mental vision.

The poems ends by turning towards Byron's more meditative poetry:

> I lov'd him in my early years,
> When faintly was his praises caroll'd
> And now, when pressed with many cares,
> I wander with the 'Pilgrim Harold'.[66]

Shelley's *Queen Mab* and 'The Mask of Anarchy' were the poems most frequently reprinted and excerpted in Chartist poetry columns. In his life of Shelley, Medwin says that Owenites considered *Queen Mab* to be 'the gospel of the sect', and Shaw recalled hearing an 'Old Chartist . . . confess that . . . it was through reading Shelley that he got the ideas that led him to join the Chartists. A little further inquiry elicited that *Queen Mab* was known as the Chartists' Bible'.[67] Most obviously, much Chartist linking of intervention and poetry derives from and makes explicit Shelley's assertion in the *Defence of Poetry* that 'The most unfailing herald, companion and follower of the awakening of a great people to work a beneficial change in opinion or institution, is Poetry.'[68] And from an amalgam of Shelley and Byron arises a Chartist programme for poetry in the future:

The destinies of mankind, rise and fall of empires, the uprooting of prejudice, the overthrow of despotism, and man himself standing in the presence of Nature and of God, with all his passions, his doubts, his rare properties and inconceivable wretchedness, will become the chief if not the sole theme of poetry amongst democratic nations.[69]

In a review of Watson's edition of 'The Mask of Anarchy' W. J. Linton writes that the poem 'is not to be looked on in the light of a political essay – except inasmuch as poetry and universal policy are synonymes'.[70]

Yet it is important to insist that it was not only the communitarian and interventionist side of romanticism that influenced Chartist poetics; Shelley was also an important influence by way of his more meditative poetry. Many Chartist poems do in practice attempt to link meditative idealism to the interventionist goals of the movement, by transforming the individualist into a communitarian intention, within a poetic discourse that draws on the landscape poetic built in the period of sensibility and romanticism, rather than the more public languages of antiquity, republicanism, or satire. For it was as much by way of the image of the poet as by his writing that the romantics serve Chartist purposes. Both Shelley and Byron exemplified lives of defiance and of personal heroism, and were also examples of selves whose expression of subjective alienation aesthetically mirrored the objective alienation of workers and worker-poets, while their poetics of euphoria offered a utopian promise as well.

Wordsworth may have been instrumental in shaping the poetic which would then become available to Chartist poets, yet his own history as political apostate made him a more problematic poetic figure for Chartist poetic theorists. One critic in 1839 produces an apologia for Wordsworth's poetry: 'Look at his poems altogether, and consider the spirit of them altogether, and they are Radical – deeply, essentially, entirely Radical.'[71] But another idiolect of Chartism declares, even in its latter moments:

In announcing [Wordsworth's] death, we must acknowledge that we are not impressed with any heavy sense of sorrow . . . Unlike those Great Spirits [Burns, Byron, and Shelley], Wordsworth passes from amongst us unregretted by the great body of his country-men, who have no tears for the slave of Aristocracy and the pensioned parasite of Monarchy.[72]

Within this formulation of a poetic tradition which identifies the voices of the people and those of the great poets writing in English, Chartist poetry in its first years is recognisably martial, impersonal, and, as Isobel Armstrong notes, masculinist, using the category of the man as a yardstick of political puissance and solidarity, and noticeably sparse on women poets.[73] In the period after the agitations of 1839–42 (whose central events were the Newport Uprising of 1839 and the strikes, demonstrations, and agitations of 1842), and after those of 1848–51 (in what we might call 'second wave' Chartism), we find a newly complex poetry of defeat and hope.

The defeat and the hopes of the 1790s had led to a splitting of the reform movement into middle-class solutions, and the fragments of ultra-radicalism. The defeats of Newport and of 1848 generated a poetry which attempted to incorporate and use devastation as a motor for illumination and development. An 1845 poem exhorts its readers, 'Never give up! It is wiser and better / Always to hope than once to despair.' In the 1850s, Ernest Jones's 'The Poet's Death' internalised this sentiment along literary lines, 'Hail to the veteran from the Titan-fight! / Hail to the heart that dies but grows not old.'[74] The voice and valence of hope grow more elegiac through the late 1840s and 1850s, and are then turned into a utopian aspiration, reformulated as a programmatic element of Morris's socialist poetics.

This elegiac mode makes its claim to print-culture status, using the conventions and forms associated with the five-beat line of iambic pentameter, and the historical genres of elegy and sonnet. To show the Chartist elegiac mode at work, it is instructive to look at a few of those poems which were written in response to the events at Newport. The Chartist elegy, coupled to the communitarian poetic rhetoric of the commoners as trustees of the land, leads into that part of the landscape dominated, in most accounts of romanticism, by the aesthetic ideology of transcendence. Landscape and consciousness are associated in the Wordsworthian poetic; land, poetry, and nationhood are continually identified in the nineteenth-century arguments of class consciousness. One only needs to think of the imperialist mandate of Palgrave's *Golden Treasury* or of Matthew Arnold's assertion that the glory of British nationhood was best measured by its poetry.[75] Though Arnold and Palgrave are in one sense collusive in the explicit separation of politics and poetry, they are nonetheless eager to have aesthetics serve politics. Chartist poetic theorists think quite differently: the glory of British poetry lies in the tradition of popular sovereignty that, they argue, has always been the central purpose of English poetry. This assertion allows the Chartist poet to appropriate the landscape of personal meditation for the uses of the class, and such a poetic claim simultaneously reaches back before romantic landscape atemporality to the tradition of topographical poetry which used the visible remains of history in the landscape as a set of general moral markers, a tradition which had been virtually overgrown by the detemporalising and individualising picturesque sensibility of meditative poetry.[76] By returning the poetry of place to the events which take place at its site, this Chartist poetry rolls back the picturesque dehistoricising of landscape, while preserving the metaphorical power of such naturalisations. The Chartist poetic landscape is revisioned from the perspective of the working class imagined as 'the people':

> Tis the voice of the people I hear it on high,
> It peals o'er the mountains – it soars to the sky;
> Through the wide fields of heather.[77]

The links amongst pictured rurality, a people's tradition, and a poetry associated with that tradition are later articulated by the Chartist poet and orator Gerald Massey in his 'Our Land', with its refrain, 'For our rare old land, and our dear old land! / With its memories bright and brave! . . . Sing O! for the hour its sons shall band, – To free it of Despot and Slave.' The forward movement of a democratic impulse is linked to the antiquity of the soil, which is in turn linked to the poetry inspired by that land, where 'Freedom's faith fierce splendours caught, / From our grand old Milton's love.'[78] In the face of the economic hardships accompanying industrialisation, it was an easy poetic move to draw upon an idealised picture of rurality to build up the utopian vision of a possible future, and to modify that idealisation by repeopling the landscape with a history of labour.

In some cases, Chartist poems invoke the landscape in order to disengage it from the proprietorship of the ruling class: 'earth, its mines, its thousand streams . . . The mountain-cleaving waterfall / . . . God gave, not to a few, but all, / As common property'.[79] In others, the land is figured more brutally as the sanguinary battle-site of class struggle:

> There is blood on the earth, all wild and red –
> It cries to our God from the freeman's bed!
> It will not fade or be washed away – [80]

There is, nonetheless, an evident problem within the retrospective perspective embedded in the use of the landscape as a central motif. This was apparent in Davenport's poetry of the 1820s, and it was true again in this category of Chartist poetry. For in communitarianism lay a contradictory model: the dream of a political movement and the obstruction built into its very antiquated character, since the categories of the 'people's tradition' on the one hand, and the working class under capitalism on the other, are not congruent. This does not mean, however, that Chartist literary activity was doomed by its anachronistic forms and motifs. Rather, it suggests that the contradictions within Chartism were produced in the context of the dynamics of disparate persons and groups identifying themselves through the political category of Chartism. The often stubborn attachment to nativism within Chartist poetry does act as a political *encumbrance*, a mood that George Meredith captures ironically in 'The Old Chartist' in the 1860s: 'Whate'er I be, Old England is my dam! . . . I'm for the nation! / That's why you see me by the wayside here, / Returning home from transportation.'[81]

But certainly from the perspective of those Chartists penally exiled from Britain because of their activities, the contours of the vanished landscape appeared attractive, generating a Chartist poetic linked to geographical rather than temporal nostalgia. For the transportation of the defeated leader of the Newport Uprising, John Frost, to Tasmania, or as it was then called, Van Dieman's Land, was a rich source for topical Chartist poetry.[82]

The Newport events are considered to be the main example of a planned insurrection by Chartists. In the aftermath of the unsuccessful insurrectionary event, once the Queen's Troops had occupied Newport on 5 November 1839 and arrested the putative leaders William Jones, Zephaniah Williams, and John Frost, there was a national campaign to save these men from being hanged and quartered, the result of which was that they were shipped to the newly opened penal colony near Port Arthur, Tasmania.

A significant number of John Frost transportation-exile poems appear in the national Chartist press, next to another popular topic of poems on the Uprising, the death of a child-martyr, George Shell. A series of meditative sonnets, 'Sonnets Devoted to Chartism', published throughout 1840 in the *Northern Star* by one of the Newport Chartists under the pseudonym of 'Iota', linked the two heroes together in a sequence of landscape meditations, beginning, 'Once more I visit thee, sweet rural walk.'[83] The anecdote of George Shell was widely disseminated. This young Chartist had written a poignant letter to his parents the night before the insurrection, ending, 'I shall see you soon; but if not, grieve not for me. I shall fall in a noble cause. My tools are at Mr. Cecil's, and likewise my clothes. Yours truly, George Shell.'[84] The romanticised pathos of the Shell story has remained literarily affective into the twentieth century and is echoed in a 1934 Anglo-Communist boys' book, *Comrades for the Charter*, in which the certainty of defeat is juxtaposed to Chartist idealism, as the dying boy, with tears in his eyes, gasps 'We are winning, aren't we?'[85]

In Iota's sonnet beginning ''Tis long since last I came this pleasant way' (Sonnet 1), Shell is given an elegiac context amidst a set of poems chiefly concerned with the landscape within which the Newport Uprising took place. Iota participates in the association of the continuity of land and poetic glory: 'Some future bard shall sing thy triumph, Shell ... Thy patriot spirit hovering o'er the land / that gave thee birth' (Sonnet 2). The sequence of eight poems as a whole belongs to the landscape meditative mode, presenting that vague ahistorical antiquity that picturesque landscape imparts to the rougher facts of historical confrontations. Iota excuses the 'Patriot' Frost from insurrectionary intentions. No, he was searching for justice, '[Frost] wandered o'er this pleasant way, / With heart-felt ardour for his country's weal . . .' (Sonnet 3). 'His country' is the nation figured as a sweet rurality, and is meant to be sharply juxtaposed to the terrifying sublimity of the penal landscape in Australia where Frost serves his time even as Iota writes his sonnets. In Iota's 'Stanzas Addressed to the Patriot's Wife – Mrs. Frost', the prophetic speaker asserts, 'He shall return.'[86]

John Watkins, a Chartist poet who wrote 'Lines on Shell', also wrote a play about Frost, extracts of which were published in 1841 in the *Northern Star*.[87] Watkins's poetic persona, Frost, utters a soliloquy filled with the agony of separation from that land which, however needful of change, remains the natural possibility for futurity. In this Chartist vision of Tasmania, art asserts instead the descent of the human into a terrifying and unfathomable nature, a sublime of terror: 'In such an irresponsive wilderness', Watkins writes, 'Man is authoriz'd to torture man, / And so exults in his most savage power . . .'[88] Watkins implies that British soil would act as a human break upon cruelty because it is, in accordance with a romantic conception of the dialectic of nature and mind, *responsive*.

To those in penal servitude in Australia and Tasmania, the picturing of British landscape *was* particularly sweet. In *The Fatal Shore*, Robert Hughes cites an on-going tradition of convict ballads of exile and rural loss: 'It's oft-time when I slumber I have a pleasant dream, / . . . I've been roving down by a sparkling stream; / In England I've been roving . . . / But I wake broken-hearted upon Van Dieman's land.'[89] And in this next example, an anonymous poem on Frost's transportation very literally occupies one of Moore's Irish Melodies.

> He [Frost] recalls the scenes of his dear native land,
>   The hearts who to life had entwined him;
> And the tears fall uncheck'd by one friendly hand
>   For the joys he has left behind him.[90]

This Chartist appropriation of Moore's text foregrounds the political content of the relationship between the exiled class leader and the beauties of his native land by linking Frost's individual sorrow to a collective potentiality of transformation: 'Nor soon shall the tears of his country be dried, / Nor for long shall its efforts desist.' In Moore's earlier version, we are given rather a solitary female mourner who will soon join her Irish patriot lover in death and her song will be lost in the grave.[91]

William Hick included a poem about the exiles in his 1840 *Chartist Songs and Other Pieces*, internalising place as commitment:

> The people's friends in dungeons pine;
> And some are banish'd 'far away,'
> Whose only fault, whose only crime,
> Was that, to break despotic sway.
>
> But ah! one lesson has been taught,
> Which ne'er shall fade from memory's dome;
> To trust alone in *native thought*,
> For deeds of honour yet to come.[92]

In *The Prelude* materials of 1805, Wordsworth argued for a link between nationality and landscape on the liberal model of the poet as solitary representative speaker of the national consciousness. In his poetry, the transition from self to nation takes place through a process whereby self is first alienated from nature and then returns to her. In his poem addressed to 'Frost, Williams, and Jones', Hick produces a utopian dream of the return of the natives:

> Away, away, she flies across the ocean,
> Bold and free, bold and free
> The steersman cheers, and every hand's in motion,
> Blythe and free, blythe and free!
> And proudly on, they breast the wave;
> And soon they reach the *convict* grave;
> And to the patriots good and brave,
> Quick they flee, quick they flee.
>
> Again, rejoice! We come to give you freedom,
> The mandate see, mandate see;
> The millions call you back to come and lead 'em
> Till they're free, till they're free.
> Your chain has gone; you are slaves no more;
> And soon afloat, where the billows roar,
> You speed to your native shore,
> And be free, and be free.[93]

The history of the image of Britain as it was appropriated by convicts and settlers in Australia provides an interesting mirror to the domestic politics of the romantic landscape. The reality of Tasmania offered a landscape of agonising sublimity to the political convict which contrasted with a picturesque calmness of the dream of home; but for the military and the apparatus of the ruling class, the prison sublime was planted over with cuttings from the British romantic picturesque.

George Thomas Blaney Boyes, a nineteenth-century colonial auditor and artist in Tasmania, attempted to encourage both local gardening and painting, hoping thereby to 'raise the standards of public taste' and stave off what he considered to be the encroaching barbarity from the influence of convicts on the children of settlers in Tasmania. For the military settler family, this aesthetic was a mode of linkage back to Britain as well as a method of obscuring the presence of the penal world. For the Chartist prisoner, on the other hand, the imagination of a picturesque Britain was an appropriative reply to the terror of prison life. The sublime of servitude was foregrounded by John Frost himself when he returned to Britain in 1856. He lectured throughout the United States and Britain on the topic 'The Horrors of Convict Life', calling work in the Tasmanian mines the 'hardest kind of labour that any man could endure' in an alien environment.[94] What is striking in Frost's lectures is that he draws no parallel between working-class servitude in Welsh mines and penal servitude in Tasmania. One senses that for the Chartist exile (and Frost remained a committed Chartist until his death), the affective power of a poetic picturesque landscape had displaced the realities of the southern coalfield of Wales. Oscillating between different intentions and interests, the poetic convention reveals its affective plasticity. The Chartist elegy works as both a collectivised version of the historical genre of individual elegy, and as the historicised version of the actual experience of spatial exile.

The use of the landscape poetic was helpful to Chartist poets insofar as it linked, however marginally, the contemporary struggle to a communitarian past located in the countryside. It was helpful when it intersected with a vision of the future built on the premises of popular sovereignty, and when it was given poetic shape in images of the nation as belonging to a people defined as the universalising of the working class. But the landscape poetic was a hindrance to the extent that it mystified the relationship between a rural past and a proletarianised present. And the irony of that rural myth becomes acutely palpable to us when we see it used to assuage homesickness amongst the transportees. The reality of the mines in Wales was not much less oppressive than that in Tasmania, though the nativist language offered a poetic terrain belonging not to the coalfield, but to a generalised British romantic landscape.

The Spencean poetic had invoked a version of the nation that unevenly interconnected native constitutionalism with the Franco-American promise of republicanism, and which emerged from a vernacular idiom of patriotism, meeting a new discourse of international natural rights. The Chartist nativist landscape poem will also be altered through the development of a more international vision of the 'people's' tradition on a global scale, and the meanings of the Chartist struggle will become increasingly implicated in events going on in Europe as well as England. Certainly one strand of communitarian poetry which begins in Chartism and moves off into internationalist republicanism has its roots in nativist landscape poems, as ideas of commonality are unmoored from the literal commons and become the characteristic of a labouring class that crosses national boundaries. Davenport's poems of the later 1840s, calling on workers 'of every state' to 'feel as brothers in their common fate' exemplify how being a Chartist might be a matter of being a European 48er as well.

After the European and domestic defeats of 1848, the idea of a 'people's' cultural tradition becomes all the more implicated in a wider world. This is marked in Chartist poetry as we move from the 1830s through the 1850s, most often depicted by reference to liberation struggles in Italy, France, Germany, and, closer to home, the oppression of Ireland. Gerald Massey's poetry of the post-1848 period highlights the internationalism of the struggle: linking together the revolutionary upsurges in the 'bravely beautiful' France, 'gallant Hungary', and 'Rome – where Freedom's heroes bled' with the nativist 'Spirit of Cromwellian might' at home, he asserts to his 'brothers of the bounding heart', 'We'll tread them down yet – curse and crown, Czar, Kaiser, King, and Slave.'[95]

The politico-material experience of defeat and exile, which generated literary forms of retrospection and elegy, coincided more or less with the beginnings of a new stage of Chartist poetry. And this passage also represents a movement from the practice of Chartist poetry as a more or less collectivised poetic activity, to a focus on individual figures. This focus, which I will reiterate in the following chapter by detailing the poetic practice of three Chartist poets, enacts within Chartist practice a division of knowledge between poetry and politics, which is also a division of labour within the movement. These divisions, however, are not simply an elegiac falling-off from a first world of undivided light; they are also a productive development, enabling the naming of a Chartist aesthetic and the elements of a Chartist canon.

CHAPTER SIX

Labour's Laureates: Allen Davenport, Thomas Cooper, and Ernest Jones in 1846

Out of the large numbers of people calling themselves 'Chartist Poets', a small number came to be recognised as central within the Chartist press, reflecting internal recognition of accomplishment. In the wake of significant political changes, a process of poetic stratification set in. The events of the 1839 Newport Uprising had precipitated a set of poems of defeat and exile, and the elegiac component of Chartist poems increased, augmented by the extended prison poem, associated in particular with Thomas Cooper's *Purgatory of Suicides* (1846) and Ernest Jones's *The New World* (1850, 1857). The genre of prison poetry makes a place for Jones and Cooper in the tradition of Newgate poetry associated with Thelwall and the English Jacobins of the 1790s. By 1850, the ratified 'Chartist Poets' comprised most crucially Cooper and Jones, alongside Gerald Massey, who contributed to both Harney's *Red Republican* and Jones's *Notes to the People*, and something of a fellow-traveller, W. J. Linton, who had begun his literary-agitational work in 1839 with his journal, *The National*.[1]

After the popular interventionist poetics of 1839 and the early 1840s, the distillation of the 'Chartist Poets' as individualised figures from out of what had been a collectivised poetic project, enacts both a falling-away from the base of the movement and a corollary division of cultural labour, punctuated by the upsurge of 1848. Cooper and Jones manifest a division of labour within the movement, yet both were themselves closely tied to the political activism of the campaign; that is, their work as Chartist poets cannot easily be extricated from their place within the political hierarchy of the movement. Poetics is at once differentiated from politics, recapitulating the division between poetry and politics within the hegemony of liberalism, and yet poetics is also critical to the shaping of politics. So the differentiation is productive. The need for aesthetic evaluation of poetry – which poems and poets are good – enables Chartism to acknowledge its own work in forming a corpus, even a canon.

At the same time, this period saw the opening up of Chartism to what

James Epstein recently characterised as a 'double vision': aiming for the continuity of the struggle of the demands of the Charter in a changing domestic and international conjunction, but also needing to imagine and structure more clearly the relationship between the Charter movement and the labour movement in general.[2] In the course of the 1840s, the shape of the Chartist poetic and its production of a 'people's tradition' becomes rather more complexly constructed. Some of the confidence was lost that had been demonstrated in 1839 and 1840 in papers such as *The Chartist Circular* about the formulation of an autonomous class poetic, bound to the autonomy of a social and political movement. This was due, in part, to the interest shown by those increasingly stratified Chartist poets in the liberal poetic milieu adjacent to their own, and also through their desire to be known as accomplished; and, in part, by the demoralisation of the activist movement after the spate of arrests and imprisonments that attended the great upsurge of activity in 1842, which witnessed 'the nearest thing to a general strike that the century saw'.[3]

Yet the shaping of an independent Chartist poetic continues: Shelley and Burns are reprinted less often, but invoked to encourage and point to the rôles and potential of a contemporary cohort. And the growth of a recognisable Chartist poetic pantheon also enabled its chief practitioners to bid for a place in the growing liberal intellectual formation. So, though Thomas Cooper was crucial in appealing to rank and file Chartists to come forward as poets at the beginning of the decade, by the mid-1840s he was more chary of the principle of total inclusion. And Ernest Jones, who in the late 1840s and 1850s came to occupy Cooper's rôle in the poetico-politics of Chartism, aimed to build a bridge between Chartist poetry and the realm of 'liberal' democratic poetry.[4] *The Labourer: a Monthly Magazine of Politics, Literature, Poetry*, edited by Jones and O'Connor in 1847 and 1848, as a cultural supplement to the *Northern Star*, continues to appeal to the political power of poetry in a Shelleyan style along similar lines to that of the Glasgow *Chartist Circular* in 1839 and 1840: 'The people mould a poet, but a poet directs a people.'[5] But *The Labourer*'s choice of poems comes almost entirely from the ranks of contemporary Chartist poets, and most often in epic, didactic, and ruminative iambic pentameter form – the form of aesthetic rather than interventionist poetry, in the metres of print rather than oral culture. Furthermore, the journal's 'Literary Review' articles exhorted the members of the liberal poetic milieu to join literary forces with the Chartists. For example, Jones prints 'democratic' excerpts from Browning, and then calls on him and other 'great minds of the day, come among the people, write for the people and your fame will live forever'.[6]

If Allen Davenport's poetry stands at the threshold of the Chartist poetic, Ernest Jones (1819–69) is the poet of its apex and dissolution. Davenport links Spencean poetry to Chartism, and Jones links Chartism to both the liberalism of the later part of the century and to the Socialist poetics of the 1880s and 1890s. His work offers an interesting example of the traffic between the individualist and the communitarian poetic traditions in the 1840s and 1850s. On the one hand, Jones was able to infuse the developing genres of Chartist poetry – the hymn, the prison poem, the marching song, all the genres of the mass movement poetic of 1839–42 – with an intense sense of the subjectivity of experience, producing, counter to the notion of the necessarily individualised character of lyric experience, a poetic of collective lyricism. On the other hand, his social origins amongst the military and minor gentry made his work more sus-ceptible to an exchange with the middle-class liberal poetic environment than the works of an artisan poet such as Davenport. As we will see, Jones's biographical example enacts the challenge posed to the old, customary inheritance standard of social origin by the voluntarism of choice and self-creation, liberating personality as a matter of identification.

Between the two poets stands the figure of Thomas Cooper (1805–92), who rose from within the columns of grass-roots level activist poets, the consummate autodidact who first organised his comrade-poets into a coherent corps, and then dominated the movement as 'Labour's Laureate' at the very moment when he was about to secede from active participation in the politics of the movement.[7] The following discussion of Jones, then, begins by placing him in relation to Davenport and Cooper, in conjunc-tion with the changing meanings of poetry within Chartist poetic theory and practice. And the warrant for the juxtaposition of the three poets within their own milieu is the curious concatenation of their works in the pages of the *Northern Star* in 1846.

The year 1846 was a crossroads year in the fortunes of Chartist poetics. Jones, who would determine the orientation of the movement for the next fifteen years, made his decisive intervention into Chartist poetry and politics in May 1846. Cooper, who had in 1843 put together the *Shakespearean Chartist Hymn Book* on behalf of the Leicester Chartists, now in 1846 abandoned his attempts to formalise and organise grass-roots Chartist poets, at the same time as he was being fêted and acknowledged as the 'Chartist Poet' in the pages of the *Northern Star*.[8] In August 1846, Cooper was expelled from the Chartist Convention in Leeds, on a motion moved by Ernest Jones, most likely on behalf of Cooper's antagonist in that year, Feargus O'Connor. During these same months the *Northern Star* was making much of the aged Allen Davenport as a grand old activist and poet of the movement, and Davenport and Cooper both publicly eulogised each other in poetry. This trio of poets forms a fascinating *de facto* literary grouping, and in their work and rivalries the varying claims of individualist and communitarian poetics correspondingly vied with each other under the Chartist banner.

Allen Davenport's poetry is interesting, in part, for the way in which it offers a counter-aesthetic to the picturesque within the poetics of an urban romanticism; Ernest Jones's is interesting for the way in which it assimilates the poetics of inner life to urgency of collective action. Davenport imbues the romantic landscape of the solitary walker with the claims of collective life, and Jones opens out the group identity to encompass the desiring impulses of interiority. Though Jones brings to Chartist poetry the lineage of lyric individualism and Davenport brings that of oral cultural forms, they also share the double inheritance of romanticism: both call on the cosmopolitan voice of Shelley as well as the landscaped, rural, and nationalist voice of Wordsworth, inflected by Goldsmith and Crabbe. But while Davenport's poetic emerges from Spenceanism, moves into an 1820s retrospective, and then re-emerges in the Land Plan period of the Chartist movement, Jones's politico-poetic career begins *ab ovo* in 1846, nurtured in German romanticism and Byronism. Davenport's political path takes him from Spenceanism to Chartism, while Jones travels from Chartism to Democ-Soc politics to, in the later 1860s, Liberalism.[9]

But Davenport and Jones met on the literary road to O'Connorville, the first Chartist Land Plan estate, at Herringsgate, near Watford.[10] Davenport was a strong supporter of Feargus O'Connor's plan to provide smallholdings and cottages to labourers in a 'back to the land' movement, and it made a bridge between his Spencean past and the industrial present, a contemporary version of 'the people's farm'.[11] For Jones, support of O'Connorville was part of his brief as a new member of the movement, and he participated in the opening ceremonies, giving a speech at the site; in September he was named by O'Connor as 'Secretary to the Second Section of the Land Society'.[12] Davenport and Jones each wrote poems which appeared in the *Northern Star* in August 1846 to celebrate 'Labour's Procession to Labour's Own Land', from Hyde Park Corner to the estate, 'to redeem the soil for the whole people', rescuing it 'from political and social bondage'.[13] Davenport's poem, not surprisingly, hearkens back to the Spencean vision of the land, even though the actual deployment of the land was very different under the Chartist scheme from that under the nationalisation plan of Thomas Spence himself, for Spence's was a communitive scheme of joint ownership, while the Chartist plan was a smallholdings idea, which at its peak, had 70,000 subscribing members.[14] O'Connor's vision of the Land Plan owes something to the individualist element within romanticism, in which the idea of the land as a respite for the self as individual recasts the Spencean plebeian notion of the community. The structure of feeling within which the Chartist Land Plan operates was shaped, at least in part, by way of romantic lyric positioning of the self in nature. The major support for the Land Plan, which was first adopted as a notion in 1845, came, though not exclusively, from highly industrialised factory towns, particularly around Manchester, with a good proportion as well of craftsmen and artisans of various kinds.[15] Just as Davenport's rural poetry was written in a period of retrospect after the radical activity of the late 1810s, so the Chartist Land Plan reintroduced the land question in a pastoral tone into working people's politics, and offered a way to forge closer links amongst the disparate people who answered to the name 'Chartist' from 1842 onwards.[16]

Davenport's poem announces itself as a ballad, written in a four-stress oral metre, and it imaginatively produces O'Connorville as the culmination of a journey through both time and space. Goldsmith's exiled villagers are assembled together with emigrants from Ireland (the famine was raging in 1845 and 1846), and they all march together under the banner of the 'British Chartists' to O'Connorville, 'land of the free, / The patriot and reformer':

> Bold was the genius that first plan'd
> That scheme of reformation,
> There is no road but through the land
> To man's regeneration!
> The Jubilee has come at last![17]

There is a nice ambiguity here about whose name is to occupy the place of that bold genius: certainly Davenport is thinking of Spence, and the term 'Jubilee' is millenarian, hearkening back to the 1790s, whilst the proximate referent is O'Connor. But the confusion allows the Land Plan to travel from the rhetoric of late eighteenth-century millenarianism to both the Chartist present and on into the future, as time and space coalesce: 'This land is ours up to the sky, / For ever and for ever.'[18] Read amidst the other poems of 1846, there is no question that this is the poem of an older generation, and that Davenport's is the voice of 'an old and esteemed friend, who has spent at least fifty years of his life in labouring to promote the freedom and happiness of his fellow men'.[19]

At seventy-one, Davenport was more than forty years older than the twenty-seven-year-old Jones, whose 'O'Connorville' poem appeared on the front page of the newspaper, under a large illustration of the estate, and next to a long article describing the procession to the settlement. Jones's poem serves as an official commemorative poem of the day of the 'Grand Demonstration to the Peoples' First Estate'.[20] Jones's poem is written in meditative, iambic pentameter verse. His precursor poet is Crabbe, and he makes a claim to share Crabbe's voice of rural empiricism, while drawing on the revolutionary sources within romantic idealism to produce a critique of Crabbe's dour vision. Jones continued to show interest in Crabbe's work, and in the 1850s, when editing *Notes to the People*, he chose Crabbe as the first in a series on 'The Poets of England'. In fact, excerpts from Crabbe make up the greatest number of non-Chartist poems in that journal's two-year life.[21] Jones's 'O'Connorville' opens on Crabbe's bleak note: rising from his sickbed, which 'yields man slumber, but denies him rest', the mechanic enters the urban oppression of the labouring day. The 'grey finger' of the day 'points the marches of time', coercing the worker to 'the long day slavery's cheerless length'. But today the events are different, and he, along with countless others, march off to O'Connorville. As the workers travel back to the countryside, Jones reverses the familiar tropes of landscaped beauty by metaphorising their economic meaning to the labouring poor: 'English deserts ... / Called *parks*, by grandeur, – but, by truth, a *waste*'.[22] As in Davenport's poem, the poem is structured as a journey, but in Jones's version, the relations between landscape and labouring identity are figured as romantically reciprocal and inter-subjective: the young and old, 'as they leave the smoky towns behind, / Breathe the full blessing of the freshening wind'. Nature in Jones's poem is instinct with the *anima mundi*, different from, but incorporating the discourse of abundance: a moving impulse that 'winds the river like a silvery band, / To bind the scattered glories of the land'. The language of the poem is hardly touched by urban republicanism, but instead suffused with the image of custom's cottage, along with a re-enchanted earth: 'The grateful soil, / That bears its produce for the hands that toil'. While Crabbe's poetry debunks the illusions of rural pastoralism, Jones's 'O'Connorville' girds Crabbe's empiricism to the notions of the 'One Life' endorsed by Wordsworth and Coleridge, but in this case fastened to an immediate and materialised holism. Jerome McGann has made a convincing case for the manner in which Crabbe performed an empiricist critique of romanticism.[23] For his part, Jones produces a romantic critique of Crabbe, but a romanticism grounded in the synthesis of natural abundance, rather than the transcendence of consciousness, and leading not out of the social world, but rather, enriched, back into it.

Jones's poetry is, in fact, marked throughout his career as a Chartist poet by the double trajectory of romanticism, implying both communitarian identity formation, and that of the voluntaristic self. His first published poems in the pages of the *Northern Star*, which coincided with his entry into the political arena as an activist, are immediately recognisable within and conform to the conventions of the communitarian Chartist song and ballad. But because these poems by Jones were written after Chartism had already experienced both its first flowering and its significant defeats in the experiences of 1839 and 1842, there is a super-added elegiac character to them. They emanate a sense of belatedness, which colours their optimism, and which renders them both more self-conscious than the anthems of 1839 and less hopeful than the indignant poems written just after the Newport Uprising: 'Though bleak may be the furrows, / the seed is in the soil.'[24] 'Our Summons' describes how the labour of agricultural workers is used not only to provide luxuries for the rich, but to undermine their own identities and subjectivity: to 'build for broken hearts / the petty parish hell', as well as to 'dig the grave, / Where the dying miner delves'. Although the poem makes reference to the by now well-worn trope of the Norman Yoke to suggest a history of struggle, its chief resource is its immediate depiction of the alienation of labour, the alienation of interiority undergone as labourers are 'Machines cast to neglect, / When your freshness has been used'.[25] Jones's focus on the experience of labour as individual alienation is evident in many of these poems: 'With the wearing of the bone and the drowning of the mind; / [we] Sink like shrivelled parchment in the flesh-devouring soil.'[26]

The four poems which make up Jones's 1846 'Our' sequence: 'Our Summons', 'Our Destiny', 'Our Warning', and 'Our Cheer' attempt to render a feeling of a subjective collectivity – a shared sense of calling, out-come, and power. The songs are noteworthy for the intensity of their sense of collective desire, as well as of collective power, and, importantly, the power of collective revenge. This is appealed to particularly against those radical reformers who have been exposed as being inimical to the interests of labourers. Jones warns that the workers shall both constitute the 'people' and define the people as workers, and that if they are resisted, they 'shall sweep, / Like a mighty Devastation / Of the winds upon the deep'.[27] Jones builds up the figures of social identity, opening up a liberated space of interiority within the realm of the exploited. He also draws upon Shelley's version of intervention, echoing Shelley's frequently reprinted 'Men of England' stanzas, and calling on 'Men of the honest heart' and 'Men of the stalwart hand' to their toil:

> Tis not to dig the grave,
> Where the dying miner delves;
> 'Tis not to toil for others
> But to labour for *yourselves*.[28]

In Jones's assertions of a collective identity in his first experiments within the Chartist poetic, there is something of an attempt to build a place for his own consciousness within that collectivity. Jones poetically carves out a place for his lyrical singularity to become part of a larger collective subjectivity, as he reaches across from his élite educated background to the political movement in front of him. Through his attempt to forge his own links with a movement to which he has become affiliated rather than into which he has been born, Jones brings the resistant edge of individualism to bear on the residual voice of the tradition of song and oral lyrics. He overcomes his own alienation from his class origins by asserting the 'we' voice in his Chartist series. His poetic project is important for the way in which it holds onto the communitarian version of identity from an earlier period, and reinvents it as a possible position for the voluntaristic self to choose. This takes place within poetic conventions that bear the impress of the tradition of radical lyrics from Spence to the myriad poets of 1839 Chartism, but also indicate a possible lyrical outcome linked to contemporary lyrical practice.

Nonetheless, it would take Jones's personal experience of imprisonment and repression, writing his poems 'in his own blood' for him to feel sufficiently integrated into the movement. His assimilation into the milieu constitutes a central element in the narrative of his own poetic vocation within Chartism.[29] But Jones easily picked up and worked within the idiom of Chartist poetry, leaping across the literary élite's habits of condescension.

While Davenport's 'O'Connorville' might be an emblem of a poetic world on its way out, Thomas Cooper, about fifteen years older than Jones, was the near-contemporary whose power as both poet and activist was, as well, a chief model and rival. In Jones's poetic relationship with Thomas Cooper, we can observe another aspect of the generational shifts within the movement. For if Davenport was the voice of the Spencean background to Chartism, Cooper's was the embodiment of the 'Chartist Poet' proper. Although Cooper was to leave this wing of the radical political movement behind, operating as an 'independent Chartist', a Mazzinian, and as a Christian Socialist, he retained the title of 'Chartist Poet', and used it to broker his way into some literary renown in London, to some extent trading on his radical chic.[30] Cooper had a respectful, if at times patronising attitude towards Davenport, eulogising him, and invoking him in order to stake his own claim as a poet, but he was in direct political and poetic competition with Jones. In 1846, Jones was instrumental in Feargus O'Connor's political defeat of Cooper. Jones, surely acting of behalf on, or in accordance with O'Connor's wishes, offered a motion to expel Cooper from the Chartist movement, after Cooper had behaved obstructively at the 1846 Convention.[31] Cooper and O'Connor had seriously fallen out over how to take forward the demands of the Charter: in particular, the question of physical force, and the rôle of O'Connor's Land Plan in the larger political movement. Involved as well in the collapse of their comradeship, it would seem, was O'Connor's botched plan to publish Cooper's prison poem, *The Purgatory of Suicides*. The Convention of the summer of 1846 was, as John Saville says, 'O'Connor's Conference', a moment to consolidate his leadership. Ernest Jones was only just entering the movement, but on a meteoric rise to prominence as both poet and leader.[32] Though social and political historians of the movement have not addressed the question in this manner, my claim here is that a poetic rivalry was part and parcel of the hostility between the men, and that this was played out in the Chartist Convention fracas. Poetry was important to the public work of Chartism, and it also influenced the internal politics of the movement.

In personal history and background, Thomas Cooper was much closer to Allen Davenport than he was to Jones, and Cooper sealed his sense of the legacy in his dedicatory stanzas to Davenport, written after the older poet's death in late November 1846. Just as Davenport had allied himself to Spence through his elegiac stanzas on Spence, so Cooper places himself in the lineage through the set of braided sonnets. The sonnets are subtitled, 'By a Brother Bard and Shoemaker', making the claim for their affinity by heritage as well as that between the artisan trade and poem-making: 'Yes, he of whom I speak, my humble friend, / A poet, too, philosopher – and more'.[33] Born in 1805, Cooper spent his childhood in Gainsborough, near the Trent. Like Davenport, his childhood was bare of luxury, as his mother worked irregularly both as a dyer and a boxmaker, and like Davenport, Cooper learned the trade of shoemaking. He was active in Methodist chapel and Sunday school, and this experience of Methodist and congregational singing was central to his Chartist poem-making in later years.[34] Thomas Cooper joined the Chartist movement in Leicester in 1842, and immediately built the local group into one of the largest sections in

England. Right from the start he associated literature with the political movement, and he insisted that his Charter Association be called The Shakespearean Association of Leicester Chartists.[35] Like his precursor Davenport, Cooper became passionately interested in poetry as a boy, and he exhibits the same combination of bravado and shame. He aimed to master the whole of English poetry: 'I thought it possible that by the time I reached the age of 24 I might . . . commit the entire "Paradise Lost" and seven of the best plays of Shakespeare, to memory.'[36] But he is soon over-whelmed by what he has memorised: 'All this practice seemed to destroy the desire of composing poetry of my own . . . The wondrous knowledge of the heart unfolded by Shakespeare, made me shrink into insignificance.'[37] The Chartist movement offered Cooper an opportunity to further his work as poet as well as activist, and at the high point of Chartist agitation he had his fellow members, who numbered 2,500, reading and writing as well as mobilising politically. The result was the *Shakespearean Chartist Hymn Book*.[38] In 1842, the year in which, Dorothy Thompson writes, 'more energy was hurled against the authorities than any other of the nineteenth century', Cooper was arrested for his involvement in a set of strikes in Staffordshire, and he began a two-year prison sentence in 1843.[39] His work before entering prison had been both politically and poetically at the heart of Chartist intervention, chiefly organisationally, including his presenta-tion of a Welsh song to O'Connor, 'The Lion of Freedom', which was widely popularised in the movement.[40] While in prison, Cooper wrote *The Purgatory of Suicides*, an epic-length Spenserean-stanza visionary poem of progress and reform. In his autobiography, Cooper recounts that he had written about one hundred lines of the poem before going to jail, and that as he did not know if the authorities 'would ever yield to allow me the use of my books and papers, I thought I could defeat their purpose by composing the poem and retaining it in my mind'.[41] Cooper's anecdote of how he turned from his plan, which had been to write the poem in blank verse, to writing it in a Spenserean-stanza, is reminiscent of the way Davenport blurred the boundaries between print and oral cultures. The blank-verse ideal of a Miltonic epic was impossible to undertake in jail, where Cooper had to memorise his lines in order to preserve them: 'when I had composed the four opening lines, I found they rhymed alternately. It was a pure accident – for I always purposed to write my poem in blank verse'. But Cooper recoups this fall from print to oral conventions when he decides to 'try the Spenserean stanza', which the example of Byron had shown 'to be capable of as much grandeur and force as the blank verse of "Paradise Lost."'[42]

Although, as we have seen, the movement had generated poems dealing with exile and prison written in prison, which had inflected the propaganda poems in a new direction, Cooper's book-length poem took Chartist poetry into a far more literary avenue than before, and as Bouthaina Shaaban writes in the only extended discussion of Cooper's *Purgatory*, the work, with its dense allusiveness and recondite knowledge is 'an almost impossible text for working-class men [to have made sense of] and not a very easy one for middle-class readers either'.[43] Cooper's poem is a ten-book dream vision poem, in which a Shelleyan visionary is transported to an extraterrestrial vantage point where he observes both the tyranny of autocracy through the ages, and, as well, observes the possibility of a new world; however, he then awakes, 'to find my home / A dungeon'.[44] With this poem, Cooper shifted poetic gears from the interventionist to the retrospective and elegiac. After the defeats and imprisonments which followed on from the agitation of 1848, it would be Ernest Jones's *The New World* which would provide the major Chartist prison poem for the following period, and it is noteworthy that his long poem both takes a rather more hopeful view of the possibilities of social change, and is also less mediated by literary allusiveness.

So in 1846 Cooper was half in and half out of the movement, leaning towards the more élite and liberal stratum of poetical activity. And this is paralleled by his mixed relations to O'Connor as the year went on. While he had earlier been a physical-force Chartist, in prison Cooper moved to a moral-force position, and began to distance himself from O'Connor. He was against O'Connor's Land Plan, and thought that O'Connor was siphoning off Land Plan subscribers' monies to support the *Northern Star* instead.[45] This accounts for the absence of any Cooper poems on the topic in a year of the *Northern Star*'s focus on it, which included the reprinting of Spence's land poems.[46] It also appears that O'Connor half-heartedly tried to arrange for the *Northern Star* publisher, McGowan, to undertake the printing of *The Purgatory of Suicides*, but then rescinded the offer, leaving Cooper to find his literary patronage outside the movement altogether. Cooper then called upon and was helped in this effort by Disraeli.[47] Cooper was soon preoccupied with the interest shown in his work by the radical Unitarian, W. J. Fox, whose *Monthly Repository* had earlier been supportive of a certain strain of working-class poetry; an interest which no doubt also urged Cooper towards a more politically liberal position.[48] As he narrates this period in his *Life*, it was the letter of praise he received from Carlyle and his subsequent visit to Wordsworth which established Cooper's trajectory into the high literary world.[49] Cooper's anecdote of

Wordsworth is illuminating, for he tells the story of his visit to Wordsworth in such a way as to signal his own place in a tradition which can include both himself and Wordsworth (he tells us that Wordsworth had read his poem and praised it), and which links him to Wordsworth politically as well. Wordsworth joins Cooper in his developing criticism of O'Connor and physical-force Chartism: "'You were quite right", he said; "I have always said the people were right in what they asked; but you went the wrong way to get it."'[50] Their encounter ended in mutual admiration of Tennyson.[51]

The picture of himself that Cooper painted when he wrote his reminiscences in the 1870s pivots around this entry into the élite literary world. The Chartist movement seemed to him to have hardened into O'Connor's personal scheme, and over the next twenty years Cooper moved in and out of the various radical political milieux, sometimes wearing the identity of a Christian Socialist, sometimes a Republican, and sometimes as the hoary 'Old Chartist'. For once the mass force of the Chartist movement was truly felt to have abated, a mythic version of the 'Old Chartist' became available to respectable society through illustrations, such as Sandys' mass-produced print of the same name, and Meredith's dry poem, 'The Old Chartist'.[52] In 1853, Cooper was still able to reaffirm himself as an old Chartist, appealing to fellow veterans to 'gather once more around the old flag'.[53]

In broadest terms, then, Jones and Cooper were on opposite social trajectories, the déclassé gentleman and the aspiring autodidact. Yet both men, like Davenport before them, forged their poetic vocations through a revised version of poetry as political intervention. When their own political careers foundered or went into abeyance in keeping with the demise of Chartism itself, they aimed towards the liberal respectability that was now characterising poetry and politics. But while he was an activist, and while in prison, Cooper was unimpeachable, and paid a substantial material and cultural cost for his commitments. When he was offered a place at Cambridge in exchange for renouncing his Chartism, Cooper replied:

I would not degrade or falsify myself by making such a promise ... if you shall ensure all the honours the University could bestow, although it has been one of the great yearnings of my heart – from a boy, I might say – to go to a University.[54]

And though one part of Cooper's poetic activity was drawing him, after his imprisonment, nearer to the liberal hegemony, in 1846 he was nonetheless still actively involved in the Chartist poetry promoted in the pages of the *Northern Star*. In the 3 January issue, Cooper inserted a short item calling on all 'rhyming brethren' within the movement to submit their poems for a 'collection of patriotic minstrelsy, that could be used in our public meetings for congregational singing' and that would serve as a second volume of the Hymn Book he had assembled in 1842.[55] In his appeal, Cooper mixes together the rhetoric of oppositional patriotism, the mythic dimensions of a suppressed bardic tradition long associated with oppositional patriotism, and the experience of Methodist hymn-singing, which had provided the main fund of Cooper's agitational poetics before his imprisonment. Juxtaposed to his later recollections of this period, what becomes visible is his sense of how the poetic mission of the movement was bifurcating into 'high' and 'low' components, and as he was now the author of a massive and erudite epic poem, he assumed the rôle of educator and anthologist. While reserving the final decision for inclusion in the volume for himself alone, 'for if this business be left to many, there might be some difficulty in determining what to insert, and what to reject, and the collection might be a mere hodgepodge besides', Cooper eagerly casts the net amongst the whole of the committed: 'I trust that everyone who possesses any degree of a poet's nature, and prides himself on the name of Chartist, will be forward to contribute.'[56]

Only two issues later, however, a letter appeared from another Chartist, John Mathias, writing in from Rotherhithe, Surrey, complaining of Cooper's 'arbitrary censorship of the different contributions which may be sent'.[57] Mathias goes on to make the poetic point rest upon a political principle: 'Mr. C., as a Chartist, knows our principles to be, that all shall legislate for all. If a song book is wanted, let a committee be chosen who can settle the merits of the different contributions in verse.'[58] This is an interesting moment, because, as the *Northern Star*'s editor defends Cooper's work, he defends the idea that not all Chartist poetry is equal, and that there are aesthetic reasons to make claims about selection beyond that simply of enthusiasm. The editor replies indignantly to Mathias, supporting Cooper as an 'honour to his class and party'.[59] The following week Cooper defends himself, but also takes the opportunity to wash his hands of the entire endeavour. He urges his correspondent to 'see the difference between one man arrogating to himself the right to "legislate for all", and a poor rhymer offering to select from the contributions of his brother rhymers pieces proper to form a volume'.[60] Cooper is clearly offended by the attack, promises that he 'can certainly spend my time much more beneficially, in a pecuniary and personal sense' and then withdraws from the project.[61]

From then on, Cooper's will be the rôle of the Poet Laureate of Chartism, distinguished from the rank and file of 'rhyming brethren', and he will be as interested in being known as such amongst the liberal literary worlds as amongst his Chartist 'brother rhymers'. An index of the strength of liberalism in the 1850s will be the growing nostalgic cachet of the Chartist poet. His reply to Mathias is also noteworthy for its allusion to Allen Davenport: 'I cannot omit expressing regret that such poetry as that which has been sent to me by Allen Davenport . . . should not be, at once, given to the world.'[62] Cooper here hints at the formulation of a corpus of Chartist poets in which Davenport is a chief originary figure, Cooper his heir.

Later in the year, in July 1846, Davenport published an appreciative poem to Cooper, 'The Midnight Dream', saluting the *Purgatory of Suicides* as 'A Prison Rhyme' that might awaken the world 'from its profound repose', and ignite a new generation to 'Truth'. But Davenport writes as if in rather too much awe of the achievement. Cooper's transition from the congregational Chartist song to the poetry of reflection in the lengthy *Purgatory* has its drawbacks. Davenport admits in his dedication that though 'I have not read it all' he is sure that 'I have read enough to know that such a poem could emanate from no common mind.'[63] Davenport's own desires for entry into literary respectability are etched into his language here, as 'common' crosses over from his use of it in 'The Poet's Hope' to mean a collective 'common fate' to the class-inflected meaning of common as 'crude'. Davenport interprets Cooper in relation to his own self-conception of being both part of the community and also standing apart, a sole self.

In May 1846, a large commemorative event took place to celebrate the one-year anniversary of Cooper's release from prison. At this festive dinner Cooper was publicly heralded in the Chartist Hall in London as 'Labour's Laureate, the Poet of Chartism' by a group of two hundred people.[64] Letters were read honouring Cooper's achievement, including ones from recognised members of the middle-class reform movement, W. J. Fox and Douglas Jerrold. Cooper was lauded for 'emerging from his prison, after suffering bodily pain and mental anguish for upwards of two years, with that gem [*The Purgatory of Suicides*] under his arm, which had given Chartism "a local habitation and name". (Loud cheers).'[65] Having been central in promoting the general production of poetry within the movement, Cooper is now apotheosised as the Chartist poet par excellence. His work is compared with that of those writers who wrote *about* but not *from* the movement, 'journalists, preachers, and novelists', who 'had either presented monsters altogether unlike Chartism, or mock portraits which wanted vitality, but it was reserved for Cooper to diffuse abroad the real essence of Chartism, clothed in the language of genius (Loud Cheers).'[66] Cooper 'was then presented with a poetic crown of laurel, and an olive branch.' At the end of the speeches, Feargus O'Connor, apparently hedging his bets, rose, 'rapturously applauded', according to his newspaper's account, and made the point that 'the tongue of scandal had been busy in asserting that he (Mr. O'Connor) was opposed to this night's proceedings, than which nothing could be more false'.[67] O'Connor was not blind to the cultural significance of Cooper as a *bona fide* 'Chartist Poet', whose very functioning in that capacity lent intellectual credibility to the movement, and O'Connor aimed to stay in amicable relations with Cooper. Yet only a few months after this O'Connor saw to it that Cooper was out of the movement, using as his weapon the *newer* and more charismatic 'Chartist Poet', Ernest Jones.

For Jones was a very explosive weapon indeed, whose power derived from his combination of personal, poetical, and political resources. In his 'Songs for the People' series, all published in the spring of 1846, Jones unexpectedly reinvigorated the collective poetic model of the 1839–40 period, but with a literary confidence that Thomas Cooper only attained after years of autodidacticism and experiment. But if Jones arrived on the scene with literary skill, and quickly became O'Connor's political apprentice, he nonetheless had to prove himself as an activist.

Jones's appearance in the pages of the *Northern Star* in 1846 disrupted the rather elegant mirroring and mutual admiration of Allen Davenport and Thomas Cooper, in which Labour Laureate saluted the Old Spencean-Chartist. Jones's intervention was as a ruling-class renegade, allying himself with what he saw as the new class forces. The first mention of Ernest Jones in the Chartist press occurs in a letter to 'Brother Chartists' on the front page of the *Northern Star*, 9 May 1846, in which he offers himself as a delegate to the next Convention, and explains that his principle desire is to 'see a government that governs for the general good, instead of individual interest'.[68] This is followed on the Poetry Page of the same issue by a short article about him, 'A New Poet', in which a combination of reticence and enthusiasm meets this newly self-proclaimed Chartist: 'Mr. Jones feels that he has a mission to perform, and we doubt not but that some one or more localities will accept his services, if on closer acquaintance his views are found in accordance with those held by the great body of the Chartists.'[69] Jones's poetic vocation as a Chartist was inextricably tied to his political activity. This was certainly a romantic inheritance, but one which, in the context of a mass movement, he was able to make good on through avenues of popular poetics unavailable to Wordsworth, or Shelley, or Byron. The *Northern Star* article goes on to quote sections of Jones's *My Life*. This poem, which was written in the year before Jones's passage to Chartism, is a narrative romance set in an aristocratic ambience, and is prefaced by some interesting passages which describe the reasons why a gentry youth might defect from his destined social path. Jones explores the lack of opportunity for moral public behaviour amongst the ruling élite: so, youth begins idealistically, and is then corrupted by convention and social conformity:

> At first I have beheld him burn,
> Then stand – then waver – and then turn!
> How few could brave – how few could shun
> The many bearing on the one.[70]

The poem as a whole echoes Byron as it focuses on the alienation of self-identity, with its corollary impulse towards self-irony. The very opening of the poem, which is not cited in the *Northern Star* extracts, employs the axioms of romantic individualism: 'My life has been a wild, strange life.' Imaged as a solitary, yet aware that all the people of his élite milieu have an emptiness at their core, Jones speaks as the representative of individual isolation. 'There's prison-life in open plain, / Without a dungeon or a chain.'[71] The ennui, however, can be broken by the desire to struggle for 'freedom', where freedom is conceived as an abstraction, a matter of consciousness. Along with 'The Better Hope', a poem which appeared the following year in his pamphlet, *Chartist Songs*, this poetic material is the closest thing we have to an autobiographical account of the motivations behind Jones's turn to activism in 1846.[72]

There was no obvious reason for Jones to shift from the idler comforts of the ironic stance to the difficulties of agitational optimism. For though Ernest Jones was born in what Allen Davenport had called that 'perilous year' 1819, in Berlin, his parentage was élite. His father was an English Major who had fought at Waterloo, and his mother came from a landowning family in Kent.[73] He was ripe for admission into the ranks of Radical Toryism, but he refused that narrative telos.

We might say that Jones matured politically at a moment when social origin, or place in the narrative of sociality meets up with the voluntarism of identification – Jones's experience of *a priori* inwardness allows him to *choose* to identify with the working class. Jones's path was downwardly mobile: this is in no small measure to be attributed to his schooling in romanticism. He was available, that is, to the democratic and utopian and communitarian claims of Chartism via his grounding in the double trajectory of romanticism. And Chartism itself was invigorated by the intellectual resources and cosmopolitanism that Jones brought with him along with his acute sensibility. As John Belchem and James Epstein have recently argued: 'The independence of the gentleman leader, committed only to the programme and forces of radicalism, mirrored radicalism's own independence and reliance upon the support of an oppressed and excluded "people."'[74]

Jones had a particularly intense experience of inwardness, developed and trained through his early awakening to poetic vocation. As a child, Jones's literary ambitions had been indulged by his parents, and in 1830, when he was eleven years old, his father arranged for the publication of a volume of the boy's *Infantine Effusions*. A letter from his father to the publisher boasts of the work as being 'superior to those [juvenilia] which were published of our celebrated poets, Cowley and Pope, at 12 and 15 years of age'.[75] Jones's earliest work is marked by German romanticism, and marbled with veins of nationalism and royalism as well. A set of verses written on the French Revolution encapsulates this style. He writes of Marie-Antoinette, 'O! Beauteous! Murder'd – injured, Martyr'd Queen! / The heart vibrates to grief o-er thy last scene! / With pity in its inmost core, will bleed.'[76] But his pre-Chartist poetry is important less for its subject matter than for the kind of free-floating sentimentality that pervades his idiom. When the family returned to London in 1838, Jones brought with him a manuscript of verses, and he appears, from his unpublished diaries between 1839 and 1845, to have devoted himself to his literary aspirations, while training as a barrister and making a good marriage. Jones's poetry and his diary from this period, suggest the self-consciousness of the romantic which offered to him an apprenticeship in interiority that he later infused into the ballad rhythms and popular customary rhetoric of plebeian communitarian lyric forms. Between 1840 and 1842 some of these poems appeared in the periodicals of the conservative élite in London, such as *The Court Journal*, poems which included the forgettable lines of 'To Her': 'To love, and to love hopelessly, / It is a bitter lot.'[77] Jones's pre-Chartist poetry aims for a timelessness-in-time atmosphere, and imposes romantic subjectivity upon renaissance themes of the immortality of poetry, as for example, in a 'Song', which describes the contest between time and the poet, in which the poet's 'sign' may 'survive the wreck': 'Thus man erects, and plans and forms, / But time, like ocean's wrath in storms, / Destroys what he has done.'[78]

But the twenty-year-old who wrote in his diary in 1839, 'Splendidly splendid day of Splendour. There is an air! There is a sky! There is a gentle breeze! There are perfumes! Splendidly splendid day of Splendour', was not consistently successful in getting his work published: a few years later, now twenty-three years old, he writes in his diary on 3 August 1842, 'Refusals and misses', 'Numberless refusals of work ... by almost *all* the magazines and publishers'.

In 1846, Jones's life changed utterly. There is little mention of politics in his diary before 1846, with the exception of a letter written to the Anti-Corn Law League in 1844.[79] The first indication of a public intervention comes in an entry for 28 January: 'I went to McGowan, Printer of *Northern Star* ... Spoke over the Chartist organisation. Gave a copy of "My Life."' His diary then notes attendance at various Chartist meetings. A few months later, on 5 May, Jones called on O'Connor, and his article and poem appeared in the 9 May issue of the paper. Given the hostility between O'Connor and Cooper at the time, O'Connor may well have seen in Jones a possible successor to Cooper as the 'official' Chartist poet, and this may have been part of the reason why Jones's career within the movement took off so rapidly. Jones's 'gentlemanly' mien may have been part of his appeal for O'Connor, whose own 'bearing was decidedly aristocratic'.[80] In 1847, *The New Quarterly Review*, which had earlier given a kind review to Jones's *My Life*, made this succession explicit which was then quoted in the *Leeds Times*:

As poet, [Jones] has taken the place of Thomas Cooper ... Ernest Jones is in every respect the greater poet of the two. He is infinitely more vigorous, and more pointed, and yet far more ideal and imaginative when he so pleases.[81]

The article goes on to describe Cooper's *Purgatory of Suicides* as 'lengthy and inartistic'.[82]

The spring and summer of 1846 were exhilarating seasons for Jones. He immersed himself in the democratic and radical world of London, going to many meetings, including a Bastille Day anniversary celebration put on by the Fraternal Democrats, and on 18 July he was elected 'Permanent Chairman' of the Polish Committee.[83] No doubt these opportunities arose in response to his increasing prominence as Feargus O'Connor's protégé, and as gentleman and internationalist. Through this same period, Jones's poems appear fast and furiously in the *Northern Star*, opening up a new zone of poetic activity between the nostalgic poetics of Davenport and the increasing high-handedness of Cooper. Jones's two streams of work – political and poetical – supported each other. Jones's talents and skills as a poet give him a clear-cut task within the Chartist propaganda, filling Cooper's place with ease and with new energy. Jones not only wrote the 'Our' sequence, in ballad measure, but also contributed experimental poems such as 'The Cornfield and the Factory', which appeared in the *Northern Star*'s June 1846 'Feast of the Poets' feature. This poem juxtaposes a first section of varying rhythms, describing a village scene of great merriment, to a second section which shows how factory life blots out the sun:

> The very sun shines pale on a dark earth
> Where quivering engines groan their horrid mirth,
> And black smoke-offerings, crimes and curses, swell
> From furnace-altars of incarnate hell![84]

In the midst of this active period, when the pages of his diary sizzle with excitement about meetings and speeches and demonstrations, is the short, sharp entry for 3 August: 'Expelled Cooper.'

The Leeds Chartist Convention, which Feargus O'Connor had convened to take place shortly before the demonstration and dedication of the O'Connorville estate, was a critical moment for the movement. It was on this occasion that Cooper and O'Connor publicly broke. Cooper was deeply suspicious of the Land Plan, and he tried to disrupt the proceedings. Only the day before Jones had given a rousing public speech at a mass meeting of over 25,000 people at Blackstone Edge, a site on the Pennine moors where mass meetings had been held throughout the Chartist agitation, which he then commemorated with a song which appeared in the *Northern Star* a few weeks later:

His style of oratory was just suited for such an occasion. He had a fine sonorous voice which could be heard at a long distance; his command of language was superior to most; his delivery was fluent, impressive, and often impassioned. His song, commemorative of that great gathering, [was] sung with enthusiasm at the Chartist meetings of 1846, 1847, and 1848.[85]

Blackstone Edge, like other sites of mass meetings, was a sublime landscape, and emphasised the orator as romantic freedom-fighter, who aimed to remind the mass of its rights to the land.[86] Jones's 'Blackstone Edge' song, like many of his other poems, is noteworthy for the way in which it reinforces the imagery of industrialisation, now interweaving artisan themes and topics with those of a more clearly urban proletariat, and so marking the chasm between the people's farm and the factory. Jones specifies more clearly than did Davenport or Cooper a poetic which draws on the rhetoric of class division:

> Though hunger stamped each forehead spare,
> And eyes were dim with factory glare,
> Loud swelled the nation's battle prayer,
> Of – death to class monopoly.[87]

It is not surprising that his pride and enthusiasm would have led him into the Leeds Convention with a sense of mission, and of power. O'Connor profited by that confidence, and Jones, though new to the movement, did the work of moving the expulsion, arguing that Cooper was being obstructive to the proceedings, as he kept raising demands for O'Connor to produce financial accounts.[88] So it happened that the new Chartist poet unseated the old, and their interaction at the Convention was spoken in the rhetoric of poetic rivalry. When Cooper made the claim that since Jones was 'a man of genius' he should be ashamed of moving the expulsion, Jones replied, filled with his experience of Blackstone Edge: '[I have] been in the highways of Chartism and seen thousands of the veritable though not enrolled Chartists on Blackstone Edge, and heard the thunder of their cheers.'[89] This episode is structured in the image of the Byronic hero: unknowable as a self, but capable of great bravery, and inspiring to those who struggle for freedom. The confrontation between the two men has an almost mythic status in the narrative of poetic vocation. According to Howell's account:

In the matter of courage, and in a modified sense, temper, no two men were better matched than Jones and Cooper. Cooper was inflexible, firm to a degree. Jones was hot and fiery, and equally firm. Cooper paid Jones a high compliment, 'as a man of genius,' an indication of his own recognition of him, as writer, and orator . . . The faults of Jones in this connection were faults of zeal, of youth, and inexperience in political turmoil.[90]

But faulty or not, Jones's public work that day put him into a competitive relationship with Cooper, and one result was Jones's instantiation as chief Chartist poet. A few weeks later the O'Connorville celebrations took place, where Jones again made a speech, and saw, that same week, his commemorative poem printed on the front page of the *Northern Star*. On 30 September he records in his diary that O'Connor has named him Secretary to the Second Section of the Land Society. We also learn from this entry that the strain and excitement of the spring and summer had taken its toll on him, and he had just arisen from being confined to bed for a month.[91]

While there remains some obscurity about the catalysts that led Jones to become an activist Chartist, there is no question that once he became a Chartist he blossomed as a poet, and acquired a strong sense of where his poetic intervention might take him. In one of the fullest entries in his diary from 1846, he expresses this desire and plan:

I am pouring the tide of my songs over England, forming the tone of the mighty mind of the people, Wonderful! Vicissitudes of life, – rebuffs and disappoint-ments countless in literature – [?] toil of business – dreadful domestic catastrophes – domestic bickerings – almost destitution – hunger – labour of mind and body – have left me, through a wonderful providence of God, as enthusiastic of mind, – as ardent of temper, – as fresh of heart – mind as strong of frame, as ever! I am prepared to rush, fresh and strong, into the strife or struggles of a nation, to ride the torrent, or guide the rill, if God permits.[92]

After his illness in September, Jones began attending Chartist meetings, and also saw the publication of a pamphlet of his songs as *Chartist Poems*, which went through at least five reprintings between October and the close of the year.[93]

'The Better Hope', the opening poem in the collection, offers insights into Jones's notions of the poet's mission as a political poet. He again describes himself as an aristocrat, 'With a rich old name', brought up in 'My father's house, in the lordly square, / [...] cold in its solemn state'. He recounts that he had aimed to go into the 'laughing world', but discovered as

> I wandered past hamlet and town,
> I listened for laughter and song:
> But man with a frown cast humanity down,
> And tyranny gloried in wrong.

While the opening sections of *My Life* were suffused with the ironic Byronic disappointment in sociality, in 'The Better Hope' Jones offers a more concrete explanation for alienation; namely, the results of the oppression of industrialism:

> For a giant had risen all grisly and grim,
> With his huge limbs, loud clattering, and vast,
> And he breathed his steam-breath – through long channels
> of death
> Till the soul itself died on the blast.

Frightened, the speaker is at first tempted to return to the comforts of his father's house:

> Then I looked back for my cold quiet home
> As the hell-bound looks back for the grave;
> But I heard my soul cry – who but cowards can fly
> While a tyrant yet tramples a slave?

The final lines of the poem adumbrate the voice of William Morris in his *Pilgrims of Hope* sequence, as the outsider joins forces with the labouring class:

> Then I bound on my armour to face the rough world,
> And I'm going to march with the rest,
> Against tyrants to fight – for the sake of the right,
> And, if baffled, to fall with the best.

1846, then, exhibits an interesting moment in the vicissitudes of Chartist poetry and poetics, as the *Northern Star* stages an engagement amongst the poetic work and values of three poets: Davenport, the old-timer; Cooper, the achieved autodidact, and Jones, the refugee from the élite seeking a rôle in the politico-poetics of social and political change.

The cultural meaning of Chartist poetry has shifted from being an organic element of a grass-roots movement to a particular branch of work of the movement, with its own complement of experts. Davenport's language is no longer readily available to the contemporary world, except insofar as Spencean land ideas coalesce with those of O'Connor, within the romantic-derived poetic language of the abundant landscape. In an obituary in the *Northern Star* Davenport's poetry is patronised:

If, in the lists of poets, we cannot rank Allen Davemport very high, we may at least award him the high praise that his simple verses were always devoted to the advance of virtue, intellect and freedom.[94]

Cooper has moved towards the liberal literary milieu, and we can begin to see how the inchoate ideologies, or perhaps more precisely, the 'structures of feeling' of individualism and communitarianism within interventionist poetics ally themselves, within Chartism, to the political practices which will merge into the political milieux of Liberalism and Socialism.

But the process is dialectical as well, and Jones's reinvigoration of the collective song of the 1839 period is heightened and deepened by his insights into the romantic affirmation of the isolated self, whose consciousness is now yoked back to the collectivity in struggle. The story of Jones's poetico-political career between 1847 and 1869 traces the shifting fortunes of the communitarian poetic within the tradition of romanticism as a corollary to the diminishing fortunes of Chartism in relation to Liberalism. Though the narrative of his poetic ends with Jones's return to the sentimentalism of his pre-Chartist œuvre, the impact of his poetic experimentation offered a strong element of continuity to the next generation.

If 1846 was Jones's *annus mirabilis*, 1847 was also a year of immense literary and political activity for him, and one in which he took an even fuller political rôle in the movement. Benefiting from his popularity as a literary voice, Jones and O'Connor that year together edited and published *The Labourer* (1847-48), as a literary supplement to the *Northern Star*. The purpose of the journal is stated in a prefatory article:

Convinced that all which elevates the feelings, or heightens the aspirations, can but strengthen the political power of a people, we have placed poetry and romance side by side with politics and history.[95]

The poetry which appears in *The Labourer* was written for the most part by Jones himself, augmented by some poems by the prolific and extremely talented W. J. Linton, a republican whose work appears across the democratic press from 1839 through the 1880s. There is nothing of Thomas Cooper's work in the supplement. The journal is severely regulated aesthetically. Jones may have received many unsolicited poems, in the custom of the *Northern Star* in the earlier period, but none are published, and there is a cold reply to a correspondent who appears to have attempted to pass his work off as Linton's, using Linton's pen-name, 'Spartacus', and offering a poem called 'A Court Fool'. Jones tartly replies: 'No "Court Fool" could have written the verses with that signature, [for] any "Spartacus" [the slave who led a rebellion against the Romans] is worthy of the name he assumes.'[96]

The Labourer was launched in an economically difficult year in Britain, and the unrest which had characterised the period between 1838–42 was to be repeated in 1847–48. Jones was alert to the power of literary presentation in shaping the face of the movement, and the voice of *The Labourer* and, indeed, Jones's work generally in this period aimed to speak in the language of a general democratic literary movement, but with a focus on the situation of the workers as a source of agency. Alongside Jones's increased attention to the situation of the industrial workers, and to formulating the terms of the contest as that between labour and capital, a result of his acquaintance with both Marx and Engels, Jones exerted his poetic rhetoric to link the experiences of workers in factories with those of agricultural labourers.[97]

One of Jones's most striking poems in the *The Labourer* is 'The Factory Town', a poem which argues that the factory workers have the power, at their urban places of production, to transform the world of the countryside, and to reclaim the land. Though this poem is written in four-beat song measure, its very great number of stanzas means that it was not likely to have been sung. It uses the oral form as an atavistic, not an active form, and its intended audience appears to encompass both activists and literary readers. The poem also offers a measure of the distance travelled from the categories of plebeian communitarianism of Shelley's 'The Mask of Anarchy' to mid-century working-class solidarity as it translates Shelley's argument for passive resistance into a contemporary, dialectical counterpart. Shelley's crowd is mown down by the State; in Jones's poem the power of working factory hands is sufficient to win the combat without exerting physical force:

> Fear ye not your masters' power;
>   Men are strong when men unite;
> Fear ye not one stormy hour;
>   *Banded millions need not fight.*[98]

In his pre-Chartist poem, *My Life*, Jones had concluded the opening reflective section by describing how his poetic craft had changed as his sense of social dismay had increased: 'I've half unlearned the Poet's art / And only kept the Poet's heart.'[99] He suggests that the poetry of print culture had to be unlearned. The power of 'The Factory Town' arises from Jones's ability to translate the expressive capability of individualist subjectivity into the shapes of the collective experience. Jones begins by providing images for the alienation of labour in industrial production, in which the difference is effaced between the human body and what it makes. The alienation is double: first, the labourer's labour is separated from him, and reified into the made products, and then again as he himself is reified, and deprived of his self-identity:

> Yet the master proudly shows
>   To foreign strangers factory scenes:
> 'These are men – and engines those –'
>   'I see nothing but – *machines!*'

Jones then draws on the expressivity of romantic landscape imagery, in which a correspondent breeze between inner and outer worlds is harnessed, not to the inclusive sympathetic mutuality of self and landscape, but to a sublime activity against oppression:

> And the winds with anthems ringing,
>   Cleaving clouds, and splitting seas,
> Seem unto the People singing:
>   'Break your chains as we do these!'

The poem attends to the factory worker's mental processes. This is the 'thought-treasure' that is robbed from the deadened brains of child operatives. In the false moralism of the economy of boss and labour, the despair that leads the factory workers to suicide is reckoned to be a sin:

> Still, the reign of guilt to further,
>> Lord and slave the crime divide:
> For the master's sin is *murder*,
>> And the workman's – *suicide!*

While the central sections of 'The Factory Town' probe at the meaning of consciousness on the shop floor, the conclusion of the poem winds round to the communitarian rhetoric of the commoner's fantasy. For the end result of the factory workers' revolt will be a return to the farm, in the image of O'Connor's Land Plan. The Spencean poetic of landscape abundance is assimilated to the Chartist Land Plan, but the modernity of the stanzas that had described the alienated subjectivity of factory labour stands out sharply against the recourse to the 'happy village ... smiling o'er the plain, / Amid the corn-field's pleasant tillage, / And the orchard's rich domain!' In places, the imagery of a proletariat with power starkly transforms the sentimentality of the pastoralism:

> with rotting roof and rafter
> Drops the factory, stone by stone,
> Echoing loud with children's laughter.

One feature, then, of Jones's contribution to the poetic of Chartism, was his transmuting of custom-based communitarian poetry into more obviously industrial and class-based poems, and endowing them with a firmer sense of the agency of the workers, though working with a poetic vocabulary that had been available for over seventy years. The terms of 'master' and 'slave' now refer to the waged relation of boss and worker; the village now refers to the smallholdings scheme of O'Connor's Land Plan. One result of this is that Jones helped create a poetic of community which is voluntaristic rather than inherited. For Jones, the legacy of plebeian communitarianism has been intertwined with the hegemony of lyric solitude: the song bears the mark of the subject. What is gained in the transaction is an unmooring of collective affiliation from either customary filiation or social origin – the family, the parish, the counters of the moral economy – and its recovery as choice and solidarity. And this refiguring of the customary plebeian as an urban proletarian made possible two significant modifications. First, it opened up a place for an increased attention to the individual: the Land Plan itself was more open to the notions of individual achievement and privacy. But it also allowed a refiguring of the nationalist discourse of customary rhetoric (which, in places, is functionally indistinguishable from Tory Radicalism) into the language of internationalism. In this way, within the dialectic of romanticism, the individualist voice of subjectivity harnessed to the residues of the customary, opens up the insularity of that customary collectivity to voluntary association, and renders it liable to the internationalist language of socialism: 'My country is the world, and the nation I belong to is the most numerous of all; the nation of the oppressed . . . To me the world forms but two camps: the rich and the poor – and in the latter I am a soldier'.[100] Jones's poetry of solidarity through choice suggests as well that the on-going division of Chartist poetic labour, through which he came to occupy a position as poet-leader, needs to be set against and not assimilated to the alienation of labour that his poetry traces and tracks.

As editor of *The Labourer*, Jones was now in a position to make literary policy as well as poems, and the journal ran a regular 'Literary Review' article. His characterisation of Shelley in one of these articles offers an apt description of his own poetical project in the late 1840s: Shelley 'had the happy power of never swerving from a practical aim in his most ideal productions'. Later in this same essay, Jones sounds a note which William Morris will develop: 'A man can be practical enough – and *common-place*. A man can be ideal enough – and *unintelligible*. Few attain the height of combining the Beautiful with the Useful.'[101]

Jones was working his way towards a more complexly interrelated social and economic analysis, in which the class lines between working class and owning class are more visibly present to him, and the constitution of classes more explicitly discrete. From this level of analytical confidence, Jones makes the case that other sectors of society should recognise their identity of interests with the workers: the movement needs to 'show to all sections of the community, how their interests are identical with those of the working classes'.[102] Confident of the coherence of the working class as an entity and an agent, Jones is able, in *The Labourer*, to make a stronger appeal to the literary world outside the boundaries of Chartism proper. In contrast to Thomas Cooper, who was pursuing personal recognition within liberal literary circles, Jones admonishes those liberal democratic poets also to choose Chartism:

Chartism is marching into the fields of literature with rapid strides . . . Its poetry is, indeed, the freshest and most stirring of the age . . . Yet, from many we have expected more . . . What is Robert Browning doing? . . . Has he nothing to say for popular rights? Let him . . . ascend into the cottage of the poor.[103]

While Cooper looks for affirmation from the literary élite, Jones's confident positioning as a gentleman radical allows him to make a larger claim, and to promise the movement's affirmation of the liberal poets if they will cross over to Chartism:

We say to the great minds of the day, come among the people, write for the people, and your fame will live for ever.[104]

Here Jones affirms the meaning of 'the people' as the labouring class, and disputes the contemporary liberal assertions of 'the people' as the middle class.

Jones was active in the Chartist agitation of 1848, the year that marks the last surge of a mass platform for the Chartist programme.[105] Jones was a principal marcher and speaker in the large demonstration on Kennington Common, and he delivered the third petition to the House of Commons, a document so long it had to be carried in three hansom cabs, as the mass demonstration was dispersed and disabled by the massive government policing presence.[106] Reprisals began a few weeks into May and June. Jones was arrested in Manchester on 6 June 1848, a few days after giving a speech at Bishopsgate.[107] Tried with five other London Chartists for riot and sedition, he was committed to jail for a two-year sentence of solitary confinement.[108]

Jones's poetry prior to his imprisonment in 1848 engages chiefly with the genres of the Chartist hymn and song, in which he aimed to imagine and lyricise the experience of the group struggle, modified by his own steeping in the lyricism of romantic solitude. His prison poetry moves towards defining a collective subjectivity and identity from an opposing source, his individual experience in jail. In his prison lyrics, Jones draws on the resources of the group to find solace and overcome his sense of personal isolation: his very body becomes the scene of a drawing together of multitudes, as his mind, and then the circulation of his blood are magnified and expanded:

> They told me 'twas a fearful thing
> To pine in prison lone:
> The brain became a shrivelled scroll,
> The heart a living stone.
>
> . . .
>
> Like conquerors bounding to the goal,
> Where cold, white marble gleams,
> Magnificent red rivers! Roll! –
> Roll all you thousand streams![109]

Jones's prison experience left a deep mark on his poetry. He returns to speaking about his own identity, convinced now that he truly shares a comradely link to others' suffering oppression. He published his prison poems as a group in *Notes to the People*, the journal he started in 1851, shortly after he was released from prison. The poems are prefaced with a dedica-

tion to 'Fellow Sufferers': 'Brothers! accept the offering of a fellow
captive.'[110] The assertion of his identity with workers, which had been
willed by Jones up until this point, now becomes a truth of his shared
experience with fellow prisoners. In places, his prison poems return to the
earlier romantic conventions of Byronic solitude:

> Loud shouts have beaten on my tingling brain;
> Lone prisons thrilled the fevered thread of life;
> The trophies perish – but the wrecks remain!
> And burning scars survive the dizzy strife.[111]

But in other places it is the bearing of his experience amongst comrades
which grounds the poem, and any incipient solipsism is rescued by this
experimentation with correspondent subjectivities. For example, in
'Earth's Burdens', the poem's speaker listens to the voice of the earth.
Romantic maternal Nature is enlarged, and Jones deepens the figure of
Shelley's Earth in 'The Mask of Anarchy':

> But man upon my back has lain
> Such heavy loads of stone,
> I cannot grow the golden grain;
> 'Tis therefore that I groan.
>
> And where the evening dew sank mild
> Upon my quiet breast,
> I feel the tear of the houseless child
> Break burning on my rest.
>
> And thick and fast as autumn-leaves
> My children drop away;
> A gathering of unripened sheaves
> By Premature Decay.[112]

Alongside the lyrics, the chief poetic achievement of Jones's period in
prison is his long poem, *The New World*. Following in the 'Chartist prison
poem' pattern set by Cooper, Jones's epic surveys the whole of human
history as the history of oppression and tyranny. Jones published the text
when he was released from prison as an admonitory poem for the United
States, and then reprinted it in 1857 as a single volume, on the occasion of
the Indian Mutiny.

The New World authorises Jones to take up fully his place as the new
Laureate of Labour. It aspires to the level of the public poem, with its
global sweep, and its provenance in prison demonstrates the poet's
suffering: 'You and I have suffered together in the same cause', he writes to
the 'unenfranchised subjects of the monarchy'.[113] *The New World* is written

in pentameter, distancing itself from Chartist hymnody and appealing to a literary version of Chartist poetics. The importance of writing is emphasised in his descriptions of the privations he suffered in jail. According to contemporary anecdotes, when Jones was denied pen and ink, he made pens 'by finding occasionally a feather from a rook's wing, that dropped in the prison yard'. And in 1851, when a petition was presented to the House of Commons by his friends calling for an investigation of his treatment in prison, evidence was given that '"The New World" was written in prison with the twig of a broom for his pen.'[114] When the poem appeared in *Notes to the People*, Jones augmented the anecdote, writing that it had been 'written chiefly with my blood while a prisoner in silence and solitude'.[115]

The New World is a survey of civilisation, beginning with the Afghan wars of 1842, and imagining the end of British domination in the subcontinent. The English are driven off Lahore into the ocean. The history of British capitalism and imperialism, and the possibility of its reiteration in the United States is then displaced into the projected history of the now emancipated Hindostan. Monarchy is first overthrown by oligarchy, which is in turn overthrown by the rule of middle-class traders, followed by the force of labour, and the instantiation of a new world of peace. The globalism of the poem and its analysis of British imperialism is part of the internationalism which began to permeate the Chartist movement in the period beginning with the revolutions of 1848, and modifying some of the older rhetoric patterns of domestic oppositional patriotism.[116] *The New World* combines satire and sentiment, along with a utopian conclusion that reaches beyond the customary vision of the land to an international cosmopolis, which ultimately becomes not merely global, but cosmic.

> Then shall the eye, with wide extended sight,
> Translate the starry gospel of the night;
> And, not as now, when narrower bounds are set,
> See, but not read the shining alphabet.[117]

In his millenarian conclusion, there is the commerce of language as well as the 'lengthening leisure' which 'gladdens greatening wealth': 'One language then endearingly extends / Shall tongues be strangers still, when hearts are friends?' When he images the final rising of the people, the image he chooses is that of the interchange between language and flesh – the word made flesh in a political, secular sense:

> Grandly and silently the People rose!
> None gave the word, they came together brought

> By full maturity of ripened thought.
> Truth sought expression: – there the masses stood,
> In living characters of flesh and blood.[118]

While Jones was incarcerated, the Chartist movement outside the prison was becoming something very different; for after 1848, it began fully to separate out into the political constituencies which formed party political Liberalism and Socialism. At the heart of the debates that motivated discussion was the ineluctable question of relations with the middle-class reform movement.[119] Because the mass platform had been first lost, and then renounced through the repression of 1848, the Chartist press became an increasingly important place to agitate for the Charter, and for 'something more', that is, democratic and social ideals that explicitly yoked social demands to political ones.[120] The left constituency centred around Julian Harney, who blossomed as a journalist during the time Jones was in prison. Harney founded the extraordinary journal, the *Red Republican* whose first issue made the claim:

Chartism in 1850 is a different thing from Chartism in 1840. The leaders of the English Proletarians have proved that they are true Democrats ... They have Progressed from the idea of a simple *political reform* to the idea of a *Social Revolution*.[121]

Harney's journal was the site of the related currents of internationalism and socialism. The languages and rhetoric of Louis Blanc and of Marx found their way into this rhetoric, and offered a glimpse of French democratic and socialist aspirations.[122] Harney's paper first published the Communist Manifesto in translation.[123] Although it is impossible to locate the first use of the slogan, it was in the *Red Republican* that the call for 'Chartism and something more' became part of the regular discourse of the movement. This slogan is filled with the materials of romanticism: a yearning beyond language, a sense of supplementarity to what is available, a utopianism that is evocative rather than articulated.

With that slogan, the Chartist Conference of 1851 passed a platform astounding in the range of social issues it took up beyond the political ones of the six points, including nationalisation of the land, separation of Church and State, and education for all, up to and including university education.[124] The internationalism of the 'Red Republicans' was openly committed to social rights and to elements of state intervention, distinct from the middle-class intellectual support of the liberal nationalist revolutionary movements in Germany and Italy.[125]

This was the milieu Jones entered in July 1850. Fluent in German as well as English, and having been educated in Europe, Jones was well suited to remain at the forefront of a 'socialised' Chartism. He advertised the forthcoming publications of his poems in the 10 August issue of the *Red Republican*, noting that the only attention Thomas Carlyle had paid to him was that he 'congratulated me on my imprisonment, because Tothill Fields was just the place to write a book in', thereby distinguishing himself from the apostate Cooper who had felt so proud to be recognised by Carlyle.[126] Harney gave a lot of space to Jones's effort, reviewing his prison poems 'with unfeigned delight'.[127] And Harney takes satisfaction in the apparent neglect of Jones's poetry in the liberal poetic press: he writes that it may be that their reviewers had never heard of Jones, but it may also be because Jones's name is 'to quote the reviewers own words – "tabooed in what are regarded as respectable literary circles."'[128]

The assertion of an independent poetic milieu is part of the formulation of social Chartism, and in the search for a social supplement to Chartism, we see a revised emergence of the communitarian impulse of romanticism which had found one form in Spenceanism and another in the Land Plan. In the 1850s, the strand of romantic lyricism whose origins lay in versions of identity born out of customary practice, and which took the form of a transpersonal collective political identity in Chartist poetry of the late 1830s and early 1840s, now translated into a new, socialised form, and, bearing an internationalist tone, motivates a resurgence of interest in the internationalist romanticism of Byron and Shelley. Late Chartist poetics unstably reconciles the divergence of individualism and communitarianism, for internationalist socialism demands the voluntarism evident in Shelley and Byron, while remaining tied to the collectivism of mass identity. From choral song to prison lament, 1850s Chartist poetry operates to educate rather than agitate: in both politics and poetry itself. Jones takes this task very seriously in his *Notes to the People* (1851–52), and its successor, *The People's Paper* (1852–58), aiming to re-establish the claim of an alternative poetic tradition 'to elevate and form the poetical mind of the country'; Jones asserts that he will foreground Shelley and print his poems.[129] Along with Shelley's poems, Jones reprints Byron's maiden speech to the House of Lords, and calls it 'democracy in action', while his poems were 'democracy in song (impelling, it is true, the actions of others)'.[130] He issued a series of poetic broadsides to accompany the *People's Paper*, written in the measures of Chartist song; the most famous of these is 'The Song of the Low', with its caustic tag, 'We're far too low to vote the tax, / But we're not too low to pay.'[131]

While many of Jones's poems were orientated towards radical working people, he also published some volumes which are written for the liberal literary milieu, to which he was becoming an increasingly interesting figure. Jones worked to maintain his distance from the growing middle-class reform movement, but from the mid-1850s until his death in 1869, he struggled with the increasing hegemony of liberalism as a mode of thinking both politically and socially, and as the dominant literary arena. It was impossible to resist. Arguments put forward by historians suggest that the economic boom meant a concomitant decrease of worker unrest in the period, that the voluntary associations fostered in the previous ten years bore fruit in ameliorative ends, and that liberalism itself was abandoning its pure *laissez-faire* stance and moving towards being interventionist in social life.[132] The value of the voluntaristic version of personal identity forged in alliance with the individualistic lyric self was matched by the increase in political and social voluntarism as well, which was the basis of the self-help and improvement schemes of the 'respectable' period of assimilation of working-class sociality. The proximity of this stratum of life to that of radical anti-hegemonic agitation is evident in Jones's life and work. Though he had called for a 'Labour Parliament' during the strike by the Preston textile workers begun in 1853, by 1858 Jones was urging some kind of class alliance, and between 1857 and the end of his life, Jones entered into the newest phase of the reform movement by brokering alliances with the middle-class movement. On 16 April 1857, he wrote: 'There can be no doubt as to the wisdom of allying with the middle classes and their leaders if they offer such a measure of reform as we can be justified in accepting', while also aiming to maintain the independence of his movement. By the end of 1858, the Chartist movement had broken down, while the Liberal reform movement was in the ascendancy, focused around John Bright's advocacy of household suffrage for boroughs and ten pound suffrage for the counties.[133] In 1864 Jones became a member of the Reform Union; in 1865, when it was renamed as the Reform League, Jones became a vice-president.

In the mid-1850s, in the ambience of popular liberalism, critics in the established papers and journals began to review Jones's work favourably. The defeat of the independent Chartist movement meant that its artifacts were now available for de-politicised, aesthetic presentation, and the Liberal appeal to ex-Chartists accommodated Jones's poetics. The victory of the individualist model of the lyric was assured, evident in this comment in the *Morning Chronicle*, 3 January 1856:

From many of our readers [Jones's] extreme political opinions would meet with but little sympathy – not so, however, his poetry. It is no part of the duty of a critic to mix up the two characters, and he must be bigoted indeed who would decline to award well-merited praise to Mr. Jones.

For his part, in the preface to *The Emperor's Vigil*, Jones steps towards that world:

The author cannot refrain from expressing his admiration of the liberal and impartial spirit evinced toward him, in a literary point of view, by the press.[134]

Jones begins to rewrite his literary history as a path towards poetic prominence unlinked to his vocation as a Chartist poet:

since, when first venturing, as an unknown writer, on the paths of literature, he at once met with the most generous encouragement ... and the same feeling of justice [was] displayed [by the 'great critical authorities of the day'] in not condemning the poet in the person of the politician.[135]

In 1857, when Jones reprinted *The New World* as *The Revolt of Hindostan* (in the manner of Shelley's *The Revolt of Islam*), the inside cover was filled with squibs about Jones's poetical felicity. Central to this distinction between Jones's poetics and his politics, was the image of the poet himself, as representative of either the brutal mass or the solitary lyric speaker:

[Jones] does not grind with strong torpid force like a street musician, nor shout out stale tropes and measured sentences like a hired mountebank in the marketplace. But you see his brow swell out with full veins, and his lip tremble, and his eye sparkle, as the scene he describes rises before him.[136]

Jones is assimilated to Byron and Shelley, produced here as figures of individual autonomy, not of collective political liberation. Of course, because Byron and Shelley were both dead before the debates around the 1832 Reform Bill were resolved, they were liable and available to all sides in the subsequent arguments about Reform. Kingsley may have fretted about Shelley's impact on militant Chartists, but after Jones's death, a eulogy in *The Times*, reprinted from the *Express*, grouped Jones together with Shelley and Byron under the label of those 'liberals' who were 'ardently, almost transcendently, liberal in their belief as to the possibilities open to Humanity'.

And Jones's 1850s poetry is, indeed, stocked with Shelleyisms: in 'The Poet's Prayer to the Evening Wind', he mimics Shelley's 'Ode to the West Wind':

> Wild rider of grey clouds, beneath whose breath
> > The stars dissolve in mist, or rain, or sleet;
> Who chariotest the scudding years to death,
> > Beneath thy driven tempests' clanging feet.[137]

The lyric speaker of the poem concludes by asking the wind to teach him to be 'a bard', 'Singing the same great bold unfearing song'.[138] This poem, like 'The Poet's Mission', and 'The Poet's Death', in the same volume, speaks in a language of the elegiac mode, in retreat from the politico-poetic power of Jones's poetry of the late 1840s and early 1850s; all are grouped together in the volume under the rubric 'Echoes from Within', highlighting the inwardness of the lyric speaker. The obvious borrowing from Shelley suggests Jones's own unsureness about what constitutes his current poetic purpose. When he writes *about* song, rather than composing in its conventions, he signals its redundancy as an efficacious genre, and marks the present marginality of the Chartist poetic as an independent poetic project. 'The Poet's Mission' and 'The Poet's Death' reiterate the theme of the 'death of the bard', familiar from the eighteenth century from Gray's 'The Bard' through Scott's 'Lay of the Last Minstrel', an idealised and elegiac representation of the poet as having once been central to social and political experience, but now peripheral to the goings-on of the world.[139] The Bard is always in a position of solitude and defeat: 'Slow down the tide of the departing years, / The venerable shadow flits along.' In 'The Poet's Mission' Jones makes the case for poetry as perform-ing the work of preservation – the traditional use of the immortality of poetry topic – while eschewing its interventionist function. 'The Bard' now produces the new world in poetry, no longer producing poetry for the new world:

> Who is it rivets broken bands
> And stranger-hearts together,
> And builds with fast-decaying hands
> A home to last for ever?[140]

Most significantly, while the Bard is capable of inspiring others, his own rôle is distant from the place of political engagement: he 'makes others strong with his own strength, / And then flits back to Heaven'.[141] In these poems Jones echoes his pre-1846 poetic voice: atmospheric, vague, and lacking a poetic purpose. Jones's entry into the liberal literary model signalled the end of his creative period as a poet. Ultimately Jones was more useful to liberalism politically than it was to him poetically.

As Margot Finn argues, in the later years of the nineteenth century, the liberal political milieu often rethought its past history in such a way as to merge the divergent goals of liberalism and Chartism within one trajectory, in order to win working-class support.[142] Jones died in 1869, while standing as a Liberal for a Parliamentary seat. The obituaries and speeches made at his funeral are noteworthy for the manner in which the speakers insist not only that Jones was a Liberal, but that he had always been one; i.e., arguing that there had been a continuity rather than a conflict between his political life in the mid-1840s and that of the 1860s. And Liberal constituencies continued to celebrate Jones's birthday as that of one of their own.[143]

But looking at Jones's life and work as poet-activist, his central formation was as a social Chartist, a prototype of the socialist of the 1880s and 1890s, and a poet precursor to internationalist Anglo-Communists such as W .H. Auden. It may be most appropriate to return now to the Newport Uprising, and its after-life in radical circles. In 1856, after years of exile in Australia for his part in the 1839 insurrection, John Frost returned to Britain, Jones heralding his pardon in the *People's Paper*: 'In plain terms after having made him powerless to fight against that Government, he has leave granted to be free.'[144] Frost was enlisted as one amongst the European exiles who turned out in force for the welcome procession: 'There might be seen the flower of foreign democracy, the men who had fought at the barricades of Paris, Berlin, Vienna, and Milan.'[145] Internationalist though this 1856 welcome was, the force of Chartist Uprising poems of 1839 peeks through as in a palimpsest, and conveys with it the language of nativist radicalism. The song written by Jones and sung at the event invoked the British past: 'Give us one glorious day / Of Cromwell's time.'[146] A cruel leader in *The Times* called the crowd of at least 20, 000, 'a few dreary democrats', and called Jones's song 'doggrel'.[147] His purchase on establishment praise was clearly dependent on the suitability of his poetic subject matter and form.

Though Jones's poetry in the 1850s, under the hegemony of the liberal lyric, moves into that negation of intervention which characterises his bard poems, and which aims to merge into the poetry of solitary meditation, the legacy of his use of the inwardness of romantic individualism had other outcomes. Jones was able, in his prison poems, and *The New World*, to harness the individualism that appears as despair in poets such as Clough and Arnold, and link it again to the romantic internationalism of Byron and Shelley in a manner unavailable to the modern liberal poets themselves. Jones's Chartist poetry worked with the double trajectory of romanticism to produce, at its best, a striking communitarian identity for its time, while drawing upon and making a social sense of the claims of inwardness and the 'deep self' thrown up by romantic individualism. The street agitations in London and their accompanying songs and poems in the 1880s demonstrated that the liberal hegemony in both politics and poetics were still being challenged through a poetic tradition leading from the 1790s onwards, while mutating and shifting into contemporary contexts.

CHAPTER SEVEN

W. J. Linton and William Morris
Republican and Socialist poets

The power of Chartist poetry demonstrates the way in which the communitarian lyric in the tradition of romanticism was itself driven through the interactive structure of individualist and communitarian models of identity. The versatility and flexibility of Chartist poetics can be measured by its ability to weave together the forms of print and oral cultures, to integrate the poetics of intervention with those of introspection, and to name itself as both an innovation and a tradition. This dynamic continues, even whilst the ascendancy of the inward solitary lyric theorised by Mill persisted through the last quarter of the nineteenth century. The supervention of Liberalism upon Chartism, as both party politics and as an explanation of identity formation, is a well-known narrative, though recently historians have interpreted that relationship as one of continuity rather than rupture.[1] But the Chartist tradition also opened pathways into radical republicanism and Socialism, where the communitarian lyric might briefly balance.

This final chapter examines the work of two poets within whose political poetics the dynamic engagement of romanticism is again played out, but in the changed circumstances of the post-Chartist world. William James Linton (1812–97) has remained a relatively unknown figure in literary history, but he was one of the most prolific poets and editors working in the radical print tradition from about 1840 through the 1870s. Though he was never a socialist (in fact, he spoke against socialism), he was a revolutionary republican, with a strong commitment to a social agenda and to the nationalisation of the land. He came to maturity in the Chartist movement, and his poetry was published in major Chartist newspapers and periodicals. William Morris (1834–96), the other figure in this chapter, came to Socialism through Liberalism, and brought with him the confidence earned through his accomplished career as a poet. Though the central attempt to shape a version of a counter-cultural poetic tradition was over by the end of the 1860s, elements of the intention appear throughout the nineteenth century, and we can see both Linton and Morris as part of a continuity linking them, most proximately, to Ernest Jones, and as well, to the vigour of interventionist song. This was a crucial part of the fabric out of which Morris worked as the poet of both *Chants for Socialists* – a set of songs for congregational singing at Socialist events – and his narrative poetic sequence, *The Pilgrims of Hope*.

Linton and Morris barely knew one another, but they are interesting mirror figures. Both men were poets and artist-artisans, and both also devoted energy as well to their callings as political activists, writers, and journalists. While Ernest Jones's literary achievement was inextricable from his experience as a Chartist activist, both Linton and Morris had autonomous reputations as craftsmen. (Linton had rather more reputation than financial success as an engraver.) Born into a family on the border of 'the middling sorts', Linton began his political life having been drawn towards the orbit of W. J. Fox and the liberalism of the *Monthly Repository*. Then, through his association with the radical publisher James Watson, from the late 1830s he was involved in the formation of London-based moral-force Chartism, alongside William Lovett and Henry Hetherington.[2] In the 1840s, Linton became a Mazzinian republican, and from that position began to promote and develop his own programme for an 'English Republic', blending voluntaristic individualism shorn of liberal economics with communitarian aspirations stripped of socialist politics. In fact, Linton's political philosophy makes him most like our contemporary communitarians: concerned with the balance of responsibility and right, 'liberty and duty', in which liberty fosters aspiration, and 'Aspiration gives birth to Duty.'[3] Linton's version of individualism, to which he remained committed through his career, was born out of a critique of competitive individualism: but it trapped him in contradictions which left him politically unmoored, and by the end of his life, distanced from both Liberals and Socialists.

William Morris, to us the more familiar figure, came from a privileged, upper-middle-class family. His political life began as a Gladstonian Liberal, and he moved to a resolutely anti-individualist Marxist Socialist position on both politics and art: 'a reform in art which is founded on individualism must perish with the individuals who have set it going'.[4] Linton and Morris both participated in the late nineteenth-century re-covery and extension of the internationalist theme that had been part of the 1790s vision of social and political change, while both also held onto and developed a nativist poetic and artistic intervention. For Linton, the French revolution of 1848 was crucial to his own version of public poem-making; for Morris, younger than Linton by twenty-two years, the London radical practice in the 1880s of celebrating the anniversary of the Paris Commune of 1871, was the source of his narrative poem, *The Pilgrims of Hope*.[5] The Paris Commune represented to Morris and others the link between working-class liberation and internationalism: 'a torch lighting us on our way towards the complete emancipation of labour, and breaking down of the wall of national rivalries'.[6]

Linton and Morris each had an important aesthetic and political impact on the chief designer of the Socialist movement, Walter Crane, who began his training as an apprentice engraver with Linton in January 1859. In the 1880s, influenced by William Morris, Crane became a committed Socialist and Marxist.[7] Crane remembered Linton as a 'true socialist at heart, with an ardent love of liberty and with much of the revolutionary feeling of '48 about him'.[8] It was easy for Crane to confuse Linton's radical republicanism with Socialism, for the 'feeling of '48' had merged the two in the idea of the 'Social and Democratic Republic' that Jones, Linton, and Julian Harney made central to their positions in the early 1850s.[9] Crane's designs for Morris's Socialist League and the Hammersmith Socialist Society focused the visual culture of the movement, working in concert with the poetic and polemical materials into which Morris poured his energy.[10] The origins of Crane's style can be found in the designs that Linton contributed to late Chartist publications such as Harney's *Red Republican* and his own *English Republic*, a linear style that combined a Blakean sinuosity with the French influences of 1848. And Morris's great poem of socialist desire, *The Pilgrims of Hope*, evolved in the pages of the periodical of the Socialist League, *Commonweal*, out of the Chartist-styled *Chants for Socialists* into a revised kind of lyrical ballad, one which combined the narrative teleology of the ballad tradition and the depth psychology of the inward lyric. Linton's earlier sequence of 'Hymns for the Unenfranchised' was a forerunner of this genre, bringing together a narrative movement coupled with a sequence of moments in lyric time, exploring lyric interiority.

Linton and Morris were shaped in the tradition of romanticism: they were both influenced by Shelley, and between them, they were responsible for assimilating Blake to the radical poetic tradition. The Shelleyan voice appears in many of Linton's political lyrics and he used excerpts from Shelley in his many periodicals, while Shelley's poetics also secured the ground for both Morris's *Chants for Socialists* and *The Pilgrims of Hope*. When we reach the end of the nineteenth century, it also becomes possible to specify a lineage from Blake through Linton and to Morris of angry,

Heading for newspaper, *Red Republican*, 1850.

talented, urban artisan poet-radicals, all strikingly holistic in their approaches to the relation of art and work.

Robert Gleckner and Shirley Dent have both studied Linton's relation to Blake.[11] Linton engraved plates for Gilchrist's *Life of William Blake*, and, Gleckner argues, 'It is difficult to imagine a more Blake-like man and career', for Linton, sharing some of Blake's cantankerousness, worked against the division of art into discrete areas of the visual and the verbal. He printed and illustrated many of his poetic works, often combining the processes of composing, engraving, printing, and illustrating.[12] His attention to the usefulness and beauty of the artifacts he made places him close to Morris, who is himself often seen as a companion artisan-poet to Blake, a comrade in the outspoken criticism of, in Blake's vocabulary, 'Druid Altars', in Morris's, English 'Shoddy'. Linton did not entirely approve of Blake's major poems, calling them 'literary incoherences', but he acknowledged Blake's 'artistic imagination', and, as Shirley Dent is proving, he integrated pieces of Blake's work into his own.[13] Linton may well have recognised a poetic filiation in the prophetic style of Blake's long poems, precedent for *Revelations of Truth*, Linton's pastiche of Lamennais's *Paroles d'un Croyant*. In late life, Linton wrote a fond parody of Blake's 'Tyger', 'To a Spider', which shifts Blake's perspective from the macro- to the micro-cosmic: 'In what distant deeps or skies / Grew those rare geometries?' and acknowledges the sublimity of tininess as well as power.[14] Morris evinced a more overtly enthusiastic response to Blake, and he included Blake along with Shakespeare, Coleridge, Shelley, Keats, and Byron, in a list of 100 books published in the *Pall Mall Gazette*, as one of the six 'Modern poets' worth reading.[15] Morris copied out a stanza from Blake's 'A Poison Tree' in at least three letters, in each to offer reconciliation with comrades with whom he had temporarily fallen out.[16] In an essay published in 1919, 'Socialism in Song', Bruce Glasier, a socialist poet and friend of Morris includes Blake in the pantheon of the 'Socialist Poets': 'The movement has made use of and has popularised songs by Blake, Shelley, Ebenezer Elliott, Ernest Jones and the Chartist singers . . .'[17] The long view available to Glasier in 1919 surveys the tradition, and not only includes Blake, but assimilates Chartist poetry to the Socialist canon. Glasier's own 'We'll Turn Things Upside Down', draws on the millenarian voice of seventeenth-century radicalism in a song convention also influenced by Jones's 'Song of the Low'.[18] It is notable that in late nineteenth-century Socialist use, the category of 'poetry' is often supplanted by that of 'song'. That is, Glasier and others claim a popular tradition for their counter-movement, yet tacitly acknowledge the loss of a claim to a literary one. At the same time, the authorship of song is emphasised, foregrounding particular songmakers, the scaffolding of print-culture reputation propping up the oral-culture genre.

But though Linton and Morris may have worked with elements of the same tradition, they followed very different trajectories. Linton's move from Chartism into radical republicanism fitted him into an even older nativist republican tradition which, linked to his position on the Land Question, made him a late nineteenth-century heir to the Spenceans. But his commitment to Mazzinian republicanism (itself a formation compounded of European romanticism and Byronic individualism) and to a voluntarist version of identity required him to replace the communitarian assumption of an embedded personal identity with one built of volitional virtue: selves must be taught to cultivate their social beings, out of a sense of 'duty' rather than to claim a 'natural right'. For his part, Morris took on the challenge of formulating a Socialist poetic out of the Marxist theory of social determination and the romantic desire for a re-imagined future: what E. P. Thompson calls the mix of 'necessity and desire'.[19]

Neither Linton nor Morris had the sorts of audiences that were available to the Chartist interventionist poets. Both fell outside the mass movement of the working class: Linton moved to the United States in the late 1860s and the Socialism of Hyndman and the Social Democratic Federation that Morris joined was a minority grouping that eschewed the trades union movement. My concentration here on Linton and Morris as individual poets itself emphasises how the falling-off of mass intervention throws individual poets into focus, repeating the overall movement of Chartist poetics, but at a later date, and in a more circumscribed arena.

W. J. Linton's politico-poetic life did not, however, start in isolation. His work as lyricist and editor began in 1839 in the midst of Chartist activism, when he edited for six months a weekly journal, *The National: a Library for the People*, legatee to Thomas Spence's *One Pennyworth of Pig's Meat*. The periodical was designed 'to consist mainly of selected extracts from such prohibited works as were beyond the purchasing-reach or time for study of working-men'.[20] The thematically arranged extracts and lessons would educate the working class and help shape a culture commensurate with the civic subjectivity implied by the political goal of the franchise. *The National* is a brilliant attempt to fashion a people's cultural milieu, in which Linton improves upon the simple concatenation of precedents by grouping materials thematically. For example, like Spence, but unlike most Chartists, Linton promoted universal suffrage, and some of the most striking numbers of *The National* are sets of texts on women's emancipation: 'We demand that women should possess all social and political rights that are possessed, or ought to be possessed by men.'[21] The poetry printed in *The National* included extracts from Chaucer, Spenser, Herrick, and Milton and from the democratic strain amongst the romantics. Linton published poetry by Shelley, Keats, Hunt, Wordsworth, Coleridge, and a bit of Tennyson. Linton included only a few poems from the ranks of his contemporary political poets, with most room reserved for his own poems.

The public conclusion to Linton's politico-literary life came in 1895, two years before his death, when he presented twenty volumes of his *Prose and Verse Written and Published in the Course of Fifty Years, 1836–1886* to the British Library. While these volumes might be ·classified bibliographically as scrapbooks, they inhabit a literary terrain somewhere in between private and public worlds, and somewhere in between the world of mechanical reproduction and that of artisan craftsmanship. To make each volume, Linton cut out and pasted onto octavo paper almost every one of the published poems, articles, and editorials of his long career: poems, polemics, and editorial commentary from the many journals and newspapers with which he was associated from his first published poems of 1836 extending through the 1880s. The collection as a whole is a curious hybrid: each bound volume has a printed title page and table of contents, denoting its status as a published book (these are housed in the main book collection of the British Library), and each one is inscribed, 'Presented to the British Museum by W. J. Linton, 1895'. Yet every volume is unique: the pasted-in clippings are in places annotated with information about republication, while red inked rubrics accompany some'of the groups of poems. These volumes are pervaded by what Walter Benjamin called 'aura': they are singular artifacts made by a labour of love. In a letter to Richard Garnett, then Keeper of Printed Books at the British Museum, Linton called the set, 'an entirely unique collection of my own writings printed and published during fifty years'.[22] Yet at the same time the collection is suffused with a kind of ersatz reproducibility: the paradox of a one-off *Collected Works*. The collection makes a poignant counterpoint to the 1839 *National*. The earlier anthology assembled extracts from different authors into a cheap periodical meant to reach thousands of readers, and to forge a collective identity. The later *Prose and Verse* assembles one man's work into fifty irreproducible volumes, which, since 1895 have been rarely examined, except by archivists and researchers.

Virtually none of Linton's poetry has survived into our own period; however, when a series of anthologies appeared in the last quarter of the nineteenth century, aiming to define and canonise the central poets and poetic themes of the immediate past, a few of Linton's poems were included. For example, Alfred H. Miles edited a twelve-volume series of the *Poets and Poetry of the Century* between 1891 and 1897, in which he included works by both Ernest Jones·and Linton. But none of the Linton poems included demonstrates any species of his political poetics. In fact, Arthur Bullen's brief biography of Linton, which prefaces the selection, though calling him by the fairly fluid term 'radical', makes no mention of Linton's life as a Chartist and republican. Linton was a friend of Bullen, who also published Linton's *Memories* in 1895, so it seems likely that Linton authorised the choice of rather listless lyrics. These are pretty and slight love lyrics, and place his work comfortably within the authority of the lyric of solitude. Linton's presentation of his *Prose and Verse* to the British Museum binds his two poetic ambitions together: to leave a complete record of his life as a radical poet-artisan, and to be accepted as a lyric poet in the closed circle of the Reading Room. He hoped, as his letter to Garnett shows, to be 'allowed a place in the Museum Library'.[23]

Linton began as a Chartist on the 'respectable' side of the movement. He had attended the London meetings of 1837 and 1838, which first called for, and then produced the People's Charter, and at a meeting on 8 May 1838, he listened to the 'Corn Law Rhymer', Ebenezer Elliott, who had been taken up by Mill and W. J. Fox in the *Monthly Repository*.[24] Linton's enthusiasm for the Chartist project led to his first major intervention into the shaping of the counter-cultural field with *The National*, which was subsidised by James Watson, a long-lived radical London publisher.[25] The rhetoric of the journal took up and amplified the sense of class division. He wrote a series of 'Letters to the Working Classes of Great Britain and Ireland, the Millions without Political Existence', in which he makes the claim that 'We have been deceived by the Reform Bill', and that the middle class 'hate and fear the productive class'.[26]

From the first, Linton opposed Feargus O'Connor's interpretation of Chartism, and Linton attributed to O'Connor that 'hot and angry talk' that 'broke up the coherence and the *morale* of the party'. More seriously, he laid at O'Connor's door the motivation for the Newport Uprising, that 'insane attempt at insurrection in South Wales'.[27] But though he disapproved of the 'physical force' Chartists, who he distinguished from the 'real Chartists – Hetherington, Watson, Lovett', Linton attempted to ameliorate the plight of Frost and the Newport rebels, helping to compose the petition for a reprieve.[28] And one of his most compelling 'Hymns for the Unenfranchised', was 'The Song of the Scattered', which belongs to the grouping of Chartist Newport exile poems, freighted with the elegiac ambition of comradely restoration:

> Where shall we meet our friends again?
>   The convict ship has sail'd,
> Through the broken foam, to the felons' home:

> For the star o' the rebel paled.
> Welcome! although we meet to share
>   The patriot's exile-pain,
> Till the world turn round, till the unripe Care
> Blush sunnily: no matter where,
>   So that we meet again![29]

In 1881, when Linton wrote a retrospective account of the Chartist movement, he placed the London group of Hetherington, Lovett, and Watson
at its centre, and described O'Connor as one 'whose demagogic egotism
did more than anything else to discredit, mislead and ruin the cause . . .'[30]
But while he wrote often against O'Connor and against O'Connor's
lieutenant-poet, Ernest Jones, Linton found himself in some of the same
late Chartist publications as Jones, particularly in the post-1848 period,
when the Chartist alignments were rearranging themselves, and the force
of liberal power was increasing. Linton and Jones were members of rival
delegations to the French Provisional Government in the late winter of
1848, but Jones published many of Linton's poems in *The Labourer*, and the
two worked together for a time on Julian Harney's *Friend of the People*
when Harney fell ill.[31] Both men shared the republican's reverence for the
memory of Oliver Cromwell.[32]

   While Ernest Jones's poetic is noteworthy, in part, for the way in which it
infuses the voice of the collective with an urgency of interiority, Linton's
poetic enacts the contest of self and community in quite a different
manner. His poetry searches for a way of highlighting the autonomy of the
self, while being inflected by a strong sense of class-consciousness. Some
historians call Linton a 'middle-class reformer', but his biographer
demonstrates that Linton oscillated between middle-class and working-
class literary milieux throughout his life.[33] Much of Linton's polemical
writing is about teaching the inward self to enter into 'The Social and
Democratic Republic: The absolute sovereignty of the whole people,
directly exercised for the social organisation of the whole people, for the
better government of society'.[34] He argued that the struggle for 'individual
liberty' had been accomplished with the overcoming of feudalism; now it
was time for the 'struggle for individual equality'.[35] By the 1850s, Linton
articulated a theory of affiliated sociality, dependent upon his celebration
of the inward self, but linked to a theory of virtue as the conduit into social
responsibility. Linton dispenses with the residue of the customary embedded self that was knitted into the communitarian poetics of earlier phases
of the interventionist lyric, and which Jones wrestled with in his Chartist
poetry. Linton's theory of poetry takes as given the autonomy and *a priori*

asociality of identity, and then presses hard towards a sense of the social as affiliative. This leads him to theorise a set of virtues, which he outlined in the *English Republic* as the means by which persons ought to make social and political choices. Linton's emphasis on the volition of the self towards sociality, and away from self-interest, is very powerful in his political lyrics. So it is noticeable that Linton's best poems are those which take up and engage with the problem of finding a voice for the claims to collective civic subjectivity: the 'poet's mission' is to read 'Your heart-streams, brothers mine!'[36] When Linton writes the poetry of isolated subjectivity, his lyrics lapse into nondescript, almost anonymous efforts: 'The Dirge of Love', 'Nought', and 'To His Love', are reminiscent of Ernest Jones's senti-mental, abstract, pre-Chartist poems. 'To the West Wind' reduces the valence of Shelley's sublimity to a flimsy domesticity: 'O happy Wind! love-laden with her sighs'.[37] Yet it was precisely this anodyne quality that Clarence Stedman praised in his 1867 study of *Victorian Poets*: though Linton had begun as a Chartist poet who 'relieved his eager spirit by incessant poetizing', with the publication of *Claribel and Other Poems*, 1865, he had produced 'a collection of more finished poetry', aiming to 'commemorate the growth, maintenance, and final strengthening by death, of a pure and sacred love'.[38] In an appreciation of Linton's work in 1879, H. Buxton-Forman noted both that Linton's poetry had 'found no sufficient praise', and as well, that his best poems were his non-political ones: 'His practical, active, aggressive republicanism is among the principal factors in keeping him from that fulness of poetic attainment for which he has the capacity.'[39]

But in 1839, newly entered on the politico-poetical project of Chartism, Linton published twenty-two political sonnets in *The National*, all signed 'One of the People'. These poems belong to the tradition of the five-beat print-culture poetic. Shelley's is the most obvious influence in these poems. For example, in 'The Enthusiast', Linton reworks Shelley's 'Lift not the Painted Veil', as Linton's speaker lifts the 'veil which the Mysterious wears; / And looked on – the Ubiquious Misery.'[40] The other striking influence on Linton's poetry in this period is the French liberal Catholic, democrat, and messianic revolutionary writer, Félicité Robert de Lamennais, from whom Linton adopted a biblical anaphoric style, which reverberates against Spence's and Blake's 1790s prophetic writings.[41] Linton's long prose poem, *Revelations of Truth*, is written in the same loose prophetic line as Blake's, and it carries the biblical line forward in counter-cultural poetics to Walt Whitman and Allen Ginsberg:

Man hath bartered Truth and Healthfulness and Power and Love,
    for a handful of glittering dirt.
He hath swallowed molten gold: and his heart is consumed.

      . . .

I see another land: it is rich and fertile, and abounding in the fruits
    of the earth; but the dwellers in that beautiful country are squalid
    and miserable, pining in the most abject poverty.[42]

Alongside these derivative poems are the series of songs and lyrics signed after the leader of the Roman slave insurrection, 'Spartacus', which were the poetic spine of Linton's main interventionist poetry, continued in Linton's next publication, the *Odd-Fellow*, which he worked on with Hetherington, and later, in the *English Republic*.[43] The 'Spartacus' songs and poems belong to the nativist rhetoric, many employing tropes familiar from the 1790s. The labourer is figured often as a slave, as in the 'The Slave's Hymn', in which the group calls out to 'Liberty', 'We have wasted till we are / As an echo of Despair.'[44] The voice is nativist also as it ventriloquises Wat Tyler in the metre of Shelley's 'The Mask of Anarchy': 'Rouse thee, Freedom! from thy grave – / Even from Custom's charter'd cave.'[45] In 'A Song for the Next Rebellion', Linton redeploys the rhetoric of the Norman Yoke:

Up! up! ye toil-worn English slaves: if blood must needs be shed,
Let it be England's tyrant lords', and not the famine-sped! –
Ay, hand to hand, and foot to foot, close fast with Tyranny: –
Our Saxon Thor is lord again: our England shall be free![46]

These songs were serially printed under the rubric, 'Hymns for the Unenfranchised', and they represent Linton's conscious use of the hymn tradition, widely spread through Methodist chapels, as a secularised mode of poetic-political intervention.[47] These poems mimic oral hymnody, but have been invented and produced within a print-culture pedagogy for the working person. Linton takes up the four-beat line when he writes texts which would equally serve as visual and oral performances.

In 'The Coming Days', Linton draws the notion of the English 'freeman' with equal rights for men and women, 'hand in hand', into a vision of a 'Commonwealth of earth'.[48] The song belongs to the same genre as Morris's later 'Chant', 'The Day Is Coming', which also imagines a time of a commonwealth of freemen in very similar language.[49] Linton writes quite a number of texts he called Chants or Chaunts, poems which are meant to be spoken collectively, but without music. 'Why Should We Not Be Free? A Chant' is characteristic of the oral poetic practice, employing many elements of repetition in stress, vocabulary, and rhythmic patterning.

> Why should we not be free?
>   The sea
> Rolls up the shingley shore
> Its everlasting roar,
> Unstay'd by Tyranny:
> Why should not man be free?[50]

Many of the songs in the *Odd-Fellow* work through the Chartist-Shelleyan idiolect. Linton takes on the language of power and force that he found in Shelley, and his commitment to both individualism and the social whole led to his reiterated image of individuals building up into an avalanche of power. In his 1839 'The Gathering of the People: a Storm Song', Linton outlines a set of images he will return to again. In this poem Linton interestingly reverses the expectation of metre between oral and print modes. He has used a five-beat, ten-syllable rhymed pattern, but broken it up as stanzas which allude to balladry or to the chant, and with the kinds of elision and syncope associated with oral performance poetry:

> Gather ye silently,
>   Even as the snow
> Heapeth the avalanche;
>   Gather ye so!
>
> Gather ye so,
> In the wide glare of day,
> Sternly and tranquilly;
>   Melt not away!
>
> Flake by flake gather;
>   Bind ye the whole
>   Closely together –
> One form and one soul!
>
>   Are ye all gather'd?
>   Welded in one?
> Hark to the thunder-shout!
>   Now roll ye on!
>
>   Roll ye on steadily;
>   Steadily grow;
> Swifter and swifter roll!
>   Who stays you now?
>
> Leap from your hill of right;
>   Burst on the plain!
> Ye were born in those valleys:
>   There shall ye reign.

> Roll on in thunder!
> Man's buildings are there:
> Lo! they mocked at your movement;
> Now hide their despair!
>
> Roll, roll, world-whelmingly!
> Calm, in your path
> Glory walks, harvest-ward:
> God rules your wrath.
>
> 'It is accomplished:'
> Melt we away!
> The phoenix To-morrow
> Is child of To-day.
>
> Gather ye silently!
> Even as the snow
> Buildeth the avalanche,
> Gather YE, Now!

This poem appears many times in Linton's œuvre; he took advantage of its ambiguous metrical status to shape it visually on the page. In 1848, he revised it as 'A Song for the People's Charter Union'. In this version, Linton regularises the metre, and re-punctuates the poem so that the enjambment of lines three and four cuts right across the singing rhythm:

> Gather ye steadily, even as the snow
> Heaps the strong avalanche, flake by flake, so
> Leap forth in your millions, your union complete:
> Hark to the echoes that follow your feet!

And he returned to it again in 1851 in the *English Republic*.[51] Shelley's example is always close by in Linton's poetic. In 1850, Linton wrote a long pastiche of the poem, 'The Jubilee of Trade', employing Shelley's stanza form. In this poem, Commerce is killed by the very disease of which it is the central cause:

> So the Plague grew more and more,
> Till it clomb unto the door
> Of the Commerce-God, where He
> In his Heaven sate gorgeously.
> . . . .
> Till the Plague which He became
> Choked itself, and – as a flame
>
> In its own smoke and stench – He died
> In the very fulness of his pride:
> And men were without Trade, and free
> In the Heaven of Love's wide charity.[52]

Like Allen Davenport and others who invoke Shelley, Linton raises him above even Shakespeare: 'Higher than Hamlet the Promethean Hymn / Of the far future Shelley hath unhid.'[53] Linton's great compliment to James Watson was that he 'seems indeed ... to have been a prose Shelley, with the same gentleness of nature and chivalrous zeal against Wrong; like Shelley also in his public spirit, in his generosity.'[54]

In the 1840s, Linton's nativist Chartism was significantly inflected by the mood of internationalism, and he began to take an interest in, and actively support European nationalist causes. He met Mazzini in 1841, and retained a lifelong attachment to his brand of republicanism.[55] As Eugenio Biagini points out, Linton was easily attracted to Mazzini, for 'At the root of his popularity in Britain there was that same Leveller zeal, Puritan moralism ... which had formed the basis of Cromwell's success as a radical symbol.'[56] Linton was active in the People's International League in 1847, along with Thomas Cooper, and other refugees from O'Connor's Chartism. In the mid-forties, Linton reviewed Cooper's *Purgatory of Suicides* in the *Illuminated Magazine*, one of the more moderate journals with which he was involved.[57] Linton praises Cooper's poem, but adds, testifying to the increased and apparently ineluctable separation of the political from the aesthetic: 'With the author's political or theological opinions we have not thought it well to meddle.'[58]

In the aftermath of 1848 Linton found his place and voice as the craftsman of the symbols and rhetoric of an English Republic, interpreted through a range of social as well as political issues. And it was then that he articulated to himself the goal of an interventionist poetic: what he called 'the real travail of my soul', was 'the Cause of the People – in ... literary or poetic ... Action'.[59] Linton's republicanism is marked by its intransigent anti-Liberalism, its will to contextualise England in a global arena, and its commitment to the political poetics of republicanism. In the anthem he printed many times, 'Our Tricolour', Linton imagines a 'true English flag', made up of the '*blue* of skies serene', and 'Albion's *white* / Dear cliffs for freedom', and 'GREEN below – our rights of Man, ocean-wide, republican'.[60] He joined in the internationalism inspired by 1848 and linked his nativism to it as an interlocking structure of fraternal national independence: 'Milton himself, if living now, would take counsel of Mazzini.'[61] Linton's biographer, F. B. Smith, argues that the journal the *English Republic* (1850–55) 'is the fullest and most venturesome transposition of European republicanism into English'. Linton called for universal suffrage, complete state-supported mental and physical education, presented along with a humanist religion which would bind the selves of the nation into a coherent whole.[62]

In the early 1850s, Linton, like Ernest Jones, worked with Julian Harney on the *Red Republican*, and his designs created the style of the English version of 'The Charter and Something More' in much the same way as Walter Crane's designs would shape the appearance of Socialism in the late 1880s and 1890s. Harney's journal aimed to integrate the vision of a social republic into the programme of nativist Chartism. An editorial in the *Red Republican* asserts: 'The Charter, the means; and the Democratic and Social Republic – the end – such is the "programme" of the *Red Republican*'.[63] Nevertheless, Linton persevered in distancing himself from socialism as construed by Harney and the French socialists.[64] He remained committed always to a voluntaristic theory of identity, but never to a *laissez-faire* economics. That is, he had a modern liberal notion of self, but it was deeply imprinted by the anti-liberal social ideology of his political milieu. In the third of his ten letters on 'Republican Principles', which were printed first in Harney's *Red Republican*, and then reprinted in the *English Republic*, Linton describes infancy as a self-involvement prior to entry into sociality: 'The child lives for itself; is (*or should be*) employed, not for Humanity, but for itself.'[65] The combination of these selves into 'Humanity', with an organic telos beyond pure growth counterpoints Linton's sense of the unencumbered self: 'We believe in the progressive development of human faculties and forces in the direction of the moral law which has been imposed upon us.'[66] Linton cuts across a liberal version of identity with a social version of economic life: 'The *Laissez-faire* (the *let-alone*) system can only suit those who have no recognition of humanity as a whole, nor knowledge of any relation between men except that of buyers and sellers, whose sole business is personal gain.'[67] In a poem on 'Free Trade', he writes 'Free to sell, and free to buy, – / Free to toil for famine wage'.[68]

Linton was eager to distinguish his theory of personal identity from what he called the 'Selfish principle'. He criticises a version of 'Liberty' that 'has been deduced from the absolute sovereignty and sufficiency of each'.[69] In its place he aims for an idea of 'duty', which is evinced in 'the eternal sacrifice of Self upon the altar of Humanity'.[70] Perhaps without realising it, Linton borrowed from the French socialist Charles Fourier the category of 'harmony', which had also inflected the vocabulary of the Owenite communitarians: Humankind must be understood as a 'whole, which ought to be harmonized together'.[71] Linton asserts the priority of a voluntaristic self, and then goes on to account for an affiliated sense of community: this self is not considered embedded in customary culture, but is linked to a set of social goals, personally experienced as what Linton calls 'aspiration'.[72] So, from within the individualist paradigm, Linton elaborates an internal dialectic, which reproduces the contest of self and sociality within the self. The second volume of the *English Republic* contains a series of articles intended to educate the individual into social responsibility: 'Personal Conduct', 'Honesty', 'Valour', 'Gentleness', and 'Self-Possession' are the virtues that Linton aims to inculcate into the new republicans.[73] Unlike the late eighteenth-century poets whose proximity to customary culture offered them the materials out of which to make claims for a communitarian identity, Linton proposes to build his version of social good out of individual will and virtue. So it is that he comes up against the contradictions that have recently been re-explored by philosophers such as MacIntyre, Sandel, and Taylor; namely, how to renovate emotivism, and discover how to bind inward constitutive goods to external social organisation.

Though Linton was in favour of private property, he was vehemently opposed to the private ownership of land: 'the State (the Government of the whole People) is the real owner of the Land'.[74] He retained the communitarian attachment to an idea of the 'people's farm'. In this way he was to the left of O'Connor's vision of the small property-owners of the Chartist Land Plan. In the brilliant sequence of poems in the *English Republic*, 'Rhymes and Reasons against Landlordism', Linton addressed the issue of the land by way of a set of poems about abuse of ownership in Ireland and England. Some of these poems ring with the themes of the Spencean poetic:

> But earth, its mines, its thousand streams,–
> And air's uncounted waves,
> Freighted with gold and silver beams
> To brighten lowliest graves, –
> The mountain-cleaving waterfall, –
> The ever-restless sea, –
> God gave, not to a few, but all,
> As common Property.[75]

Linton's 'The Parks' is a wry riposte to Felicia Hemans's often reprinted 1827 *Blackwood's Magazine* poem, 'The Homes of England'.[76] Linton inhabits Hemans's metre to counterpoise the productive land of abundance to the beauty of the landscaped park:

> Those Parks, despite their beauty's worth,
> And memories proudly worn,
> We value less than common earth
> That grows the peasant's corn;

> We'd raze their bowers and plough them o'er,
>> Ay! 'confiscate' the best,
> Ere one of England's Martyr Poor
>> Should hunger unredresse'd.[77]

While Hemans's poem imagines an amiable juxtaposition of classes – 'The free, fair Homes of England! / Long, long in hut and hall', each in their appropriate homes – Linton focuses on the system of land ownership which supports these homes, and equably suggests in a note to the poem: 'We will not plough up the Parks, but keep them as the holiday-grounds of the People; and when the noble and gentle owners, disgusted at the sight of happy faces, give up their mansions, we will make them the homes of the aged and infirm, and the banqueting-halls as lecture-rooms.'

This sequence of poems has a collective narrative force: each addresses a particular event or issue, but together they make a narrative succession in which solidarity is first developed, struggle takes place, defeat is suffered, but the contest continues and moves on: 'Each footstep is a fall, – move on thy way! / Try again!'[78]

> Hold together, flinch for nought!
> Set thy foot by mine, my brother!
> Shield of each one shade the other!
>> Well resolved is bravely fought:
>> Well begun is half-way wrought:
>> Hold together, halt for nought![79]

Linton is alert to the interchange of oral- and print-culture poetics. On the one hand, he uses metres that can be sung and lifted from the sequence into the performative arena of the meeting. On the other hand, by shaping a narrative, he invites a private solitary reading. The 'Rhymes and Reasons against Landlordism' presents a genre which solves the problem of both meeting the affective needs of the individual through lyricism, and the narrative aims of the collective struggle.

The final poems of the sequence produce a utopian vision of the land reclaimed: first in the 'Irish Harvest Song',

> O by the strength of our despair,
>> Our unrequited toil,
> By God who gave us choice of death
>> On our own soil, –
> Reap, though our reaping-hooks be swords, and let
>> The robber-born
>> Glean plenteously our scorn.[80]

These final poems are framed in a rhetoric that produces the belated medievalism pervasive in Socialist poetics and design, most obviously in work by Morris and Crane. The language of Linton's 'English Reapers', 'Harvest-Home', and 'The Happy Land' sounds much more like the 1890s 'Merrie England' rhetoric promoted by Robert Blatchford through the working-class journal, the *Clarion*, than it does like Blandford's or Davenport's rhetoric of the common treasury. The plebeian transpersonal voice operates as something of a retrospective ornament in Linton's poems.

Yet the poems do belong to the engagement that this study has been following through the long nineteenth century. Linton's utopian poems work with themes which Allen Davenport had taken on in the early 1820s in a similar mood of political retrospection. And Chartist poetry then re-complicated a category already concentrated within romanticism as lyric subjectivity, redeploying it as community, and recovering the roots of the poetic in customary mutuality. Ernest Jones reconnected this communitarian impulse to the vestigial but still available residues of the customary so as to elicit the possibility of a voluntary, chosen association. The Chartist landscape poetic re-conceived some of the elements of solitude, personal meditation, and the drive towards interiority as a transpersonal solidarity. For Linton these elements are now linked together as an unstable combination of the elegiac and the anticipatory. Ernst Bloch, the twentieth-century theorist of 'Hope', argues for the constructive capacity of elegiac formulations. The utopian function, he argues, 'operates as the successive continuation of the implications in the cultural constellations of the past gathered around us as non-past'.[81] This focus on 'Hope', crucial in the final poems of Linton's sequence, will also be the fulcrum for William Morris's version of what Bloch describes as 'anticipatory illumination'.[82]

In 'Harvest-Home', the idea of the future is cast on the mould of an idealisation of the past. And this is parallel to a doubling back and ornamenting of an idea of the land.

> The autumn winds are flinging
>   The sunshine on the grain;
> And the merry reapers, bringing
> Load after load, are singing
>   Of Freedom's harvest gain.
> Pile up the sheaves, boys! ho, boys!
>   The harvest is our own:
> There's none fears now to sow, boys!
> When each is free to grow, boys!
>   A harvest for his own.
> Pile up the sheaves, boys! ho, boys!
>   A harvest for our own.[83]

The last poem of the sequence, 'The Happy Land', is built upon the earlier ones, and only takes on its force within a republican argument by virtue of the narrative momentum which makes this final poem a utopian presentation of the English Republic.

> The Happy Land!
> Where in the golden sheen of autumn eves
> The bright hair'd children play among the sheaves;
> Or gather ripest apples all the day,
> As ruddy-cheek'd as they.
> O happy, happy Land![84]

Perhaps Linton believed his own version of rurality, for having fallen out with Jones and other late Chartists, he moved in 1852 to Brantwood, an estate in the Lake District, where he worked on the *English Republic*, aided in 1854 by a group of young republican acolytes.[85] The 1860s were unhappy and unprofitable times for Linton. The Liberal hegemony had swallowed up many of his former Chartist colleagues, while he went through difficulty getting work as either editor, writer, or engraver. His second marriage, to Eliza Lynn Linton, was a disaster, and his children from his first marriage began to sicken and die.[86]

Linton emigrated to the United States in November 1866, at the age of fifty-four. It proved to be a gratifying move, and he was soon part of the American intelligentsia around New York's Century Club. He secured an appointment at the Cooper Institute, where he taught wood engraving, and in 1869 he was invited to Boston to speak about republicanism to such American liberals as Whittier and Phillips and Bronson Alcott.[87] In the 1870s Linton was living in Connecticut, in a house he called 'Appledore', where he set up his own press, and in which he wrote an important history of engraving, *Masters of Wood-engraving*.[88] But he stayed abreast of what was going on in England and on the Continent, and spoke in the voice of an earlier era. In a letter to the *National Standard* (USA), Linton wrote: 'I am one of that unfortunate party stigmatised – no less in America than elsewhere – as *Red Republicans*. I am one of the original lot, my republicanism dating some thirty years back . . . '[89]

Linton responded with great enthusiasm to the Paris Commune of 1871. While Marx saw the Commune as the forerunner of revolutionary socialism, Linton felt that it signalled the start of the true republic.[90] He defended it in letters to newspapers in the United States, and his biographer tells us that he read a dozen French and English daily newspapers.[91] Unlike the British liberal world, which repudiated the Commune, Linton defended it. When pushed, he even assimilated Red

Republicanism to Communism: the colour Red 'denotes that the Communists and the Republicans are ready to give their lives for their principles . . . '[92] But Linton distanced himself from what he considered to be the errors of communism, which he later assimilated to the trades union movement as well: 'I am as little in accord with Communism as with Trade Unionism – twin children of the same mistake – yet I am free to think that even "Communists" have suffered enough from misrepresentation and calumny without need of this further pebble from the hand of an English working man.'[93] In a pamphlet published from articles he had written for the Boston periodical, *The Radical*, Linton attacked what he called 'anarchic individualism', promoting instead 'the new gospel of *Communion*, the *Duty* of fellowship . . . The hermit must quit his cell for active citizenship'.[94]

By the late 1870s, Linton had retreated from active polemics about the political questions of the day.[95] Living in the United States, he missed an important moment for the revived anti-Liberal republicanism that was a feature of 1870s radical politics in England. Antony Taylor argues that 'plebeian republicanism . . . gained its strongest support during the trough of unpopularity of the Liberal government of 1868–74, and made particular targets of the great doyens of Liberalism, Gladstone and John Bright'.[96] But Linton was interested in the Eastern Question: the campaign in which Gladstone helped build his Liberal-Labour constituency through antagonism to Disraeli's support of the Turks against the Russians in 1877–78.[97] Those opposed to this alliance included both persons from the older republican tradition and those from the growing Socialist movement: Linton was in political company with Marx and H. M. Hyndman, the organiser of the Democratic Federation.[98]

And it was the agitation around the Eastern Question that served as the first step in the politicisation process that led William Morris into revolutionary Marxist Socialism. The song Morris wrote for a public meeting held at the Exeter Hall in London in January 1878 marked the beginning of his work as an interventionist poet. As was the case for Ernest Jones before him, Morris's entry into political life was simultaneously poetic and political, for the meeting was also the occasion of his first political speech. Morris described it the next day in a letter to his wife, Jane:

As to the agitation: I must confess I have been agitated as well as agitating: you will have got the newspapers by this time with a sort of report of our proceedings including the speech of me, & its – may I call it amicable indiscretion . . . ['Wake, London Lads'] went down very well, & they sang it well together: they struck up while we were just ready to come to the platform & you may imagine I felt rather excited when I heard them begin to tune up: they stopped at the end of each verse and cheered lustily . . .[99]

Set to the tune of 'The Hardy Norseman', the song shows Morris to be familiar with the rhetorical traditions of the popular political song: he mobilises the language of the sun ('The bright sun brings the day') and of the native republic:

> Think on your Sires! how oft and oft
>   On freedom's field they bled,
> When Cromwell's hand was raised aloft,
>   And Kings and scoundrels fled.[100]

A few weeks after this event, Linton sent a letter to the *Newcastle Weekly Chronicle*, in which he satirised Morris's effort by adding his own stanza to the song, urging the 'London lads' to 'Sleep on, brave lads! (What call indeed, / To startle slumberers so?)', and to dream of the oppressions throughout Eastern Europe wrought by 'Poland's gentle foe', i.e., Russia. He then adds his own satirical condemnation of the anti-Turk feeling: 'Down with the Turk! he is safe to die; / Give him a kick as you pass him by!'[101] This antagonistic 'collaboration' between Linton and Morris ironically evokes the Poetry Page of the Chartist *Northern Star*, where poet-activists corresponded through verse. Here, of course, the two poets are employing the same rhetoric to make antithetical political points, but having been schooled in it, Linton assumes the continuity of the inter-ventionist poetic tradition, and works within what he takes to be a still lively network of issues, newspapers, and poetic conventions.

There is, however, no evidence that Morris ever saw Linton's letter, either in the *Chronicle* or carefully cut out and preserved in Linton's *Prose and Verse*. Morris knew little of Linton, though presumably Walter Crane had spoken about his apprenticeship in Linton's workshop. Other sources tell us that those close to Morris, including Arthur Mackmurdo and Emery Walker, saw Linton as an important contributor to the 'democratic principle' in art.[102] There is one letter from Morris extant (26 October 1883), a reply to a letter from Linton, though it is unclear if Morris had any idea with whom he was corresponding.[103] The letter intimates that Linton has asked about the Democratic Federation, and Morris asks, 'will you not join our organisation which as far as I know is the only active Socialist body in England?' But the chief purpose of Linton's letter was to ask for permission to reprint a few of Morris's lyrics in a multi-volumed collection of *English Verse* that he was editing with Henry Stoddard.[104]

That collection shows that by the late 1870s, in Linton's mind there was a large gap between political and lyric poetry. In an introductory essay to that volume of the series called *Lyrics of the Nineteenth Century*, Linton and Stoddard declare that the great lesson learned by the early poets of the century was 'to shut their books, and look into themselves'.[105] Their essay concludes with an astonishing reduction of Shelley's poetic purposes, describing him as 'of too etherial a mould for the material England of the Georges'.[106] The volume includes a few of Linton's own poems, 'Bridal Song' and 'Iphigneia at Aulis', both quite unrepresentative of Linton's largely interventionist lyricism. He did include 'The Happy Land', the final poem of the sequence from the *English Republic*.[107] But in the context of asocial lyricism, the poem is shorn of its place at the end of a cumulative poetic argument about harnessing the past to the possibility of a republican future. The Morris lyrics which Linton included are also quite anodyne.[108]

Linton had occupied a vital place within the Chartist poetic milieu and had been published even by his political enemies. Within the argument of this study, Linton provides an interesting example of how the hegemony of individualism became a strand in an otherwise social lyric construction. But under the impact of the liberal cultural authority, Linton was diminished to a minor figure in high-culture poetics. Buxton-Forman did the most to offer Linton a place in a tradition of liberal poetry, arguing that Elizabeth Barrett Browning must have read Linton's Shelleyan 'Dirge of Nations' before writing 'Casa Guidi Windows', and that Swinburne drew upon that poem when writing his 'Ode to the Proclamation of the French Republic'.[109] Just as Ernest Jones's poetry had been interpreted in the light of contemporary cultural politics, so was Linton's intransigent social republicanism turned into something quite different in Buxton-Forman's presentation: 'Intense patriotism is the leading characteristic of Mr. Linton's poetry, for the violent republicanism we have dwelt upon is rather accidental to the political situations in which he has found himself.'[110]

Linton focused on the autonomy of the self as the precondition for forging social harmony; William Morris aimed to bind a plebeian communitarian identity to the science of society. His compelling combination of medieval elements with contemporary social science characterises Morris's socialist communitarian aesthetic. But Morris had also been schooled in, and had practised the poetic art of lyrical inwardness, so his poetry acknowledges and aims to make sense of the contest of individual and communitarian identity formation. At his most revolutionary, Morris is also the most romantic: insisting upon the contest of self and community as a chief issue for humans in his world, and for both the politics and art that humans make. But Morris enters the debate struggling against the dominance of the individualist model. He repeatedly asserted the power of the trans-personal as the foundation of both politics and art: 'it was the collective people, and not a few miraculous individuals who have produced all worthy, that is all genuine, art in the past'.[111] For Morris, art is 'man's embodied expression of interest in the life of man', and 'however much [that interest] might be broken by grief and trouble of individuals', art is 'the expression of pleasure in life generally'.[112] In addition to all that Morris learned from Ruskin, from his fellow Pre-Raphaelites, and from the canonical romantic poetics, he also learned from and contributed to the communitarian tradition of interventionist lyricism. Oral and printed radical songs, the complex project of social subjectivity undertaken by Ernest Jones, and the generic experiment devised by Linton are part of the politico-poetic context out of which emerged Morris's *Pilgrims of Hope*.

The thirteen poems which, with their concatenation of song and classical metres, lyric and narrative elements, make up *The Pilgrims of Hope* trace out the complex emotional designs discernible within political, sexual, and comradely entanglements in the setting of the British socialist and labour movement and the Paris Commune of 1871, setting against one another the individualist claims of feeling and the collective ones of social change.[113] By commemorating a recent historical event and invoking it as an aspiration as well as a memory, Morris's poem, serialised from March 1885 to July 1886 in the Socialist League journal, *Commonweal*, offers a 'glimpse of the coming day', made visible through the power of 'hope', a category of practical value for Morris, as it was for Linton, capable of redeeming the past in a revolutionary future. In this way, Morris appropriates the romance genre for contemporary use: 'I have heard people mis-called for being a romantic', he wrote, 'but what romance means is the capacity for a true conception of history, a power of making the past part of the present'.[114] Morris was more self-aware than was Linton, and more poetically self-confident than Ernest Jones. So it was easier for him to acknowledge his relation to the romantic tradition, and to work both within and against it, and not to find it troublesome to knit together a poetic which responded to the claims of both inner self and social teleology, locating in the narrative impulse of the medieval romance a counter-weight to the inwardness of romantic lyricism.

The Pilgrims of Hope as a narrative sequence interweaves a personal dialectic of identity and a public one of history. The hero and heroine, Richard and his wife, move from the agricultural plebeian culture of the countryside to an artisanal life in London, where they become Socialists. Though Richard is appalled by the poverty and exploitation that he finds in the 'grim net of London' (II), he does not create a false memory of the rural life left behind, for 'enough and to spare had I seen / Of hard and pinching want midst our quiet fields and green' (III). The contrast he makes is between the capitalism that pervades both city and country and a Socialist alternative, not a nostalgic contrast between city and country. At an open-air propaganda meeting, Richard gets into a scuffle with a heckler, and ends up in prison. He is then taken up by Arthur, an activist from a bourgeois background, and while the two men develop a good political relationship, Arthur falls in love with Richard's wife, which precipitates a crisis amongst the three of them, setting at odds the claims of their personal and their political lives.[115] Morris is here able to make good on the impulse of a communitarian poetic interwoven with the exigencies of autonomous selves; namely, to assert that the existential choices of the inward self are shaped by and help to shape the external constitutive goods which produce social goals and teleologies. Narratively, the personal crisis is resolved by the three comrades going off to join the Paris Commune, where Richard's wife and Arthur are both killed. Richard then returns to England to raise his son and organise for the Socialist future. Though he settles in the countryside of his youth, the breach that has opened between Richard and his past life makes him more aware of himself as a self cut adrift: 'Strange are they grown unto me; yea I to myself am strange' (VIII). But his experience has made him more aware of himself as potentially powerful within the activity of a collective, which is now decisively linked to the city. Separated from the plebeian past, Richard must use his voluntarist capability to choose the modern version of a constitutive good: namely, the urban site of collective organisation. For it is in the city, in Paris, that Richard sees, albeit briefly, the materialisation of his Socialist yearning: 'Such joy and peace and pleasure!' In the Paris Commune Richard sees 'what few have beheld, a folk with all hearts gay . . . / I say that I saw it now, real, solid, and at hand' (XI). In these lines we hear a late nineteenth-century romantic voice answer Wordsworth's recollection of 1791, when he too sought in French revolutionary possibility a place for a grounded transformation of the world,

> Not in Utopia . . .
> But in the very world which is the world
> Of all of us, the place in which, in the end,
> We find our happiness or not at all.[116]

By looking at *The Pilgrims of Hope* at the end of the argument which this study has undertaken, I am making a claim for the specifically romantic aspect of Morris's Socialism, and this returns us to the view of romanticism set out by E. P. Thompson in 1955 in his *William Morris: Romantic to Revolutionary*. In the two editions of that biography, Thompson offered readings of nineteenth-century romanticism which aimed to recover from within it a revolutionary tradition consistent with revolutionary practice.[117] In his 1976 revision of the study, Thompson invited critics to consider the book with an eye to its presentation of the issue of romanticism: 'But I would hope that one part of [the volume's] structure – the part least noted by its critics – might receive a little attention before it is pulled down: that is, the analysis of Romanticism and of its trajectory in Morris's life.'[118] In order to show how *The Pilgrims of Hope* can be understood as a lyrical sequence in addition to a narrative one, I want to pause and consider Thompson's view of English poetic romanticism.

Thompson argues that romanticism begins as 'a passionate protest against an intolerable social reality', which atrophies in the course of the century into 'little more than a yearning nostalgia or a sweet complaint'.[119] Thompson argued strongly in his 1976 edition that if the original indigenous tradition of revolutionary 'desire' had been listened to by British Marxists, the crisis-ridden history of 'scientific' Marxism might have had quite a different outcome. But whether in the 1955 discussion, in which Morris moves from being a romantic to being a revolutionary, or in the 1976 version, in which Morris's romanticism is understood as a significant gesture towards an English Marxism that 'failed to reciprocate', the terms of the discussion of revolution and romanticism generally, and particularly the case of William Morris, were unquestionably set by Thompson in the 1950s, and came to be taken as assumptions by the 1980s.[120]

In the revised version of the biography, Thompson specifies Keats as the chief poetic influence on Morris's own 'youthful revolt'. Thompson views Keats's late romantic achievement as 'the acute tension between the richness of the life of the senses and the imagination and the poverty of everyday experience', and applauds 'Keats's struggle to reconcile the two': the Victorian appropriation of the medieval romance, via Keats, as a template for mid-century romanticism expressed the mid-century revolt against the industrial age.[121] However, Thompson goes on to argue, this revolt, much enervated from Wordsworth's and Coleridge's first burst of Jacobin romanticism, as well as from the republican internationalism of the second-generation romantics, Byron and Shelley, resulted in the aestheticisation of the central poetic movement of the century.

Thompson's argument is developed sequentially. Keats comes after Shelley, as inward-turning comes after social engagement: 'Art [for Keats] was no longer conceived, as by Shelley, as an agent in man's struggle to master nature and discover himself. Art (if we set aside a lingering faith in its refining moral influence) was conceived as a compensation for the poverty of life.'[122] Morris enters the scene as a defender and builder of this Keatsian revolt and is then, through his engagement with the socialist movement, himself transmuted: 'Morris, the Romantic in revolt, became a realist and a revolutionary.'[123] But as John Goode has pointed out, Thompson's 1976 revision of the Morris biography included a reduction in Thompson's analysis of romanticism; most importantly, the excision of the extended discussion of Shelley.[124] Goode finds the warrant for this deletion in Thompson's remark that 'while in the 1880s Morris was to carry forward all that was most positive in the Republican and internationalist traditions of Byron and Shelley, in the 1850s these seem to have exercised only a passing influence on his conscious mind'.[125] And yet for Thompson this 1880s return to the 'positive' presents a different sort of problem, because, although he organises his biography around the vindication of the romantic lineage for an understanding of the genius and contribution of Morris's work, he does not actually think that Morris's explicitly socialist verse is very good, preferring to focus on the importance of *A Dream of John Ball* and *News from Nowhere* as the significant productions of the later work.

For Thompson the deficiency of the 1880s poems is precisely how much they 'rely upon words, images, rhythms coined in the romantic movement' and therefore 'cannot be said to lay the foundations of a poetry of "revolutionary realism"'.[126] So, even though he admires Morris's political ambitions and local motives in *The Pilgrims of Hope*, Thompson observes that it is marked by 'weakness in construction [and] technical slackness bred of haste and lack of concentration'.[127] Thompson has not been alone in making a negative assessment of the sequence. In 1899, in the first major biography of Morris, J. W. Mackail wrote that a few of the sections of the poem would 'stand high among [Morris's] finest work', but that it was mostly characterised by 'weakness and unreality'.[128] More recently, the editor of Morris's letters, Norman Kelvin, has argued that in *The Pilgrims of Hope*, Morris 'failed to create in poetry a language that would describe, express, and idealize – transform into an epic of modern time – a social-political event that had captured his imagination', and therefore Kelvin has 'ranked it decidedly below his earlier major poems'.[129] Even in one of the very few extended discussions of the poem, Michael Holzman writes from the assumption that the poem is a failure: 'We can also account for its failure as a work of art, a failure of the form to contain the conflict between the topical subject matter of the poem and the personal emotions that flowed into it when Morris began to write about the period around 1870.'[130] Running through all these remarks is a desire for a sequence with a narrative in it to be a 'realist' narrative.

There is, however, another tradition of appreciation of the poem, one which precisely does attribute to it the virtue of that 'revolutionary realism' which Thompson invokes. In 1897, describing Morris's proto-Socialist and Socialist materials written and printed between 1878 and 1890, Buxton-Forman looks first at Morris's pamphlets and activist songs – *Chants for Socialists* – and goes on:

but a far higher effort than these is the poem of modern life called *The Pilgrims of Hope*, which lies buried in the first two volumes of *Commonweal* ... Although this was privately reprinted [by Buxton-Forman], the poet has kept it by him to render it more perfect in form; but whether he has left any revision or not, the poem will ultimately rank among his leading works, and is likely to remain, for another generation of English readers, the most remarkable thing in the distinctly militant literature of the Socialist movement among us.[131]

Morris's friend and comrade, Bruce Glasier, a leader of the Socialist League in Scotland and a resolute believer in the political efficacy of poetry, was the first to devote full critical attention to the text, calling *The Pilgrims of Hope* a 'proletarian epic'. Glasier argued: 'Of all his poetical writings [*The Pilgrims of Hope*] is the most objective or realistic, and it might be said to be of all modern poems the most modern in ethical feeling.'[132] The most significant recent reading of the poem, Florence Boos's 'Narrative Design in *The Pilgrims of Hope*', has begun the recovery of the poem by tracing the interweaving of internal and external problems in the poem: '[the] balance of interior vision and historical reality provides evidence that struggle and resistance within these cycles may yet achieve some of our deepest human purposes'.[133] Boos makes the case that an apparent lack of integration between the private and public themes of the poem in fact respects the complexity of Morris's understanding of revolutionary struggle and personal identity.

Glasier aimed to establish the poem within the realist, not the romantic literary tradition. And in its evocation of the conflicts between personal and political commitments, the poem does indeed in part belong to the traditions of English realism; furthermore, as a poetic undertaking within realism, it has affinities with, though it also constitutes a rejoinder to, George Meredith's 1862 poetic sequence, *Modern Love*. When Richard, the protagonist of *The Pilgrims of Hope*, realises that his wife and Arthur have fallen in love, he visualises 'the sharp and bitter pain / As the sword 'twixt the lovers bewildered in the fruitless marriage' (x). We feel that we are very close here to Meredith's image in *Modern Love* of the loveless married couple lying together like medieval effigies, wishing for the 'sword that severs all'.[134]

But though *The Pilgrims of Hope* belongs to and investigates what Glasier calls 'the deeper moral vicissitudes of modern human existence', it does so within a framework which suggests larger and more social sources and solutions to existential problems.[135] The deep pessimism of Meredith's sonnet sequence is assuaged in *The Pilgrims of Hope* by Morris's appeal to a social good, and the possibilities of a socially redemptive 'hope'. The poem is not sacrificial or transcendent; rather it suggests an alternative understanding of love relations within a larger network of social relations. It is because of their revolutionary commitment that, unlike the estranged couple in Meredith's sonnet sequence, the feeling which wraps together Richard and his wife 'was not wrath or reproaching, or the chill of love-born hate' (x).

Glasier uses the categories of realism and epic to make sense of *The Pilgrims of Hope*, and Morris does suggest an epic tradition with his martial theme, his ambition to assert the epic claim for a new civilisation. His use of both an alliterative metre which suggests Anglo-Saxon epic and a line that has echoes of the classical hexameter attests to his awareness of the traditions he was working with. But *The Pilgrims of Hope* is also centrally indebted to romantic and lyrical traditions; and these enable Morris to supply the non-transcendent, social solution to the problems the poem poses. Thompson's complaint that in returning to Shelley's 'Ode to the West Wind' in 'The Message of the March Wind', the opening poem of *The Pilgrims of Hope*, Morris was trying to recover an outmoded poetic is not adequate to the aspect of that tradition that Morris was engaged in when he entered Socialist politics and helped to shape Socialist poetics. Morris himself thought very highly of the poem: on 10 February, he wrote to Jane Morris that it was 'not bad I think'; two weeks later he called it 'the best short poem I have written'.[136] Three points should be noted here: first, the importance of Shelley's poetic to an on-going tradition of political poets makes Morris's place in that tradition contemporary and not atavistic. Second, Morris's yoking together of the communitarian poetic with the romantic presentation of inwardness make this poem exemplary of an on-going dialectic of the individualism and communitarianism whose form in the 1880s took the rhetorical shape of an argument about individualism and collectivism.[137] And third, the presentation of this romantic power replies to and criticises the *weak* romanticism of that late Victorian poetic which concentrated almost entirely on the inward, isolated self. Once we substitute the notion of an on-going romantic dynamic for Thompson's implicit model of the movement's blossoming and withering, we are in a better position to see how, for example, the modernist poetics of Anglo-Communism execute another turn of this romantic dialectic.

The presence of the romantic tradition is a positive factor, rather than a liability, in Morris's political poetic. And in addition to Shelley's influence, we find in Morris's Socialist poetry evidence as well of the even earlier revolutionary romanticism of Blake. The London of 'The Bridge and the Street', the second poem in *The Pilgrims of Hope*, and one of those which uses a four-beat oral song metre, is Blake's London, with the trammelled and 'charter'd' river running through it as the sign of both constraint and possibility: 'On each side lay the City, and Thames ran between it / Dark, struggling, unheard 'neath the wheels and the feet' (II). The war-machine which the bourgeoisie has outfitted to destroy the barricades of the Paris Commune is a machine of those 'wheels within wheels' of Blake's fallen Jerusalem. And the bitter speech of Richard when he is released from prison reverberates against Enion's lament at the end of the second Night of Blake's *The Four Zoas*, where Wisdom can be bought only 'in the desolate marketplace', and Experience bought with the price 'of all that a man hath'.[138]

But the crucial aspect of the romantic tradition that Morris drew upon in the 1880s was not the influence of the republicanism and internationalism that Thompson associates with the rationalist individualist traditions of Byron and Shelley (i.e., that which is most properly associated with liberalism) but that of popular radical and Chartist songs. As I noted earlier in this chapter, by the 1880s and 1890s the struggle to claim and shape an alternative, 'people's' literary canon had been abandoned, but a strong impulse remained to focus on and develop the rôle of the interventionist song.[139] The proliferation of Socialist hymn books and song books, and the absence of Socialist poetry anthologies is witness to the gap between high and low culture, poetics and song, which it had been part of the Chartist literary mission to refute. *The Pilgrims of Hope* is a fascinating text partially because it grew out of the popular genre of Morris's *Chants for Socialists*, songs he composed and printed in *Justice* and *Commonweal* between 1883 and 1884. These were songs which served the same functions as had Chartist songs.[140] But Morris's *Chants* exhibit self-consciousness about the interaction between oral and print modes in a period of mass literacy. His use of the category of 'chant' emphasises this awareness: the form suggests something between speech and song. In 1919, Bruce Glasier would describe the songs in an anachronistic language. He says of Morris's songs that, 'The best mode of rendering the verses would be to chant them to the accompaniment of a harp or lute, as the old minstrels did their *chansons de geste*.'[141] By that point, the life of the interventionist poetic had been severely reduced: on the one hand, the Socialist movement produced a proliferation of songs meant to be sung at meetings; on the other hand, there was a depletion of poems as autonomous forms available for either oral performance or print publication. The coy antiquarianism of Glasier's comment registers the inefficacy of the genre in his own time and world. He takes the patently literary character of this poem and medievalises it in order to preserve some link to an oral tradition; but the anachronism of his claim suggests that these poems belong to coterie, rather than congregational experience.

Both E. P. Thompson and Chris Waters focus on the degree to which the *Chants for Socialists* carry forward what they consider to be romantic conventions. Thompson writes that 'the poems caught fire in the hearts of the comrades ... whose previous knowledge of romantic verse had accustomed them to the material which Morris used'; and Waters writes that the popularity of Morris's *Chants* 'rested less on their expression of socialist convictions than on the way in which they conveyed those convictions through forms of imagery that would have been familiar to those knowledgeable of romantic verse'.[142]

Appreciative as these two comments are of Morris's talent, neither takes into account how much the version of romantic verse that Morris draws upon was in fact the communitarian impulse within romanticism which had fuelled the poetics of political and social movements from the 1790s onwards. Morris draws more on the version of romanticism developed in Ernest Jones's poetics than directly from an autonomous romanticism as we understand it as the voice of the individualist lyric. Morris recovers and develops the communitarian aspect of romanticism, knitting the influence of his immediate political predecessors in Jones and the Chartist poets together with the Pre-Raphaelites' discovery of Blake's radical poetic. All this was part of his response to what he felt was the vitiating individualism of late nineteenth-century capitalism.

One of the *Chants*, 'The Voice of Toil', first published in *Justice*, is a direct inheritor of Jones's 'Our' series: Morris creates a collective subjectivity in Jones's vein, and freights it with Blake's understanding of the entanglements of psychological and political oppression:

> Where home is a hovel and dull we grovel,
> Forgetting that the world is fair;
> Where no babe we cherish, lest its very soul perish;
> Where our mirth is crime, our love a snare.[143]

Chris Waters has studied the frequency of Morris's *Chants* in Socialist songbooks compiled between 1888 and 1912, and virtually all of them contain Morris's work. Cooper's 'Truth Is Growing', and Jones's 'The Song of the Lower Classes' were also reprinted in Socialist songbooks.[144]

Morris's 1892 'May Day' chant, which enacts an exchange between 'The Workers' and 'The Earth' revives Shelley's communitarian Earth from 'The Mask of Anarchy', who again asks, 'Are ye few? Are they many?' reiterating her admonition in the earlier poem: 'Ye are many – they are few!' The poem asserts the importance of poetic tradition itself, the necessity of linking the narratives of the past to those of the present and the future: 'Many years were we wordless and nought was our deed', say the workers, 'but now the word flitteth from brother to brother'.[145]

'The Day Is Coming', similar to Jones's 'The Better Hope', asserts the importance of recovering narrative forms to make sense of identity in relation to a past and in relation to the future. In this sense Morris returns to the place of narrative within lyric, balladic forms. But the context is very different from when Wordsworth worked through this problematic in the 1790s. By making explicit residual elements of customary culture in the context of the voluntaristic self, Wordsworth was signalling that culture's dissolution. Morris, linking the voice of narration to the collective, links it as well to the capabilities of a collective affiliation achieved through voluntaristic choice, in the manner of Jones: 'Why, then, and for what are we waiting? there are three words to speak: / WE WILL IT.'[146] In 'All for the Cause', Morris asserts that the narratives of political martyrdom are neither nostalgic nor irrelevant: 'E'en the tidings we are telling was the tale they had to tell, / E'en the hope that our hearts cherish, was the hope for which they fell.'[147]

The first two poems in *The Pilgrims of Hope* are written in song metre, after which Morris takes on a complex and interesting metrical intention. The verse of the rest of *Pilgrims of Hope* is written in a six-beat stress metre. As Derek Attridge points out, the underlying pattern of six-beat metres is three beats, one unrealised beat, repeated; hence, a variant of the four-beat line.[148] Morris draws on the four-beat metre, but needs a line suited to narrative that is somewhat more adaptable. And at the same time, the metre suggests a variation of an imitation of a classical hexameter. The alliteration suggests an Anglo-Saxon nativist poetic mode; the

hexameters, an international classical epic mode. *The Pilgrims of Hope*
reaffirms the communitarian poetic at the same time as it links together
print and oral metres, and also links together song and epic. In *The Pilgrims
of Hope*, Morris reaffirms, albeit in a minor key, a *literary* as well as a *song*
culture. And this work has the same sort of hybridity to it as the Linton
sequence of 'Rhymes and Reasons'. So, while it is true that *The Pilgrims of
Hope* makes sense within the realist tradition, its poetic intention seems
more closely linked to the tradition of romanticism. Given Morris's keen
antagonism to the principles of architectural restoration, it is unlikely that
he was concerned to 'restore' romantic poetics. Rather, he was aware of
the transpersonality of tradition: as he wrote of designers, the poet 'be he
never so original . . . [is] under the influence of *tradition*; dead men guide
his hand even when he forgets that they ever existed'.[149]

At the same time, there is a particularly 1880s flavour to Morris's
verse which is absent in both Jones and Linton, steeped as it is in that
atmosphere Stephen Yeo has described as 'the religion of socialism'. 1880s
Socialist rhetoric bears an encrustation of Victorian sentimentality, rather
than the romantic engagement of competing theories of identity. This
voice skews some of the romantic influence. For example, Fred
Henderson's poem 'The Cry', which brings Christ together with the
speaker observing the city 'Where weary faces drifted up and down',
emerges from Blake's London, but bears an almost pre-Raphaelite
aura.[150] Even though it was Morris who invoked the 'religion of socialism',
his poetry struggles against the flat edge of this piety.[151] Rather, in the
'Message of the March Wind', the speaker laments the irrelevance of most
art to those who work in what Richard later calls 'city squalor and country
stupor' (v):

> The singers have sung and the builders have builded;
> The painters have fashioned their tales of delight;
> For what and for whom hath the world's book been gilded,
> When all is for these but the blackness of night? (i)

Richard then vows that 'from henceforth no fair words shall be hiding /
The night of the wretched, the days of the poor' (ii). *The Pilgrims of Hope*
goes on to recover a possible poetic: one which will harness the truth of the
past to build for 'the day to be' (xiii). Morris's version of the 'conversion'
experiences of Socialism is about the making of personal identity:
Richard learns that he is both an isolated self, and also one amongst many,
recognised by his comrades: 'he spoke like a friend long known; and lo! I
was one of the band' (v).

In the autumn before he began work on *The Pilgrims of Hope*, Morris wrote to Fred Henderson in the dialect of the interventionist poetic. Henderson had found himself, Morris wrote, 'confronted by the rising hope of the people, and have been able to declare yourself a soldier of the Cause ... believe me this is better than mere poetry-writing, for you will find something to do in the movement & doubtless will fill your place worthily ... you will find you will add such backbone to your poetry by your work in the Cause as will make it indeed worthwhile to write poetry'.[152] The focus on the poet as a special type of person was anathema to Morris. He argued that poets should take up their part in the general burden of work: a poet 'will write better poetry and not worse if he has an ordinary occupation to follow'.[153] As in the Chartist history of the literature of the 'people', Morris was concerned with the transindividual aspect of creation, both in craft and in poetry. Epic poems are the greatest, Morris writes: 'They are in no sense the work of individuals, but have grown up from the very heart of the *people*.'[154] Morris welcomed literary scholarship that shifted the authorship of the Greek epics into collectivity: 'Modern research has made Homer a dim and doubtful shadow to us, while it has added clearness to our vision of the life of the people of that time, who were the real authors of the Homeric poems.'[155] But Morris was not centrally interested in the construction of a people's poetic in the way that Ernest Jones had been, and he never made the same global claims for the political work of poetry as had the radical poets of thirty years earlier. Morris wrote on 6 November 1885 to Henderson: 'But now language is utterly degraded in our daily lives, and poets have to make a new tongue each for himself'. Morris here suggests that the individualism of contemporary poetry is a reflex of political defeat, which has infiltrated the very building blocks of communication. There is a suggestion here of a poetic Babel, all poets speaking unintelligibly to one another.

Morris's decision early in the process of composition to let the lyrics of *Commonweal* develop into a narrative is matched in the later numbers of the sequence by his decision to open up the nativism of the first poems to the internationalism of the Paris Commune. At the poem's thematic centre stands the complex image of the Paris Commune – an image of a revolutionary fusion of the values of communitarianism with the assets of urban life. Because of his own access to the communitarian tradition, Morris is able to make palpable not only the contemporary political links between the Commune and the struggle for Socialism in Britain, but also the connections between the values of the Commune and a set of values already deep in a British tradition. Morris is, able, in other words, to 'English' the Paris Commune, make it congruent with a nativist tradition. Morris is able to allude to the communitarian tradition within the social movements of Spenceanism and Chartism without reproducing them, drawing upon but not copying his precursor styles. It has been argued that in *The Pilgrims of Hope* the contrast created between the city and country is rather facile, 'practically the equivalent of that between capitalist oppression and revolutionary freedom'.[156] If that were true, then the poem might well be viewed as simply a recapitulation of the theme of 'romanticism as a criticism of industrialism'. Yet rurality is never posited as a revolutionary goal in the poem, but rather as the first moment in a spiralling dialectic, and the political possibilities that are seen in the city mean that it is not a simple repository of negative value. It is not city versus country so much as capitalism – agricultural or industrial – that Morris attacks in this poem.

The image and memory of the Paris Commune was an important screen onto which British Socialism came to project its own representations and fantasies. The end of the century as a political episode was a period of crisis within liberalism, its privileges under pressure from the new trade unions of gasworkers and railway workers, unmoored from the compromises made by the trade union leaders of craft unions in the mid-century. And Liberalism had to deal with the politicisation of Socialism. The theorising of collectivisation gave a new turn to the deeper tradition of community. The roots of this shift lie back in late eighteenth-century plebeian 'recalcitrance', but its later nineteenth-century form is predicated on an analysis of capitalist relations, in which the antidote to individual alienation is the choice of association made possible by the paradoxical collectivity of the workplace: site of both personal alienation and collective solidarity. Morris's access to contemporary theories of society, which permeated both Liberal and Socialist groupings, offered him the ability to see how elements of the 'moral economy' of plebeian communitarianism were forerunners of the 'sciences' of society with their social and political attention to 'collectivism'.

Within the London milieu, the scramble amongst Socialists and Liberals for the support of the working class was compounded by the difficult relationship between trade unionists and Socialists.[157] Because both the Social Democratic Federation and Morris's wing of the movement, the Socialist League, were busier formulating their political positions than linking up with the newly forming unions, the Liberals for a period managed to resolve their crisis by evolving what was called 'the new liberalism', aiming to bridge the gap between working class and middle class by channelling the push for labour representation through its own party forms, and thereby both hastening its own decline, and also weakening the autonomy of the labour movement by dosing it with liberal ideology. Stefan Collini has analysed the way in which a debate between 'individualism and collectivism' permeated the spectrum of political parties: collectivism by the end of the 1880s was employed not only by the 'avowedly Socialist organisations' but, for the 'radicalism of Liberal proposals and legislation'.[158]

For the Socialist movement, the Paris Commune survived as an image of purity. The Commune, moreover, conveyed a particular poignancy, as one aspect of the long nineteenth-century romantic dialectic was the persistence of a communitarian motive within urban popular poetics and politics. This element was made explicit in the Commune, offering an image of a people's self-government which, while resembling the practices of the medieval and rural communes, was contemporary, urban, and suffused by a new sense of power amongst the labouring poor.

Within the Leninist tradition, the Commune occupies the position of fulcrum for the revolutionary narrative stretching from 1789 to 1917. For Marx himself, one of the most crucial aspects of the Commune was the way in which it demonstrated the dialectical *reconstruction* of the form of the primitive commune as the communal structure of the future. In *The Civil War in France*, he writes:

It is generally the fate of completely new historical creations to be mistaken for the counterpart of older and even defunct forms of social life, to which they may bear a certain likeness. Thus, this new Commune which breaks the modern State power, has been mistaken for a reproduction of the medieval communes.[159]

Just as agrarianism as an element in an urban plebeian politics was not a simple desire to 'return to the land', so the Commune bore traces of medievalism but transformed them in the context of an urban heterogeneity of artisanal, industrial, and newly displaced rural workers.[160] In a first draft of the pamphlet, Marx wrote that the Commune 'was a revolution against the State itself, of this supernaturalist abortion of society, a resumption by the people for the people of its own social life'.[161] So, the anti-hierarchical aspect of the Commune, whose meaning for workers' real lives bore absolutely no resemblance to the oppressive hierarchy of the feudal commune, nonetheless did bear a genealogical relationship to continuous plebeian traditions. These are what Victor Shanin, discussing Marx's pamphlet, calls 'vernacular traditions':

To all those steeped in Hegelian dialectics, children resembled their grand-parents more than their parents. The 'primary' commune, dialectically restored on a new and higher level of material wealth and global interaction, entered Marx's images of the future communist society, one in which once more the 'individuals behave not as labourers but as owners – as members of a community which also labours'.[162]

The heterogeneous elements within the Commune were ideologically represented by and through languages of class as well as languages of custom and enlightenment rationality. And these elements show a kinship with the same uncertain mix which had peopled London in the 1790s.

The Commune, then, offered itself to Morris as a representation both external to England, and also internal, by virtue of an analogous vernacu-lar structure. While both Socialists and Liberals in Britain called upon the memory of the French Revolution throughout the nineteenth century, the Commune was an image that was claimed almost exclusively by the Socialist movement in the 1880s and 1890s. Though British radicals and liberals had supported the city of Paris and the republic against the Prussian invasion, they soon rallied around the bourgeois Thiers govern-ment in Versailles, which was the instrument of the brutal repression in April 1871 of the artisan and working-class Commune.[163] Central English intellectuals were straightforwardly in support of the Thiers government, including Carlyle, Eliot, Browning, and Tennyson, who deplored the 'red fool-fury of the Seine'.[164]

W. J. Linton's support of the Commune has then to be put in the context of a more general liberal repudiation of it, and understood as part of the complexity of his version of republicanism. Linton's wife, Eliza Lynn Linton, wrote an interesting novel about the Commune in 1872, *The True History of Joshua Davidson, Christian and Communist*, which adumbrates in some respects Morris's evocation of the Commune. In her novel, a young woman, Mary Princep, becomes part of and is sacrificed to the revolutionary movement, operating as an index of the Commune's re-publican purity, as well as a foil to the allegorical narrative of Joshua Davidson, a Christian Socialist martyr. The novel went through three editions within three months of publication.[165]

In England, it was primarily the International and the Positivists who came out in support of the Commune itself. That the General Council of the International Working Men's Association would issue a pamphlet as incendiary as Marx and Engels's *The Civil War in France*, suggested to the Liberals that the International, hardly heard of before, might pose an immediate threat to Britain. The Commune and the International were thus linked in Liberal and Conservative circles, and were the objects of hundreds of attacks in the press, which thereby put Karl Marx on the intellectual map in Britain for the first time. In 1871 and 1872 British politicians and establishment intellectuals claimed that the International had been at the heart of the Paris events, and that it was planning, from its offices in High Holborn, to organise a similar insurrection in Britain.[166] Eleanor Marx recalled near the end of her life that in 1871 there had been a prevalent 'condition of perfectly frantic fury of the whole middle class against the Commune ... It was proposed – quite seriously – that the Communards who had taken refuge in England should be handed over to the doctors and the hospitals for purposes of vivisection'.[167]

The influx of Communard refugees did have the immediate effect of augmenting the internationalist orientation of the post-Chartist period in the London radical sphere, and a tradition was initiated of a yearly commemoration of the Commune.[168] These anniversaries served a practical purpose in the political excitement of the 1880s and 1890s, providing a rallying point and a platform for the often warring factions within the Socialist movement. These meetings often included exiles from the Commune itself, including famous French revolutionaries, such as the *pétroleuse* Louise Michel.[169] With the arrival in London of Russian anarchist exiles such as Kropotkin and Stepniak, and their inclusion on the platforms, these events gave evidence of an international movement.

Morris's own participation in the Commune anniversary commemorations began in 1884, on the first anniversary of Marx's death, and the thirteenth of the Commune, when the London Socialist community sponsored a march and rally at Highgate cemetery. Morris wrote to Jane Morris that he had been 'loath to go, but did not dislike it when I did go'. The marchers were refused entry into the cemetery, 'so we adjourned to an uncomfortable piece of waste ground near by and [the "International"] was sung and the speeches made'.[170] Over the course of the next seven years, Morris was to continue to participate in Paris Commune celebrations, and to use *Commonweal* as a site for returning to the history of the Commune and bringing out its lessons for readers. In the month following the 1886 commemorative meeting Morris introduced the topic of the Commune into *The Pilgrims of Hope*. In fact, though scholars and commentators write about the sequence as if the poem were 'about' the Paris Commune, the subject of the Commune is only introduced in poem No. XI, 'A Glimpse of the Coming Day'. As one reads through the successive numbers of *Commonweal*, it seems likely that Morris, preoccupied with the anniversary celebrations, realised that in drawing on this historical event he might locate exactly the dramatic turning-point that the sequence needed, a way of demonstrating a potential material and social solution to the personal problems raised in the poem. The inability of the three friends to resolve their emotional relationships is subsumed into the more pressing circumstance of making the conditions under which a resolution might even be dreamt of. We are not left with a certain knowledge that Richard himself has resolved the question, but rather that individual issues must be answered within the scope of collective ones. The Paris Commune offers Richard the vision of a new geography in which a rational collective urban life might emerge from the communitarian impulse:

> So at last from a grey stone building we saw great flag fly,
> One colour, red and solemn 'gainst the blue of the spring-tide sky,
> And we stopped and turned to each other, and as each at each did
>   we gaze,
> The city's hope enwrapped us with joy and great amaze. (xi)

Morris finished his verse sequence by reminding his readers of the purpose of the romance, to make the past a part of the present, and thus available for the future. To his child, and other children, Richard affirms the power of hope to draw from the past to build the future: 'Year after year shall men meet the red flag overhead, / And shall call on the help of the vanquished and kindness of the dead' (xiii). At the end of the last installment of the poem in *Commonweal*, entitled 'The Story's Ending', Morris added 'to be concluded'. Yet he never added another section. Mackail notes this as evidence that the poem simply fell apart. I think it more likely, given the title of the section, that Morris was suggesting that the sequence would truly end when its predicated 'hope' was fully realised in the political and social sphere.

Morris's use of the linked lyrical-narrative form suggests its place as a lyrical balladry for his time. Like Meredith's *Modern Love* and Clough's *Amours de Voyage*, Morris writes something like a novel in verse; but like Wordsworth's *Lyrical Ballads*, he forces the explicitation of the relationship between the communitarian version of identity as choice, and the solitary depth of modern inwardness.

Conclusion

I have ended this study with William Morris's Socialist poems, and with the ghost of Wordsworth's *Lyrical Ballads*. Though this suggests some circularity, the dialectic of romanticism does not end in the 1890s. It continues to lead a more and less attenuated life, flowering in moments of political upheaval, disappearing almost entirely at other times, and shifting its locus amongst many different kinds of political projects, fanning out from the labour movement and into the CND, the campaigns against imperialist intervention, the Women's Liberation Movement, and a proliferation of socio-political identity groupings.

One episode which deserves full treatment in a study of twentieth-century poetry is that of Anglo-Communism, most seriously exemplified in poems by W. H. Auden. In ballads such as 'As I walked out one evening', and 'Miss Gee', Auden reinvents the lyrical ballad for the twentieth century.[1] These poems speak from the depth of a deracinated inwardness. While Wordsworth's 'Simon Lee' has the sympathetic narrator to make sense of his difficulties, the narrator of 'Miss Gee' is hollow, cynical: 'She passed by the loving couples / And they didn't ask her to stay.' But Auden's version of communitarian romanticism still urges him on to locate external goods in a collective engagement:

> O stand, stand at the window
>   As the tears scald and start;
> You shall love your crooked neighbour
>   With your crooked heart.

The redeployment of the lyrical ballad in Auden's poetic is compounded of a modernist impersonality, which recapitulates the impersonality of plebeian balladry, while burning out the sentiment of the late eighteenth-century humanitarian ballad, replacing it with a corrosive psychoanalysis of interiority, where 'motives like stowaways / Are found too late'.

Auden repudiated his greatest poem in the communitarian tradition of romanticism, 'Spain', but it continues to be reprinted and read. 'Spain' evokes 'The beautiful roar of the chorus under the dome' which exalts a collective human sublime at the same moment as it pokes fun at human habits and hobbies, 'the exchanging of tips on the breeding of terriers.' The pilgrims in 'Spain' are less hopeful than Morris's, for they feel themselves to be more fully determined by their destructive psychic impulses: 'And our faces, the institute face, the chain-store, the ruin / Are projecting their greed as the firing squad and the bomb.'

The self-awareness of Auden's communitarian position places him, like Ernest Jones, in the lineage of Byron, composed 'Of Eros and of dust'. In 'September 1, 1939', Auden's voice is situated in the already-elegiac: he sits 'alone and afraid', the decade's hopes are dashed, and his immediate geography is the city of anomie, New York. Unlike the Chartist exiles in Van Dieman's Land, Auden in exile does not mystify the English landscape. In this poem, Auden ironises the claims of the dialectic of romanticism by positioning against each other a collective nightmare of fascism and the enervated inwardness of modern individualism. But Auden also insists on the inescapable ambiguity of both desiring 'to be loved alone' and knowing that 'We must love one another or die.'[2] The poet is poised where the 'Just / Exchange their messages', and even though 'Beleaguered by the same / Negation and despair', he aims to 'Show an affirming flame.' In this attenuation of the romantic, the competing claims of the individual and the collective are equally compelling and insufficient.

A companion study to this one would explore the residual life of the romantic engagement well into the twentieth century. The rush of poetry written within the mining community during the Great Strike of 1984–85 is one such episode. Alongside it, the place of interventionist poetics in the women's movement, and lately, in the revitalisation of oral poetics through British Afro-Caribbean, Asian, and Irish culture suggests pathways in which residual romanticism is interwoven with other, global poetic resources.

By returning to Thompson's version of romanticism in the final chapter, I have circled back to the opening of this study, which originated in a criticism of Thompson's elevation of the 'Jacobinism-in-recoil' at the expense of other voices. For though the main movement of this study has been to make a place for poets and poetic intentions which have been under-represented in our normative accounts of romanticism, my aim has also been to suggest ways of thinking about romantic lyricism as a dynamic which can accommodate both canonical and non-canonical romantic poets, and so recover our sense of both the variety and the coherence of the romantic project. At the start of this work I cited Thompson's remark that Blake was the singular example of a poet who threaded together the discourses of artisan radicalism and romanticism: 'After William Blake, no mind was at home in both cultures, nor had the genius to interpret the two traditions to each other.'[3] I hope to have shown that there was in fact the vigorous interchange that Thompson had wished for. But the fact that such an interaction did exist suggests as well that it has not yet had the efficacy that Thompson imagined it would produce. We remain pilgrims of hope.

Notes

INTRODUCTION. ROMANTIC STUDIES AS A UNIFIED FIELD

1 Stuart Curran has given a good accounting of the assumption of the anti-generic orientation in romantic poetry in *Poetic Form and British Romanticism* (Oxford: Oxford University Press, 1986), 4, 21, 207. But see as well the arguments of Jean-Luc Nancy and Philippe Lacoue-Labarthe about the modern status of the romantic fragment in *The Literary Absolute: the Theory of Literature in German Romanticism*, trans. Philip Barnard and Cheryl Lesser (Albany: State University of New York, 1988) and 'Genre', *Glyph* 7 (1981), 2: 'Romanticism will always be more than a period . . . in fact, it has not yet stopped in-completing the period it began'.

2 Jerome McGann, *The Romantic Ideology* (Chicago: University of Chicago Press, 1980), and Marjorie Levinson, *Wordsworth's Great Period Poems* (Cambridge: Cambridge University Press, 1986).

3 Marilyn Butler's *Romantics, Rebels, and Reactionaries: English Literature and Its Background, 1760–1830* (Oxford: Oxford University Press, 1981) gives an excellent reading of the continuity between enlightenment and romantic practice.

4 Jacques Barzun, *Romanticism and the Modern Ego* (Boston: Little, Brown, 1944).

5 Frank Kermode, *Romantic Image* (London: Routledge and Kegan Paul, 1957); Bloom, *Poetry and Repression: Revisionism from Blake to Stevens* (New Haven: Yale University Press, 1975); Nancy and Lacoue-Labarthe, *Literary Absolute*.

6 Butler, *Romantics*; Curran, *Poetic Form*; *Romanticism: an Anthology*, edited by Duncan Wu (Oxford: Blackwell, 1994); *The New Oxford Book of Romantic Period Verse*, edited by Jerome McGann (Oxford: Oxford University Press, 1994); *Women Romantic Poets 1785–1832*, edited by Jennifer Breen (London: Dent, 1992); *The New Oxford Book of Eighteenth Century Verse*, edited by Roger Lonsdale (Oxford: Oxford University Press, 1984); *Romantic Women Poets, 1770–1838*, edited by Andrew Ashfield (Manchester: Manchester University Press, 1995); *Nineteenth Century Women Poets*, edited by Isobel Armstrong and Joseph Bristow, with Cath Sharrock (Oxford: Oxford University Press, 1997).

7 Margaret Homans's two volumes on nineteenth-century literature were the pioneering discussions of the silenced romantic woman. See Margaret Homans, *Women Writers and Poetic Identity* (Princeton: Princeton University Press, 1980) and *Bearing the Word: Language and Female Experience in Nineteenth-Century Women's Writing* (Chicago: University of Chicago Press, 1986). Both Homans and Susan Wolfson have done considerable work on the problems faced by Dorothy Wordsworth. For a fascinating response to Homans, see Wolfson's 'Dorothy Wordsworth in Conversation with William', in *Romanticism and Feminism*, edited by Anne K. Mellor (Bloomington: Indiana University Press, 1988), 139–165.

8 Stuart Curran, 'The Altered "I"', in *Romanticism and Feminism*, edited by Anne Mellor, 185–207; Donna Landry, *The Muses of Resistance: Labouring-Class Women's Poetry in Britain, 1739–1796* (Cambridge: Cambridge University Press, 1990); *Women Romantic Poets*, edited by Breen.

9 See Nicola J. Watson, *Revolution and the Form of the English Novel, 1790–1825, Intercepted Letters, Interrupted Seductions* (Oxford: Clarendon Press, 1994); Gary Kelly, *Women, Writing, Revolution 1790–1827* (Oxford: Oxford University Press, 1993); Mary Favret, *Romantic Correspondence: Women, Politics and the Fiction of Letters* (Cambridge: Cambridge University Press, 1993).

10 Jerome McGann, *The Poetics of Sensibility* (Oxford: Oxford University Press, 1997).

11 McGann, *Romantic Ideology*; Levinson, *Wordsworth's Great Period Poems*; Raymond Williams, *Marxism and Literature* (Oxford: Oxford University Press, 1977); Raymond Williams, *Culture and Society* (London: Chatto & Windus, 1958); Terry Eagleton, *Criticism and Ideology* (London: New Left Books, 1976).

12 Malcolm Chase, *'The People's Farm': English Radical Agrarianism 1775–1840* (Oxford: Clarendon Press, 1988); James A. Epstein, *Radical Expression: Political Language, Ritual, and Symbol in England, 1790–1850* (Oxford: Oxford University Press, 1994); Kevin Gilmartin, *Print Politics: the Press and Radical Opposition in Early Nineteenth-Century England* (Cambridge: Cambridge University Press, 1997); Iain McCalman, *Radical Underworld: Prophets, Revolutionaries and Pornographers in London, 1795–1840* (Cambridge: Cambridge University Press, 1988); Jon Mee, *Dangerous Enthusiasm: Blake and the Culture of London* (Oxford: Oxford University Press, 1993); David Worrall, *Radical Culture: Discourse, Resistance and Surveillance, 1790–1820* (Detroit: Wayne State University Press, 1992); E. P. Thompson, *Witness against the Beast: William Blake and the Moral Law* (Cambridge: Cambridge University Press, 1993). For a version of this encounter in eighteenth-century America, see Michael T. Gilmore, *Cambridge History of American Literature*, edited by S. Bercovitch (Cambridge: Cambridge University Press, 1994), vol. I, *1590–1820*, 591–629.

13 Mee, *Dangerous Enthusiasm*, 51.

14 E. P. Thompson, *Customs in Common* (London: Merlin Press, 1991); J. M. Neeson, *Commoners: Common Right, Enclosure and Social Change in England 1700–1820* (Cambridge: Cambridge University Press, 1993); Peter Linebaugh, *The London Hanged: Crime and Civil Society in the Eighteenth Century* (Harmondsworth: Penguin, 1991); Deborah Valenze, *The First Industrial Woman* (Oxford: Oxford University Press, 1995).

15 Alasdair MacIntyre, *After Virtue* (London: Duckworth, 1981).

16 Charles Taylor, *Sources of the Self* (Cambridge, MA: Harvard University Press, 1990).

17 Neeson, *Commoners*, 300.

18 Fredric Jameson, *The Seeds of Time* (New York: Columbia University Press, 1994), 67.

19 I am extrapolating from Derek Attridge's classifying of English metre into four-stress and five-stress systems, in which he makes the point that five-stress

poetics is determined, fundamentally, by its difference from the plurality of four-stress metres. Derek Attridge, *Poetic Rhythm: an Introduction* (Cambridge: Cambridge University Press, 1995), 63.

20 Cited in Dennis Donoghue, 'The Book of Genius: Harold Bloom's Agon and the Uses of Great Literature', review of *The Western Canon: the Books and Schools of the Ages* (New York: Harcourt Brace, 1994), *Times Literary Supplement*, 6 January 1995.

21 Taylor, *Sources of the Self*, 174.

22 For an interesting discussion of the issue of romantic exclusions, see 'Introduction', *At the Limits of Romanticism: Essays in Feminist and Materialist Criticism*, edited by Mary A. Favret and Nicola J. Watson (Bloomington: Indiana University Press, 1994), 1–20.

I THE COMMUNITARIAN LYRIC IN THE DIALECTIC OF ROMANTICISM

1 E. P. Thompson, 'Disenchantment or Default? A Lay Sermon', in *Power and Consciousness* edited by Conor Cruise O'Brien and William Dean Vanech (New York: New York University Press, 1969), 52.

2 William Wordsworth, *Poetical Works*, edited by Ernest de Selincourt and Helen Darbishire (Oxford: Clarendon Press, 1952), 2nd edn, IV, 463.

3 For the orthodox statement of (1) see Arthur J. Lovejoy, 'On the Discrimination of Romanticisms', *Essays on the History of Ideas* (Baltimore: Johns Hopkins University Press, 1948), 228–53; rpt. in *English Romantic Poets: Modern Essays in Criticism*, edited by M. H. Abrams (New York: Oxford University Press, 1960), 3–24; for (2) see René Wellek, 'The Concept of Romanticism', in *Concepts of Criticism* (New Haven: Yale University Press, 1963), 128–196.

4 McGann, *The Romantic Ideology*; Levinson, *Wordsworth's Great Period Poems*.

5 'September 1, 1939', *Selected Poems of W. H. Auden*, edited by Edward Mendelson (New York: Vintage, 1989), 88.

6 E. P. Thompson, *William Morris: Romantic to Revolutionary* (London: Lawrence and Wishart, 1955; 2nd edn, London: Merlin Press, 1976).

7 E. P. Thompson, *The Making of the English Working Class* (Harmondsworth: Penguin, 1963), 915.

8 Thompson, *William Morris* (1976), 669.

9 *Collected Letters of William Morris*, edited by Norman Kelvin (Princeton, NJ: Princeton University Press, 1987), II, 230.

10 See Terry Eagleton, *The Ideology of the Aesthetic* (Oxford: Blackwell, 1990); Blake, *Complete Writings*, edited by Geoffrey Keynes (Oxford: Oxford University Press, 1972), 621.

11 Thompson, *William Morris*; Harold Bloom, 'The Internalization of Quest Romance', in *Romanticism and Consciousness*, edited by Bloom (New York: W. W. Norton, 1970), 3–4.

12 Blake, *Complete Writings*, 466.

13 *The Letters of Percy Bysshe Shelley*, edited by Frederick L. Jones (Oxford: Clarendon Press, 1964), II, 191.

14 Shelley, *The Mask of Anarchy*, edited by Donald H. Reiman (New York: Garland, 1985); William Wordsworth, *The Prelude*, edited by Ernest de Selincourt, 2nd edition revised by Helen Darbishire (Oxford: Clarendon Press, 1959), Book II, line 278. All further references by book and line number.

15 *Poetical Works of Shelley*, edited by Thomas Hutchinson (Oxford: Oxford University Press, 1971), 579.

16 See Palgrave, *The Golden Treasury* for 'The Book of Wordsworth'; Robert Burns, 'The Tree of Liberty', *The Poems and Songs of Robert Burns*, edited James Kinsley (Oxford: Clarendon Press, 1968), II, 913.

17 Taylor, *Sources of the Self*, 175.

18 MacIntyre, *After Virtue*, 23–35.

19 Anthony Arblaster, *The Rise and Decline of Western Liberalism* (Oxford: Blackwell, 1984), 204.

20 Levinson, *Wordsworth's Great Period Poems*, 14–57.

21 John Stuart Mill, 'Thoughts on Poetry and Its Varieties', *Dissertations and Discussions: Political, Philosophical, and Historical* (London: Parker, 1859), I, 67.

22 Harold Bloom, *The Ringers in the Tower* (Chicago: University of Chicago Press, 1971), 18.

23 Michael McKeon, 'The Secret History of Domesticity: Public, Private and the Division of Knowledge', unpublished manuscript, 155.

24 Alan Liu, *Wordsworth: the Sense of History* (Palo Alto, CA: Stanford University Press, 1989), 51.

25 Bloom, *The Western Canon: the Books and Schools of the Ages* (New York: Harcourt Brace, 1994); M. H. Abrams, *Natural Supernaturalism: Tradition and Revolution in Romantic Literature* (New York: W. W. Norton, 1971).

26 Blake, *Complete Writings*, 746.

27 S. T. Coleridge, *Poetical Works*, edited by E. H. Coleridge (Oxford: Oxford University Press, 1912), 364–9.

28 See Jerome McGann's remarks on Wordsworth's *Lyrical Ballads* in *The Poetics of Sensibility*, 121–126.

29 Joanna Baillie, 'A Summer's Day'; Anna Barbauld, 'Washing Day', both in *Romantic Women Poets*, edited by Breen, 52–59, 81–84. See also Ruth L. Smith and Deborah M. Valenze, 'Mutuality and Marginality: Liberal Moral Theory and Working-Class Women in Nineteenth-Century England', *Signs* 13 (1988), 277–98.

30 John Thelwall, 'News from Toulon, etc.', *The Tribune* 1, no. 1 (1795); reprinted in Michael Scrivener, *Poetry and Reform: Periodical Verse from the English Democratic Press 1792–1824* (Detroit: Wayne State University Press, 1992), 113.

31 Gregory Claeys, *Citizens and Saints: Politics and Anti-Politics in Early British Socialism* (Cambridge: Cambridge University Press, 1989), 1.

32 Terry Eagleton, *The Illusions of Postmodernism* (Oxford: Blackwell, 1996), 84.

33 Thompson, *Customs in Common*, 2.

34 Ibid., 9.

35 Linebaugh, *The London Hanged*, 440.

36 Taylor, *Sources of the Self*, 91–107.

37 Thomas Evans, 'An Address to All Mankind', *A Humorous Catalogue of Spence's Songs, Part the Second* (London: ?1811).

38 Olive D. Rudkin, *Thomas Spence and His Connections* (London: George Allen, 1927); P. M. Ashraf, *The Life and Times of Thomas Spence* (Newcastle: Frank Graham, 1983); Olivia Smith, *The Politics of Language 1791–1819* (Oxford: Clarendon Press, 1984), 96–109.

39 E. J. Blandford, 'Nature's First, Last, and Only Will! Or a Hint to Mr. Bull.', *Medusa* (1819), 60.

40 Alun Howkins and C. Ian Dyck, '"Time's Alteration": Popular Ballads, Rural Radicalism, and William Cobbett', *History Workshop Journal* 23 (1987), 23.

41 Grossman, 'Summa Lyrica', *Western Humanities Review* 44 (1990), 53.

42 Charles Kingsley, 'Burns and His School', *Miscellanies* (London: Parker, 1859), 357.

43 See the ground-breaking annotated anthology edited by Brian Maidment, *The Poorhouse Fugitives: Self-Taught Poets and Poetry in Victorian Britain* (Manchester: Carcanet, 1987).

44 Shelley, *Poetical Works*, 234.

45 W. J. Linton, 'The Gathering of the People', *The English Republic* 1 (1851), 136–7.

46 Ernest Jones, 'Our Summons', *Northern Star*, 16 May 1846.

47 Arblaster, *Rise and Decline of Western Liberalism*, 270.

48 See Chris Waters, 'Morris's "Chants" and the Problems of Socialist Culture', in *Socialism and the Literary Artistry of William Morris*, edited by Florence S. Boos and Carole G. Silver (Columbia, Missouri: University of Missouri Press, 1990), 128.

49 Malcolm Chase, '*The People's Farm*', 3.

50 The importance of Burke to Wordsworth's poetry has been brilliantly charted by James K. Chandler, *Wordsworth's Second Nature: A Study of the Poetry and Politics* (Chicago: University of Chicago Press, 1984).

51 Alasdair MacIntyre, 'The Spectre of Communitarianism', *Radical Philosophy*, 70 (1995), 35.

2 BALLAD, LYRICAL BALLAD, LYRIC: WORDSWORTH, DYER, AND MILL

1 Martha Vicinus, *The Industrial Muse: a Study of Nineteenth Century British Working-Class Literature* (London: Croom Helm, 1974), 9; Roy Palmer, *The Sound of History: Songs and Social Comment* (Oxford: Oxford University Press, 1988).

2 Butler, *Romantics, Rebels, and Reactionaries*, 58.

3 John Clare, *By Himself*, edited by Eric Robinson and David Powell (Manchester: Carcanet Press, 1996), 98.

4 Among the most interesting see: John E. Jordan, *Why the 'Lyrical Ballads'? The Background, Writing and Character of Wordsworth's 1798 Lyrical Ballads* (Berkeley: University of California Press, 1976); Stephen Maxfield Parrish, *The Art of the 'Lyrical Ballads'* (Cambridge, MA: Harvard University Press, 1973); Mary Jacobus, *Tradition and Experiment in Wordsworth's 'Lyrical Ballads' (1798)* (Oxford: Clarendon Press, 1976); Robert Mayo, 'The Contemporaneity of the *Lyrical*

Ballads', *PMLA* 69 (1954), 486–522; Butler, *Romantics, Rebels, and Reactionaries*, 58–64.

5 Parrish, *Art of the 'Lyrical Ballads'*, 83.

6 *British Critic* 17 (1801), 131n, cited in Jordan, *Why the 'Lyrical Ballads'?* 172.

7 'Lyric', *The New Princeton Encyclopaedia of Poetry and Poetics*, edited by Alex Preminger and T.V. F. Brogan (Princeton, NJ: Princeton University Press, 1993).

8 David Lindley, *Lyric* (London: Methuen, 1985), 1–3.

9 Grossman, 'Summa Lyrica', 53.

10 Anne Janowitz, *England's Ruins: Poetic Purpose and the National Landscape* (Oxford: Blackwell, 1990), 65–72.

11 Mary Robinson, *Lyrical Tales* (London: 1800); George Dyer, 'Essay on Lyric Poetry', *Poems* (London: 1802), 1, i–xcii.

12 Butler, *Romantics, Rebels and Reactionaries*, 57.

13 Tilottama Rajan, 'Romanticism and the Death of Lyric Consciousness', in *Lyric Poetry: Beyond New Criticism*, edited by Chaviva Hosek and Patricia Parker (London: Cornell University Press, 1985), 194–208; Don Bialostosky, *Wordsworth, Dialogics, and the Practice of Criticism* (Cambridge: Cambridge University Press, 1992), passim.

14 Allan Bold, *The Ballad* (London: Methuen, 1979), 15–17.

15 For a generous selection of these poets, see Michael Scrivener, *Poetry and Reform: Periodical Verse from the English Democratic Press, 1792–1824* (Detroit, Wayne State University Press, 1992).

16 For the conservative account of Burns, see Isobel Armstrong, *Victorian Poetry: Poetry, Poetics, and Politics* (London: Routledge, 1993), 69.

17 Mayo, 'The Contemporaneity of the *Lyrical Ballads'*. Charles Ryskamp, 'Wordsworth's *Lyrical Ballads* in their Time', in *From Sensibility to Romanticism*, edited by F. Hilles and H. Bloom (Oxford: Oxford University Press, 1965), 357–372.

18 John Stuart Mill, 'What Is Poetry?', *Monthly Repository* VII (1833), 60–70.

19 Francis Turner Palgrave, *The Golden Treasury of the Best Songs and Lyrical Poems in the English Language* (London: Macmillan, 1861), vii.

20 Levinson, *Wordsworth's Great Period Poems*; Alan Liu, *Wordsworth: the Sense of History* (Palo Alto, CA: Stanford University Press, 1989); Nicholas Roe, *Wordsworth and Coleridge: the Radical Years* (Oxford: Oxford University Press, 1988).

21 E. P. Thompson, 'Disenchantment or Default? A Lay Sermon', in *Power and Consciousness*, edited by Conor Cruise O'Brien and William Dean Vanech (New York: New York University Press, 1969), 152; Chandler, *Wordsworth's Second Nature*.

22 Thompson, 'Disenchantment or Default?', 152.

23 Chandler, *Wordsworth's Second Nature*, xviii.

24 Sheldon S. Wolin, 'Hume and Conservatism', *Hume: a Re-evaluation* (New York: Fordham University Press, 1976), 242.

25 Taylor, *Sources of the Self*, 347.

26 Neeson, *Commoners*, 12.

27 Taylor, *Sources of the Self*, 305.

28 Wordsworth and Coleridge, *Lyrical Ballads: the Text of the 1789 Edition with the Additional 1800 Poems and the Prefaces*, edited by R. L. Brett and A. R. Jones (London: Methuen, 1963), 242. Further page numbers indicated parenthetically in the text.

29 For the concept of an 'habituated self', see MacIntyre, *After Virtue*, 221.

30 David Simpson, *Wordsworth's Historical Imagination: the Poetry of Displacement* (London: Methuen, 1987), Chapter 2; Z. S. Fink, 'Wordsworth's Interest in Seventeenth-Century English Republican Thought', *Journal of English and Germanic Philology* 47 (1948), 107–126.

31 David Simpson, *Romanticism, Nationalism and the Revolt against Theory* (Chicago: University of Chicago Press, 1993), 153.

32 Simpson, *Romanticism, Nationalism and the Revolt against Theory*, 152–155.

33 Kenneth Johnston, 'Philanthropy or Treason? Wordsworth as "Active Partisan"', *Studies in Romanticism* 25 (1986), 371–409; 'Wordsworth's Revolutions, 1793–1798', in *Revolution and English Romanticism*, edited by Keith Hanley and Raman Selden (London: Harvester, 1990), 169–205.

34 Marilyn Butler gave a compelling reading of the continuity of the communities of living and dead in 'We Are Seven' at a paper presented at the University of York, July 1994.

35 See in particular Kenneth Johnston's discussion of the poems of human suffering in *Wordsworth and the Recluse* (New Haven: Yale University Press, 1984); James A. Averill, *Wordsworth and the Poetry of Human Suffering* (Ithaca, NY: Cornell University Press, 1980).

36 *Chartist Circular*, 14 August 1841.

37 *Lyrical Ballads*, 48–54. Line numbers given parenthetically in text.

38 For a full discussion of Gypsies and Jews in romantic poetry, see my 'The Transit of the Gypsies in Romantic Period Poetry', in *Country and City Revisited*, edited by Donna Landry, Gerald McLean, and Joseph Ward (Cambridge: Cambridge University Press, forthcoming). For depictions of Wandering Jews, see Frank Felsenstein, *Anti-Semitic Stereotypes: a Paradigm of Otherness in English Popular Culture, 1660–1830* (Baltimore: Johns Hopkins University Press, 1995), 58–89.

39 Harold Bloom, 'William Wordsworth', *Romantic Poetry and Prose* (Oxford: Oxford University Press, 1973), 125.

40 Charles Rzpeka, *The Self as Mind: Vision and Identity in Wordsworth, Coleridge & Keats* (Cambridge, MA: Harvard University Press, 1986).

41 Liu, *Wordsworth*, 455, 51.

42 Wordsworth, *Works*, II, 115–117 ; see as well discussion by David Simpson, *Irony and Authority in Romantic Poetry* (London: Macmillan, 1979), 72–76. Thanks to Tim Burke for calling my attention to the poem.

43 Albert Friedman, *The Ballad Revival: Studies in the Influence of Popular on Sophisticated Poetry* (Chicago: University of Chicago Press, 1961), 269.

44 Ibid., 292.

45 'Essay, Supplementary to the Preface' (1815), *Prose Works of William Wordsworth*, edited by W. J. B. Owen and Jane Worthington Symser (Oxford: Clarendon Press, 1974), II, 78.

46 Arblaster, *The Rise and Decline of Western Liberalism*, 206.

47 Ibid., 200.

48 Raymond Williams, *Keywords: a Vocabulary of Culture and Society* (London: Fontana, 1976), 149–150.

49 Maidment, *The Poorhouse Fugitives*, 282.

50 F. W. Robertson, *Lectures, Addresses, and Other Literary Remains* (London: 1876), quoted in Maidment, *Poorhouse Fugitives*, 311.

51 Dyer, 'Essay on Lyric Poetry', I, 6.

52 Thomas Noon Talfourd, *Final Memorials of Lamb* (London: Moxon, 1855), I, 136, 138.

53 M. Ray Adams, *Studies in the Literary Backgrounds of English Radicalism* (Lancaster, Pennsylvania: Franklin and Marshall College, 1947), 227–266; Leslie F. Chard, *Dissenting Republican: Wordsworth's Early Life and Thought in their Political Context* (The Hague: Mouton, 1972), 158–221; Roe, *Wordsworth and Coleridge*, 85–92; Ben Ross Schneider, Jr., *Wordsworth's Cambridge Education* (Cambridge: Cambridge University Press, 1957), 150; Nicholas Roe, 'Radical George: Dyer in the 1790s', *Charles Lamb Bulletin* NS 49 (1985), 17–46.

54 Adams, *Literary Backgrounds*, 235.

55 George Dyer, *An Inquiry into the Nature of Subscription to the Thirty-Nine Articles* (?London: ?1789), 10.

56 Dyer, *An Inquiry*, 7.

57 George Dyer, *Four Letters on the English Constitution* (London: Johnson, 1812), 115.

58 Epstein, *Radical Expression*, 9.

59 George Dyer, *The Complaints of the Poor People of England* (London, 1793), 22.

60 Adams, *Literary Backgrounds*, 249.

61 Roe, *Wordsworth and Coleridge*, 92.

62 Mark Philp, 'The Fragmented Ideology of Reform', in *The French Revolution and British Popular Politics*, edited by Mark Philp (Cambridge: Cambridge University Press, 1991), 50–77.

63 Dyer, *Four Letters*, 59.

64 The exceptions are in Adams and Roe.

65 See Chapter 3, following.

66 *The Letters of Charles and Mary Lamb*, edited by Edwin W. Marrs, Jr., 2 vols. (London: Cornell University Press, 1976), I, 240.

67 As Donald Reiman points out in his edition of Dyer's *The Poet's Fate* (London: Garland, 1979), Dyer proved to be a prescient literary critic, for not only did he refer to the Pantisocracy, he also grouped together Southey, Coleridge, Wordsworth, Lamb, and Lloyd 'as up and coming writers, thus providing the first united notice of five writers who would eventually be grouped by a variety of commentators, from the satirists of the *Anti-Jacobin* to modern literary historians', vii–viii.

68 Dyer, *Poems*, I, i–xcii; II, 1–30; essays will be cited by volume and page number parenthetically in the text. For a discussion of the printing history of Dyer's *Poems*, see Harriet Jump, '"Snatch'd out of the Fire": Lamb, Coleridge, and George Dyer's Cancelled Preface', *Charles Lamb Bulletin* NS 58 (1987), 54–67.

69 Letter to Richard Woodhouse, 27 October 1818, in *Letters of John Keats* edited by H. E. Robbins (Cambridge: Cambridge University Press, 1958), I, 387.
70 Nicholas Roe, *John Keats and the Culture of Dissent* (Oxford: Clarendon Press, 1997), 27–32.
71 Dyer, *Four Letters*, 59.
72 Wordsworth, *The Prelude*, 1805, Book II, line 278.
73 Stuart Curran, *Poetic Form and British Romanticism* (Oxford: Oxford University Press, 1986), 15.
74 M. H. Abrams, in *The Mirror and the Lamp: Romantic Theory and the Critical Tradition* (Oxford: Oxford University Press, 1951), 21–26, discusses Mill in relation to Wordsworth, arguing that Mill's articulation of the 'expressive' theory of poetry drew from, but went beyond, Wordsworth's.
75 'What Is Poetry?' and 'The Two Kinds of Poetry', *Monthly Repository* VII (1833), 60–70; 714–724; reprinted as 'Thoughts on Poetry and Its Varieties', in *Dissertations and Discussions: Political, Philosophical, and Historical*, 4 vols. (London: Parker, 1859–74), I, 63–94. All further references to this essay will appear by page number parenthetically in the text.
76 John Stuart Mill, *Autobiography*, edited by Jack Stillinger (Oxford: Oxford University Press, 1971), 89.
77 Raymond Williams, *Culture and Society* (Harmondsworth: Penguin, 1960), 67.
78 Mill, *Autobiography*, 89.
79 Taylor, *Sources of the Self*, 319.
80 Mill, *Autobiography*, 88.
81 Ibid., 90.
82 Karl Britton, 'J. S. Mill: A Debating Speech on Wordsworth, 1829', *Cambridge Review* 79 (1958), 419.
83 Cited in Vicinus, *Industrial Muse*, 94.
84 John Stuart Mill, *On Liberty* (New York: W. W. Norton and Co., 1974). Page numbers indicated parenthetically in the text.
85 Gregory Claeys, *Machinery, Money and the Millenium: the New Moral Economy of Owenite Socialism, 1815–60* (Princeton, NJ: Princeton University Press, 1987), 144.
86 Arblaster, *Rise and Decline of Western Liberalism*, 268.
87 Palgrave, *Golden Treasury*, vii.

3 THE SUN AND THE TREE: LYRICS OF LIBERTY

1 For extracts from the debates of the 1790s 'Revolution Controversy', see *Burke, Paine, Godwin and the Revolution Controversy*, edited by Marilyn Butler (Cambridge: Cambridge University Press, 1984).
2 William Wordsworth, *The Prelude*, 1805, VI, 412.
3 Anthony Arblaster, 'Thomas Paine: at the Limits of Bourgeois Radicalism', in *Socialism and the Limits of Liberalism*, edited by Peter Osborne (London: Verso, 1991), 51–71.
4 Ibid., 68.

5 C. B. Macpherson, *Burke* (Oxford: Oxford University Press, 1980), 55–59, 5.

6 Neeson, *Commoners*, 24.

7 Philp, 'The Fragmented Ideology of Reform', 50–77.

8 Kevin Gilmartin, *Print Politics: the Press and Radical Opposition in Early Nineteenth-Century England* (Cambridge: Cambridge University Press, 1997), 1–10.

9 E. P. Thompson, *Witness against the Beast: William Blake and the Moral Law* (Cambridge; Cambridge University Press, 1993), 174–194; Mee, *Dangerous Enthusiasm*.

10 Anne Grant, 'Familiar Epistle to a Friend', in *Women Romantic Poets*, edited by Breen, 86–94.

11 For a representative set of these texts, see Michael Scrivener, *Poetry and Reform: Periodical Verse from the English Democratic Press, 1792–1824* (Detroit: Wayne State University Press, 1992). Many of the poems cited in this chapter can be found in Scrivener, and for those poems I have given page numbers to his volume as well as to their periodical location.

12 Jerome McGann has recently pointed to the contradictions of the enlightenment focus on the passions. See his *The Poetics of Sensibility* (Oxford: Oxford University Press, 1997).

13 M. H. Abrams, 'Structure and Style in the Greater Romantic Lyric', in *From Sensibility to Romanticism: Essays Presented to Frederick A. Pottle*, edited by Frederick W. Hilles and Harold Bloom (Oxford: Oxford University Press, 1965), 527–560.

14 ?Thomas Spence, 'Alteration', *Pig's Meat* 2 (1794), 2.

15 Robert Southey, 'The Oak of Our Fathers', *Poetical Works* (London: Longman's, 1873), 123.

16 Arthur M. Schlesinger, 'Liberty Tree: a Genealogy', *The New England Quarterly* 25 (1952), 436.

17 Mee, *Dangerous Enthusiasm*, 100–103.

18 Cited without source in James Vernon, *Politics and the People, a Study in Political Culture c.1815–1867* (Cambridge: Cambridge University Press, 1993), 320.

19 Arblaster, 'Paine', 67.

20 Thompson, *Customs in Common*, 9.

21 Ibid., 86.

22 Ibid., 96.

23 'Stanzas, to the Memory of Robert Burns', *Monthly Magazine* (1797), 53–54.

24 Donald A. Low, *Robert Burns: the Critical Heritage* (London: Routledge, 1974), 22.

25 Ibid.

26 John McVie, *The Burns Federation: a Bi-Centenary Review* (Kilmarnock: Kilmarnock Standard, 1959), 33.

27 Epstein, *Radical Expression*, 160.

28 Isobel Armstrong, *Victorian Poetry: Poetry, Poetics and Politics* (London: Routledge, 1993), 68–69.

29 Robert Burns, *The Poems and Songs*, edited by James Kinsley (Oxford: Clarendon Press, 1968), I, 209.

30 Burns, *Poems and Songs*, 'The Liberty Tree', ii, 913.

31 Chase, *'The People's Farm'*, 178, 'The Chartist Song' (c. 1840); Thomas Evans, 'The Spencean Plan for a' that', *Spence's Songs* (London: ?1811), ii.

32 British Library, Add. MS 27808, ff. 151, 204; Add. MS 27789, f. 61. Quoted in P. M. Ashraf, *The Life and Times of Thomas Spence* (Newcastle: Frank Graham, 1983), 42.

33 Gregory Claeys, *The Politics of English Jacobinism, Writings of John Thelwall* (University Park: Pennsylvania State University Press, 1995), xiv.

34 Ibid., xv.

35 Ibid., xviii.

36 E. P. Thompson, 'Hunting the Jacobin Fox', *Past and Present* 142 (1994), 94.

37 John Thelwall, 'Lines, Written at Bridgewater', *Poems Chiefly Written in Retirement* (Hereford: 1801), lines 126–132, 129; Claeys, *Politics of English Jacobinism*, xxxii.

38 Thelwall, *Poems Chiefly Written in Retirement*, 156.

39 Thompson, 'Hunting the Jacobin Fox', 102.

40 See David Worrall, 'Agrarians against the Picturesque', in *Politics of the Picturesque*, edited by Stephen Copley and Peter Garside (Cambridge: Cambridge University Press, 1994), 240–260.

41 Paul Mantoux, *The Industrial Revolution in the Eighteenth Century* (London: J. Cape, 1961), 148–149.

42 Chase, *'The People's Farm'*.

43 See Ashraf, *Thomas Spence*, 93–99; Olive D. Rudkin, *Thomas Spence and His Connections* (London: George Allen, 1927); Worrall, *Radical Culture*, 165–200; Chase, *'The People's Farm'*, 78–120; McCalman, *Radical Underworld*.

44 Claeys, *Politics of English Jacobinism*, xix.

45 Chase, *'The People's Farm'*, 174, 19; *The Nationalisation of the Land in 1775 and 1882. Being a Lecture Delivered at Newcastle-on-Tyne, by Thomas Spence 1775. Reprinted and Edited, with Notes and Introduction, by H. M. Hyndman, 1882*, edited by H. M. Hyndman (London: E. W. Allen, 1882).

46 *One Pennyworth of Pig's Meat; or, Lessons for the Swinish Multitude*, 2nd edn (Little-Turnstile, High Holborn: Hive of Liberty, 1793–95).

47 See Olivia Smith, *The Politics of Language 1791–1819* (Oxford: Clarendon Press, 1984), 96–109.

48 'The Progress of Liberty', *Pig's Meat* i (1793), 280–281.

49 Michael Turner, *Enclosures in Britain, 1750–1830* (London: Macmillan, 1984), 17; W. G. Hoskins, *The Making of the English Landscape* (Harmondsworth: Penguin, 1955), 185; Mantoux, *Industrial Revolution*, 148–149.

50 Chase, *'The People's Farm'*, 31.

51 Epstein, *Radical Expression*, 31.

52 Allen Davenport, *The Life, Writing, and Principles of Thomas Spence* (London: Wakelin, 1836), 17.

53 Thomas Spence, *The Rights of Infants* (London: 1797), 6.

54 Chase, *'The People's Farm'*, 21.

55 Thomas Spence, *The Grand Repository of the English Language* (Newcastle Upon Tyne, 1775).

56 Thomas Spence, *The Important Trial of Thomas Spence* (London, 1803), 9.

57 Spence, *Grand Repository*, title page.

58 The fullest discussion of Murray and Spence is in Ashraf, *Thomas Spence*, 17–29.

59 Ibid., 189.

60 Rudkin, *Thomas Spence*, 26.

61 Davenport, *Thomas Spence*, 2.

62 Spence, *The Rights of Infants*, 5.

63 Ashraf, *Thomas Spence*, 13; Evans, *Spence's Songs, Part the First*, claims that this ballad was 'First Published at Newcastle in the Year 1785', 6.

64 'The Rights of Man', *Pig's Meat* 2 (1794), 105. This text dates the first printing as 1783.

65 Chase, *'The People's Farm'*, 45.

66 Chase, *'The People's Farm'*, 45–78; McCalman, *Radical Underworld*, 7–49.

67 *Pig's Meat* 1 (1793), title page.

68 Marcus Wood, *Radical Satire and Print Culture, 1790–1822* (Oxford: Clarendon Press, 1994), 57–96.

69 Kathryn Sullivan, 'Events . . . Have Made Us a World of Readers: Reader Relations 1780–1830', in *The Romantic Period: The Penguin History of Literature*, edited by David B. Pirie (Harmondsworth: Penguin, 1994), 19.

70 Wood, *Radical Satire*, 88.

71 Chase, *'The People's Farm'*, 46; Allen Davenport, *Life and Literary Pursuits of Allen Davenport, with a Further Selection of the Author's Work*, compiled and edited by Malcolm Chase (Aldershot: Scolar Press, 1994), 16; Charles Cooke, *Pocket Edition of Select British Poets* (London: 1794–1804), 46 vols.

72 *Pig's Meat* 1 (1793), 33–36, 279, 280.

73 Richard Lee, 'The Rights of God', 'Sonnet to Freedom', *Pig's Meat* 2 (1794), 204, 284.

74 'Palemon, or, The Press-Gang', *Pig's Meat* 2 (1794), 140–141.

75 Ashraf, *Thomas Spence*, 59–60; Chase, *'The People's Farm'*, 63; *Pig's Meat* 3 (1795), 3.

76 'The Beggar's Petition', *Pig's Meat* 3 (1795), 194–195.

77 'The Peasant's Lamentation on the Exportation of Corn', *Pig's Meat* 3 (1795), 259; Ashraf, *Thomas Spence*, 189.

78 Chase, *'The People's Farm'*, 186.

79 Neeson, *Commoners*, 3, 5–6, 11, 12, etc.; John Clare, 'The Mores', in *Poems of the Middle Period, 1822–37*, edited by Eric Robinson, David Powell, and P. M. S. Dawson, (Oxford: Clarendon Press, 1996), II, 347–350.

80 Walter J. Ong, *Orality and Literacy: the Technologising of the Word* (London: Methuen, 1982), 37–39.

81 Lindley, *Lyric*, 31.

82 Spence, *The Rights of Infants*, 10.

83 'The Rights of Man', Evans, *Spence's Songs*, 7.

84 *An Account of the Christian Practices observed by the Churches called Glasites in Scotland, and Sandemanians in America* (Galashiels: 1832), 22, 7.

85 Spence, *The Rights of Infants*, 10.

86 Thomas Spence, 'On the Late Barren Patriotic Meetings; Particularly That on the 4th of February, 1795', *Pig's Meat* 3 (1795), 57.

87 'A New Song, Sung by Mr. Meredith, at Liverpool, on the Anniversary of the French Revolution', *Pig's Meat* 1 (1793), 82.

88 Thomas Spence, *The Meridian Sun of Liberty; or, the Whole Rights of Man Displayed* (London, 1796), title page.

89 John Thelwall, *A Letter to Francis Jeffrey, Esq., on Certain Calumnies and Misrepresentations in the Edinburgh Review* (Edinburgh: 1804), 45; quoted in Thompson, 'Hunting the Jacobin Fox', 127.

90 McCalman, *Radical Underworld*, 49.

91 'The Rights of Man', Evans, *Spence's Songs*, 6.

92 Chase, '*The People's Farm*', 70.

93 Evans, *Spence's Songs*, title page.

94 Evans, *Spence's Songs, Part the Second*, 2.

95 Thomas Evans 'An Address to All Mankind', *Spence's Songs Part the Second* (London: ?1811).

96 Christopher Hill, 'The Norman Yoke', in *Puritanism and Revolution: Studies in the Interpretation of the English Revolution of the Seventeenth Century* (London: Secker and Warburg, 1956), 91; J. G. A. Pocock, *The Ancient Constitution and the Feudal Law: a Study of English Historical Thought in the Seventeenth Century*, 2nd edn (Cambridge: Cambridge University Press, 1987), passim.

97 Epstein, *Radical Expression*, 3–29.

98 Thomas Spence, 'The Downfall of Feudal Tyranny', *Pig's Meat* 3 (1795), 249–51.

99 'Alteration', *Pig's Meat* 2 (1794), 2.

100 W. D. Grant, 'Tribute to Liberty', *Pig's Meat* 2 (1794), 43–44.

101 'Ode on Liberty', *Morning Chronicle* (17 July 1792); reprinted in Scrivener, *Poetry and Reform*, 39.

102 Joseph Gerrald, A *Convention Is the Only Means of Saving Us from Ruin* (London: D. I. Eaton, 1793), 88. Cited in Epstein, *Radical Expression*, 19.

103 *The Prelude* (1850), Book XIII.

104 Ashraf, *Thomas Spence*, 94.

105 M. Ray Adams, *Studies in the Literary Background of English Radicalism* (Lancaster, Pennsylvania: Franklin and Marshall, 1947), 227–266.

106 John Thelwall, *The Rights of Nature against the Usurpations of Establishments, etc.* (London, 1796, 3rd edn), pt. 2, 16–17, cited in Epstein, *Radical Expression*, 6.

107 George Dyer, 'An Ode', *Black Dwarf* 12 (1824), 529–532; reprinted in Scrivener, *Poetry and Reform*, 278–281.

108 George Dyer, 'Song', *Moral and Political Magazine* 1 (1796), 95; reprinted in Scrivener, *Poetry and Reform*, 127–128.

109 'The Genius of France', *Morning Chronicle* (30 November 1792); reprinted in Scrivener, *Poetry and Reform*, 43–44.

110 'An Hymn for the Fast Day, To Be Sung by the Friends of Mankind', *Politics for the People* 1, part 2, no. 4 (1794), 3–5; reprinted in Scrivener, *Poetry and Reform*, 88–90.

111 John Thelwall, 'The Cell', *Poems Written in Close Confinement in the Tower and Newgate under a Charge of High Treason* (London: 1795), 9.

112 Ibid., iii.

113 John Aiken, 'To Gilbert Wakefield, A. B. on his Liberation from Prison', *Monthly Magazine* (July 1801), 513–514; Lucy Aiken, 'To the Memory of Gilbert Wakefield', *Monthly Magazine* (October 1801), 220–221; reprinted in Scrivener, *Poetry and Reform*, 155–157, 158.

114 'On the Death of Gilbert Wakefield. Meditated in a Garden, near a Church-Yard, at the Close of Autumn', George Dyer, *Poems* (London: 1802), I, 102–109.

115 *The Prelude*, 1805, Book IX, 510, 517–518.

116 Betty T. Bennett, *British War Poetry in the Age of Romanticism: 1793–1815* (London: Garland, 1976), 67.

117 Ibid., 1.

118 Douglas Lane Patey, '"Aesthetics" and the Rise of Lyric in the Eighteenth Century', *SEL* 33 (1993), 600.

119 But see Michael Scrivener, 'The Rhetoric and Context of John Thelwall's "Memoir"', in *Spirits of Fire: English Romantic Writers and Contemporary Historical Methods*, edited by G. A. Rosso and Daniel P. Watkins (Rutherford, NJ: Fairleigh Dickinson University Press, 1990), 112–130: 'Thelwall was in a tiny minority of middle-class intellectuals who neither recanted nor moderated their earlier radicalism. Nevertheless, he wanted to make a living as an intellectual and was necessarily dependent on an anti-Jacobin public' (112); John Thelwall, 'News from Toulon', *The Tribune* 1 (1795), 166–168, in Scrivener, *Poetry and Reform*, 113–115.

120 William Keach, 'Cockney Couplets: Keats and the Politics of Style', *Studies in Romanticism* 25 (1986), 185.

121 John Thelwall, *The Poetical Recreations of the Champion* (London: 1822), 164.

122 John Thelwall, 'A Sheepsheering Song', *The Tribune* 1, no. 8 (1795), 190–192; reprinted in Scrivener, *Poetry and Reform*, 115–118.

123 *Lyrical Ballads*, 107.

124 Blake, *Complete Writings*, 151.

125 Ibid., 152.

126 Thomas Spence, *A Supplement to the History of Robinson Crusoe, Being the History of Crusonia, or Robinson Crusoe's Island* (Newcastle Upon Tyne, 2nd edn, 1782), 19–20.

127 Worrall, 'Agrarians against the Picturesque', 245.

128 Ibid., 240–260.

129 Worrall, *Radical Culture*, 149.

130 Spencean Philanthropist, 'The Wrongs of Man. Or, Things as They Are', *Medusa* (1819), 24; reprinted in Scrivener, *Poetry and Reform*, 229–231.

131 Thomas Spence, 'The Rights of Man', *Pig's Meat* 2 (1794), 103.

132 Worrall, *Radical Culture*, 149.

133 Chase, '*The People's Farm*', 1; Evans, *Spence's Songs*.

134 Worrall, *Radical Culture*, 150; Spencean Philanthropist, 'The Rights of Man, or, Things as They Were Intended to Be by Divine Providence', *Medusa* (1819), 30; reprinted in Scrivener, *Poetry and Reform*, 231–233.

135 E. J. Blandford, 'Nature's First, Last, and Only Will! Or, a Hint to Mr. Bull', *Medusa* (1819), 60; reprinted in Scrivener, *Poetry and Reform*, 234–235.

136 Deborah Valenze, *The First Industrial Woman* (Oxford: Oxford University Press, 1995), 182.

137 E. J. Blandford, 'A Real Dream; or, Another Hint for Mr. Bull', *Medusa* (1819), 67–68; reprinted in Scrivener, *Poetry and Reform*, 236–237. See Worall, *Radical Culture*, 142–146 for the only extended discussion to date of Blandford's poems, and to which I am indebted.

138 E. J. Blandford, 'A Terrible Omen to Guilty Tyrants; or the Spirit of Liberty', *Medusa* (1819), 160; reprinted in Scrivener, *Poetry and Reform*, 243.

139 Bouthaina Shaaban, 'Shelley's Influence on the Chartist Poets, with Particular Emphasis on Ernest Jones and Thomas Cooper' (Ph.D. diss., University of Warwick, 1981).

140 P. M. S. Dawson, *The Unacknowledged Legislator: Shelley and Politics* (Oxford: Oxford University Press, 1980), 40.

141 Shelley, *Letters*, II, 152.

142 *The Mask of Anarchy*, edited by Donald H. Reiman (New York: Garland, 1985). All references by stanza number.

143 Michael Henry Scrivener, *Radical Shelley: The Philosophical Anarchism and Utopian Thought of Percy Bysshe Shelley* (Princeton, NJ: Princeton University Press, 1982), 227.

144 George Edward Woodberry, *The Shelley Notebook in the Harvard College Library* (Cambridge: John Barnard Associates, 1929), 149.

145 Shelley, *Poetical Works*, 573.

146 Kenneth Neill Cameron, *Shelley: the Golden Years* (Cambridge, MA: Harvard University Press, 1974), 116–117.

147 William St. Clair, *The Godwins and the Shelleys: the Biography of a Family* (London: Faber and Faber, 1989), 394; McCalman, *Radical Underworld*, Chapter 4, 'Cannon and Rationalist Philosophy'.

148 Donald H. Reiman, 'Shelley as Agrarian Reactionary', *The Keats-Shelley Memorial Association Bulletin* 30 (1979), 9.

149 Ibid., 12.

150 McCalman, *Radical Underworld*, 101.

151 Personal communication.

152 'An Address to "The Rabble"', *Medusa* (1819), 292; reprinted in Scrivener, *Poetry and Reform*, 245–246. See also: 'The Bloody Field of Peterloo!' and 'Saint Ethelstone's Day', *Theological and Political Comet* (1819), 85–86, 125; 'On a Bloody Massacre' and 'Paddy Bull's Epistle to His Brother John', *Medusa* (1819), 292; reprinted in Scrivener, *Poetry and Reform*, 218–19, 224–5; 244, 246–8.

153 E. P. Thompson, *The Making of the English Working Class* (Harmondsworth: Penguin, 1963), 178.

154 M. D. George, *Catalogue of Political and Personal Satires* (London: British Museum, 1949), IX, 132–58.

155 Iain McCalman, 'Females, Feminism and Free Love in an Early Nineteenth Century Radical Movement', *Labour History* 38 (1980), 10.

156 Shelley, *Letters*, II, 136.
157 Homans, *Women Poets and Poetic Identity*, 4.
158 Ibid., 26
159 Meena Alexander, *Women in Romanticism: Mary Wollstonecraft, Dorothy Wordsworth, and Mary Shelley* (London: Macmillan, 1989), 34.
160 John Berger, 'The Nature of Mass Demonstrations', *Selected Essays and Articles: The Look of Things* (London: Penguin, 1972), 249.
161 Richard Holmes, *Shelley: the Pursuit* (London: Penguin, 1987), 593.
162 See Scrivener's notes on Fair in *Poetry and Reform*, 175–185.
163 McCalman, *Radical Underworld*, 19.
164 E-mail message from Michael Scrivener, 10 February 1997. This information is in a letter to Francis Place, 9 March 1831 (British Library, Add. MSS. 27808, ff. 319–321).
165 McCalman, *Radical Underworld*, 81.
166 E-mail message from Neil Fraistat: 'in a presentation of the 1821 piracy at the University of Kentucky library, Fair calls himself (as opposed to Cannon or Benbow [the others in the project]) the "Editor" of the volume.'
167 R. C. Fair, 'Ode to Religion', *Theological Inquirer* (1815), 142; reprinted in Scrivener, *Poetry and Reform*, 176–177.
168 Shelley, *Poetical Works*, 530.
169 R. C. Fair, 'The Ruined City', *Theological Inquirer* (1815), 140–142; 220–224; 300–303; 376–379. Excerpted in Scrivener, *Poetry and Reform*, 179–184.
170 For discussion of the thematic differences between the exoteric and esoteric poems, see Stephen C. Behrendt, 'The Exoteric Species: the Popular Idiom in Shelley's Poetry', *Genre* 14 (1981), 473–492.
171 Shelley, *Poetical Works*, 791.
172 Ibid., 471.
173 Shelley, *Poetical Works*, 764.
174 Ibid., 47, 75.
175 *The Early Poems of John Clare, 1804–1882*, edited by Eric Robinson and David Powell (Oxford: Clarendon Press, 1989), I, 156.
176 Ibid., 569.
177 Clare, *Poems of the Middle Period*, II, 347–350.
178 John Clare, *By Himself*, edited by Eric Robinson and David Powell (Manchester: Carcanet, 1996), 58.
179 Ibid., 57–58.
180 *The Later Poems of John Clare, 1837–1864*, edited by Eric Robinson and David Powell (Oxford: Clarendon Press, 1984), I, 574.
181 Ibid., 396–7, 397–8.
182 John Clare, *Selected Letters*, edited by Mark Storey (Oxford: Oxford University Press, 1988), to Thomas Pringle, 8 February 1832, 182.
183 Ibid., 208, 206.
184 Ibid., 215.
185 Ibid., 216.

4 ALLEN DAVENPORT ON THE THRESHOLD OF CHARTISM

1 For an exhaustive bibliography of citations of Shelley in the Chartist press, see Bouthaina Shaaban, 'Shelley in the Chartist Press', *Keats-Shelley Memorial Bulletin* 34 (1983), 41–60; 'The Romantics in the Chartist Press', *Keats-Shelley Memorial Bulletin* 38 (1989), 25–45.

2 Llewellyn Woodward, *The Age of Reform: England 1815–1870* (Oxford: Oxford University Press, 1962, 2nd edn), 78–86; Clive Behagg, *Labour and Reform: Working-Class Movements 1815–1914* (London: Hodder & Stoughton, 1991), 33; Newman Ivey White, *Shelley* (London: Secker and Warburg, 1947), II, 404–409.

3 'A Review of Modern Poetry', *New Moral World* v, no. 6 (1 December 1838), 84.

4 Although social and cultural historians of the early nineteenth century have written, if not at length, at least appreciatively of Davenport's rôle in the history of radicalism from the 1790s through the 1840s, there has been little honouring of his literary works. The fullest contemporary account of Davenport is his own: *The Life and Literary Pursuits of Allen Davenport, with a Further Selection of the Author's Work*, compiled and edited by Malcolm Chase (Aldershot: Scolar Press, 1994). But see also Chase, 'Allen Davenport', in *Dictionary of Labour Biography*, vol. 8, edited by Joyce M. Bellamy and John Saville (London: Macmillan); Chase, '*The People's Farm*'; McCalman, *Radical Underworld*; Iowerth Prothero, *Artisans and Politics in Early Nineteenth-Century London: John Gast and His Times* (Folkestone: Dawson, 1979) for details of Davenport's political activities. David Worrall provides the first literary assessment of Davenport's work in *Radical Culture*, 77–89.

5 'The Poet's Hope', *Northern Star*, 11 April 1846.

6 'The Midnight Dream', Davenport, *Life and Literary Pursuits*, 115.

7 Davenport, *Life and Literary Pursuits*, 3; 'The Poet's Hope', *Northern Star*, 11 April 1846.

8 Allen Davenport, *The Life, Writing, and Principles of Thomas Spence . . .* (London, 1836), v.

9 Chase, '*The People's Farm*', 161.

10 Ibid., 164.

11 Davenport, *Life of Thomas Spence*, v.

12 Ibid.

13 Ibid.

14 Ibid., 16.

15 Ibid., 22.

16 Ibid., 23.

17 Ibid., 23.

18 William Hazlitt, *Political Essays* (London: Simpkin and Marshall, 1822), 99.

19 *Crisis* 3 (1834), title page; John Belchem, *Popular Radicalism in Nineteenth-Century Britain* (London: Macmillan, 1996), 54–55; Claeys, *Machinery, Money and the Millenium*, xvi.

20 Arthur E. Bestor, Jr., 'The Evolution of the Socialist Vocabulary', *Journal of the History of Ideas* 9, no. 3 (1948), 260.

21 Robert Owen, *The Future of the Human Race* (London: 1853), 21; see Logie Barrow, *Independent Spirits: Spiritualism and English Plebeians 1850–1910* (London: Routledge and Kegan Paul, 1986), 19–30.

22 Davenport, *Life and Literary Pursuits*, 3.

23 Ibid., 4.

24 Ibid.

25 Ibid.

26 Ibid., 5.

27 Ibid.

28 'Hornsey Wood', Allen Davenport, *The Muse's Wreath* (London, 1827), 11.

29 Davenport, *Life and Literary Pursuits*, 6.

30 Ibid., 9.

31 Ibid., 6.

32 Ibid., 8.

33 Ibid., 14.

34 Ibid., 15–16.

35 Ibid., 16.

36 Ibid.

37 Worrall, *Radical Culture*, 82; Malcolm Chase, 'Editorial Afterward', in Davenport, *Life and Literary Pursuits*, 47.

38 Davenport, *Life and Literary Pursuits*, 16.

39 Ibid., 17.

40 Shelley, *Letters*, II, 191.

41 Davenport, *Life and Literary Pursuits*, 16.

42 *The Kings; or Legitimacy Unmasked*, in Davenport, *Life and Literary Pursuits*, 70, 71.

43 Blake, *Complete Writings*, 746.

44 *The Kings*, in Davenport, *Life and Literary Pursuits*, 77.

45 'The Topic', *Sherwin's Political Register* 2 (1817), 106; also in Scrivener, *Poetry and Reform*, 205–206.

46 'Saint Ethelstone's Day', *Theological and Political Comet* (1819), 125; also in Scrivener, *Poetry and Reform*, 224–225.

47 Belchem, *Popular Radicalism*, 51–53; James Epstein, *Radical Expression: Political Language, Ritual, and Symbol in England, 1760–1850* (Cambridge: Cambridge University Press, 1994), 100.

48 Chase, 'Allen Davenport', *Dictionary of Labour Biography*.

49 Kenneth Neill Cameron, *The Young Shelley: Genesis of a Radical* (London: Victor Gollancz, 1951), 405.

50 Mary Shelley gave a holograph of the poem to John Bowring in 1826; perhaps other copies circulated before. See H. Buxton Forman, *Shelley, 'Peterloo,' and 'The Mask of Anarchy'* (London: 1887), 16.

51 'Sonnet', *Republican*, 14 March 1823.

52 'Words to the Wind', Davenport, *Muse's Wreath*, 17.

53 'The Midnight Dream', Davenport, *Life and Literary Pursuits*, 115.

54 'An Elegy on Mr. Shelley', *The Oracle of Reason* 2 (1842), 632.

55 'Co-operation', Davenport, *Muse's Wreath*, 67.

56 Ibid., 66.
57 Ibid.
58 See M. S. Kalim's unpublished MA dissertation on *The Use of Shelley in the Writings of the Owenites during the 1830s and 1840s* (University of London, 1960), for an account of Shelley in Owenite periodicals.
59 'Matter', 'What Is Man?', Davenport, *Muse's Wreath*, 68, 61.
60 'Friendship', Ibid., 69.
61 'The Irish Emigrant',Ibid., 54–55.
62 Chase, 'Allen Davenport', *Dictionary of Labour Biography*.
63 'Hornsey Wood', Davenport, *Muse's Wreath*, 12.
64 Davenport, *Life of Thomas Spence*, 20.
65 Ibid., 19.
66 'Rural Reflections', Davenport, *Muse's Wreath*, 52.
67 'The Cottage in Which I Was Born', 'Co-operation', Ibid., 23, 68.
68 Worrall, *Radical Culture*, 88.
69 'London', Davenport, *Muse's Wreath*, 21.
70 Davenport, *Life of Thomas Spence*, 15.
71 Belchem, *Popular Radicalism*, 70.
72 Thomas Cooper, 'Sonnets to Allen Davenport', *Northern Star*, 5 December 1846; 'Death of Mr. Davenport', *Northern Star*, 5 December 1846.
73 'The Patriot', *Northern Star*, 24 January 1846.
74 'The Poet's Hope', *Northern Star*, 11 April 1846.
75 'Ireland in Chains', *Northern Star*, 25 April 1846.
76 'The Iron God', *Northern Star*, 4 July 1846.

5 THE FORMS OF CHARTIST POETRY AND POETICS

1 Dorothy Thompson, 'The Early Chartists', *Outsiders* (London: Verso, 1993), 50; Dorothy Thompson, *The Chartists: Popular Politics in the Industrial Revolution* (New York: Pantheon, 1984) is the most complete account of the movement.
2 John Belchem, *Popular Radicalism in Nineteenth-Century Britain* (London: Macmillan, 1996), 72.
3 Dorothy Thompson, 'Chartism and the Historians', *Outsiders*, 36.
4 Thompson, *Chartists*, 79–86.
5 Two comprehensive bibliographies exist for this material: J. F. C. Harrison and Dorothy Thompson, *Bibliography of the Chartist Movement, 1837–1976* (Sussex: Harvester Press, 1978); Owen Ashton, Robert Fyson, and Stephen Roberts, *The Chartist Movement: A New Annotated Bibliography* (London: Mansell, 1995).
6 Historical discussion of the various rhetorics of Chartism took off with the publication of Gareth Stedman Jones, 'Rethinking Chartism', *The Languages of Class: Studies in English Working Class History 1832–1982* (Cambridge: Cambridge University Press, 1983), 90–178.
7 Thompson, 'Early Chartists', 48.
8 *Northern Star*, 3 July 1841; for a fascinating analysis of the *Northern Star*'s

correspondence, including poetic correspondence, see Stephen Roberts, 'Who Wrote to the *Northern Star*?', in Owen Ashton, Robert Fyson, and Stephen Roberts, *The Duty of Discontent: Essays for Dorothy Thompson* (London: Mansell, 1995), 55–70.

9 John Belchem, '1848: Feargus O'Connor and the Collapse of the Mass Platform', in *The Chartist Experience: Studies in Working-Class Radicalism and Culture, 1830–1860*, edited by James A. Epstein and Dorothy Thompson (London: Macmillan, 1982), 269–310.

10 Anon., 'Chartists and Liberty', *Northern Star*, 10 April 1841; 'The State Pauper's Soliloquy', *Northern Star*, 18 January 1840; S. J., 'Nine Cheers for the Charter', *Northern Star*, 29 October 1842.

11 'Working Men's Rhymes, no. 1', *Northern Star*, 6 January 1838.

12 James Epstein, *The Lion of Freedom: Feargus O'Connor and the Chartist Movement, 1832–1842* (London: Croom Helm, 1982) offers the fullest discussion of O'Connor.

13 Though mentioned in many sources, no copy is known to have survived. See item 190, Ashton, Fyson, and Roberts, *Chartist Movement*.

14 Y. V. Kovalev, *An Anthology of Chartist Literature* (Moscow: 1956); 'Introduction', translated by J. C. Dumbreck and Michael Beresford, *Victorian Studies* 2 (1958), 117–138. I am very grateful to Stephen Roberts for giving me a copy of the Kovalev volume, a rare and most appreciated gift; *An Anthology of Chartist Poetry: Poetry of the British Working Class, 1830s–1850s*, edited by Peter Scheckner, (London: Associated University Presses, 1989).

15 Phyllis Mary Ashraf, *Introduction to Working Class Literature in Great Britain* (East Berlin: Lehrmatieral zur Ausbildung von Diplomlehrern Englisch, Part I Poetry 1978, Part II Prose 1979), 2 vols.

16 Martha Vicinus, *The Industrial Muse* (London: Croom Helm, 1974); Brian Maidment, *The Poorhouse Fugitives: Self-taught Poets and Poetry in Victorian Britain* (Manchester: Carcanet Press, 1987).

17 Isobel Armstrong, *Victorian Poetry: Poetry, Poetics and Politics* (London: Routledge, 1993), 191–198.

18 Some other studies exist as well: Stephen Roberts gives an exuberant portrait of *Radical Politicians and Poets in Early Victorian Britain: the Voices of Six Chartist Leaders* (Lampeter: Edwin Mellen Press, 1993); Ulrike Schwab's published dissertation, *The Poetry of the Chartist Movement: a Literary and Historical Study* (Dordrecht: Kulwer Academic Publishers, 1993) offers a good compendium of Chartist poets and their texts; Ian Haywood, in *The Literature of Struggle: an Anthology of Chartist Fiction* (Aldershot: Scolar Press, 1995), has opened up the rich field of Chartist fiction.

19 Thomas Carlyle, *Selected Writings* (London: Penguin, 1971), 155.

20 J. A. Epstein, 'Feargus O'Connor and *The Northern Star*', *International Review of Social History* 21 (1976), 69–80, 97.

21 'Little Jack Horner – New Reading', *Northern Star*, 29 February 1840; 'Acrostic', *Northern Star*, 2 May 1840; 'Flowers and Slaves', *Northern Star*, 16 May 1840; John Watkins, 'Prologue to a New Drama, Spoken by a Druid, on John Frost and the

Insurrection at Newport', *Northern Star*, 30 November 1840 and 2 January 1841; 'Lines Written in Prison', *Northern Star*, 25 April 1840.

22 'An Enigma for Radicals', *Northern Star*, 23 May 1840.

23 *Northern Star*, 25 April 1840.

24 'Song for the People', *Northern Star*, 13 July 1839.

25 'Chester Gaol', *Northern Star*, 12 October 1839.

26 'Politics of Poets', *Chartist Circular*, 24 October 1840.

27 Roberts, 'Who Wrote to the *Northern Star*?', 68–70.

28 William Hick, *Chartist Songs and Other Pieces, No.1* (Leeds: J. Hobson, 1840).

29 'Literary Sketches: Robert Burns', *Chartist Circular*, 20 February 1841.

30 Charles Kingsley, 'Burns and His School', *Northern British Review* 16 (1852), 164, 165.

31 Derek Attridge, *Poetic Rhythm: an Introduction* (Cambridge: Cambridge University Press, 1995), 153.

32 'To Readers and Correspondents', *Northern Star*, 18 December 1841.

33 Adam Cornford, 'Political Poetry and Formalist Avant-Gardes', *City Lights Journal* 1 (1987), 129.

34 'The Voice of the People', *Northern Star*, 4 December 1841.

35 'The Politics of Poets', *Chartist Circular* 11 July, 1840.

36 Ernest Jones, 'The Song of the Future', *Notes to the People*, 2 (1852), 993.

37 William Benbow, *Grand National Holiday and Congress of the Productive Classes, etc.* (London: 1832), 4.

38 See Eileen Yeo, 'Culture and Constraint in Working-Class Movements, 1830–1855', in *Popular Culture and Class Conflict 1590–1914*, edited by Eileen and Stephen Yeo (Brighton: Harvester Press, 1981), 154–186.

39 See Dror Wahrman, *Imagining the Middle Class: The Political Representation of Class in Britain, c.1780–1840* (Cambridge: Cambridge University Press, 1995) for a detailed discussion of the ways in which the language of the middle class was deployed.

40 'Politics of Poets', *Chartist Circular*, 11 July 1840.

41 Dorothy Thompson, 'Who Were "the People" in 1842?', *Living and Learning: Essays in Honour of J. F. C. Harrison*, edited by Malcolm Chase and Ian Dyck (Aldershot: Scolar Press, 1996), 122.

42 E. J. Hobsbawm, *Nations and Nationalism since 1790* (Cambridge: Cambridge University Press, 1990) for discussion of meeting up of traditional and revolutionary-democratic nationalism; *Patriotism: the Making and Unmaking of British National Identity*, edited by Raphael Samuel (London: Routledge, 1989), 3 vols. for the domestic tradition of patriotism; and especially Hugh Cunningham, 'The Language of Patriotism, 1750–1914', *History Workshop Journal* 12 (1981), 8–33.

43 Hick, *Chartist Songs*, 5.

44 'Literary Sketches: Sir Walter Scott', *Chartist Circular*, 13 February 1841.

45 'Politics of Poets', *Chartist Circular*, 24 October 1840.

46 'Chartism from Shakespeare', *Northern Star*, 23 May 1840.

47 *Chartist Circular*, 26 September 1840.

48 'Death of Mr. Davenport', *Northern Star*, 5 December 1846.

49 In this context, it is worth considering Patrick Joyce's argument that working-class writers in this period aimed for a universal and a non-class specific notion of humanity. See his *Democratic Subjects: the Self and the Social in Nineteenth-Century England* (Cambridge: Cambridge University Press, 1994).

50 G. S. R. Kitson-Clark, 'The Romantic Element, 1830–1850', in *Studies in Social History: a Tribute to G. M. Trevelyan*, edited by J. H. Plumb (London: Longman's, 1955), 234; F. Engels, *The Condition of the Working Class in England* (New York: Macmillan, 1958), 242.

51 Eugene La Mont, 'Universal Liberty – the Chartist Reaction', *Northern Star*, 26 September 1840.

52 Robert Southey, *Lives of Uneducated Poets* (London: 1836), 12.

53 Kurt Heinzelman, 'The Uneducated Imagination: Romantic Representations of Labor' (101–124) in *At the Limits of Romanticism*, edited by Mary Favret and Nicola Watson (Bloomington: University of Indiana Press, 1994), 119.

54 Thomas Frost, *Forty Years' Recollections: Literary and Political* (London: 1880), 14.

55 Ibid., 15.

56 Ibid., 38.

57 Ibid., 39.

58 Ibid., 45.

59 Ibid., 49, 57, 102.

60 Ibid., 34.

61 Ibid., 168.

62 Kingsley, 'Burns and His School', 154.

63 Ibid., 165.

64 Bouthaina Shaaban, 'The Romantics in the Chartist Press', *Keats-Shelley Journal* 38 (1989), 27–46.

65 'Politics of Poets', *Chartist Circular*, 19 December 1840.

66 W. L. Warren, 'Byron Defended', *Northern Star*, 24 January 1846.

67 Thomas Medwin, *The Life of Percy Bysshe Shelley* (London: 1847), I, 103; Bernard Shaw, *Pen Portraits and Reviews* (London: Constable, 1932), 244.

68 Shelley, *Prose Works*, edited by R. H. Shepherd (London: Chatto & Windus, 1888), II, 38.

69 'Politics of Poets', *Chartist Circular*, 31 October 1840.

70 W. J. Linton, *Prose and Verse Written and Published in the Course of Fifty Years, 1836–1886* (Connecticut, 1895), v, 114 (unique copy, British Library, 12269.g.11).

71 'Politics of Poets', *Chartist Circular*, 1 August 1840.

72 *The Democratic Review*, May, 1850, 473.

73 Armstrong, *Victorian Poetry*, 192.

74 Anon., 'Never Give Up', *Northern Star*, 22 February 1845; Ernest Jones, 'The Poet's Death', *The Battle-Day and Other Poems* (London: Routledge, 1855), 132.

75 Matthew Arnold, *English Writers and Irish Politics*, edited by R. H. Super (Ann Arbor: University of Michigan Press, 1973), 55.

76 Janowitz, *England's Ruins*.

77 'Voice of the People', *Northern Star*, 4 December 1841.

78 Gerald Massey, 'Our Land', *The Friend of the People*, 21 December 1850.

79 W. J. Linton, 'Property', *Prose and Verse*, x, 12.

80 'The Patriot's Grave', *Northern Star*, 9 September 1843.

81 George Meredith, *The Poetical Works* (London: Constable, 1912), 117.

82 Ivor Wilks, *South Wales and the Rising of 1839: Class Struggle as Armed Struggle* (London: Croom Helm, 1984); David Williams, *John Frost: a Study in Chartism* (Cardiff: University of Wales, 1939); David J. V. Jones, *The Last Rising: the Newport Insurrection of 1839* (Oxford: Clarendon Press, 1985).

83 Iota, 'Sonnets Devoted to Chartism', *Northern Star*, 9 May, 27 June, 1 August, 15 August 1840.

84 Shell letter reprinted in *Welsh Labour History* 1 (1970), 8.

85 Robert Geoffrey Trease, *Comrades for the Charter* (London: Martin Lawrence, 1934), 142.

86 Iota, 'Stanzas', *Northern Star*, 16 May 1840.

87 John Watkins, 'Prologue to a New Drama, Spoken by a Druid, on John Frost and the Insurrection at Newport', *Northern Star*, 30 November 1840; 2 January 1841.

88 Ibid.

89 Robert Hughes, *The Fatal Shore: a History of the Transportation of Convicts to Australia, 1787–1868* (London: Collins Harvill, 1987), 368.

90 J. H. Watkins, 'Frost', *Northern Star*, 2 May 1840.

91 Thomas Moore, *Irish Melodies* (London: Muse's Library, 1908), 104–105.

92 Hick, *Chartist Songs*, 5.

93 Ibid., 13.

94 John Frost, *The Horrors of Convict Life* (Hobart: Sullivan's Cove; rpt. 1973 of 1857), 27.

95 Gerald Massey, 'Song of the Red Republican', *Red Republican* 1 (1850), 1.

6 LABOUR'S LAUREATES: ALLEN DAVENPORT, THOMAS COOPER, AND ERNEST JONES IN 1846

1 F. B. Smith, *Radical Artisan: William James Linton 1812–97* (Manchester: Manchester University Press, 1973), 36.

2 James Epstein, 'National Chartist Leadership: Some Perspectives', in *The Duty of Discontent: Essays for Dorothy Thompson*, edited by Owen Ashton, Robert Fyson, and Stephen Roberts (London: Mansell, 1995), 42.

3 Dorothy Thompson, *The Chartists: Popular Politics in the Industrial Revolution* (New York: Pantheon, 1984), 295.

4 See Isobel Armstrong, *Victorian Poetry: Poetry, Poetics and Politics* (London: Routledge, 1993) for discussion of the 'democratic' poetic theories of the *Monthly Repository*, 112–135.

5 'Literary Review', *The Labourer* 2 (1847), 96.

6 Ibid.

7 'Soiree to Thomas Cooper, the Chartist Poet', *Northern Star*, 9 May 1846.

8 Ibid.

9 See Margot C. Finn, *After Chartism: Class and Nation in English Radical Politics,*

1848–1874 (Cambridge: Cambridge University Press, 1993), for a full discussion of the post-Chartist political milieu.

10 Joy MacAskill, 'The Chartist Land Plan', in *Chartist Studies*, edited by Asa Briggs (London: Macmillan, 1962), 326; Malcolm Chase, '"We Wish Only to Work for Ourselves": the Chartist Land Plan', *Living and Learning*, 133–148.

11 Chase, 'Editorial Afterword', in Allen Davenport, *Life and Literary Pursuits of Allen Davenport* (Aldershot: Scolar Press, 1994), 53.

12 Ernest Jones, Diary 1844–46, 17 August 1846, 30 September 1846, Manchester Reference Library, Ernest Jones Collection.

13 'Chartist Jubilee', *Northern Star*, 22 August 1846.

14 MacAskill, 'Chartist Land Plan', 317.

15 Ibid., 321, 330.

16 Thompson, *Chartists*, 303.

17 Davenport, 'O'Connorville', *Northern Star*, 22 August 1846.

18 Ibid.

19 'The Feast of the Poets', *Northern Star*, 11 April 1846.

20 'Grand Demonstration to the Peoples' First Estate', *Northern Star*, 22 August 1846.

21 'Extracts from Crabbe', *Notes to the People* 21–23 (1851–1852).

22 Ernest Jones, 'O'Connorville', *Northern Star*, 22 August 1846.

23 Jerome J. McGann, 'The Anachronism of George Crabbe', *English Literary History* 48 (1981), 559.

24 Ernest Jones, 'Our Summons', *Northern Star*, 16 May 1846.

25 Ibid.

26 Ernest Jones, 'Our Destiny', *Northern Star*, 11 July 1846.

27 Ernest Jones, 'Our Warning', *Northern Star*, 1 August 1846.

28 Ernest Jones, 'Our Summons', *Northern Star*, 16 May 1846.

29 Ernest Jones, *The Revolt of Hindostan* (London: Effingham Wilson, 1857), i.

30 Thompson, *Chartists*, 323.

31 George Howell, 'Ernest Jones, The Chartist', *Newcastle Weekly Chronicle*, 1 January 1898, in 'Pamphlets, Cuttings and Funeral Speeches of Ernest Jones', Manchester Reference Library, Ernest Jones Collection; G. D. H. Cole, *Chartist Portraits* (London: Macmillan, 1941), 212.

32 John Saville, *Ernest Jones: Chartist* (London: Lawrence and Wishart, 1952), 22–23.

33 Thomas Cooper, 'Dedicatory Stanzas to Allen Davenport', *Northern Star*, 5 December 1846.

34 Thomas Cooper, *The Life of Thomas Cooper*, edited by John Saville (1872; rpt. New York: Humanities Press, 1971), 164.

35 Ibid.

36 Ibid., 57.

37 Ibid., 63–64.

38 *Shakespearean Chartist Hymn Book*, edited by Thomas Cooper, 2nd edn (Leicester: 1843). (No copy is known to have survived.)

39 Thompson, *Chartists*, 296.

40 Thomas Cooper, 'The Lion of Freedom', *Northern Star*, 11 September 1841.
41 Cooper, *Life*, 251.
42 Ibid.
43 Bouthaina Shaaban, 'Shelley's Influence on the Chartist Poets, with Particular Emphasis on Ernest Charles Jones and Thomas Cooper' (Ph.D. diss., University of Warwick, 1981), 291. Shaaban's thesis carries out a close reading of the traces of Shelley in poems by Cooper and Jones; see also the interesting discussion of the poem by Isobel Armstrong, *Victorian Poetry*, 214–217.
44 Thomas Cooper, *Poetical Works* (London: Hodder & Stoughton, 1886), 278.
45 Cole, *Chartist Portraits*, 211.
46 Thomas Spence, 'The Land', *Northern Star*, 17 January 1846.
47 Cooper, *Life*, 264–268; Jane Ridley, *The Young Disraeli, 1804–1846* (London: Sinclair-Stevenson, 1995), 309.
48 Armstrong, *Victorian Poetry*, 30; Cooper, *Life*, 280–281.
49 Ibid., 281–282.
50 Ibid., 290.
51 Ibid.
52 George Meredith, *The Poetical Works* (London: Constable, 1912), 117.
53 Saville, 'Introduction' to Cooper's *Life*, 24.
54 Cooper, *Life*, 257.
55 Thomas Cooper, 'To Chartist Poets', *Northern Star*, 3 January 1846.
56 Ibid.
57 'Mr. Cooper's "Despotism"', *Northern Star*, 17 January 1846.
58 Ibid.
59 Ibid.
60 'Mr. Cooper and the Projected Chartist Song and Hymn-Book', *Northern Star*, 24 January 1846.
61 Ibid.
62 Ibid.
63 Davenport, *Life and Literary Pursuits*, 114.
64 'Soiree to Thomas Cooper, the Chartist Poet', *Northern Star*, 9 May 1846.
65 Ibid.
66 Ibid.
67 Ibid.
68 Ernest Jones, 'To the Chartist Body', *Northern Star*, 9 May, 1846.
69 'A New Poet', *Northern Star*, 9 May 1846.
70 Ibid.
71 Percy Vere [Ernest Jones], *My Life* (London: T. C. Newby, 1846), 2.
72 See as well his laconic 1859 comment, 'In the winter of 1845, having accidentally seen a copy of the *Northern Star*, and finding the political principles advocated harmonised with my own, I sought the executive and joined the Chartist movement', Saville, *Ernest Jones*, 17.
73 Saville, *Ernest Jones*, 13.
74 John Belchem and James Epstein, 'The Nineteenth-Century Gentleman Leader Revisited', *Social History* 22 (1997), 182.

75 Howell, 'Ernest Jones'.
76 Ernest Jones, 'Verses on the French Revolution', Manchester Central Library, Jones Collection.
77 Ernest Jones, 'To Her', *The Court Journal*, 8 January 1842.
78 Ernest Jones, 'Song', Manuscript poems, Manchester Central Library, Jones Collection.
79 Jones, Diary, 4 June 1844.
80 *Barnsley Times*, 27 May 1882, 3; quoted in Belchem and Epstein, 'Nineteenth-Century Gentleman Leader Revisited', 178.
81 *Leeds Times*, 1 May 1847, 6.
82 Ibid.
83 Jones, Diary, 14 July, 18 July 1846.
84 Ernest Jones, 'The Cornfield and the Factory', *Northern Star*, 27 June 1846.
85 Howell, 'Ernest Jones'; Thompson, *Chartists*, 242, 308.
86 James Vernon, *Politics and the People: a Study in English Political Culture, c. 1815–1867* (Cambridge: Cambridge University Press, 1993), 212.
87 Ernest Jones, 'The Blackstone-Edge Gathering', *Northern Star*, 22 August 1846.
88 Cole, *Chartist Portraits*, 212.
89 Howell, 'Ernest Jones'.
90 Ibid.
91 Jones, Diary, 30 September 1846.
92 Ibid., 8 October 1846.
93 Ernest Jones, *Chartist Poems* (London: McGowan, 1846).
94 'Death of Mr. Davenport', *Northern Star*, 5 December 1846.
95 'Preface', *The Labourer; a Monthly Magazine of Politics, Literature, Poetry* 1 (1847), i.
96 'To Correspondents', *The Labourer* 1 (1847), 192, mispaginated as 119.
97 Jones met Marx in 1847, and participated with him on a platform commemorating the 1830 Polish Revolution. Saville, *Ernest Jones*, 27.
98 'The Factory Town', *The Labourer* 1 (1847), 51.
99 Jones, *My Life*, 7.
100 *People's Paper*, 9 December 1854; quoted in Saville, *Ernest Jones*, 215.
101 'Literary Review', *The Labourer* 1 (1847), 285.
102 Ernest Jones, 'Open Letter', *Northern Star*, 1 April 1848.
103 'Literary Review', *The Labourer* 2 (1848), 95.
104 Ibid., 96.
105 John Belchem, '1848: Feargus O'Connor and the Collapse of the Mass Platform', *The Chartist Experience: Studies in Working-Class Radicalism and Culture*, edited by James A. Epstein and Dorothy Thompson (London: Macmillan, 1982), 269–310.
106 Cole, *Chartist Portraits*, 342; Belchem, *Popular Radicalism*, 91.
107 Saville, *Ernest Jones*, 31.
108 Ibid., 32.
109 Ernest Jones, 'The Silent Cell', *Notes to the People* 1 (1851), 66.

110 Ernest Jones, *Notes to the People* 1 (1851), 63.
111 Ernest Jones, 'A Prisoner's Night-Thought', *Notes to the People* 1 (1851), 63.
112 Ernest Jones, 'Earth's Burdens', *Notes to the People* 1 (1851), 67.
113 Ernest Jones, *The New World, Notes to the People* 1 (1851), 4.
114 Frederick Leary, *The Life of Ernest Jones* (London: The Democrat, 1887), 25, 26.
115 *The New World, Notes to the People* 1 (1851), 4.
116 Finn, *After Chartism*, 60–105.
117 *The New World, Notes to the People* 1 (1851), 14.
118 Ibid., 12.
119 Saville, *Ernest Jones*, 35.
120 Finn, *After Chartism*, 112–113.
121 'The Charter and Something More!' *Red Republican*, 22 June 1850.
122 Saville, *Ernest Jones*, 37; Finn, *After Chartism*, 115.
123 'Manifesto of the German Communist Party', translated by Howard Morton, *Red Republican*, 9 November 1850.
124 'Programme Adopted by the Chartist Convention of 1851', *Northern Star*, 12 June 1851.
125 Belchem, *Popular Radicalism*, 95; Finn, *After Chartism*, 75.
126 'Ernest Jones to the People', *Red Republican*, 10 August 1850.
127 'Review', *Friend of the People*, 10 May 1851.
128 Ibid.
129 *People's Paper*, 17 September 1853.
130 'The Authors of England', *People's Paper*, 15 May 1852.
131 Ernest Jones, 'The Song of the Low', *Notes to the People* 2 (1852), 953.
132 Belchem, *Popular Radicalism*, 104. Historians have recently focused attention on the continuities between popular radicalism and liberalism: see in particular Eugenio F. Biagini, *Liberty, Retrenchment and Reform: Popular Liberalism in the Age of Gladstone* (Cambridge: Cambridge University Press, 1991).
133 Saville, *Ernest Jones*, 72.
134 Ernest Jones, 'Preface', *The Emperor's Vigil* (London: Routledge, 1856), v.
135 Ibid., vi.
136 'Minor Minstrels,' *Athenaeum*, 24 May 1856.
137 Ernest Jones, 'The Poet's Prayer to the Evening Wind', *The Battle-Day and Other Poems* (London: Routledge, 1855), 125.
138 Ibid., 126.
139 Janowitz, *England's Ruins*, 65–78.
140 Ernest Jones, 'The Poet's Mission', *The Battle-Day and Other Poems* (London: Routledge, 1855), 121.
141 Ibid.
142 Finn, *After Chartism*, 310.
143 Ibid., 312.
144 'Free Pardon to John Frost', *People's Paper*, 10 May 1856.
145 'Great National Demonstration', *People's Paper*, 20 September 1856.
146 Ibid.
147 *The Times*, 16 September 1856.

7 W. J. LINTON AND WILLIAM MORRIS: REPUBLICAN AND SOCIALIST POETS

1 See, for example, Patrick Joyce, *Democratic Subjects: the Self and the Social in Nineteenth-Century England* (Cambridge: Cambridge University Press, 1994); Eugenio Biagini, *Liberty, Retrenchment and Reform: Popular Liberalism in the Age of Gladstone, 1860–1880* (Cambridge: Cambridge University Press, 1992); James Vernon, *Politics and the People: a Study in English Political Culture, c.1815–1867* (Cambridge: Cambridge University Press, 1993).

2 W. J. Linton, *James Watson: a Memoir* (Manchester: 1880), 58; F. B. Smith, *Radical Artisan: William James Linton* (Manchester: Manchester University Press, 1973), 1, 34–5.

3 W. J. Linton, 'The Selfish Principle', *English Republic* 2 (1852–1853), 129.

4 *The Collected Letters of William Morris*, edited by Norman Kelvin (Princeton, NJ: Princeton University Press, 1987), II, 230.

5 E. P. Thompson, *William Morris: Romantic to Revolutionary* (New York: Pantheon Press, 1976), 314.

6 Ernest Belfort Bax, Victor Dave, and William Morris, *A Short Account of the Commune of Paris* (London: 1886), 79.

7 Smith, *Radical Artisan*, 144; Isobel Spencer, *Walter Crane* (London: Studio Vista, 1975), 16; Peter Stansky, *Redesigning the World: William Morris and the Arts and Crafts Movement* (Princeton, NJ: Princeton University Press, 1985), 195.

8 Walter Crane, *An Artist's Reminiscences* (London: Methuen, 1907), 46.

9 Margot Finn, *After Chartism: Class and Nation in English Radical Politics, 1848–1874* (Cambridge: Cambridge University Press, 1993), 112–115; W. J. Linton, 'Republican Socialism: an Explanation', *English Republic* 1 (1851), 338.

10 Crane, *Reminiscences*, 267.

11 Robert F. Gleckner, 'W. J. Linton's Tailpieces in Gilchrist's *Life of William Blake*', *Blake: an Illustrated Quarterly* 14 (1981), 208–211; 'W. J. Linton, a Latter-Day Blake', *Bulletin of Research in the Humanities* 85 (1982), 208–227; Shirley Dent, 'Linton, Blake, and Secularism', Ph.D. in progress, University of Warwick.

12 Gleckner, 'Latter-Day Blake', 210.

13 W. J. Linton, *Memories* (London: Laurence & Bullen, 1894; rpt. New York: August Kelly, 1970) 182; Dent, 'Linton, Blake, and Secularism'.

14 W. J. Linton, 'To a Spider', *Heliconundrums* (Connecticut: Appledore, 1892), 61–62.

15 *Collected Letters*, II, 516.

16 Ibid., 308, 357, 381.

17 J. Bruce Glasier, *Socialism in Song: an Appreciation of William Morris's 'Chants for Socialists'* (Manchester: National Labour Press, 1919), 2.

18 *Penguin Book of Socialist Verse*, edited by Alan Bold (London: Penguin, 1970), 97.

19 Thompson, *William Morris*, part IV, 641–731.

20 Linton, *James Watson*, 59.

21 *The National*, March 1839; W. J. Linton, *Prose and Verse Written and Published in the Course of Fifty Years, 1836–1886* (Connecticut, 1895), III, 41 (unique copy, British Library, 12269.g.11) for Chartists' attitudes towards female suffrage, see Anna

Clark, 'Gender, Class, and the Nation: Franchise Reform in England, 1832–1928', in *Re-reading the Constitution: New Narratives in the Political History of England's Long Nineteenth Century*, edited by James Vernon (Cambridge: Cambridge University Press, 1997), 230–253, 255.

22 W. J. Linton, Letter to Richard Garnett, 23 May 1895 (British Library Archives, DH4/64, 1895, f. 202); Edward Miller, *That Noble Cabinet: a History of the British Museum* (London: Andre Deutsch, 1973), 269,273.

23 Linton, letter to Garnett (British Library).

24 Linton, *Memories*, 34.

25 Linton, *Memories*, 75.

26 *Prose and Verse*, I, 42.

27 Linton, *Memories*, 35.

28 Linton, *James Watson*, 55, 61; Smith, *Radical Artisan*, 36.

29 Linton, *Prose and Verse*, III, 136.

30 W. J. Linton, 'Who Were the Chartists?', *Century Magazine*, 1891 (*Prose and Verse*, XIX, 164).

31 Finn, *After Chartism*, 115.

32 Antony Taylor, 'Anti-Monarchism and the Radical Tradition, 1850–72', in Vernon, *Re-reading the Constitution*, 161.

33 Smith, *Radical Artisan*, 17.

34 'Liberty and Equality', *English Republic* I III (1854), 131.

35 Ibid., 121.

36 Linton, *Prose and Verse*, VI, 61.

37 W. J. Linton, *Claribel and Other Poems* (London: Simpkin, Marshall, 1865), 179.

38 Edmund Clarence Stedman, *Victorian Poets* (Boston: Osgood, 1876), 260, 271.

39 H. Buxton-Forman, 'William James Linton as a Poet', *Gentleman's Magazine* (1879), 575–592, 576.

40 *The National*, 5 January 1839, 6.

41 W. G. Roe, *Lamennais and England: the Reception of Lamennais's Religious Ideas in England in the Nineteenth Century* (Oxford: Oxford University Press, 1966).

42 *The National*, 2 February 1839, 71; 30 March 1839, 182.

43 Linton, *Memories*, 37.

44 W. J. Linton, 'The Slave's Hymn', *Prose and Verse*, III, 143.

45 W. J. Linton, 'The Voice of Wat Tyler', *Prose and Verse*, III, 148.

46 W. J. Linton, 'A Song for the Next Rebellion', *Prose and Verse*, III, 183.

47 Isobel Armstrong also notes this genre in Linton: see *Victorian Poetry*, 509n30.

48 W. J. Linton, 'The Coming Days', *Prose and Verse*, VI, 44.

49 William Morris, 'The Day Is Coming', *Chants for Socialists* (London: Socialist League Office, 1885), 3.

50 Linton, 'Why Should We Not Be Free? A Chant', *Prose and Verse*, VI, 45.

51 W. J. Linton, 'A Song for the People's Charter Union', *Prose and Verse*, VII, 165; *English Republic* I (1851), 136–137.

52 Linton, *Prose and Verse*, VI, 30.

53 W. J. Linton, 'The Poet-Prophet', *Prose and Verse*, XV, 39.

54 Linton, *James Watson*, 39.
55 Linton, *Memories*, 51.
56 Biagini, *Liberty, Retrenchment and Reform*, 49.
57 Smith, *Radical Artisan*, 65.
58 Linton, *Prose and Verse*, VI, 112.
59 Diary entry, cited in Smith, *Radical Artisan*, 93.
60 W. J. Linton, 'Our Tricolour', *Prose and Verse*, VII, 209.
61 *English Republic* 2 (1852–1853), 71, quoted in Finn, *After Chartism*, 114.
62 Smith, *Radical Artisan*, 104.
63 *Red Republican*, 26 October 1850, 145–146, quoted in Finn, *After Chartism*, 113.
64 Smith, *Radical Artisan*, 105; Linton, *Memories*, 124.
65 Linton, 'Letter III', *Prose and Verse*, X, 65.
66 Linton, 'Letter II', *Prose and Verse*, X, 62.
67 Ibid., 64.
68 W. J. Linton, 'Free Trade', *Prose and Verse*, X, 18.
69 Linton, 'The Selfish Principle', 132.
70 Ibid.
71 Arthur E. Bestor, 'The Evolution of the Socialist Vocabulary', *Journal of the History of Ideas* 9 (1948), 264; W. J. Linton, 'Republican Principles', *Red Republican*, 21 September 1851, 110.
72 Ibid.
73 *English Republic* 2 (1852–1853), 141–144, 145–148, 149–152, 153–156, 161–164.
74 Smith, 100, 105; Linton, 'Communists', *Prose and Verse*, XIX, 83; 'The Land Question', *English Republic* 2 (1852–1853), 91.
75 W. J. Linton, 'Property', *Prose and Verse*, X, 12.
76 For a vindication of Hemans's poem, see Jerome McGann, *The Poetics of Sensibility: a Revolution in Literary Style* (Oxford: Clarendon Press, 1996), 182–190.
77 W. J. Linton, 'The Parks', *Prose and Verse*, X, 46.
78 W. J. Linton, 'Try Again', *Prose and Verse*, X, 49.
79 W. J. Linton, 'The Way Out', *Prose and Verse*, X, 37.
80 W. J. Linton, 'Irish Harvest Song', *Prose and Verse*, X, 51.
81 Ernst Bloch, *The Utopian Function of Art and Literature: Selected Essays*, translated by Jack Zipes and Frank Mecklenburg (Cambridge, MA: MIT Press, 1988), 46.
82 Bloch, *Utopian Function*, 41; for a comparison of Bloch and Morris, see Ruth Levitas, 'Marxism, Romanticism and Utopia: Ernst Bloch and William Morris', *Radical Philosophy* 51 (1989), 27–36.
83 W. J. Linton, 'Harvest-Home', *Prose and Verse*, X, 53.
84 W. J. Linton, 'The Happy Land', *Prose and Verse*, X, 55.
85 Smith, *Radical Artisan*, 112–113.
86 Ibid., 149.
87 Ibid., 165.
88 R. Malcolm Sills, 'W. J. Linton at Yale – the Appledore Private Press,' *Yale University Library Gazette* 12 (1938), 43–52; for extensive discussion of this aspect of Linton's life, see Gleckner, 'Latter–Day Blake'.
89 *Prose and Verse*, XVIII, 71.

90 Smith, *Radical Artisan*, 174.

91 Ibid., 175.

92 *Prose and Verse*, XVIII, 81–82.

93 'Mr. W. J. Linton and the Nineteenth Century', *Prose and Verse*, XIX, 587.

94 W. J. Linton, *The Paris Commune* (Boston: 1871), 23, 25.

95 Smith, *Radical Artisan*, 189.

96 Taylor, 'Anti-Monarchism', 176.

97 Thompson, *William Morris*, 202–225.

98 Ibid., 208, 268.

99 *Collected Letters*, I, 435.

100 Ibid., 436n8.

101 W. J. Linton, 'Down with the Turk', *Prose and Verse*, XIX, 48.

102 Smith, *Radical Artisan*, 146.

103 'I have written to a male person, but with apologies if I am wrong, is it possibly *Mrs.* Linton I am addressing?', *Collected Letters*, II, 241.

104 W. J. Linton and R. H. Stoddard, *English Verse* (New York: C. Scribner's Sons, 1883), 5 vols.

105 W. J. Linton and R. H. Stoddard, *Lyrics of the Nineteenth Century* (New York: C. Scribner's Sons, 1883), xviii.

106 Ibid., xxvi.

107 Ibid., 201–203.

108 Ibid., 281–285.

109 Buxton-Forman, 'W. J. Linton', 585.

110 Ibid., 592.

111 William Morris, 'Artist and Artisan as an Artist Sees It', *Commonweal* 3 (1887), 291.

112 William Morris, 'The Worker's Share of Art', *Commonweal* 1 (1885), 19.

113 William Morris, *The Pilgrims of Hope* (London: 1886). All quotations from the sequence will be made parenthetically in the text, by reference to the poem number.

114 William Morris, 'Address at the Twelfth Annual Meeting of the Society for the Protection of Ancient Buildings', 3 July 1889, in *William Morris, Artist, Writer, Socialist*, edited by May Morris (Oxford: Basil Blackwell, 1936), I, 148.

115 Michael Holzman makes a good case that the poem refers to the triangular relationship amongst Jane Morris, William Morris, and Dante Gabriel Rossetti, which was taking place during the period of the Paris Commune. See Michael Holzman, 'Propaganda, Passion, and Literary Art in William Morris's *The Pilgrims of Hope*,' *Texas Studies in Literature and Language* 24 (1982), 372–393.

116 Wordsworth, *The Prelude*, 1805, Book X, lines 724–728.

117 E. P. Thompson, *William Morris: Romantic to Revolutionary* (London: Lawrence and Wishart, 1955), 2nd edn (London: Merlin Press, 1976).

118 Ibid., 807–808.

119 Ibid., 1.

120 Ibid., 786; see John Goode's excellent consideration of 'E. P. Thompson and "The Significance of Literature"', in *E. P. Thompson: Critical Perspectives*, edited by Harvey J. Kaye and Keith McClelland (Cambridge: Polity Press, 1990), 183–203; see also Perry Anderson, *Arguments within English Marxism* (London: Verso Press, 1980).

121 Thompson, *William Morris*, 1976, 2, 11.

122 Ibid., 19–20.

123 Ibid., 2.

124 Goode, 'E. P. Thompson', 183–203.

125 Thompson, *William Morris*, 1955, 31.

126 Ibid., 669.

127 Ibid., 671.

128 J. W. Mackail, *The Life of William Morris* (London: Longman's, 1922), II, 148.

129 *Collected Letters*, II, xxv, xxix.

130 Holzman, 'Propaganda, Passion, and Literary Art', 377.

131 H. Buxton-Forman, *The Books of William Morris Described . . .* (London: Frank Hollings, 1897), 111.

132 J. Bruce Glasier, 'A Proletarian Epic', *The Socialist Review: A Quarterly Review of Modern Thought* 17 (1920), 322.

133 Florence S. Boos, 'Narrative Design in *The Pilgrims of Hope*', in *Socialism and the Literary Artistry of William Morris*, edited by Florence S. Boos and Carole G. Silver (Columbia, Missouri: University of Missouri Press, 1990), 166.

134 George Meredith, *Modern Love* (London: Rupert Hart-Davis, 1948), Sonnet 1.

135 Glasier, 'A Proletarian Epic', 325.

136 *Collected Letters*, II, 386, 391.

137 Jose Harris, *Private Lives, Public Spirit: Britain 1870–1914* (London: Penguin, 1994), 11–13; Stefan Collini, *Liberalism and Sociology, L. T. Hobhouse and Political Argument in England, 1880–1914* (Cambridge: Cambridge University Press, 1979), 13–50.

138 Blake, *Complete Writings*, 290.

139 Chris Waters, 'Morris's "Chants" and the Problems of Socialist Culture', in *Socialism and the Literary Artistry of William Morris*, edited by Boos and Silver, 127–146.

140 Ibid., 128.

141 Ibid., 8.

142 Thompson, *William Morris*, 669; Chris Waters, *British Socialists and the Politics of Popular Culture 1884–1914* (Manchester: Manchester University Press, 1990), 111.

143 *Justice*, 5 April 1884; *The Pilgrims of Hope and Chants for Socialists* (London: Longman's, 1915), 66.

144 Waters, 'Morris's "Chants"', 133.

145 William Morris, 'May Day' [1892], *The Pilgrims of Hope and Chants for Socialists*, 79.

146 Ibid., 63.

147 Ibid., 68.

148 Derek Attridge, *Poetic Rhythm, an Introduction* (Cambridge: Cambridge University Press, 1995), 156.
149 *William Morris*, edited by May Morris, I, 128.
150 Cited in Stephen Yeo, 'A New Life: the Religion of Socialism in Britain, 1883–1896', *History Workshop Journal* 4 (1977), 5.
151 William Morris, 'Why Not?', *Justice*, I (1884), 2.
152 *Collected Letters*, II, 472.
153 Ibid.
154 Ibid., 515.
155 Morris, 'Artist and Artisan', 291.
156 Holzman, 'Propaganda, Passion and Literary Art', 372.
157 Paul Thompson, *Socialists, Liberals and Labour: the Struggle for London 1885–1914* (London: Routledge and Kegan Paul, 1967), 91.
158 Collini, *Liberalism and Sociology*, 33.
159 Karl Marx and Friedrich Engels, *Writings on the Paris Commune*, edited by Hal Draper (New York: Monthly Review Press, 1971), 74–75.
160 See Kristin Ross, *The Emergence of Social Space: Rimbaud and the Paris Commune* (London: Macmillan, 1988), 22.
161 Marx and Engels, *Writings on the Paris Commune*, 150.
162 Victor Shanin, 'Marxism and the Vernacular Revolutionary Traditions', in *Late Marx and the Russian Road: Marx and 'the Peripheries of Capitalism'* (London: Routledge and Kegan Paul, 1983), 255.
163 A. L. Morton, 'Britain and the Paris Commune', *Marxism Today* 15 (1971), 82.
164 Jack Lindsay, 'The Commune of Paris', *Marxist Quarterly* 11 (1954), 170, 173.
165 For more on Linton, see Nancy Fix Anderson, *Woman against Women in Victorian England: a Life of Eliza Lynn Linton* (Bloomington: Indiana University Press, 1987).
166 For a full discussion, see Kirk Willis, 'The Introduction and Critical Reception of Marxist Thought in Britain, 1850–1900', *The Historical Journal* 20 (1977), 417–459.
167 Quoted in Yvonne Kapp, *Eleanor Marx: Family Life, 1855–1883* (London: Virago Press, 1979), II, 134.
168 Morton, 'Britain and the Commune', 85; Stanley Hutchins, 'The Communard Exiles in Britain', *Marxism Today* 15(1971), 183.
169 Hutchins, 'The Communard Exiles in Britain', 185.
170 *Collected Letters*, II, 270.

CONCLUSION

1 W. H. Auden, *Selected Poems*, edited by Edward Mendelson (London: Faber & Faber, 1979), 60–63, 55–59.
2 Ibid., 89.
3 E. P. Thompson, *The Making of the English Working Class* (Harmondsworth: Penguin, 1963), 915.

Index

Cambridge Studies in Romanticism

GENERAL EDITORS

MARILYN BUTLER, *University of Oxford*
JAMES CHANDLER, *University of Chicago*